Dear Janet,
I am grateful for our years of friendship and look forward to many more. May the Lord bless you as you pursue His kingdom.
Christian

THE BIBLE IN THE U.S. CAPITAL

Inviting All People to Engage with the Transformative Power of the Bible

CHRISTIAN ASKELAND, ASHLEY CARTER, JERRY PATTENGALE, *AND* AMY VAN DYKE

THE BIBLE IN THE U.S. CAPITAL: Inviting All People to Engage with the Transformative Power of the Bible

Published by Tyndale House Publishers

Published with the assistance of The Wayne Hastings Company, LLC.
Cover design by Marc Whitaker
Interior design by Jorie Lee

Front cover image credit: Museum of the Bible photographer Alex R. Matos

ISBN 978-1-4964-8222-8

Printed in the United States of America

28 27 26 25 24 23 22

7 6 5 4 3 2 1

CONTENTS

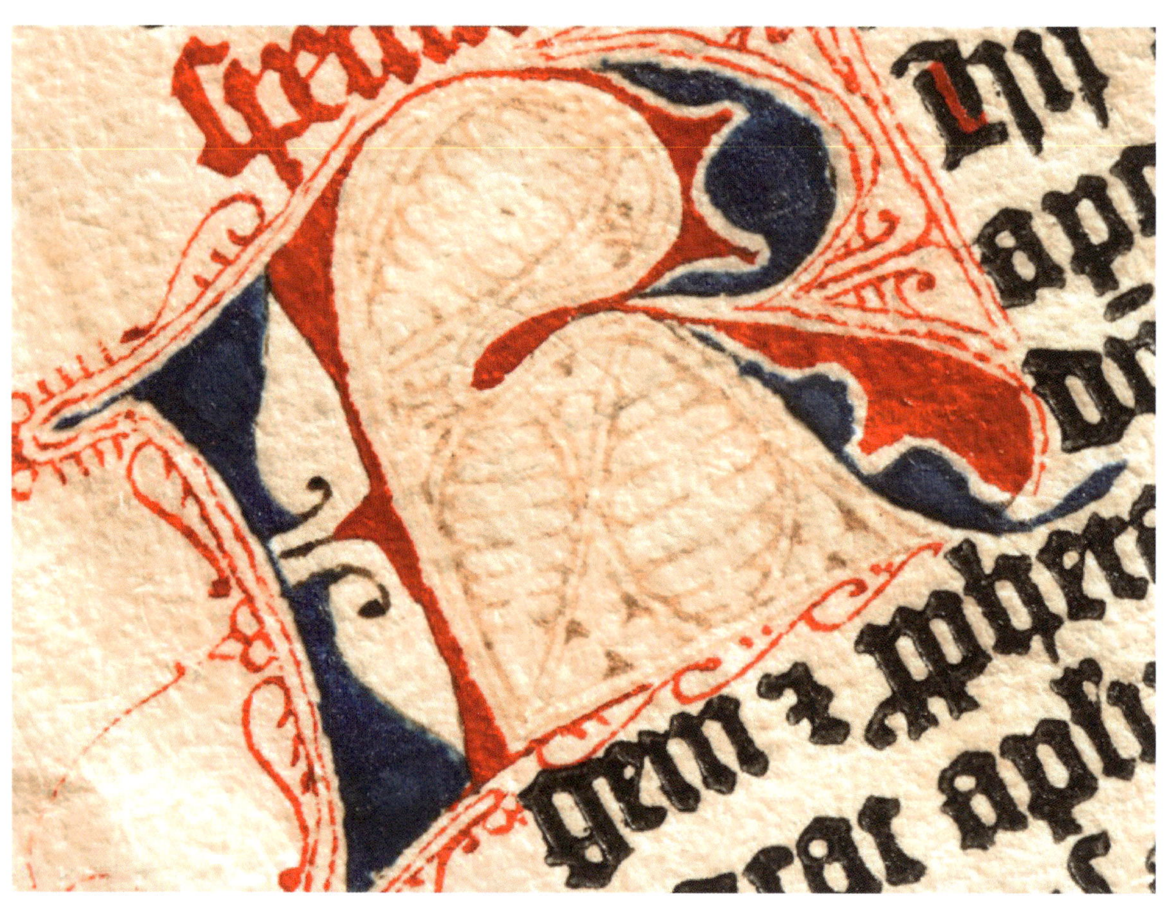

An illustrated letter added to a Gutenberg Bible page after it was printed (ca. 1454).

The cover image of the book you are reading is a close-up of the Gutenberg printing plates (that is, of the 40-foot replicas at the Museum of the Bible entrance).

FOREWORD

IN THE SIXTH chapter of the Gospel of John, Jesus's teachings drive many of his followers away. They take offense to his words, but Jesus continues to teach the truth. When the crowd has left, he asks his apostles whether they will leave him as well.

Peter responds with simplicity and candor. "To whom else would we go?" he asks. "You alone have the words of eternal life."

Countless men and women across the generations and all around the planet can testify to the exact same reality. In the Bible we find stories and songs, parables and poems, wisdom and insight that have illuminated, inspired, enriched, and transformed us. We find in this ancient book a piercing sword, a trustworthy guide, and the power of God for the salvation of all who believe. We find something we find nowhere else in all the world: the precious words of life.

The Bible also is one thing all Christians have in common. Amid our differences, even in our strife and rancor, we can all gather around the Bible at the center of our lives and communities. Of course the same is true of our Jewish friends and the Hebrew Bible, or what Christians call the Old Testament.

These are the reasons I've been captivated by the vision of the Museum of the Bible from the beginning. The museum is a remarkable place dedicated to the stories, history, and impact of this great Book of books, inviting all of us to engage the Bible more deeply. I had the privilege of watching that vision unfold from a mere idea to a construction site of steel and mud to a beautiful building in the heart of our nation's capital with world-class collections, displays, and media. The generous givers and extraordinary creative teams behind the museum have developed something that invites and educates the whole church and the world it serves.

The museum also tells the story of God's loving faithfulness with magnificent clarity. Like Jesus in John 6, it declares the truth and lets the audience make its own decisions. It bears eloquent witness to the words of life.

What's more, now the museum is becoming a place not only of learning and engaging but also of gathering and celebrating. It serves in an age of fragmentation as a place where we can come together and remember the deep and beautiful things we hold in common.

The need for these things – for invitation to engage the words of life and for celebrating the life the Word gives us – is profound. The museum is so timely and so important because it bears witness to something so eternal.

This book honors what the museum has become and all who made it so. We pray it succeeds in its mission and serves the world for many generations to come.

Timothy Dalrymple
President and CEO of Christianity Today

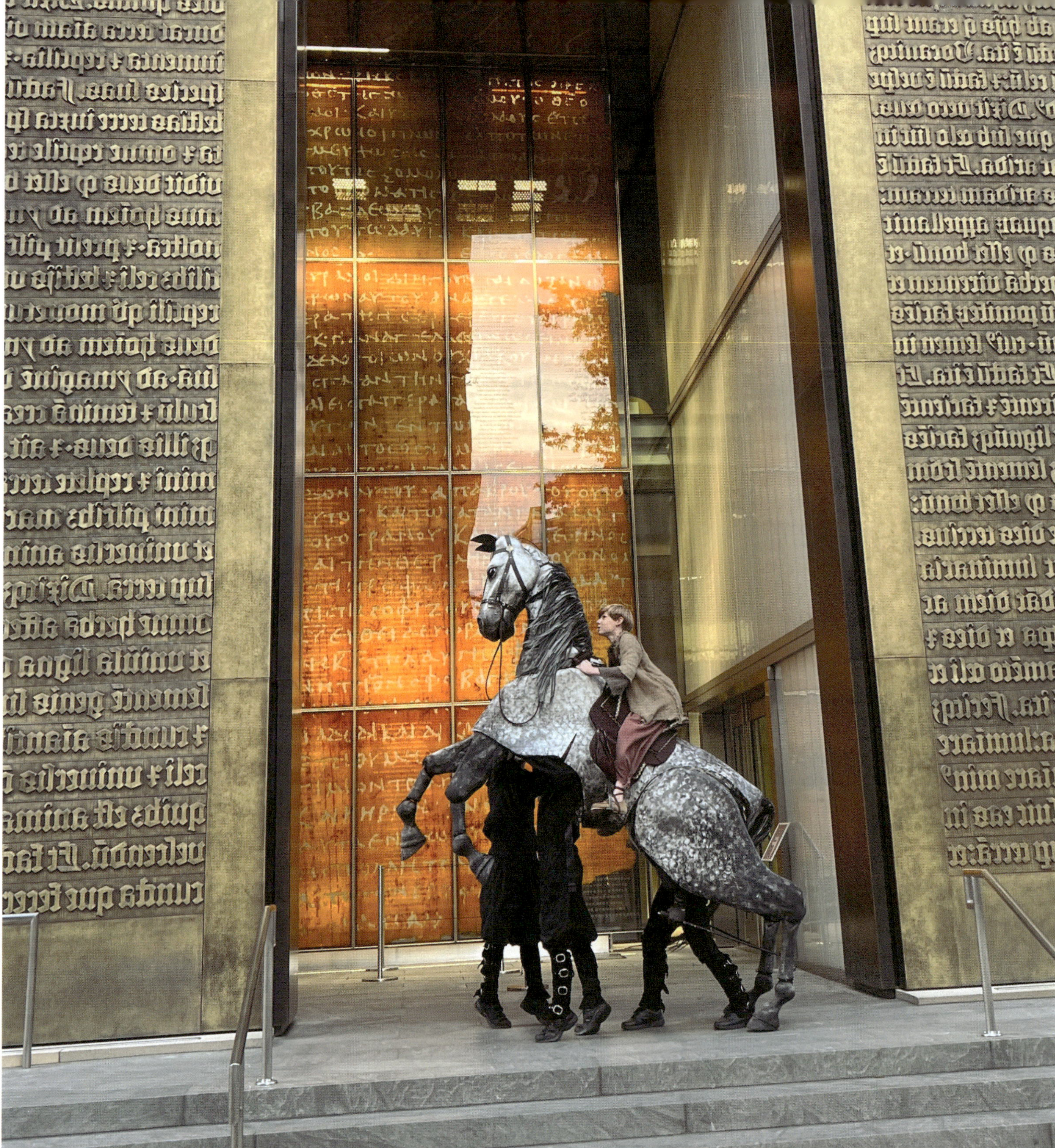

Academy of the Arts from Taylors, South Carolina, is practicing for *The Horse and His Boy* and other Narnia plays for the World Stage Theater (January – March, 2023).

FOUNDATIONS: An Introduction

Jerry Pattengale
a founding scholar of the Museum of the Bible

Five Years and Counting

Since 2017, an amazing phenomenon has occurred in Washington, DC—the Museum of the Bible has become a destination point for a wide swath of visitors. During its first five years, more than two million people trekked from across North America, and from Israel, Norway, Papua New Guinea, Rwanda, and beyond. Millions more are coming, both in person and through its expanded digital offerings, to engage with the transformative power of the Bible.

For some, it is a bucket list trip and, for many, a sacred space. At the least, it is aesthetically and creatively educational. At the most, it is also exhilarating and inspirational.

The museum's origins, development, and celebrations have played out on stages, large and small, through social media posts, countless articles, blogposts, and books. From foreign dignitaries to church leaders, diplomats, and celebrities, its guests emphasize the magnificence of the museum's structure and the message and influence of its central item—the Bible.

From its Washington, DC, location today and key museums and spaces in Israel, Cuba, Germany, Vatican City, and across America, some of its precious objects have helped tell the history, story, and impact of the Bible in various settings. Dozens of colleges have also hosted exhibits or items, and within its first two years (2010—2012), dozens of universities were involved with the Scholars Initiative studying some of these objects.

From its earliest days, the museum collaborated with more than 100 scholars worldwide and produced two versions of a Bible "curriculum" (sets of books on the Bible's history, story, and impact). Hundreds of thousands of students have used this resource in various forms and languages, and Tyndale House Publishers will be re-releasing it in new forms.

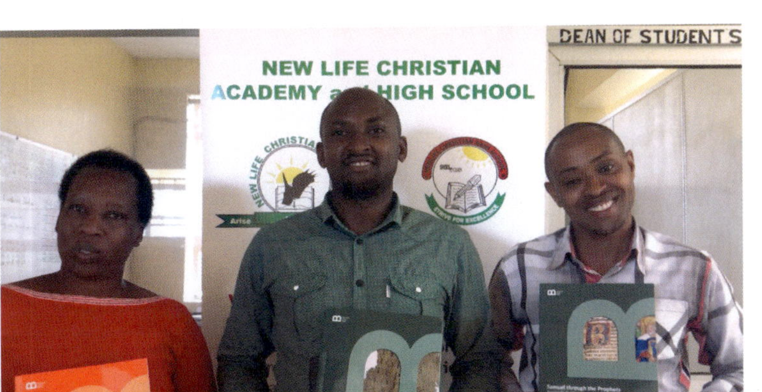

Bottom Left: During the museum's second anniversary, Peb Jackson (center) pauses with some of his special friends in one of the immersive elevators designed by some of those with him (November 2019).

Bottom Right: Teachers in Kayonza, Rwanda, praising the Museum of the Bible curriculum, September 2018. *(Picture courtesy of Africa New Life Ministries.)*

The Convening Place

We'd be remiss not to say up front that it's difficult to think of the Museum of the Bible without its partnering programs such as Women of Legacy and Inspire, with their consistent use of the museum for a wide range of events. They have come alongside the museum to offer faith-based approaches to subjects represented in the museum—often utilizing key objects. The extended list of major organizations, Christian and Jewish, private and secular, who have partnered with the museum or used its facilities is beyond our space here.

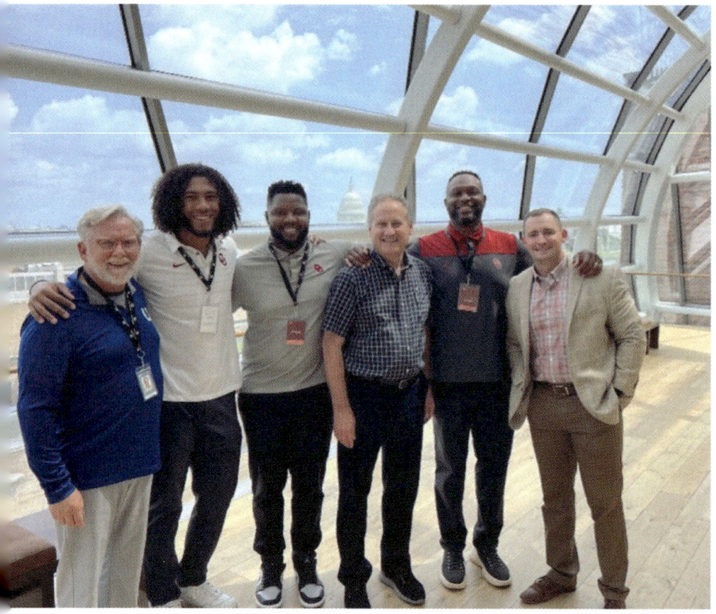

Among the numerous marquee athletes who have visited the museum are those from SOUL Mission from Oklahoma University's football program (in the middle around Steve Green, left to right) Caleb Kelly, Curtis Lofton, & Josh Norman (August 2022).

A glimpse of those unique groups linked to the museum will need to suffice. For King and Country, Matthew West, Danny Gokey, and The Gettys are but a few of the musicians involved. Roma Downey, Kirk Cameron, Denzel Washington, *The Chosen*'s staff and cast, and a litany of others are among the TV personalities who have connected in meaningful ways. The same with Nick Hall, CREATR, Shane and Shane, and a host of others in the wider Christian worship space. (We end this book with a more representative list.)

The museum's World Stage Theater has become, in a sense, like the Carnegie Hall, Radio City, and Comedy Club for different guilds. We seem only to have just begun. In the summer of 2022 Blessing of the Elders brought many African American religious leaders to the stage, from Tony Evans and James E. Ward to Claude Alexander and John Perkins. Earlier, Jack Graham, Anne Graham Lotz, Skip Heitzig, and other major expository preachers graced the stage.

It's difficult to imagine the Museum of the Bible without such amazing developments. But let us try to frame the key steps in the journey.

The Beginnings—A Museum without Walls

In 2010, Steve Green stood at his conference room table in Oklahoma City and shook hands with me; twelve years later, we are both still committed to a project worthy of life's best energies and resources. Neither of us knew what God had planned in the decades ahead. From that handshake until the massive doors opened on Washington, DC's 4th Street SW, seven busy years would ensue.

The earliest acquisitions of key manuscripts involved a Middle English-Latin commentary on the Psalms and a fragment of the Gospel of John (P39, P. Oxy. 1780). Other early key acquisitions included the Codex Climaci Rescriptus, one of the most important Greek Bible manuscripts, and Rahlfs 2110, the earliest complete manuscript of the Greek Psalms. All of these manuscripts are featured in the artifacts section of this book, but the reader should anticipate the complexity of the Codex Climaci Rescriptus, which at first glance contains a Syriac (Aramaic) text, but with the help of digital imagery contains early biblical texts in Greek and Christian Palestinian Aramaic.

The Greens collected approximately 5,000 Torah scrolls, easily the largest private collection, as well as various objects relevant to Jewish history. Continued acquisitions such the Washington Pentateuch and a codex from the Valmadonna Trust Library mean that the museum's history floor exhibition is among the top venues for Judaica outside Israel, including pieces from the Samaritan tradition, the Cairo Genizah, and a piece from the early medieval Silk Roads.

The majority of the collection interacts with the advent of the printing press, the translation of the Bible into numerous world languages and the worldwide spread of the biblical message. Visitors can interact with a Bible owned by Elvis in the same context as the earliest Bible printed by order of Congress, the Aitken Bible. Because the work of translation and proclamation is yet to be finished, the illumiNations exhibition visually challenges the patron to celebrate progress and to consider the urgency of what remains.

The collection includes artwork, which is curated by book author Amy Van Dyke, who has organized and executed many of the museum's key exhibitions. The reader will encounter images of Jesus portrayed in Tiffany glass on later pages. The collection includes a work of Salvador Dali, and visitors will encounter a replica of the Pietà. Van Dyke recently oversaw engagements related to Watchman Nee, the John Newton "Amazing Grace" anniversary and the Wiedmann Bible.

The miles trod while assembling a growing team during those years is dizzying, in the hundreds of thousands annually. The mileage was accented by the staggering numbers of objects collected. However, many were collected before the handshake and a commitment to the Museum of the Bible. In the early 2000s, an energetic group approached the Green family about assisting with a Bible museum in Dallas. The Greens loved the idea and began purchasing objects that might assist that eventual project. But the thought of a global museum of the Bible seemed to overshadow a regional one. While still acquiring special items, the family seized the opportunity to purchase around 10,000 objects at one time—especially strong in Americana. The Bible's role in the founding of America remains a strong area of interest for Steve and his wife, Jackie.

While its first seven years represented a museum without walls, it was also an exhilarating and exhausting era. Some of its great programs, objects, people, and places come from this season of growth—a time of many highs, some lows, but always forging ahead. And ultimately a time of significant accomplishments.

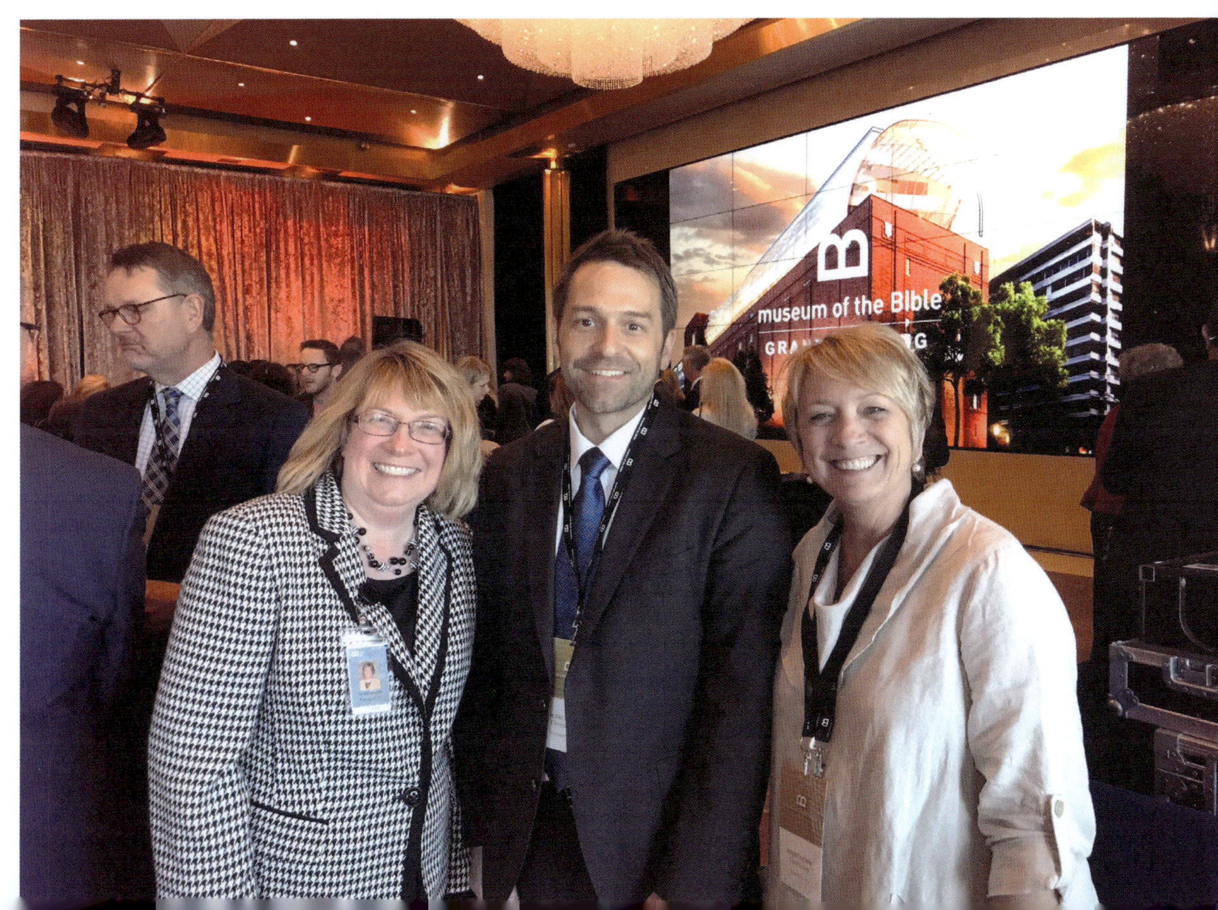

Tamara Schneider and Cindy Pattengale at the museum's opening with TV personality, David Stotts *(Drive thru History)*.

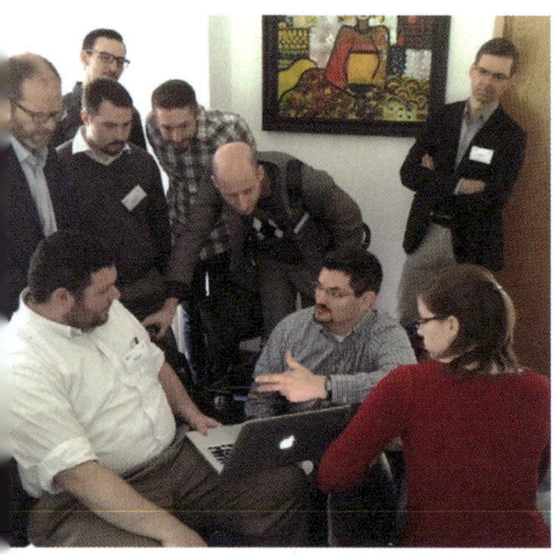

Above: Christian Askeland sharing the latest information from his research on a New Testament manuscript (The Scholars Initiative—Logos, Oxford, UK, ca. 2015). In the background is Jeff Kloha who would become the museum's Chief Curatorial Officer in 2018.

Right: Mart Green sharing with the leaders of By the Hand Club for Kids about illumiNations at the 2017 opening. This Chicago area program was one of the first adopters of the museum's Bible curriculum.

During that conference room meeting in early 2010 with Steve Green and the other scholar, the concept of the Museum of the Bible was formed. A few assistants worked in the collection's storage room, including Steve and Jackie's daughter, Lauren McAfee. Assisting with church relations was her husband, Michael—now the founding president of Inspire mentioned above. Christian Askeland was the first full-time researcher hired to assist me with Green Scholars Initiative (later renamed Scholars Initiative). Today, Christian serves as the museum's Senior Researcher and has become one of the world's leading Coptic scholars in textual criticism.

From the first traveling exhibit in 2011, *Passages* (staffed by book author Ashley Carter) included special (and usually full) lecture series. Until the museum's opening in 2017, it held some 150 special lectures with top authorities on biblical topics in various cities and countries.

The board of the Museum of the Bible may personally point readers to the Bible's value in living a fuller life and in understanding the possibility of eternal life. However, the board committed to allowing the museum and its staff to let visitors determine for themselves the Bible's importance in their own lives—while learning of its central stories and its key role and impact in history.

So, we first pause to cast the larger story. The release of this book coincides with the museum's fifth anniversary of being open—but the twelfth of its existence. The real heroes of this journey are the objects. Surrounded by creative programming, exhibits, and experiences, they collectively help all people to engage with the transforming power of the Bible.

The Religious Moorings Beneath the Museum's Foundations

While the patriarchs of the Green family are often listed as David and Barbara Green, the founders of Hobby Lobby, they would be quick to point to the real spiritual matriarch, David's mother, Marie Green. Her story, and much of what follows in this introduction, was drafted by Mac Pier and me for Pier's Movement Day organization in the fall of 2022 and adapted here with permission.

Marie Green didn't enjoy things many of us take for granted, like a car. Yet she was a passionate tither. She not only tithed her income, but she also tithed gifts of every sort. Sometimes it was a tithe of her garden produce or from the sale of knitted doilies (that she was making for ministry!). That ethic of generosity was sown deeply into her descendants.

David saw this firsthand and was reminded of their meager (but rich) journey from the hard kitchen floor that doubled as his bedroom (with a couple of assigned kitchen drawers as a dresser). His mother's piety was real, and he could touch it and it him. God assured David Green of a twin call to the marketplace and to generosity.

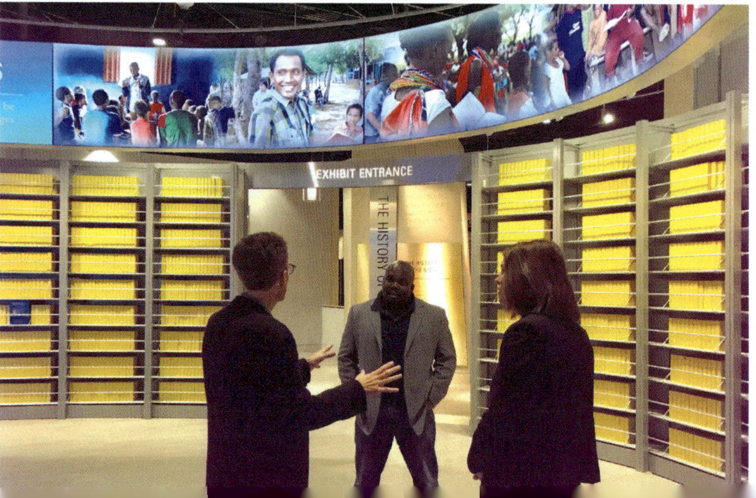

Two years after their family began manufacturing picture frames in their home, David and Barbara Green began Hobby Lobby in 1972. Fast forward to 2021. Hobby Lobby generated $7 billion in revenue, and this in the COVID aftermath. The threads of a Bible-centered life, generosity, and a call to the marketplace had set the foundation for the entire Green family. This spirit remains manifest in son Mart Green's various global ministry projects and son Steve Green's journey with Museum of the Bible. One of the hallmarks of Mart's role on numerous international projects is gathering like-minded ministries and projects to find sensible synergy—to save personal and financial resources by removing duplication of efforts. The fingerprints of this approach are manifest in projects like Every Tribe Every Nation/illumiNations collaboration and YouVersion. He summarized this in an interview for this book: "These initiatives are platforms that make their ministry partners more efficient and effective. And as for YouVersion, it's perhaps one of the most powerful tools of our lifetime—a Gutenberg moment that we got to see up close!" He also added the following about The illumiNations exhibit. "It has provided strong advocacy for the vision to 'Eradicate Bible Poverty.' It is memorable to see all 6,000+ languages on display and then to realize that 3,600 of them still don't have adequate Scripture. The visual presentation of the museum's exhibit brings that reality home for visitors in a powerful way."

The Spiritual Journey of the Chairman of the Board

It's not much of a stretch to find a strong connection between the Green family's personal religious beliefs and funding commitments. While it's possible to tell the museum's story without mentioning this, it would be an incomplete narrative. In fact, they are rather straightforward with the types of projects they consider and, in this case, their desire to have others join them in the museum's support. This love for God and the Bible (which they clearly claim as "His Word") is also reflected in their time commitments. We find this in the demanding role as Chairman of the Board of Museum of the Bible, which Steve Green has held since its founding.

He reminisced about his spiritual journey, "We attended church service weekly, and my faith became my own at age 7 or 8. As a kid I prayed, 'I want to know God better and study the Bible in more depth.' Later, I was deeply influenced at church camps. I not only enrolled in them but worked for three weeks in three other church camps."

Following high school, Steve worked for Hobby Lobby, after having joined his siblings Mart and Darsee in helping with tasks in its infancy (like assembling picture frames at home). Throughout this time, he sought formal and informal venues to study the Bible. However, he passed on college given his commitment to his family's business (and the lengthy reading lists). Ironically, years later he became a voracious reader and has even authored a few books since the museum's founding.

Capping this authoring and resource trajectory, in 2022 the Museum of the Bible signed a remarkable 180-book, ten-year deal with Tyndale House Publishers (the world's largest independent Christian publisher). It's fitting that the first release is *The World's Greatest*

Book, a second edition co-authored by both a Christian and a Jewish scholar.

Steve said, "My wife, Jackie, and I felt that God had brought us to a place in our spiritual journey to shepherd the creation of the museum. The first steps were in 2010 and formally in 2012. This was an awesome assignment from God." They shifted their priorities and began giving tremendous time commitments to the museum's future.

Determining the City for the Museum and finding a building in Washington, DC

The first major decision was the museum's location. The family was offered several properties and courted by other business owners or city representatives. However, a survey of 1,000 people nationally pointed to three top options: Dallas, New York City, and Washington, DC.

While Dallas remained on the list, Washington, DC, surfaced for two main reasons—its platform for events and proximity to many of the nation's leading museums.

Steve once commented, "We were pleasantly surprised with DC's accommodating leadership, including providing permits for us to build. The biggest challenge, however, was finding the right building and location."

Our current CEO, Harry Hargrave, remembers standing on the Capitol steps in 2012, struggling with how to find the right property. At the time, he was advising the funders and overseeing the selection and acquisition process (after a solid history of organizational and business development). It had been a year, and large properties in DC simply were rare. He asked God to provide the right place, and offered a simple two-word prayer, "Help me."

In a sense, he was nearing the end of his efforts—not wanting to continue past the year without successfully locating a building. But then it happened. Not weeks or months later—but literally minutes. After praying, he walked down from Capitol Hill to the next building in his research and "serendipitously" noticed an older, repurposed building serving as the Washington Design Center. As he was walking into his office across the National Mall after viewing that building, a call arrived from his attorney about that very place (not realizing he had just toured it)! The owners needed to show a profit for the quarter and wanted to liquidate it before the fiscal quarter ended. Though the bid wasn't

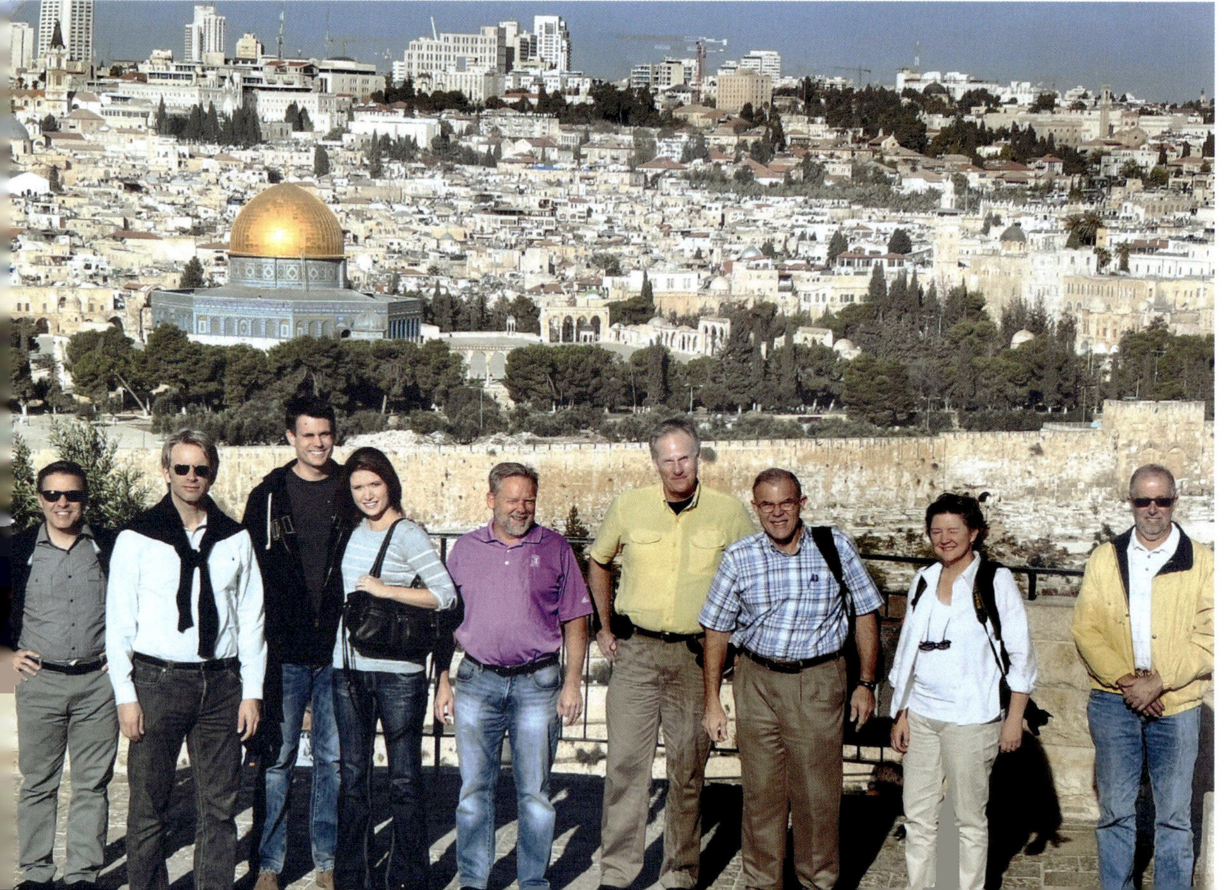

Cary Summers (then CEO, third from right) hosting the museum's various design teams for a research trip in Israel (October 2013).

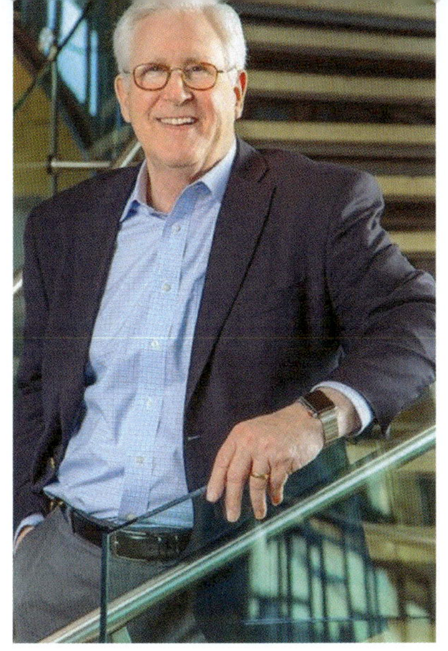

Harry Hargrave, CEO of Museum of the Bible, was a key advisor to the funders and board during the building's acquisition and construction.

the highest, it was cash, and thus the DC museum began. The entire triangular block (around a million square feet) was purchased—and is strategically located above the metro.

Built in 1922, it was originally The Terminal Refrigerator and Warehousing Company, located at 400 4th Street SW. If you can picture DC's National Mall, it's just a couple of blocks south of The National Museum of the American Indian. It was purchased on behalf of the museum in 2012, renovated over the following five years, and then in 2017, Museum of the Bible opened.

The planning team began by carefully selecting a larger group to conceive the mission and the metrics of the museum's intangible and tangible aspects. First, they organized a board of directors, which initially included the late Robert E. Cooley—the former president of Gordon Conwell Seminary. He played a critical role in amassing a mélange of influencers such as Rick Warren (of Saddleback), Anne Beiler (Auntie Anne's Pretzels), James Moore (C-Suite for Coca-Cola), Bob Hoskins (founder of One Hope), and so forth. Underpinning the tangible efforts were many of the programs already in place.

The Scholars Initiative had launched a wide-ranging research and mentoring program in 2010. The first key collaborators were at Tyndale House in Cambridge, UK, led by Peter J. Williams, and Stan Rosenberg at Oxford (the SCIO program associated with Wycliffe Hall). More than 300 key biblical language students have already gone through the Scholars Initiative's Logos Program, which includes two weeks in either Oxford or at Museum of the Bible in DC.

What is often missed when standing before the majestic Museum of the Bible is that God had already helped to orchestrate programs involving faculty and students at some 100 universities worldwide before it opened.

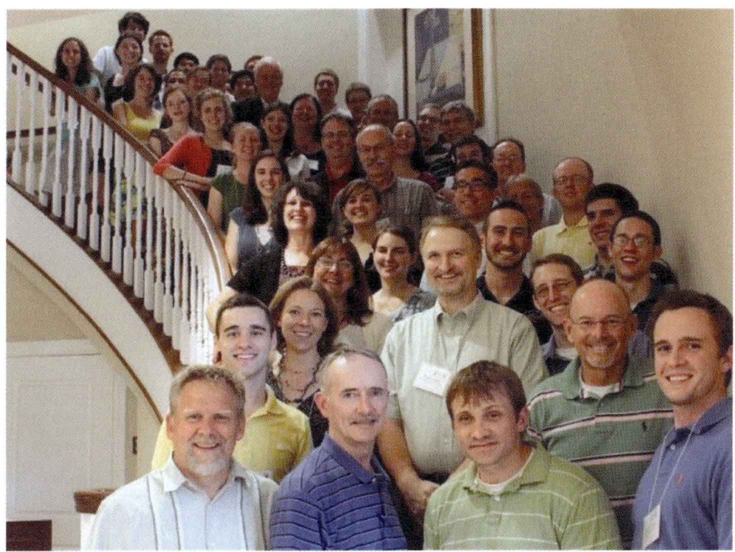

The first Logos meeting (the signature program of the Scholars Initiative). The original meeting was held at Baylor University in Waco, Texas, before alternating between Oxford University and the Museum of the Bible, DC.

The design team for that imposing DC building had experience in building presidential libraries and Disney experiences. Cary Summers, whom the board first hired to organize a traveling exhibition, *Passages*, eventually assumed the president's role and brought his entertainment background into the creative strategy of building the museum. Harry Hargrave oversaw the construction, keeping it on time and within budget.

Throughout this remarkable phase, thousands more objects were purchased, though not without a wave of media attention. Inadvertent mistakes with some of these early transactions proved invaluable for learning protocol for longtime operations. Antiquities were certainly new territory for the Greens. Some purchases made international news, both for their incredible merit and, at times, because of missteps prompted by dealers or third parties. In the end, the museum leadership navigated these unexpected ethical challenges with honor. And for perspective, dozens of other key museums and collectors made similar mistakes with the same third parties.

The Museum Opens

Prior to the museum's official opening in November 2017 were numerous hard-hat tours of the construction site. A major pre-opening event highlighted the wonderful life of Michael Cromartie, with Os Guinness and Michael Gerson as contributors.

Let us look a bit closer at the museum. It contains more than 1,000 permanent objects from the collection on display and hundreds of items on loan across seven floors. Later in this book, we include some of the key artifacts in the museum. To help put these in context, here is an overview of the floors before we turn the pages to the high-image walkthrough of its timeline and then its treasures.

- **Floor 1:** Flanking the museum's main entrance are the Gutenberg Gates. These massive 40-foot-high brass gates contain the first lines from Genesis in Latin as set in the printing bed of the Gutenberg press. The Grand Hall features a breathtaking, 140-foot-long digital ceiling that displays a series of images, such as illuminated manuscripts, nature, art, and spectacular architecture. The first floor also contains an exhibit from the Vatican, a children's gallery, a virtual reality experience, and a packed Museum Shop.
- **Floor 2:** This interactive floor communicates the impact of the Bible in world history (across many civilizations and cultures). This includes an area called Bible Now, which provides a spectacular live feed of global data. Also featured on this floor is the Bible in America exhibit, which traces its history from the first settlers to the 21st century. It also contains the Bible in the World exhibit, where guests discover the Bible's global influence in areas like film, music, literature, fashion, and government. The museum's ride, Washington Revelations, can also be found on the second floor—providing visitors with a multi-sensory tour of Washington, DC, "flying" them past biblical references in and around the nation's capital. It was designed from a prototype in Vienna, Austria.
- **Floor 3:** Here visitors are able to walk through the stories of the Hebrew Bible, immerse themselves in first-century Nazareth, and listen to the story of how the followers of Jesus became a thriving community. The award-winning Hebrew Bible experience has indeed been a favorite of more than two million visitors.

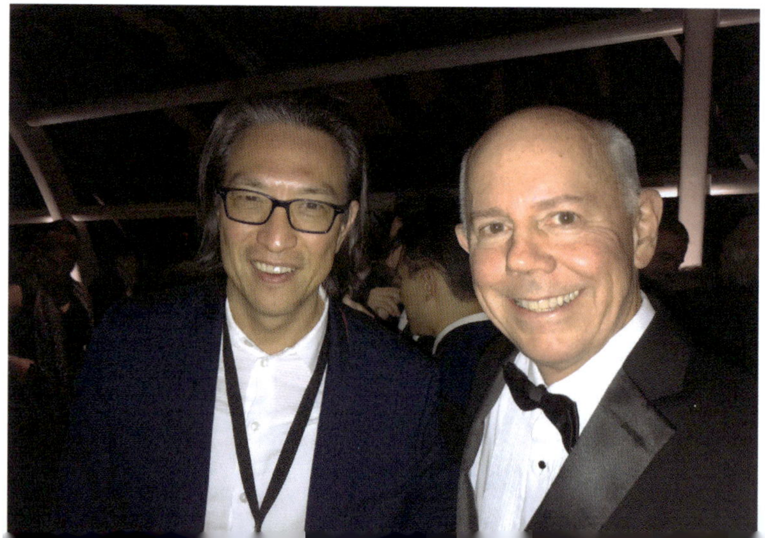

Makoto Fujimura is one of the noted artists and authors whose works have been highlighted at the museum. He is with author Tom Holladay at the museum. Tom retired from Saddleback Church in July 2022 after thirty-one years of service.

- **Floor 4:** The History of the Bible includes background on the Dead Sea Scrolls, early Greek, Latin, and Syriac texts, stunning illuminated manuscripts, early English Bible translations, and various other manifestations of the Bible in other languages. Also, the illumiNations gallery identifies known Bible translations—whether in part or whole—and languages yet to have translations of the Bible. This area is all color coded for a stunning visual of translation work.
- **Floor 5:** The World Stage Theater, rotating (temporary) exhibition space, that features a spectacular view of the city and the Capitol's rotunda. You also find here the Israel Antiquities Authority exhibit, a rare opportunity to see artifacts outside of Israel.
- **Floor 6:** The Gathering Room for meetings and events, Manna restaurant, and an outside Biblical Garden. Tucked away for speakers and invited guests are gathering spaces, lecture and green rooms, and a media production area.

The Museum's Message

As the museum was being planned, its Bible "curriculum" was already well underway. Eventually its four volumes and 108 chapters developed around three main themes for use by homeschool, private school, and trade audiences. These themes are the history, story, and impact of the Bible—the board Chair's vision for the museum as well.

The History of the Bible. On the History Floor, more than 600 scrolls, manuscripts, illuminated books, and printed Bibles, including a replica of the Great Isaiah Scroll, show how the Bible has spread across the globe and was embraced by different communities. Its powerful conclusion is the illumiNations gallery, which shows the state of Bible translation in every language in the world and anticipates a Bible in all of them by 2033.

The Impact of the Bible. Various signposts attest to the Bible's impact on world civilizations. *Life* magazine stated in 2000, the most important event of the past thousand years was the printing of the Gutenberg Bible (and thus the influx of printed books). Throughout history, we can show the impact of the Bible in most facets of culture and daily life—education, medicine, ethics, law, and spiritual life, to name a few. The second floor contains two major exhibits, the Bible in America, tracing the Bible's profound and sometimes complicated impact on American history, and the Bible in the World, which highlights the Bible's influence all around us. The Bible NOW lets guests engage with a live feed of global data related to the Bible and lets them add their own thoughts about it, too.

The Stories of the Bible: The narrative or text of the Bible comes to life in the exhibits on the third floor through living history interpreters, a dramatic walk-through experience, and a panoramic theater. Where else (besides Nazareth) can guests visit a replica Galilean village where the villagers are abuzz with the news of a new rabbi named Jesus? Or hear the story of the early followers of Jesus from the apostle John? Or walk through some of the greatest stories ever told in the Hebrew Bible, from creation to the return from exile? The Stories of the Bible floor offers guests a way to immerse themselves in the Bible itself.

The Vision for the Museum

Steve Green relayed three aspirations for the Museum of the Bible by 2033. First, that it would realize millions more visitors. Second, that media venues would allow the message of the museum to be sent to millions of people unable to attend in person. This was a goal from the beginning and considerable efforts have taken place involving digital and interactive content and resources. Third, that a considerable number of world influencers and leaders would come to a more informed understanding of how the Bible has changed our world.

A key manifestation of a confluence of his goals is Inspire—an intense day at the museum. It is designed to provide three different sessions. (1) The history of Hobby Lobby and its tie to ministries, specifically the museum. (2) The Bible's narrative. And (3) The history of the museum's creation along with a tour of the museum. Steve's goal, and those of the planning team, is *that the museum would have an impact on leaders around the world.*

Visitors spot their friends' names on the walls of donors.

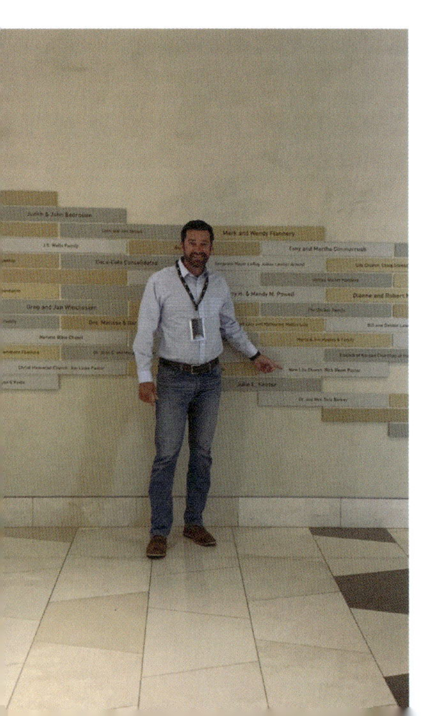

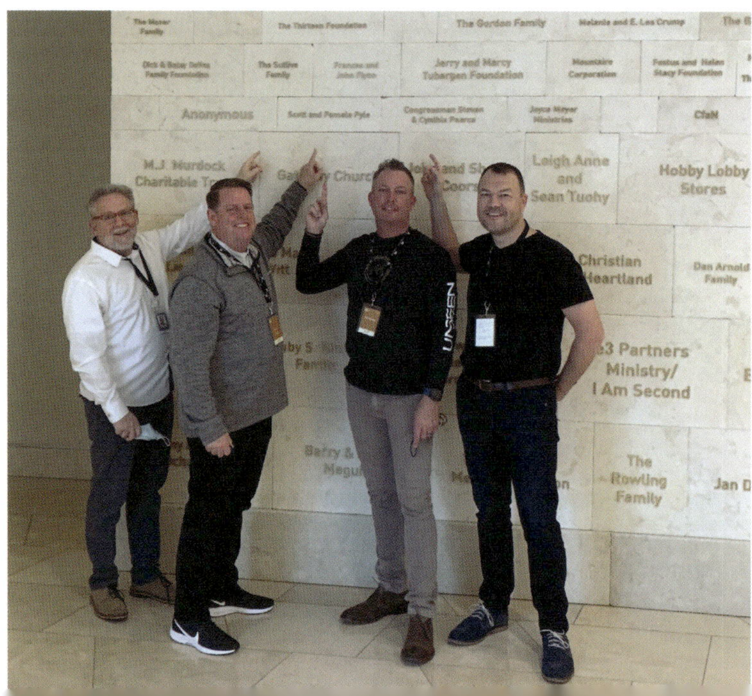

All of this was to be done in partnership with others, and more than 100,000 have joined in helping the museum to move forward.

The Journey Continues

In recent months, museum visitors have enjoyed engaging exhibits on the Magna Carta, the Chinese martyr Watchman Nee, and the Samaritans. Likewise, some wonderful venues are upcoming. Key among them are the Narnia plays with the stunning two- and three-person walking puppets. The Academy of the Arts (and Logos Theatre) from Taylors, South Carolina, are putting on forty showings of plays it wrote around C. S. Lewis's works, such as *The Horse and His Boy*. These come with the approval and blessing of Douglas Gresham, Lewis's stepson.

As this goes to press, we are excited to announce a critical new partner, CREATR Immerse. This talented group of musical and digital storytellers brings a one-of-a-kind digital experience to the World State Theater. This 360-degree immersive story will feature the creativity of the world's leading worship leaders, celebrating the role of creativity and worship throughout the Bible.

We have great faith that these new partnerships will draw a significant new audience from around the world to experience the museum. The same is true of various exhibits, partnerships, and new objects under discussion.

The following two sections will first survey the Museum of the Bible's history and next highlight approximately forty of the more than 60,000 objects in our collections.

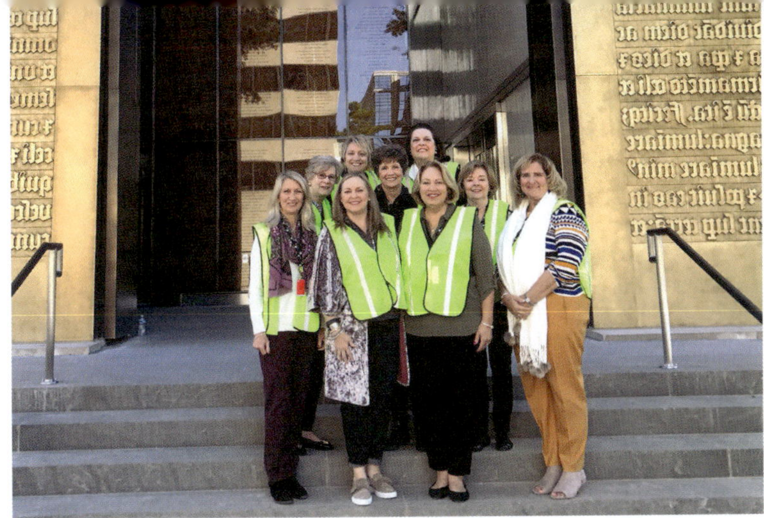

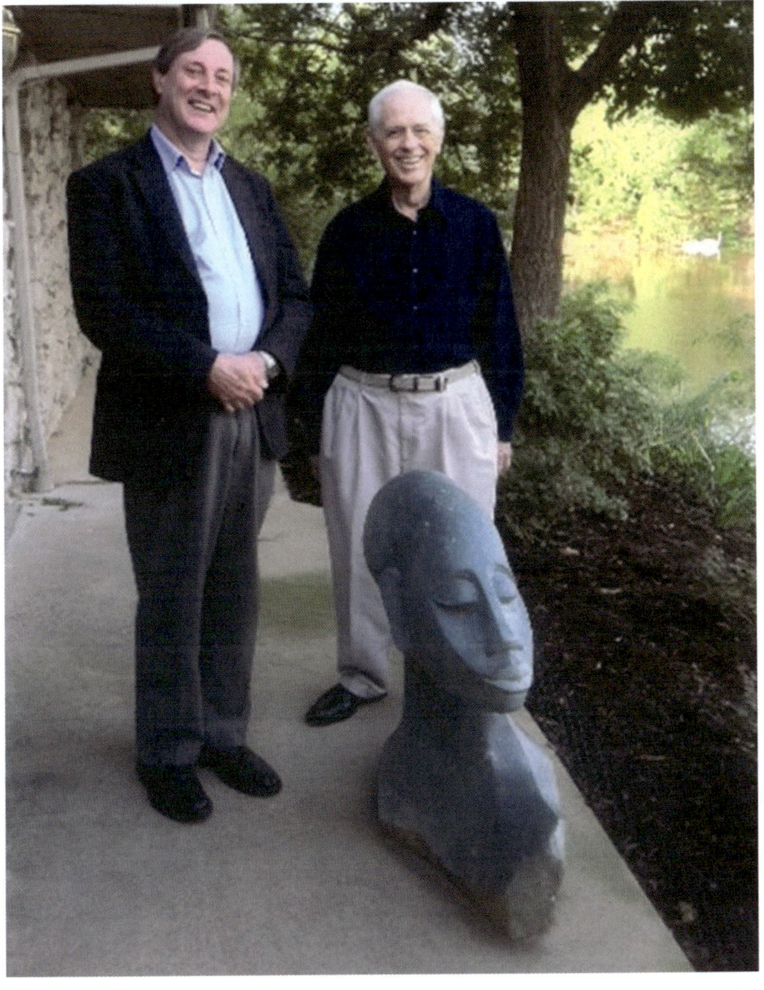

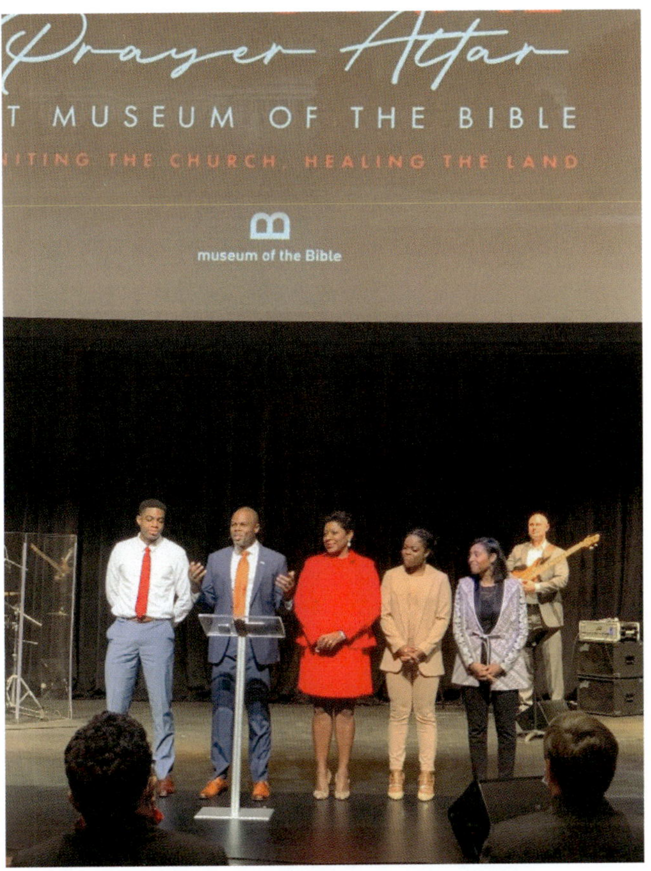

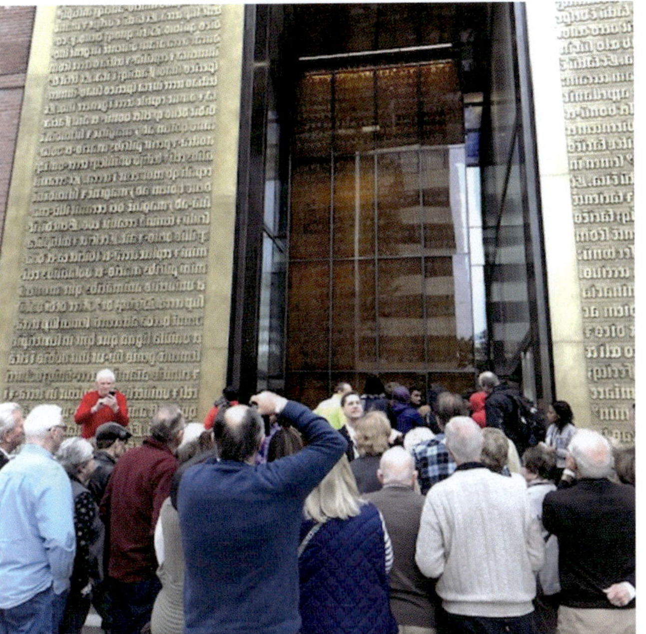

Top Left: Jackie Green (front, second from left) hosting one of her first of many groups of women at the museum (October 18, 2017).

Top Right: Pastors James and Sharon Ward hosting a National Prayer Altar in the World Stage Theater (September 29, 2021).

Bottom Left: Alister McGrath (Oxford) and the late Tom Oden at Tom's house in Oklahoma City. Both scholars were involved in the early years of the museum, and Alister continues to lecture annually for Logos—the centerpiece of the Scholars Program. Alister was in Oklahoma to speak in the inaugural Passages lecture series. You can find a hologram-like image of Alister giving a lecture on the Museum of the Bible's Impact floor.

Bottom Right: A crowd from Indiana awaits to enter on the one-year anniversary (November 17, 2018).

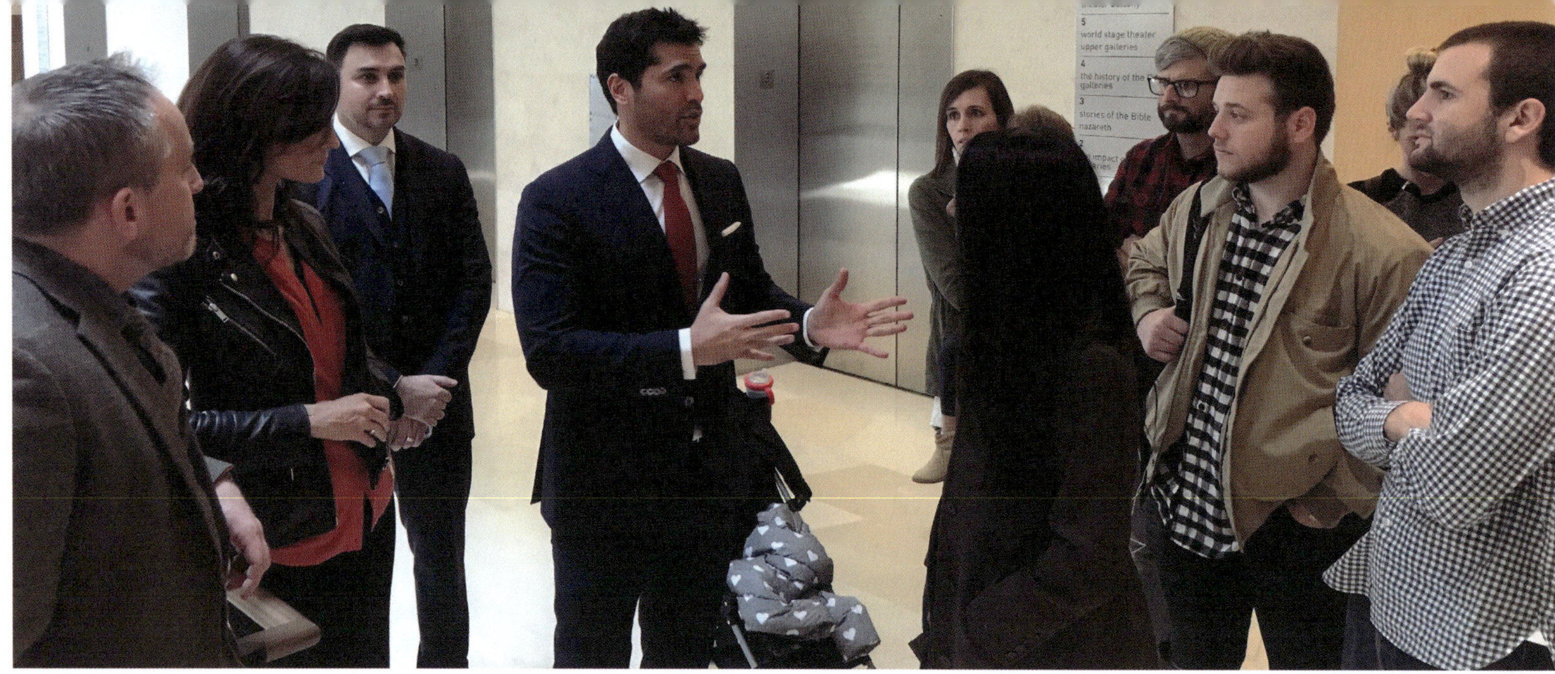

Top: Actor Eduardo Verastegui stops during the museum's opening to talk with visitors.

Center Left: One of the more than 63,000 visitors at the opening (traveling) *Passages* exhibit in the Oklahoma City Museum of Art.

Bottom Left: Ruth Graham and Candy Carson in front of the museum's "Easter Morning" window by Louis C. Tiffany.

Bottom Right: Steve Green speaking at the World Stage Theater during the museum's opening in 2017.

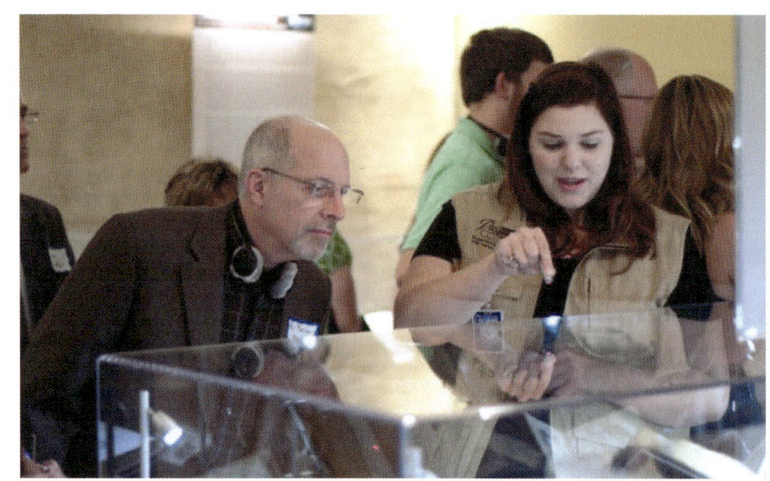

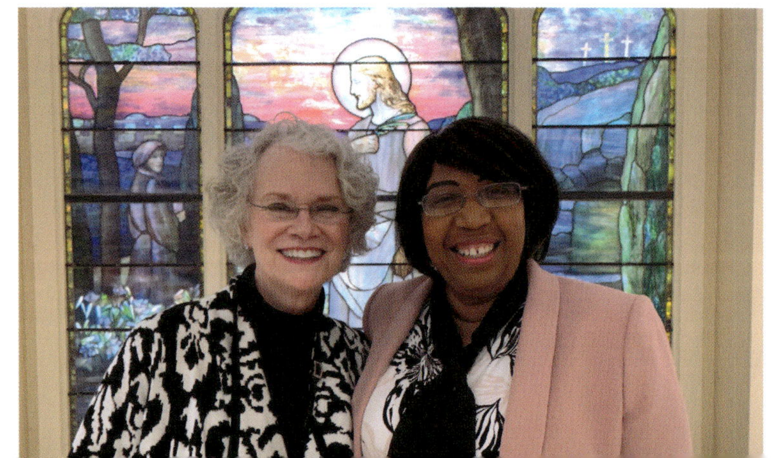

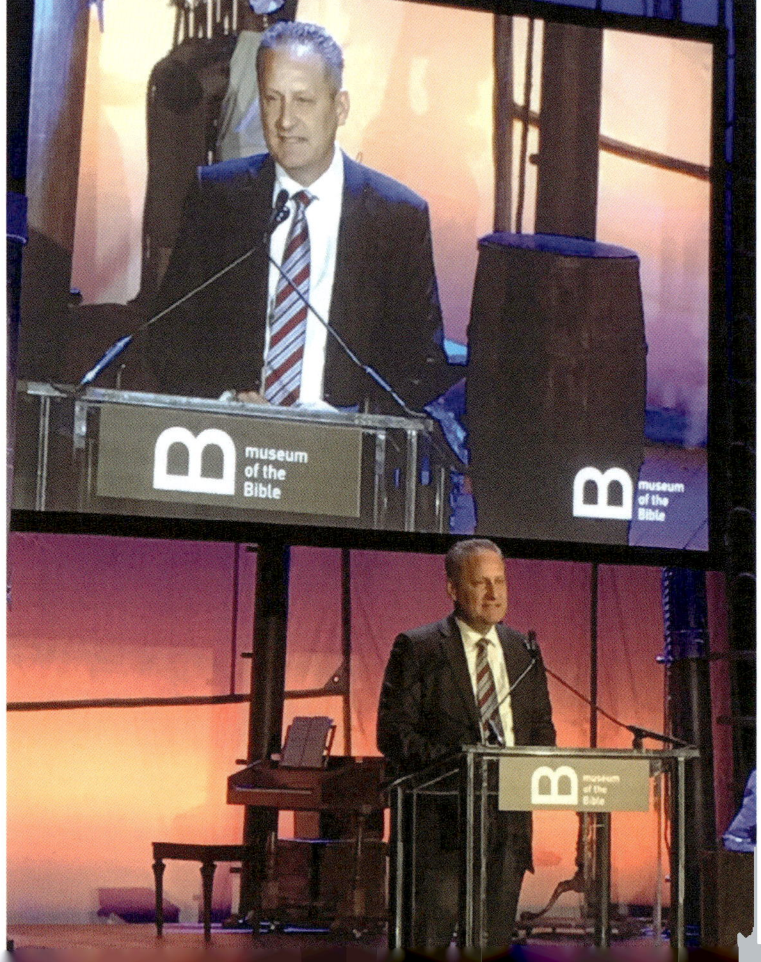

A History of
Museum of the Bible
2010–2022

September 2010

Museum of the Bible established as a 501(c)(3) nonprofit

Steve and Jackie Green both grew up in households that had been radically shaped by the Bible. Neither grew up in wealth or ever dreamed of one day overseeing the world's largest private collection related to the transmission and impact of the Bible.

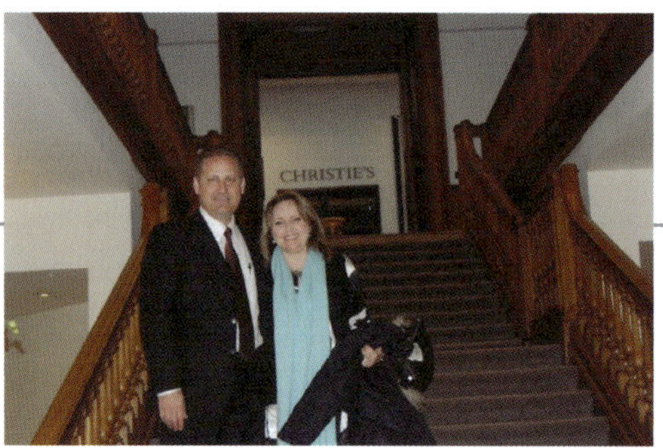

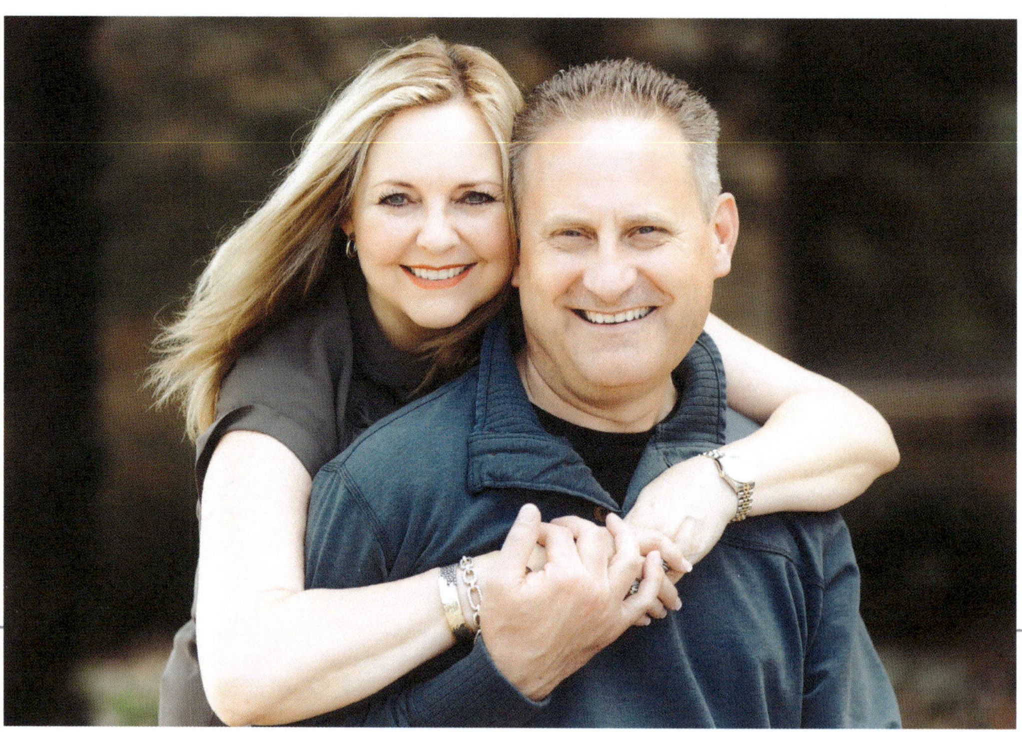

"The Bible is a book that guides our lives, influences our family, informs our business, is instilled in the foundation of our country, and continues to impact the world. We believe that every person should be knowledgeable of its history, impact, and story. That is why Museum of the Bible was created, and why we invite all people to engage with this beautiful book."

Steve & Jackie Green
Co-Founders, Museum of the Bible

May 2011

Passages: The 400th Anniversary of the King James Bible opened at Oklahoma City Museum of Art.

PASSAGES WAS A traveling exhibition featuring approximately 400 artifacts. It first debuted in Oklahoma City to celebrate the 400th anniversary of the King James Bible. Traveling to six states in five years, more than 500,000 people visited this exhibit. *Passages* was an interactive experience that presented the history of the Bible and allowed children the opportunity to explore the objects through an educational series narrated by Leo the Lion. This 30,000-square-foot exhibit invited guests to engage with the Bible through contextual settings such as an ancient Jewish synagogue, the Jerusalem chamber at Westminster Abbey, Israel's Qumran caves, and the Moon.

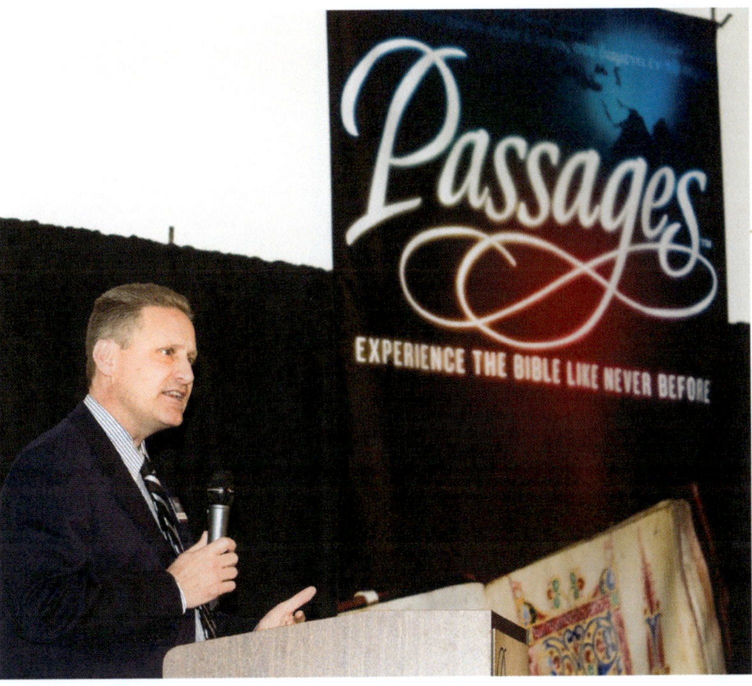

Passages visited:

- Oklahoma City, OK
- Atlanta, GA
- Charlotte, NC
- Colorado Springs, CO
- Springfield, MO
- Santa Clarita, CA

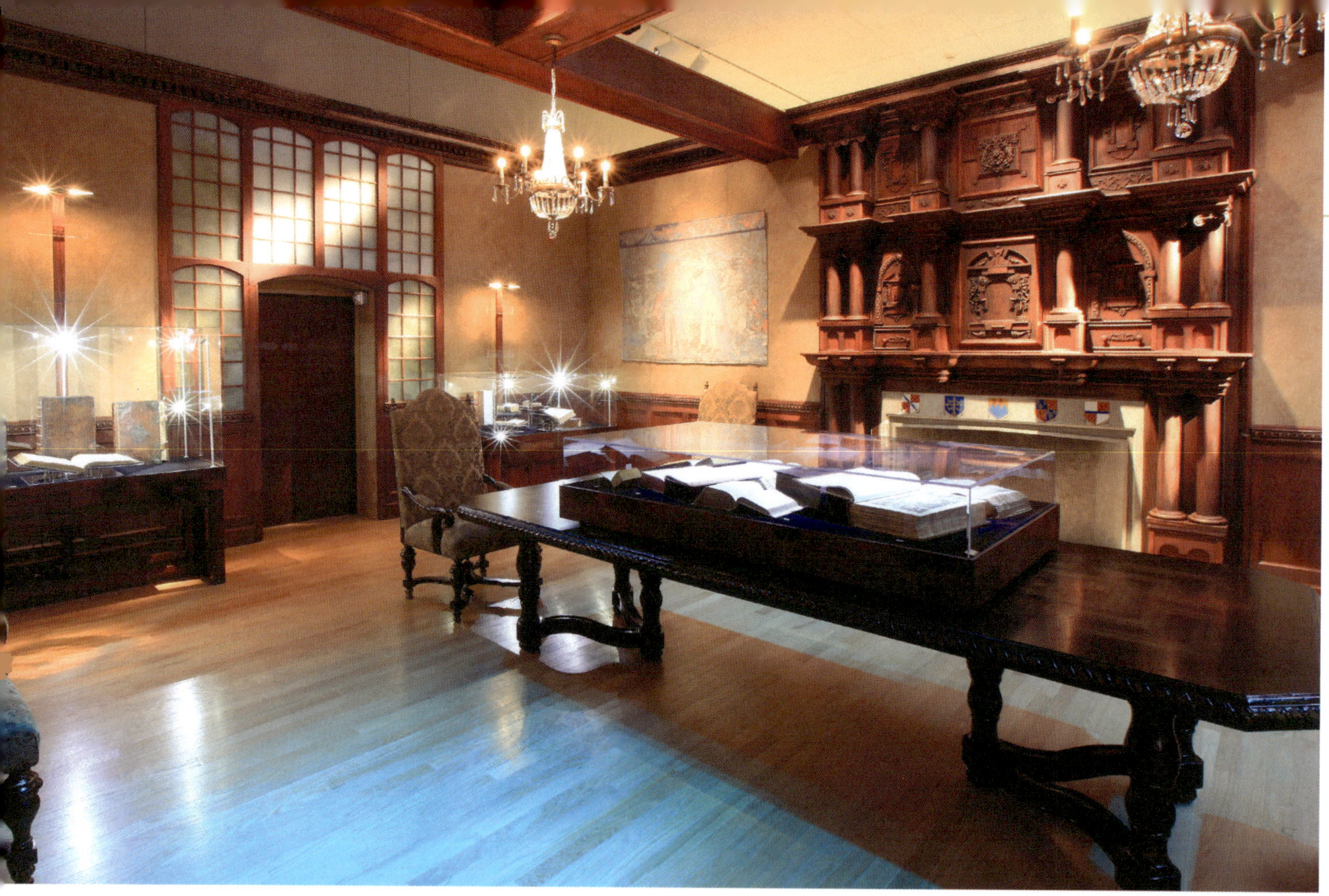

Top: The Jerusalem Chamber exhibit gallery at *Passages*.

Bottom Left: Leo the Lion in Jerome's Cave.

Bottom Right: The Lunar Bible exhibit gallery at *Passages*.

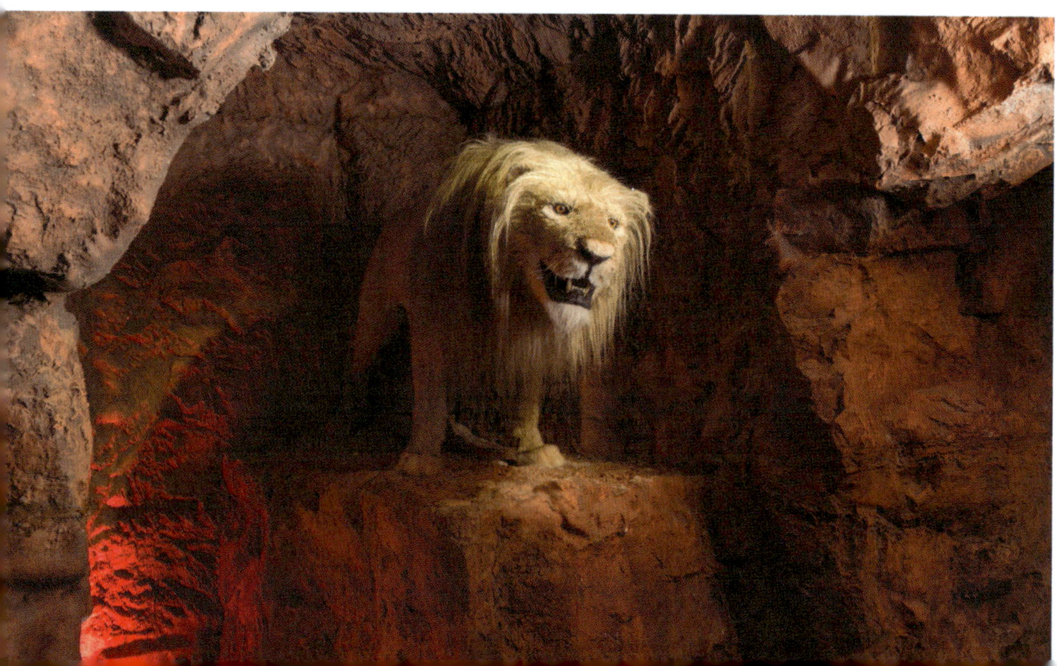

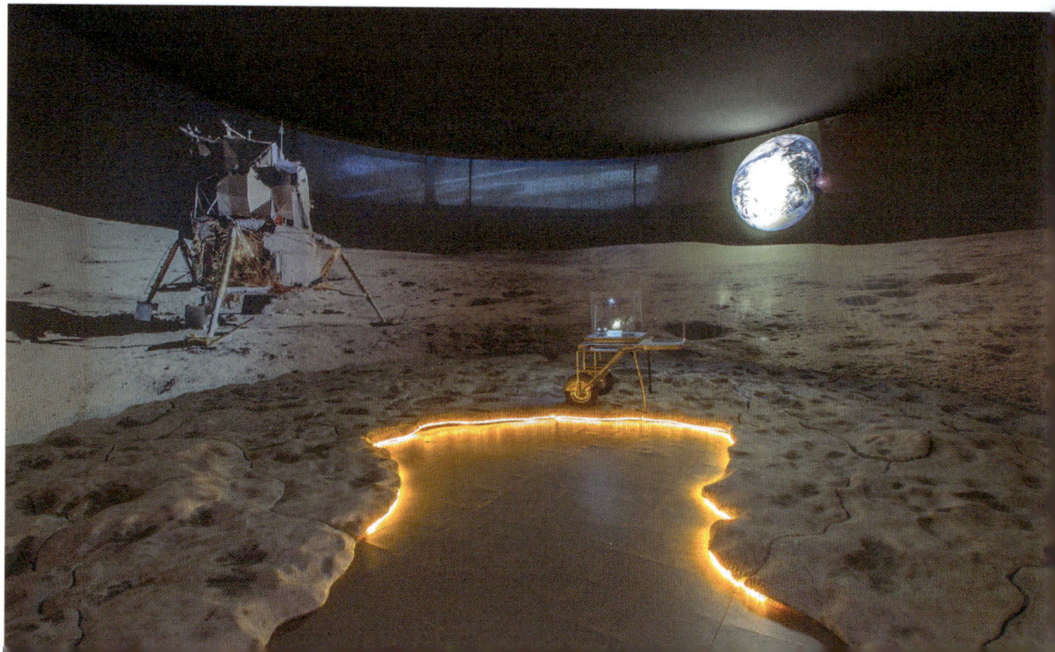

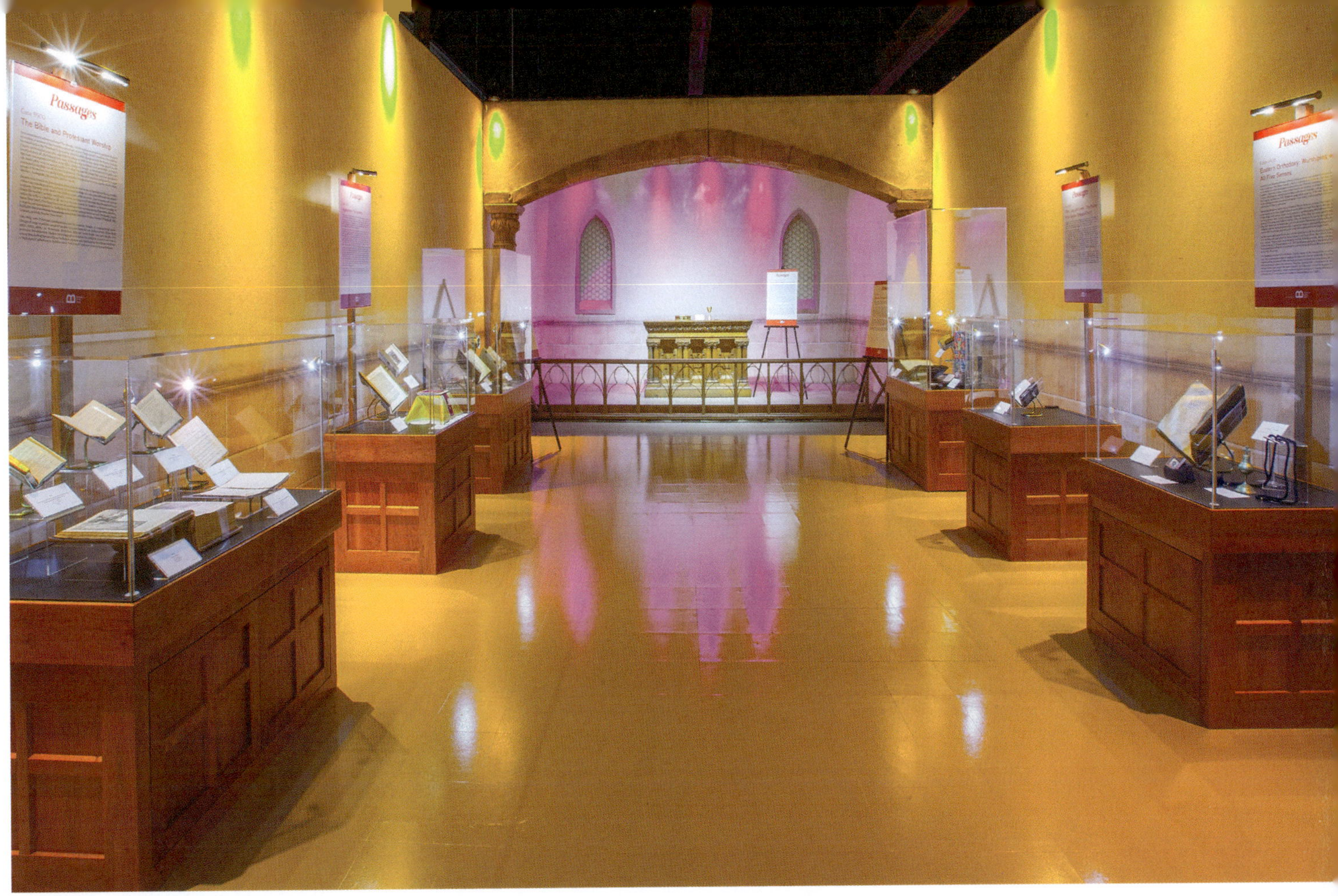

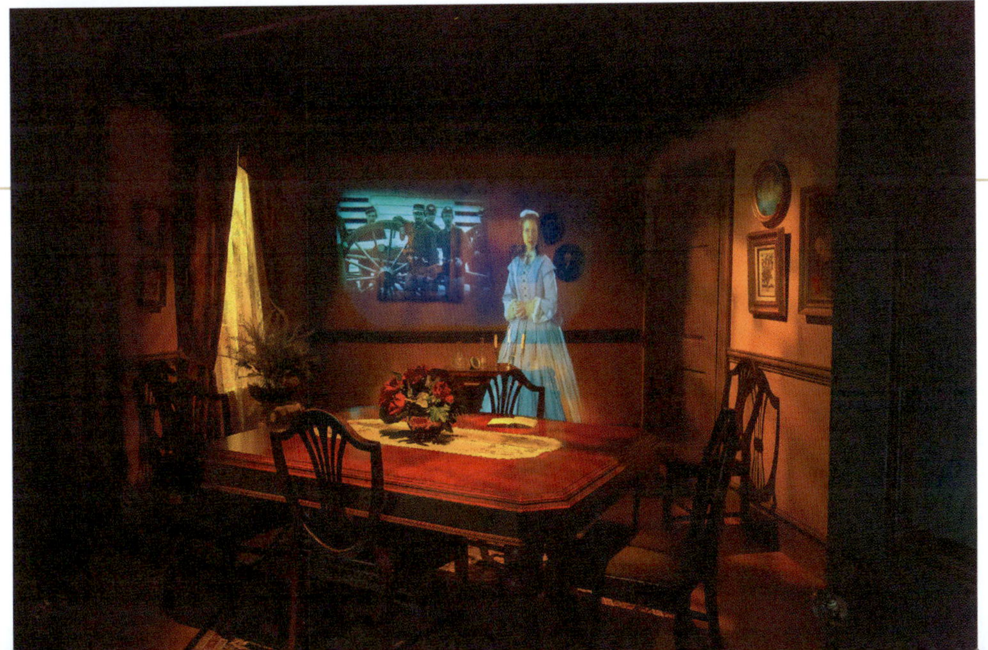

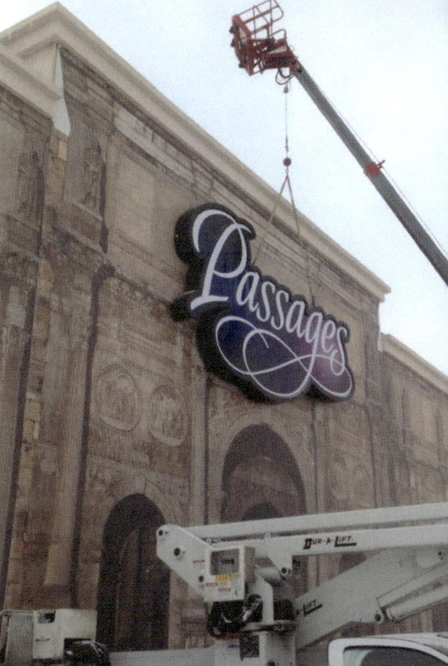

Top: The Christian Liturgy exhibit gallery at *Passages*.

Bottom Left: The Battle Hymn of the Republic exhibit gallery at *Passages*.

Bottom Right: The *Passages* sign install in Colorado Springs.

March 2012

Verbum Domini exhibited in Vatican City.

MUSEUM OF THE BIBLE'S first international traveling exhibit, *Verbum Domini: God's Word Goes Out to the Nations*, was launched in Vatican City in 2012. The exhibit highlighted more than 200 objects that reflected the Bible's global appeal and impact through the centuries.

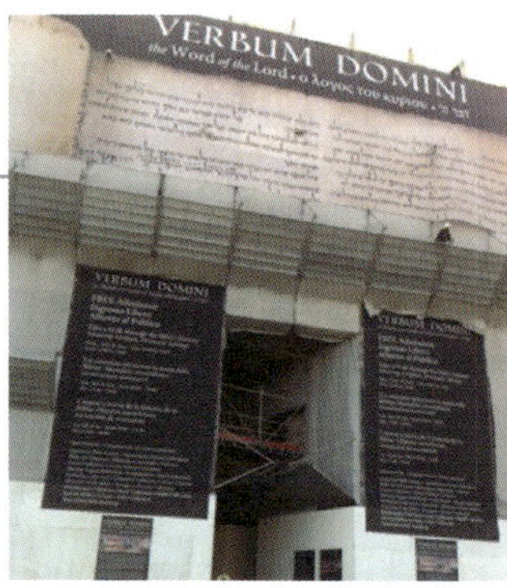

LEFT: *Verbum Domini* signage being installed outside the Vatican.

RIGHT: The Greens standing outside *Verbum Domini II* at Vatican City.

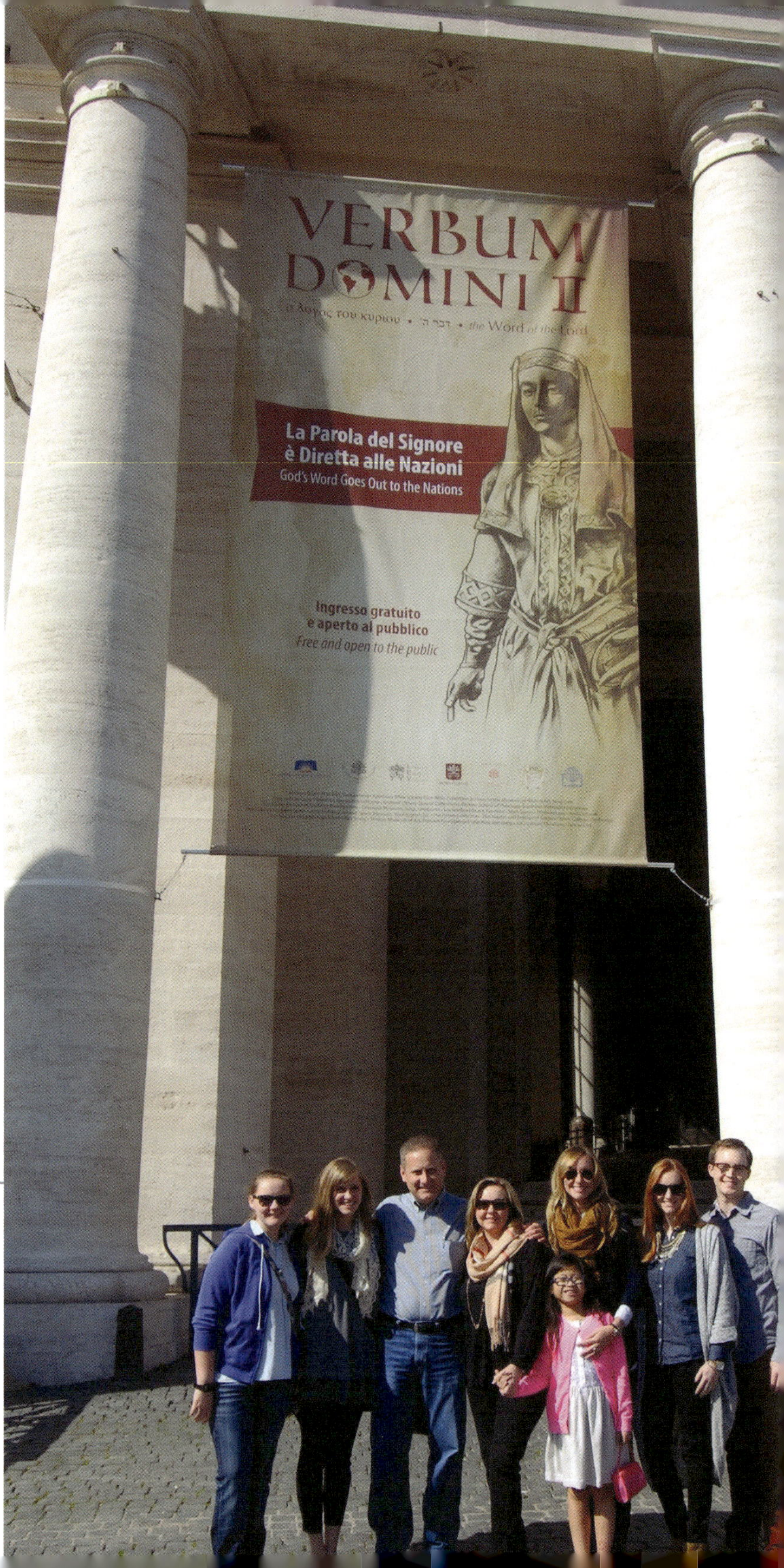

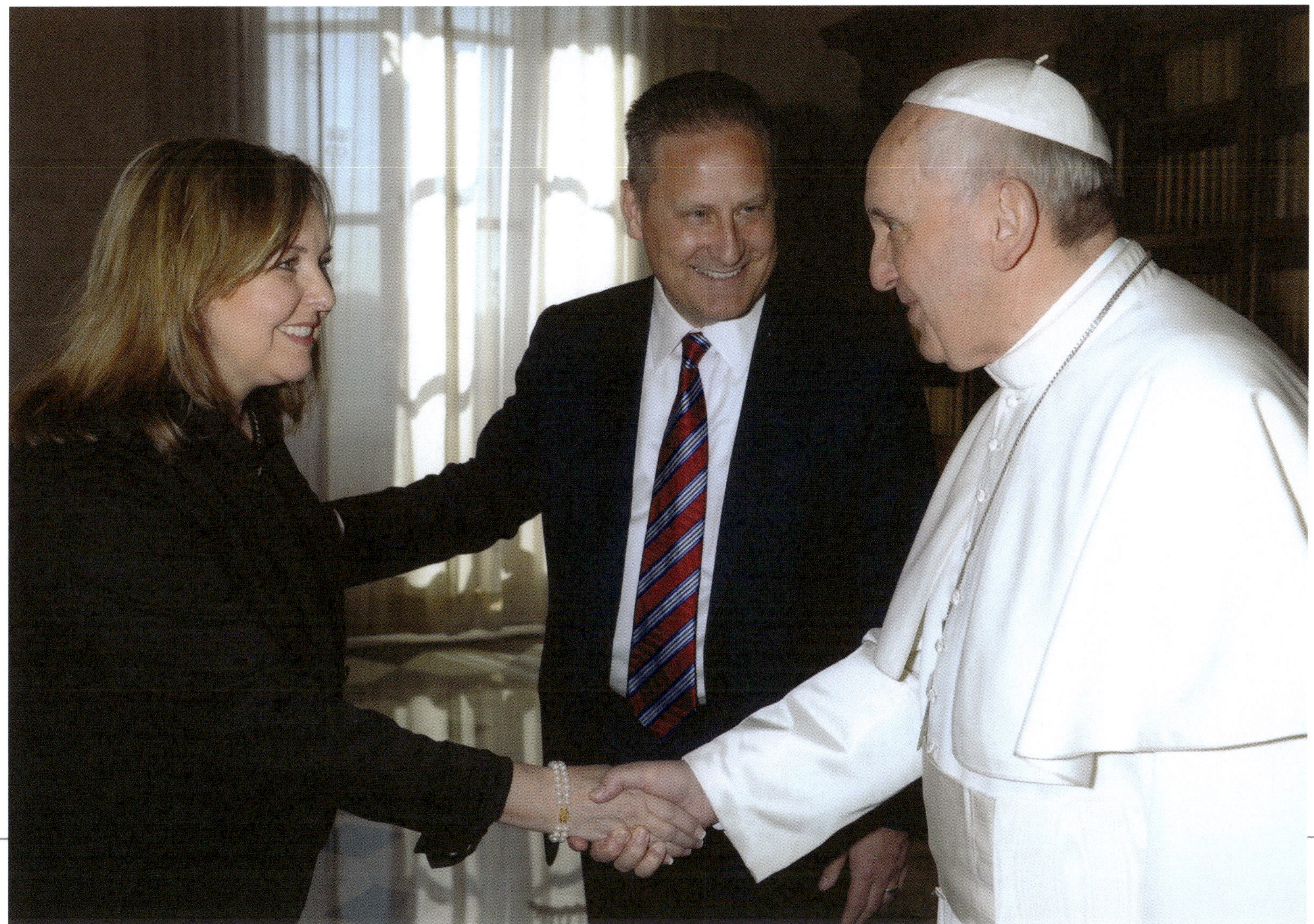

Steve and Jackie Green meeting Pope Francis.

Due to the exhibit's popularity, the exhibit returned to St. Peter's Square in 2014 with *Verbum Domini II.* In 2015, Museum of the Bible joined with the World Meeting of Families in Philadelphia to present an abbreviated version of the popular *Verbum Domini II.*

July 2012

The Washington Design Center building was purchased as the future home of Museum of the Bible.

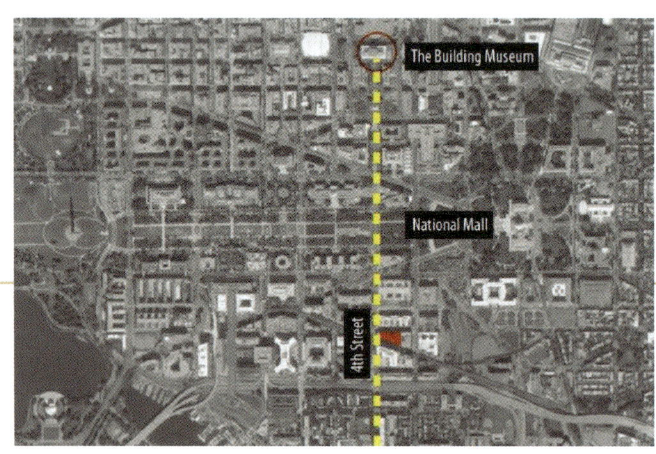

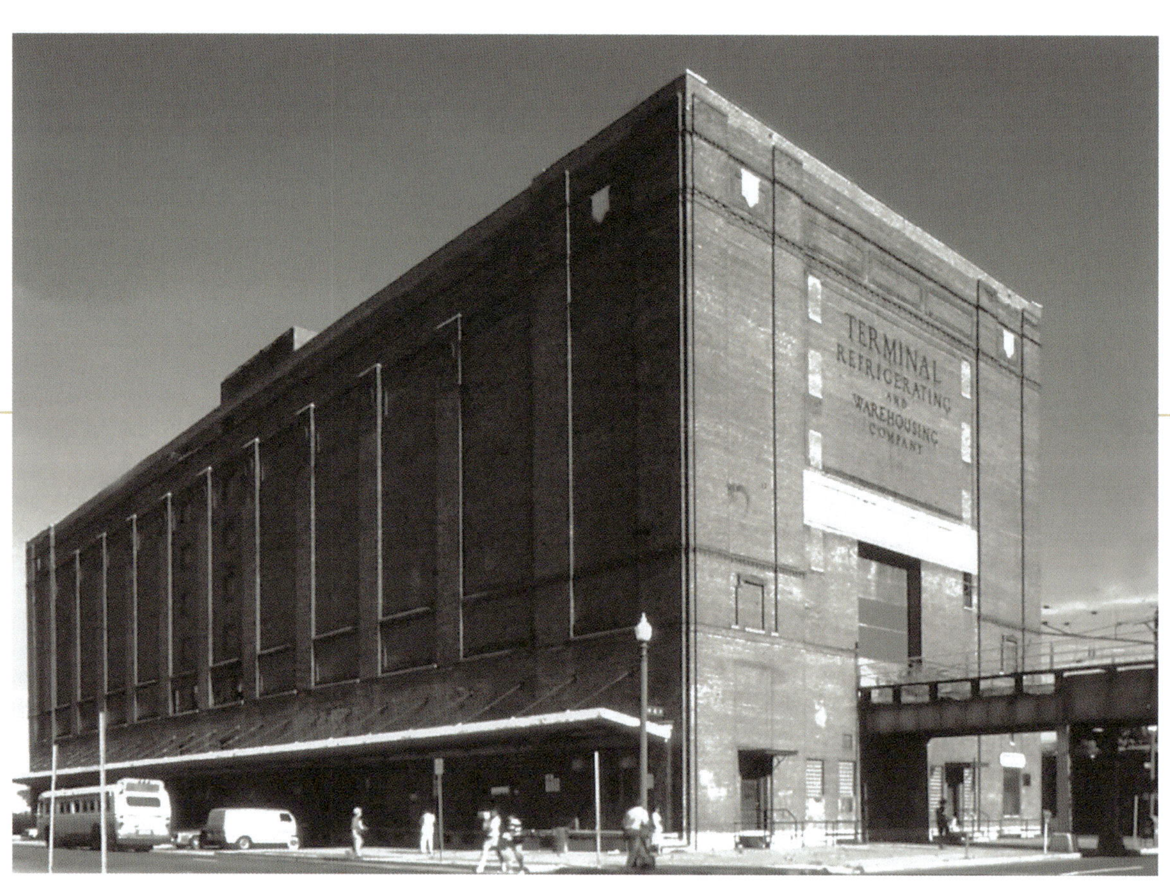

The Terminal Refrigerating and Warehousing Company Building

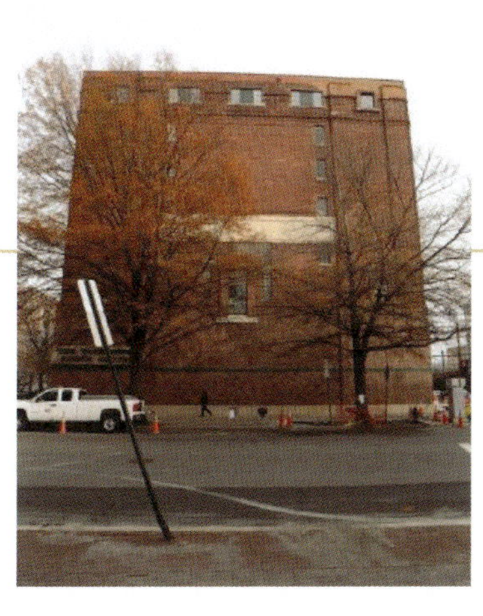

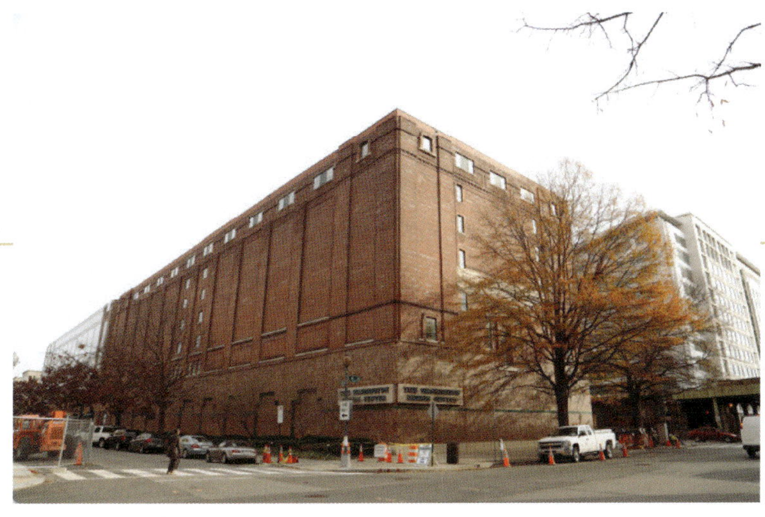

The Washington Design Center

THE OLD BRICK building has a history dating back to 1923. Originally called the Terminal Refrigerating and Warehousing Company Building, it was exactly what it sounds like: a refrigerated warehouse. For decades it served its purpose, outlasting the rapid increase in home refrigeration. Eventually, it closed, with the District of Columbia taking possession of the building around 1980. Soon after, the building was purchased, and in 1983, it opened as the Washington Design Center. By 2012, the owners needed a smaller property, and the building went back on the market, allowing the building's purchase as the future home of Museum of the Bible.

October 2013

Book of Books exhibited at Bible Lands Museum, Israel.

BOOK OF BOOKS presented the relationship between Jewish and Christian faiths by tracing the transmission of the biblical text over the past two millennia, from the Judean wilderness to the whole world. It was on display at the Bible Lands Museum in Jerusalem, Israel, for one year.

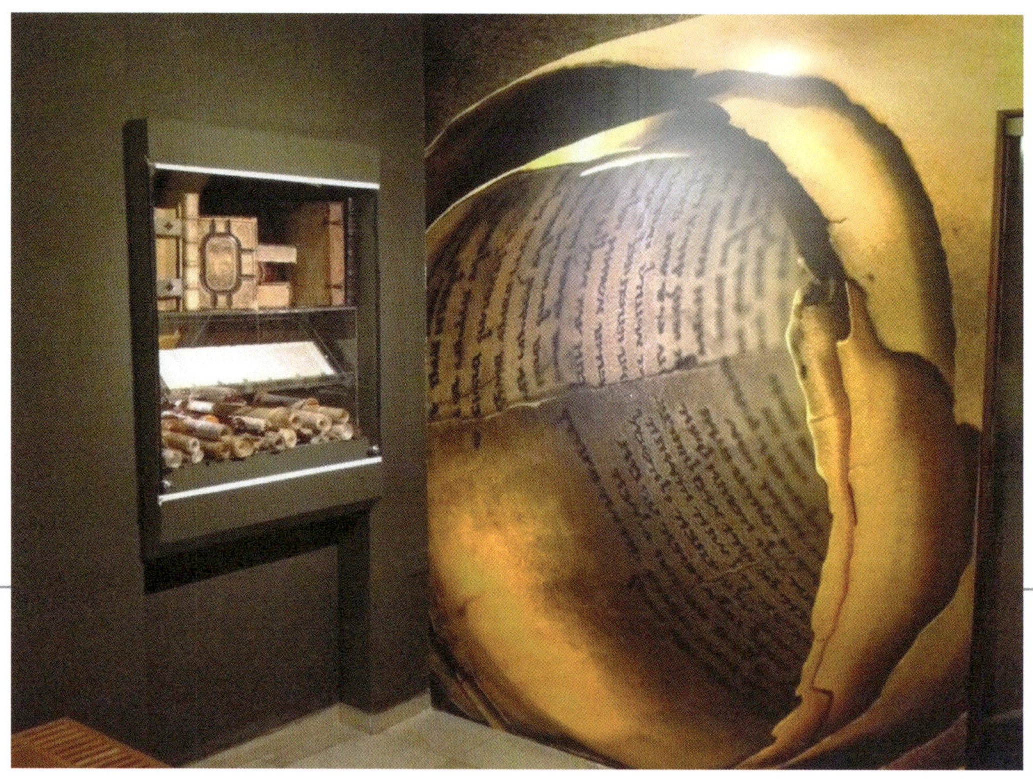

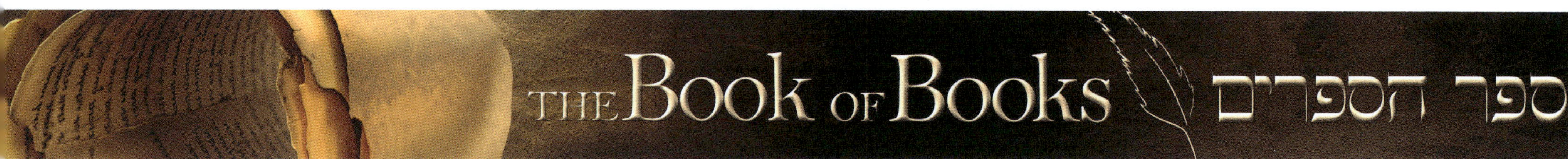

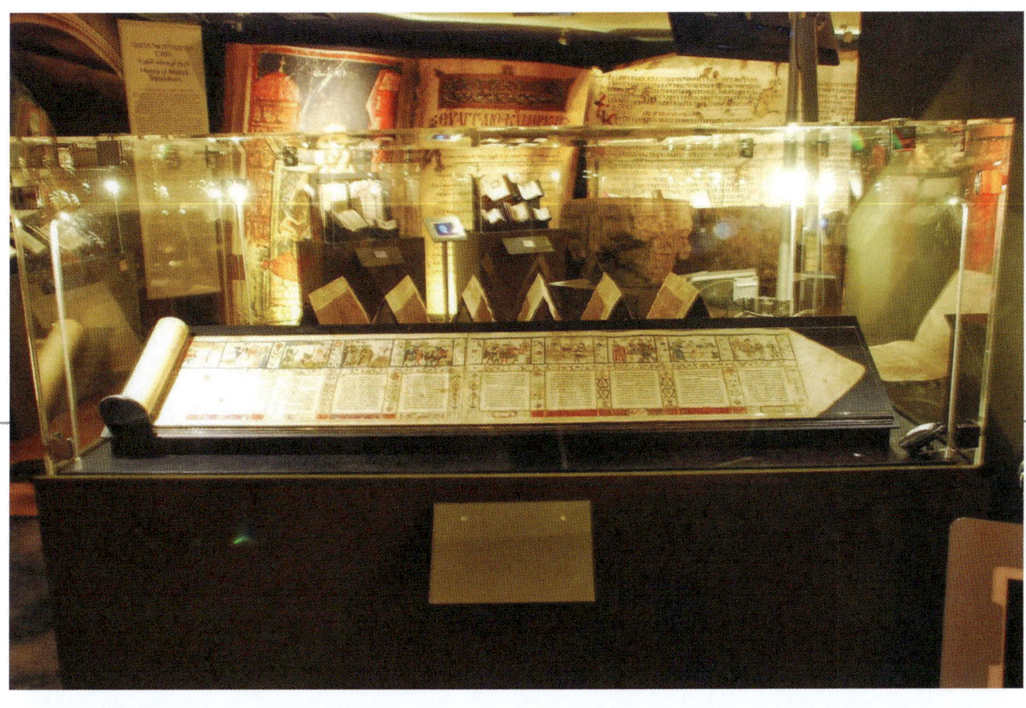

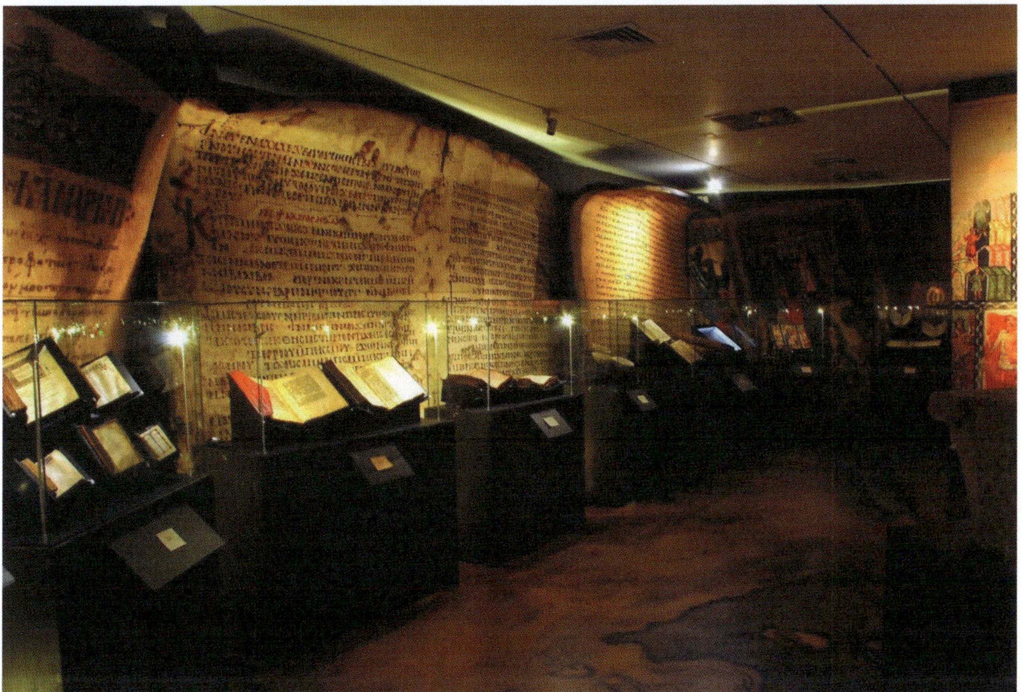

"Through a large network of scholars, such as those associated with the Green Scholars Initiative (later Scholars Initiative), and the Bible Lands Museum, we can trace the historic spread of the Bible and its impact on those societies."

Steve Green
From the Preface of *The Book of Books* exhibit guide

January 2014

***La Biblia, The Way of God in the Way of Man* exhibited in Cuba.**

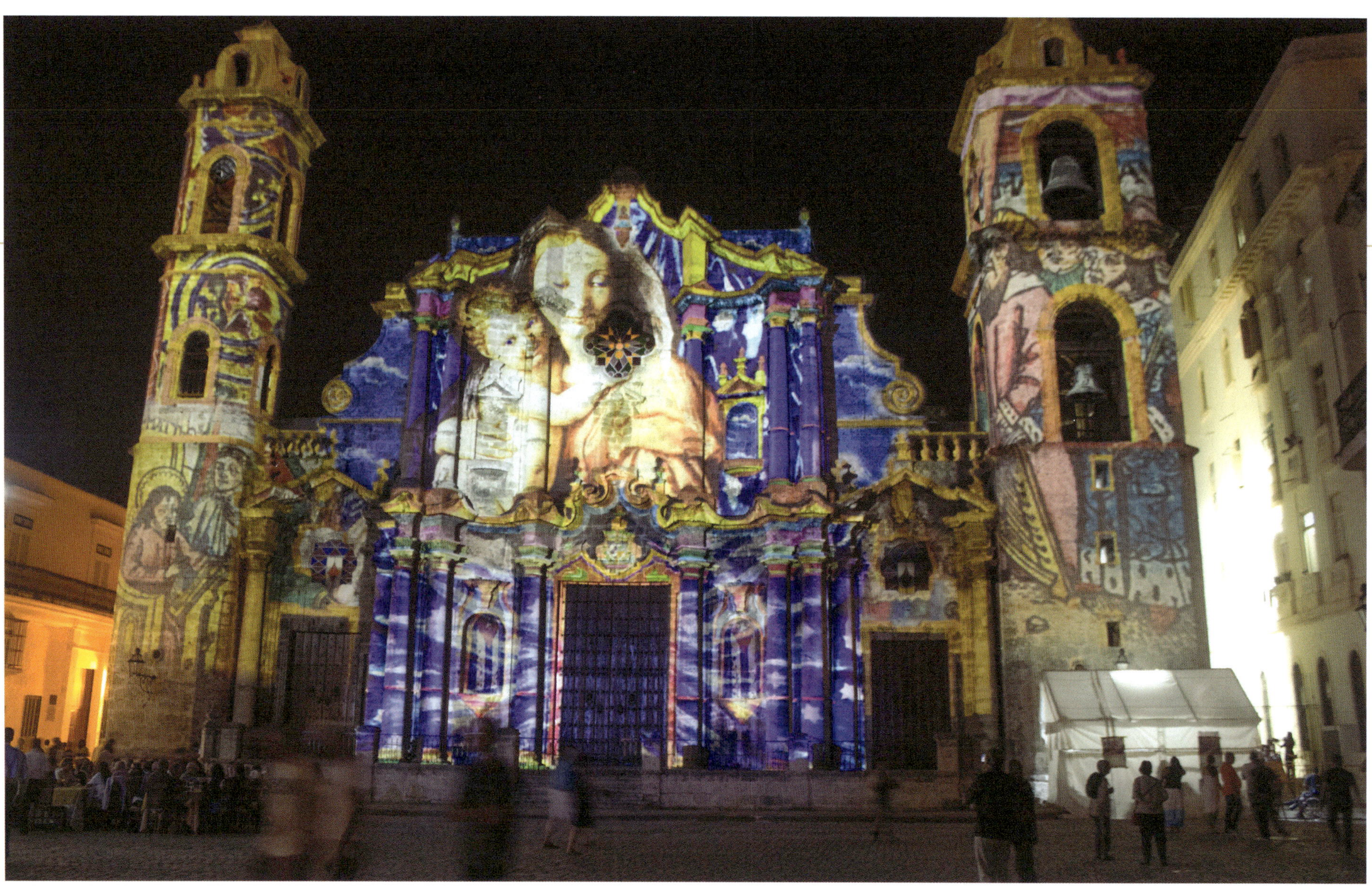

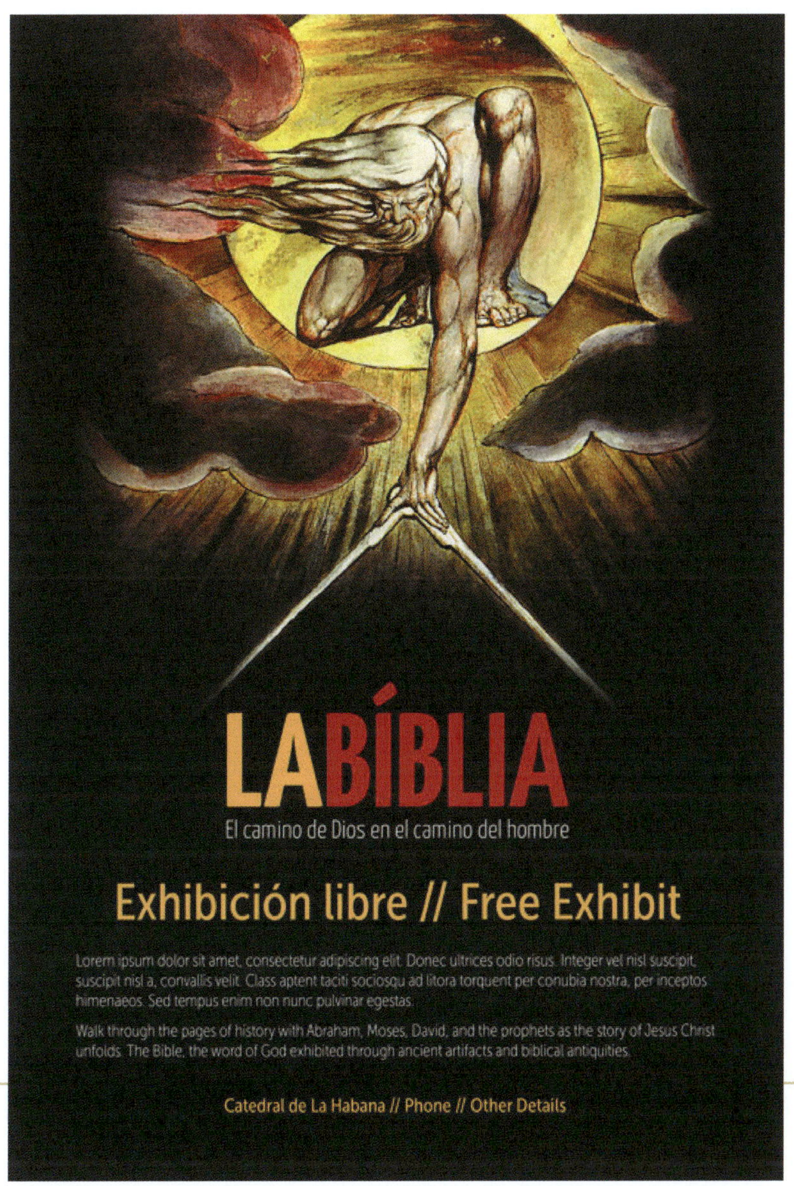

LA BIBLIA, *The Way of God in the Way of Man,* was originally on display for a three-week period in 2014 in Havana, Cuba, and drew more than 30,000 visitors. This exhibit focused on biblical history and the Bible's relevance in Cuban culture. It was so popular that the exhibit returned in 2016 to Santiago, Cuba.

La Biblia exhibit poster

October 2014

Oklahoma City fundraising event and Museum of the Bible brand release.

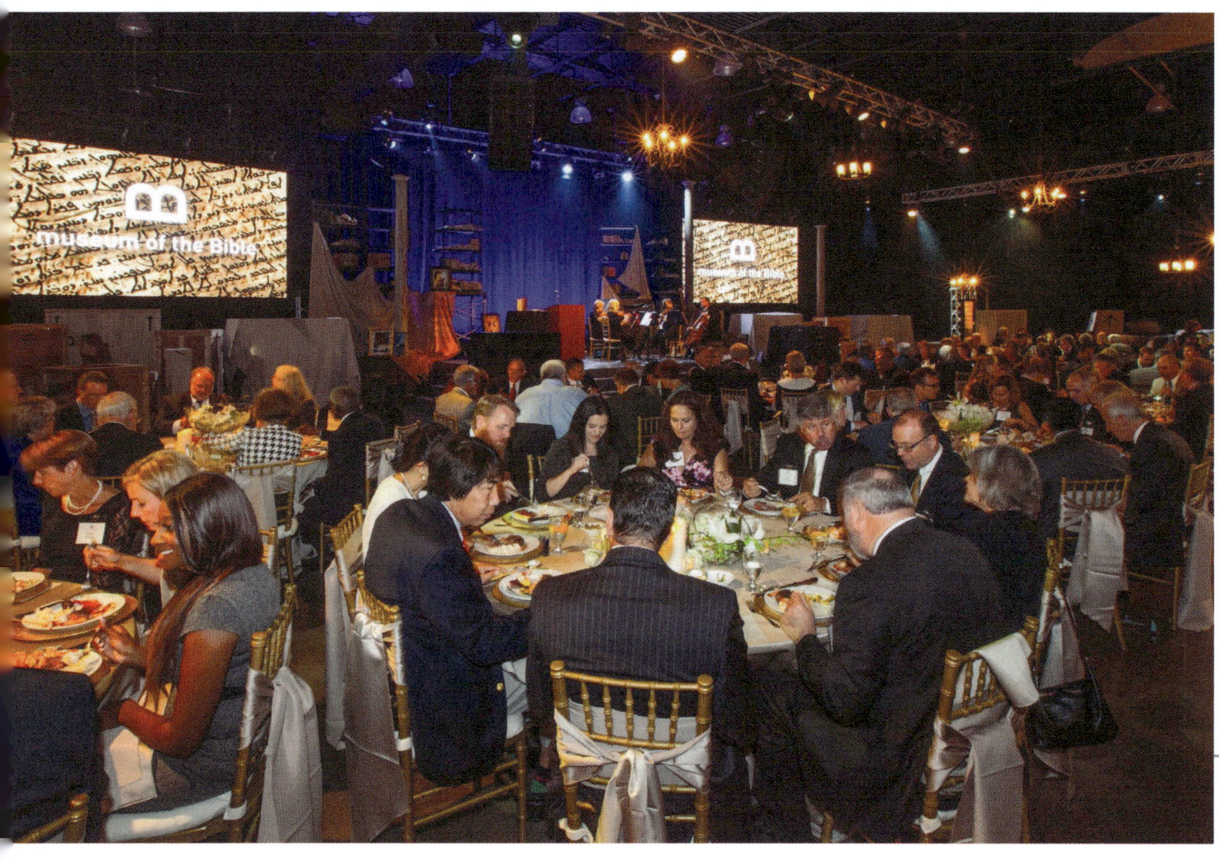

FACING PAGE: The Four Evangelists (1905) and the Easter Morning windows (1909) are by Louis Comfort Tiffany, from the Church of the Epiphany in Orange, New Jersey.

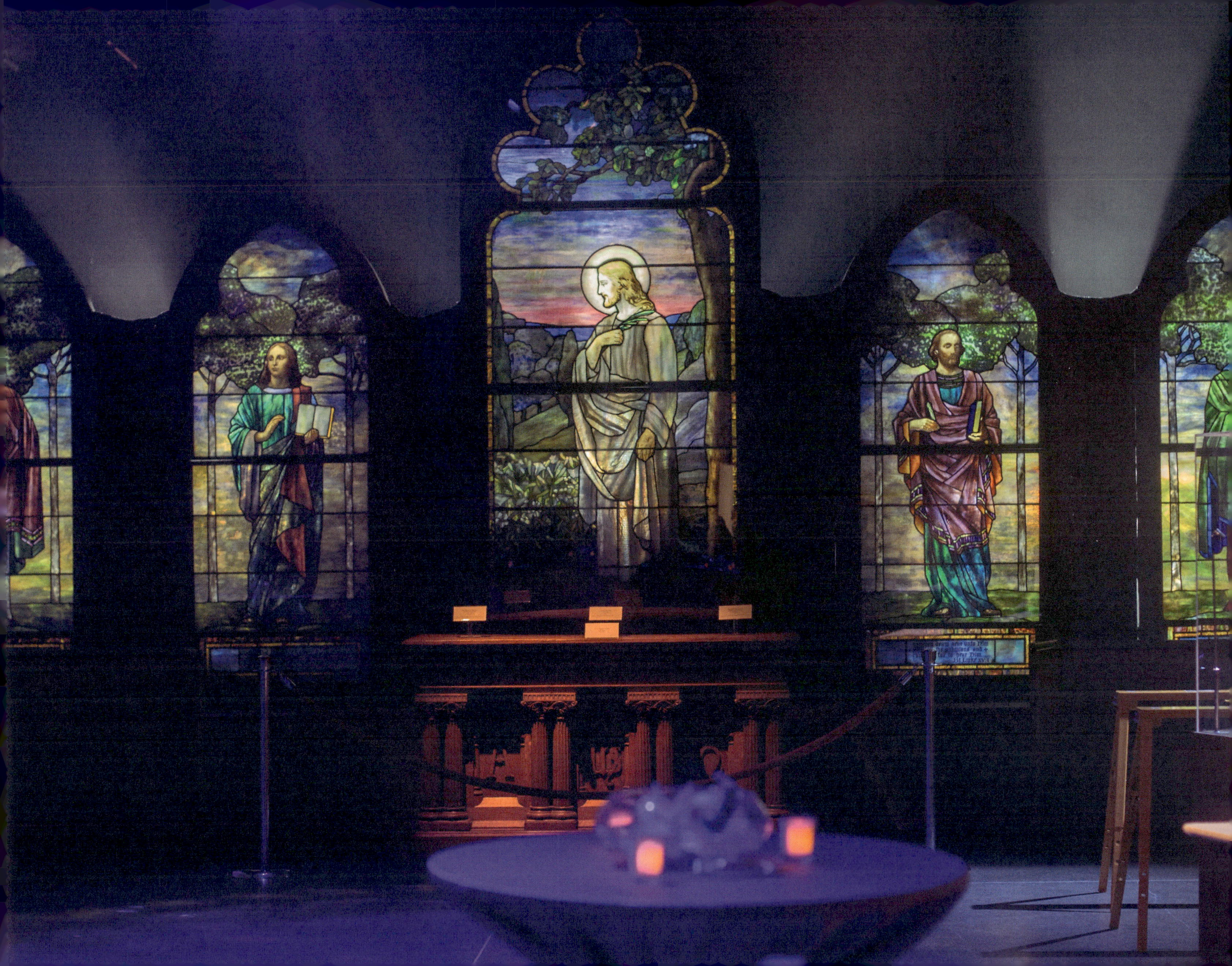

February 2015

Construction began on Museum of the Bible's building.

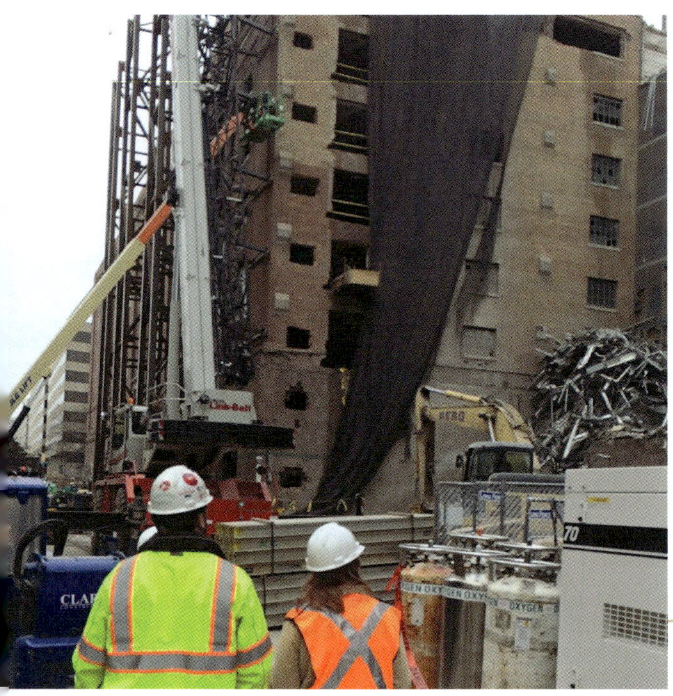

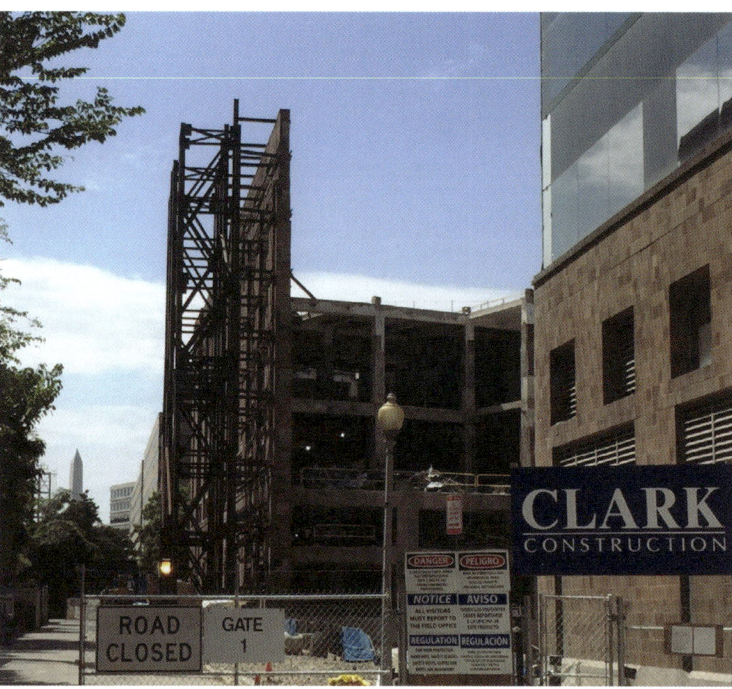

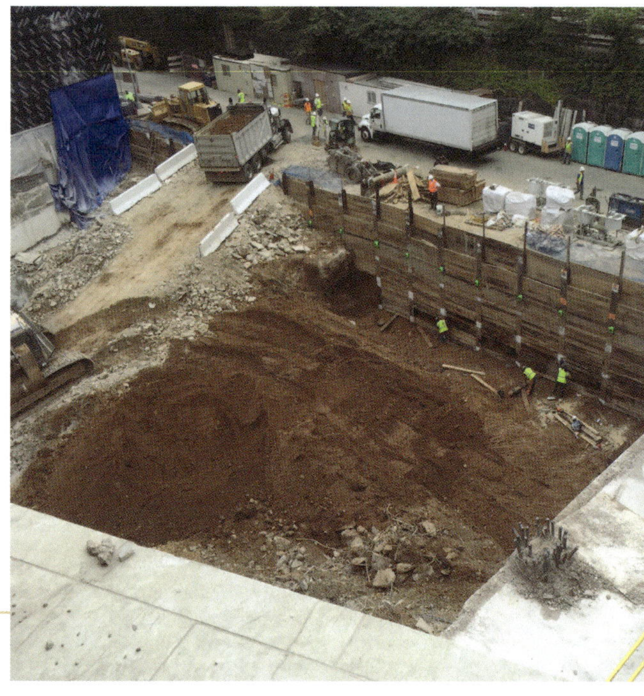

THE EIGHT-STORY, 430,000-square-foot Museum of the Bible took a giant step toward its 2017 opening in Washington, DC, beginning with surgical demolition of a 1982 addition to the historical building that would be reinvented as an international Bible museum. Museum of the Bible was built by Clark Construction, and the architectural design team was DC-based SmithGroupJJR.

The historical building presented challenges. Every other floor was removed with the outer walls held intact. This was one of the more difficult projects Clark Construction had ever undertaken.

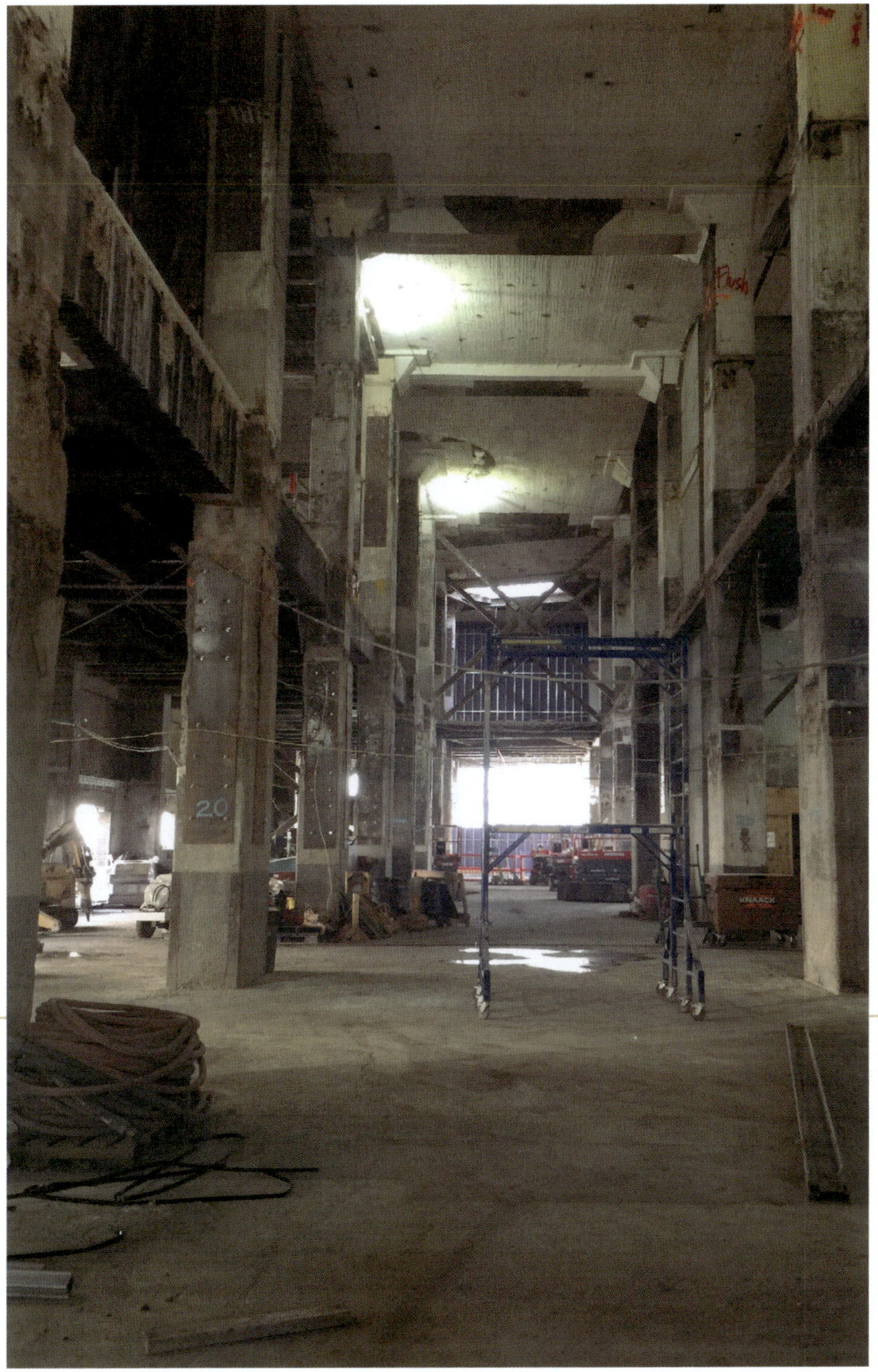

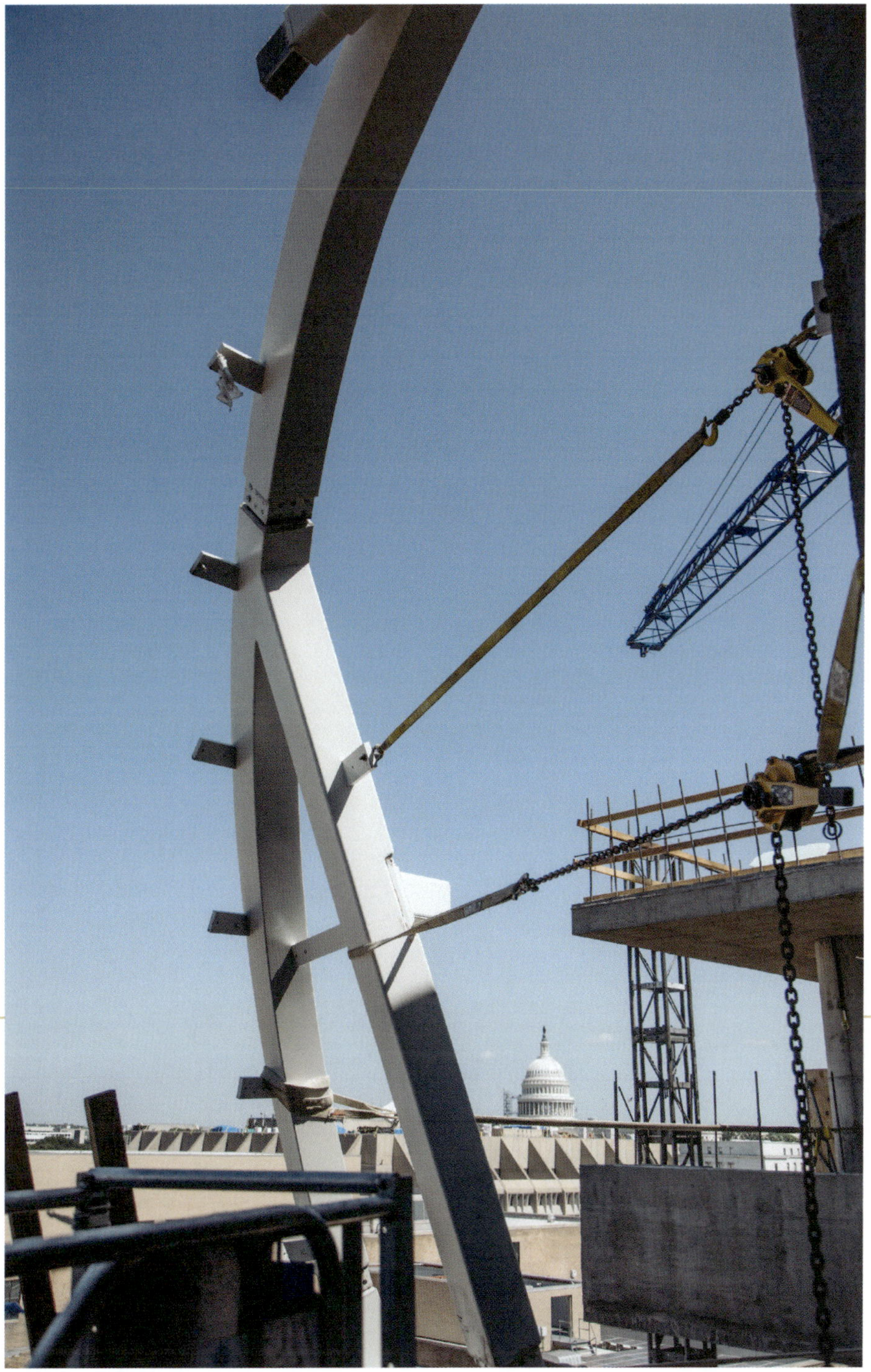

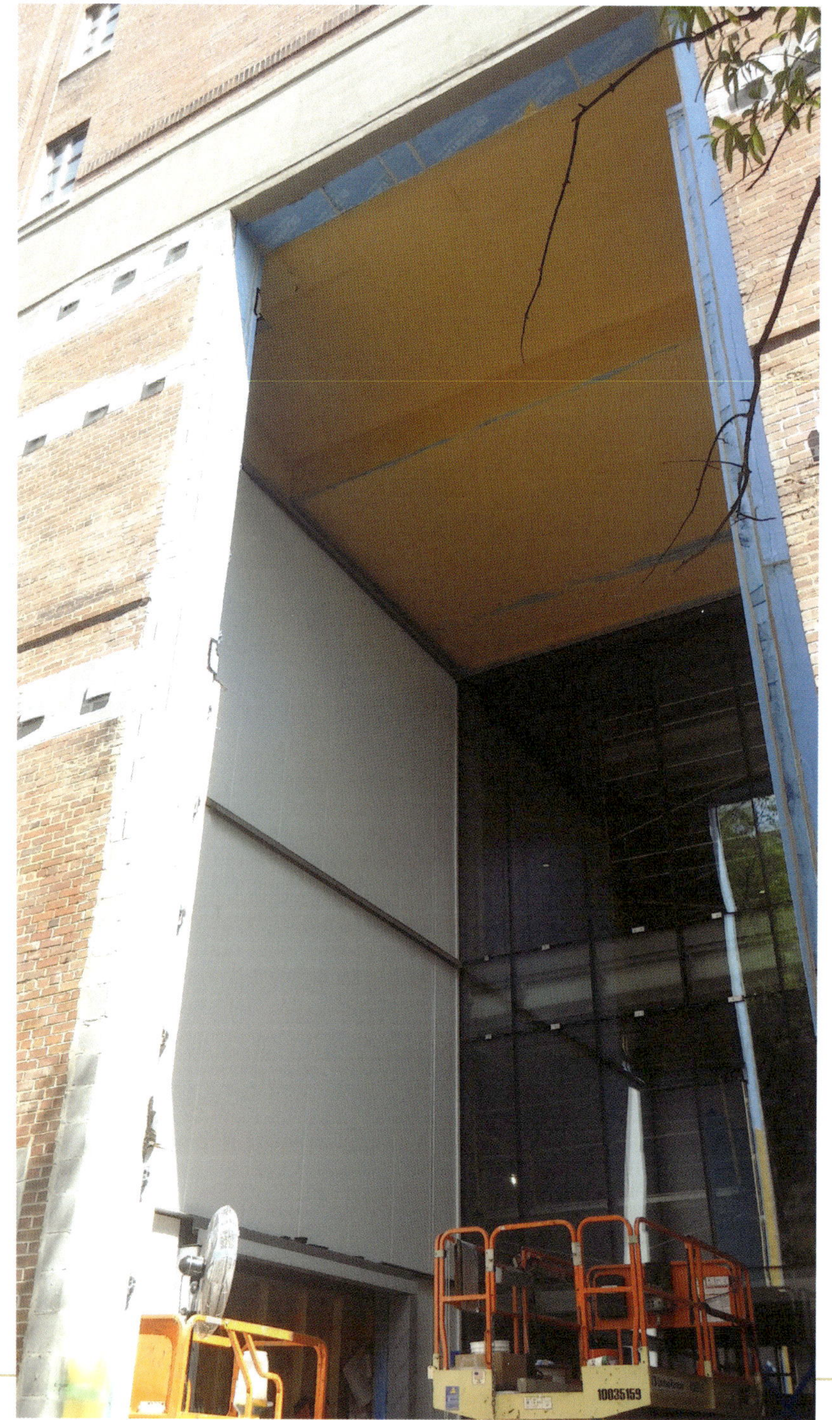

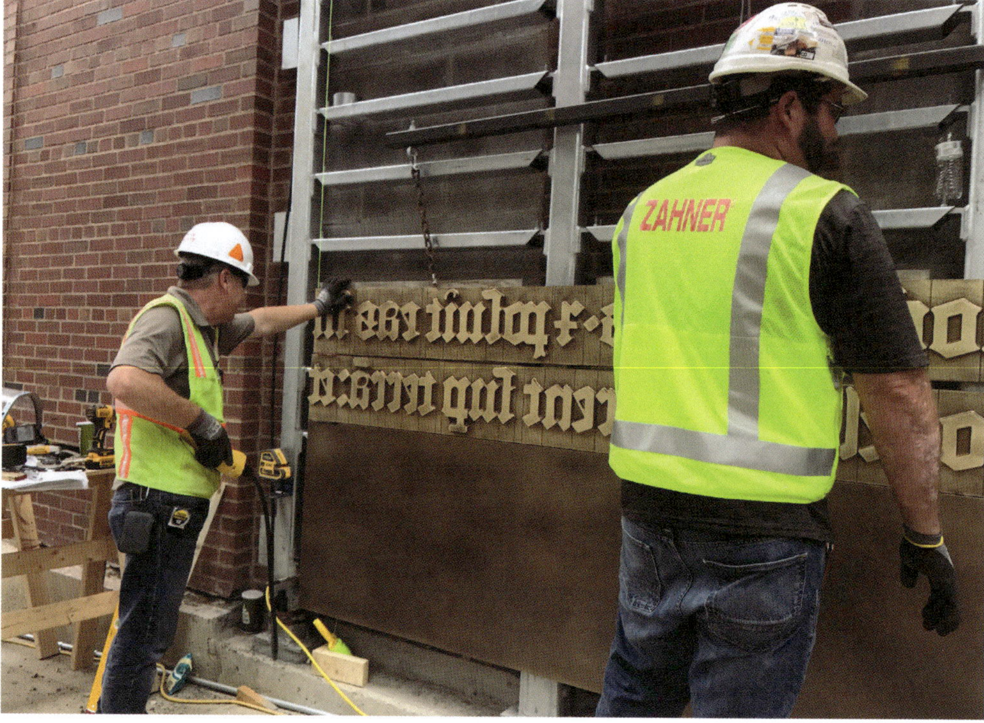

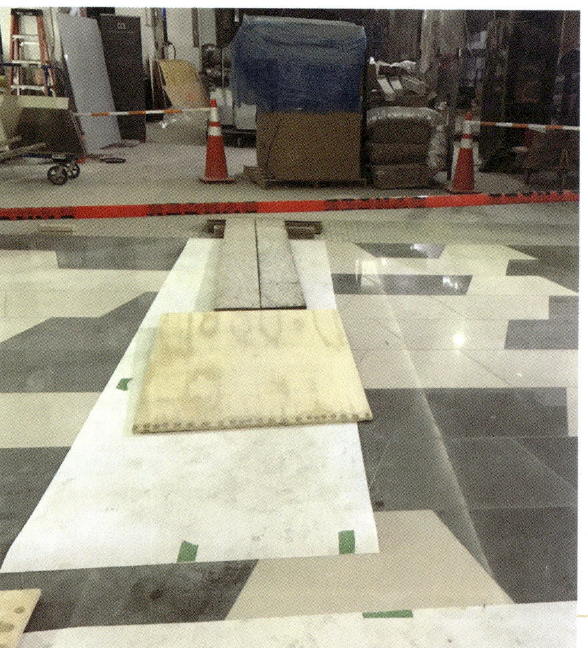

Top Right: The Gutenberg Gates are replica printing plates at the museum's entrance. They weigh 7 and 9 tons respectively, are 37 feet, 6.25 inches high, and a total of 43 feet wide. The material is 1-inch thick brass, zinc and copper alloy specially formulated in Germany, and fabricated in Kansas City, Missouri. The finalized design contains the first 80 lines of Genesis written in Latin, as originally printed in the Gutenberg Bible.

Bottom Right: Imported marble that goes from dark to white, representing darkness to light as visitors get closer to the artifacts.

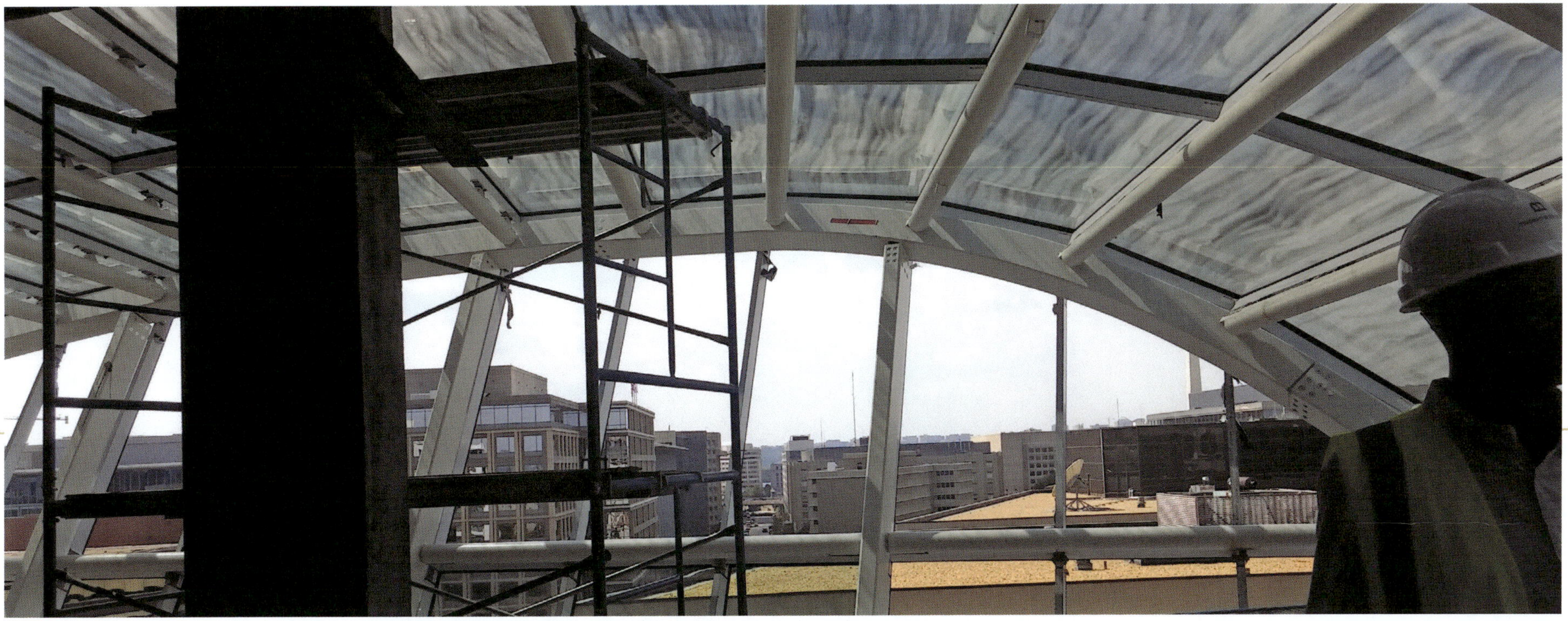

Top: Crafted in Augsburg, Germany, the landmark glass roof relies on 300 panes of six-millimeter, microscopically-etched glass and 170 steel fixtures. This cutting edge glass maximizes light, while minimizing heat.

Bottom Left: Many early guests wrote their names on the beams and added favorite biblical passages. Steve Green noted Psalm 1, and Jackie added Isaiah 40:8.

Bottom Right: Installation of one of sixteen panes of glass produced by Mayer'sche Hofkunstanstalt which reproduce a papyrus leaf containing Psalm 19 from the earliest surviving Greek Psalter (RA 2110). Upon closer inspection, the engaged visitor will find this Psalm translated into sixteen modern languages on the glass.

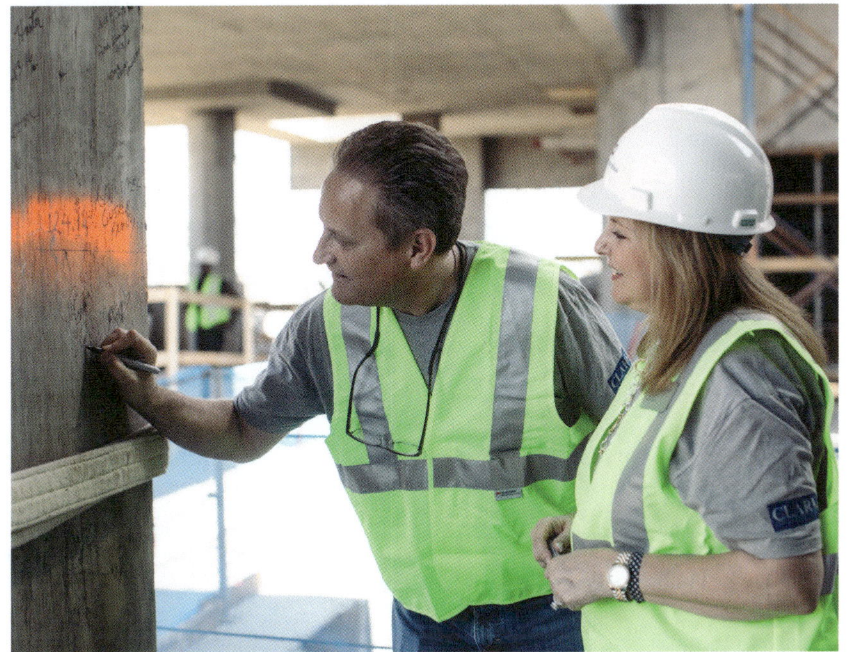

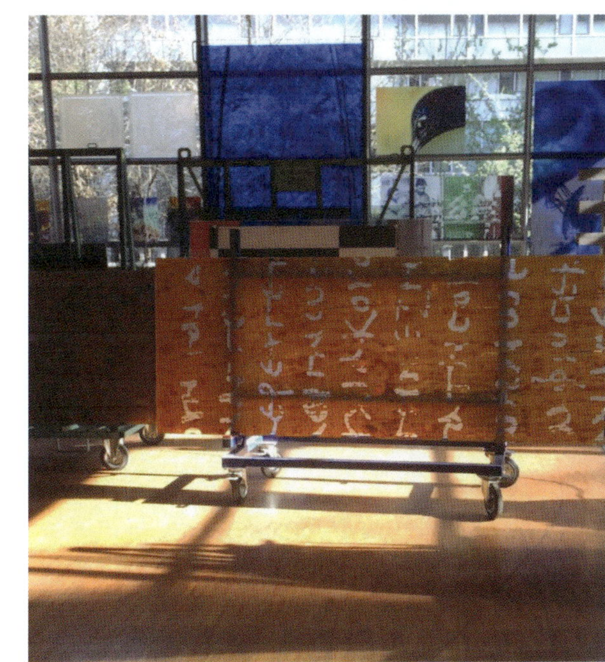

2013–2017

Designing a museum—The Impact of the Bible floor.

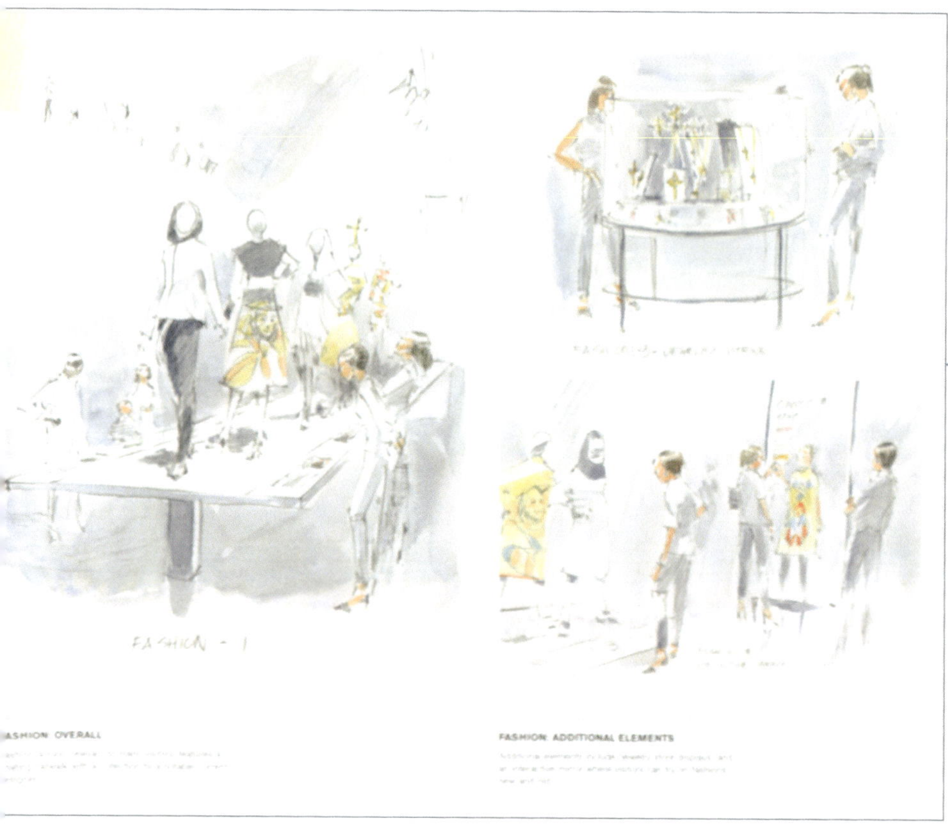

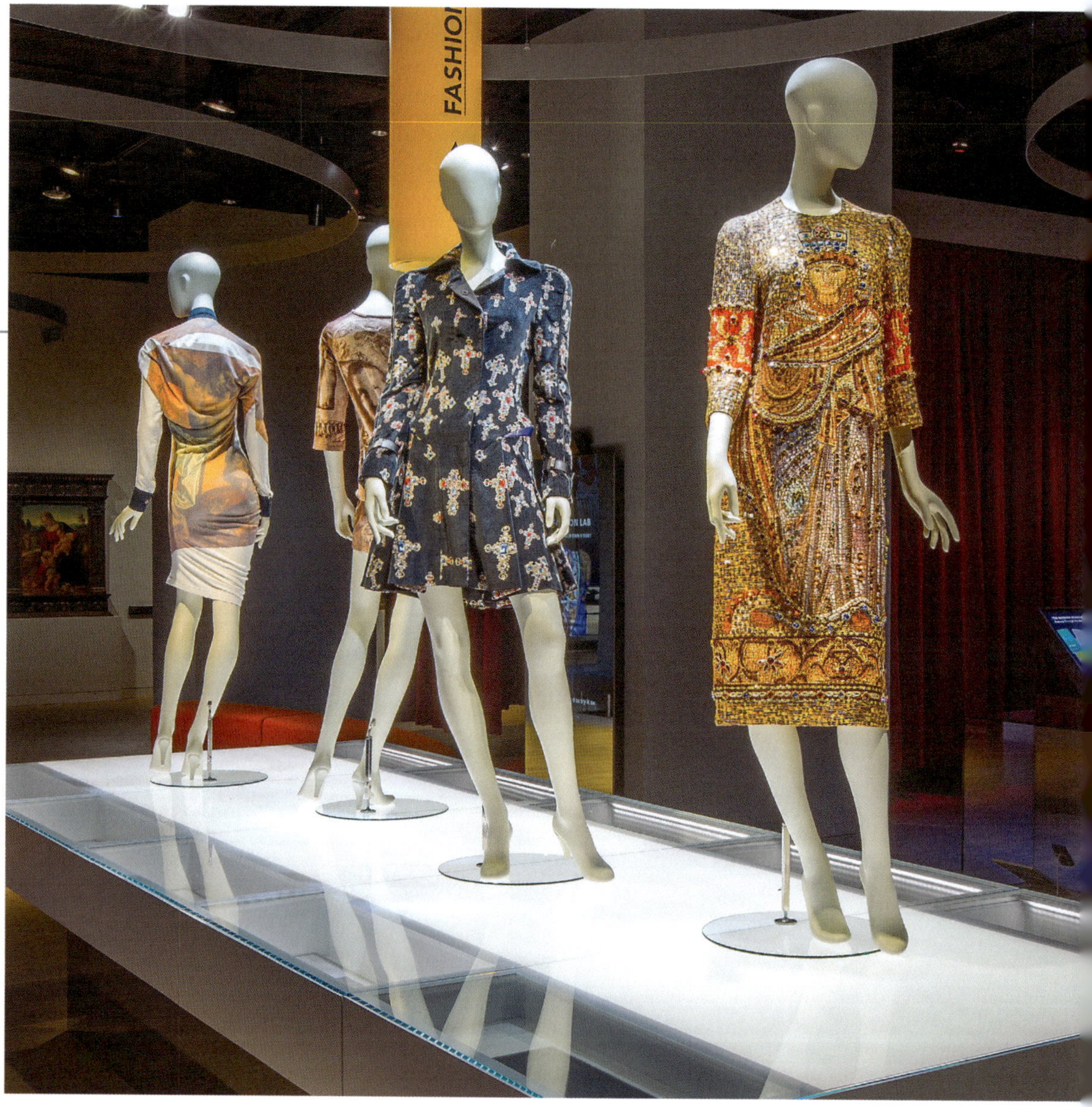

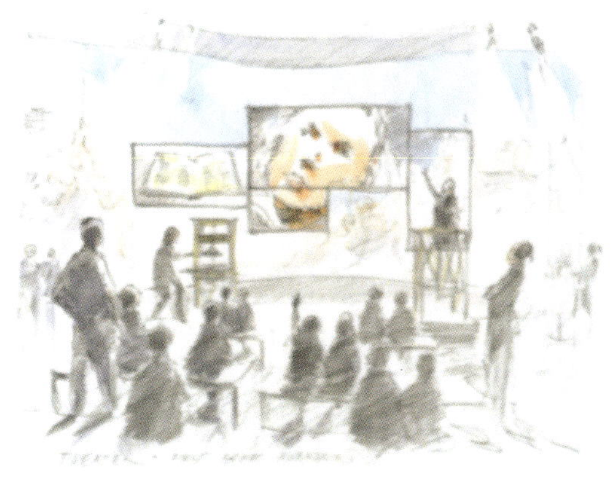

FLOOR 2 of the museum addresses the Impact of the Bible, demonstrating the enormous influence the Bible has had on nearly every aspect of life. There are three major exhibit areas: *Bible in the World, Bible in America*, and *Bible Now*. Galleries on the Impact of the Bible floor were designed by C&G Partners.

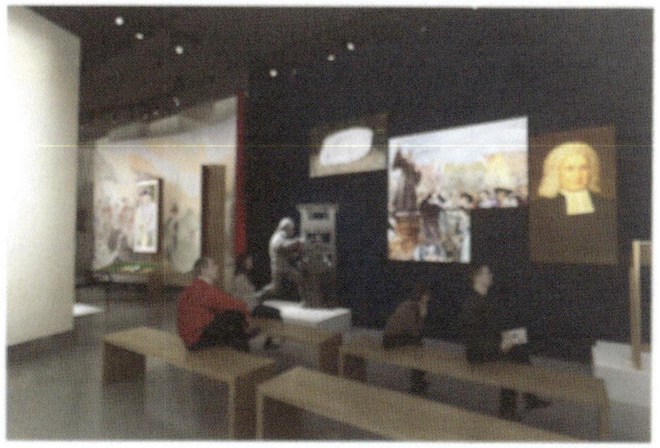

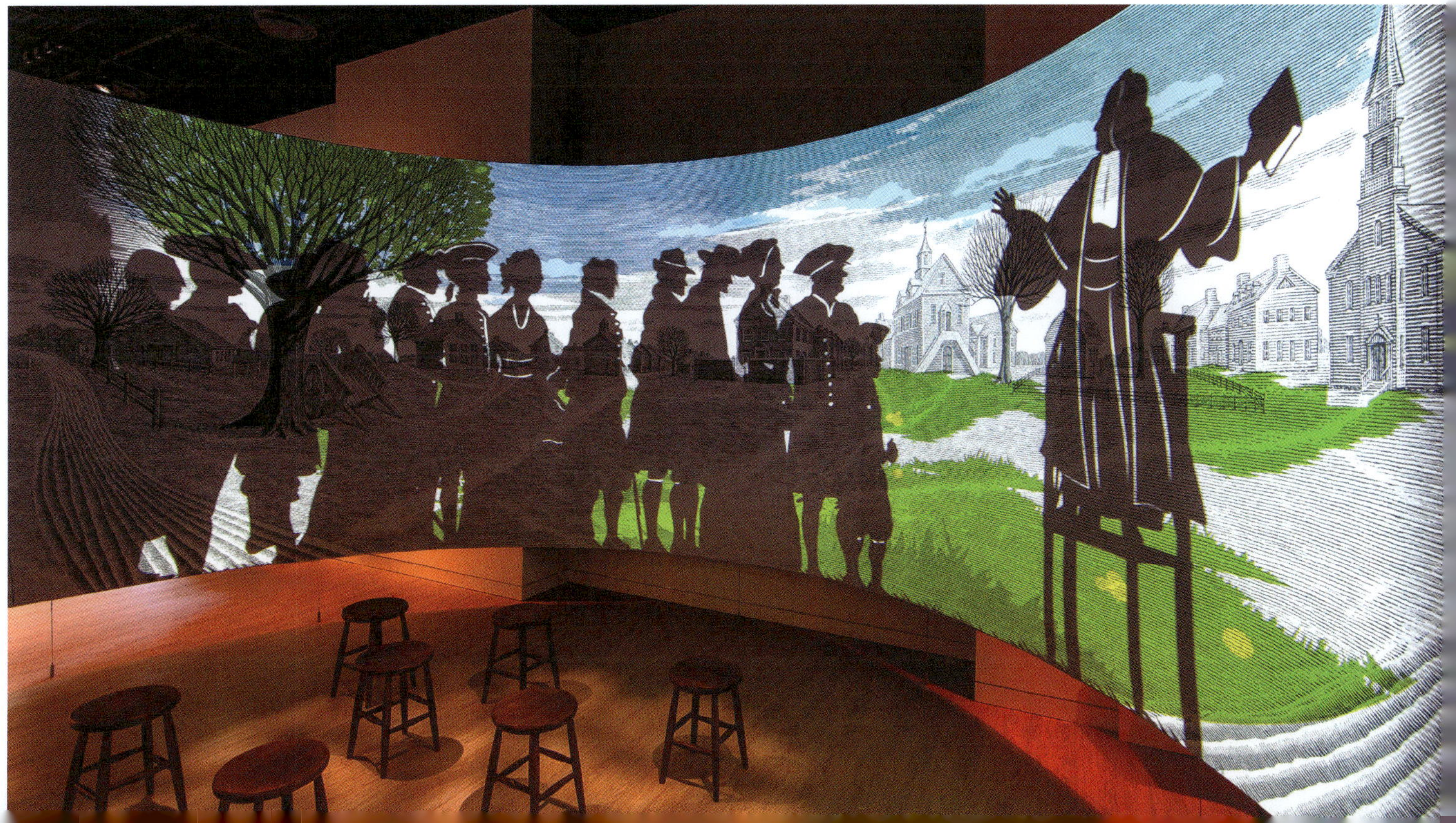

2013–2017

Designing a museum—The Stories of the Bible floor.

BRC Imagination Arts designed and created the Hebrew Bible Experience. In this thirty-minute experience, guests encounter significant narratives from the Hebrew Bible, the stories of Noah's ark, the burning bush, and Passover. In 2020, Museum of the Bible was the recipient of the Themed Entertainment Association's (TEA) Thea Award for Outstanding Achievement–Museum Exhibit for its Hebrew Bible Experience.

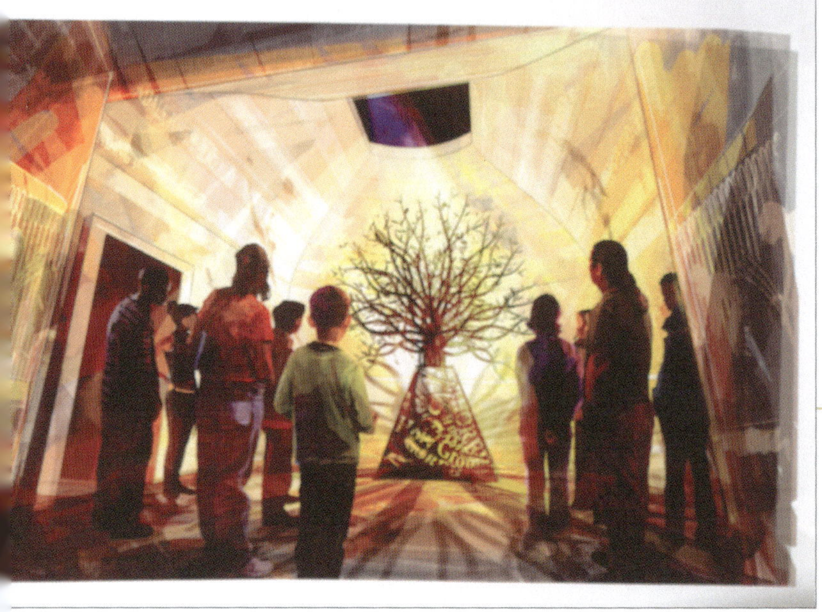

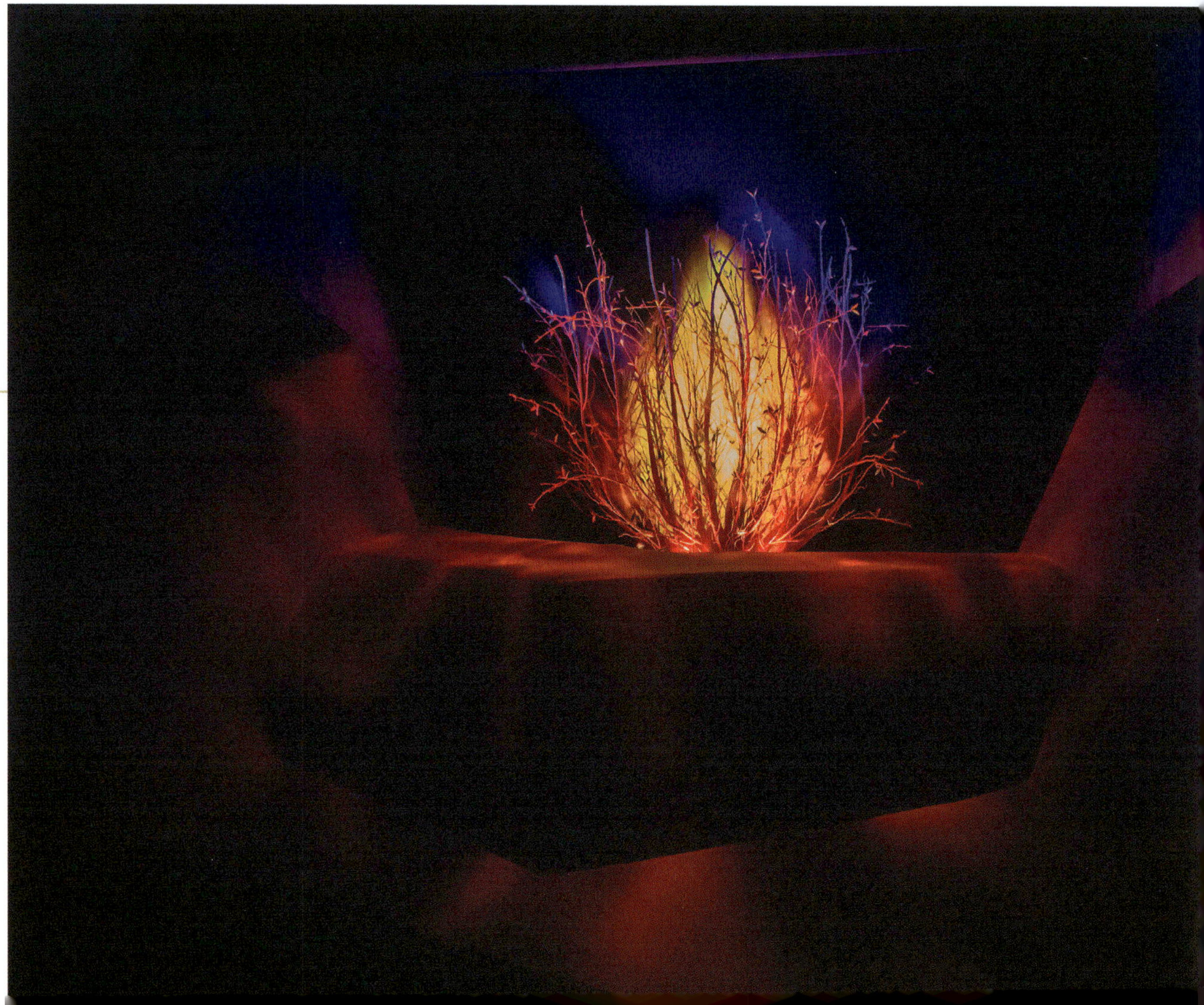

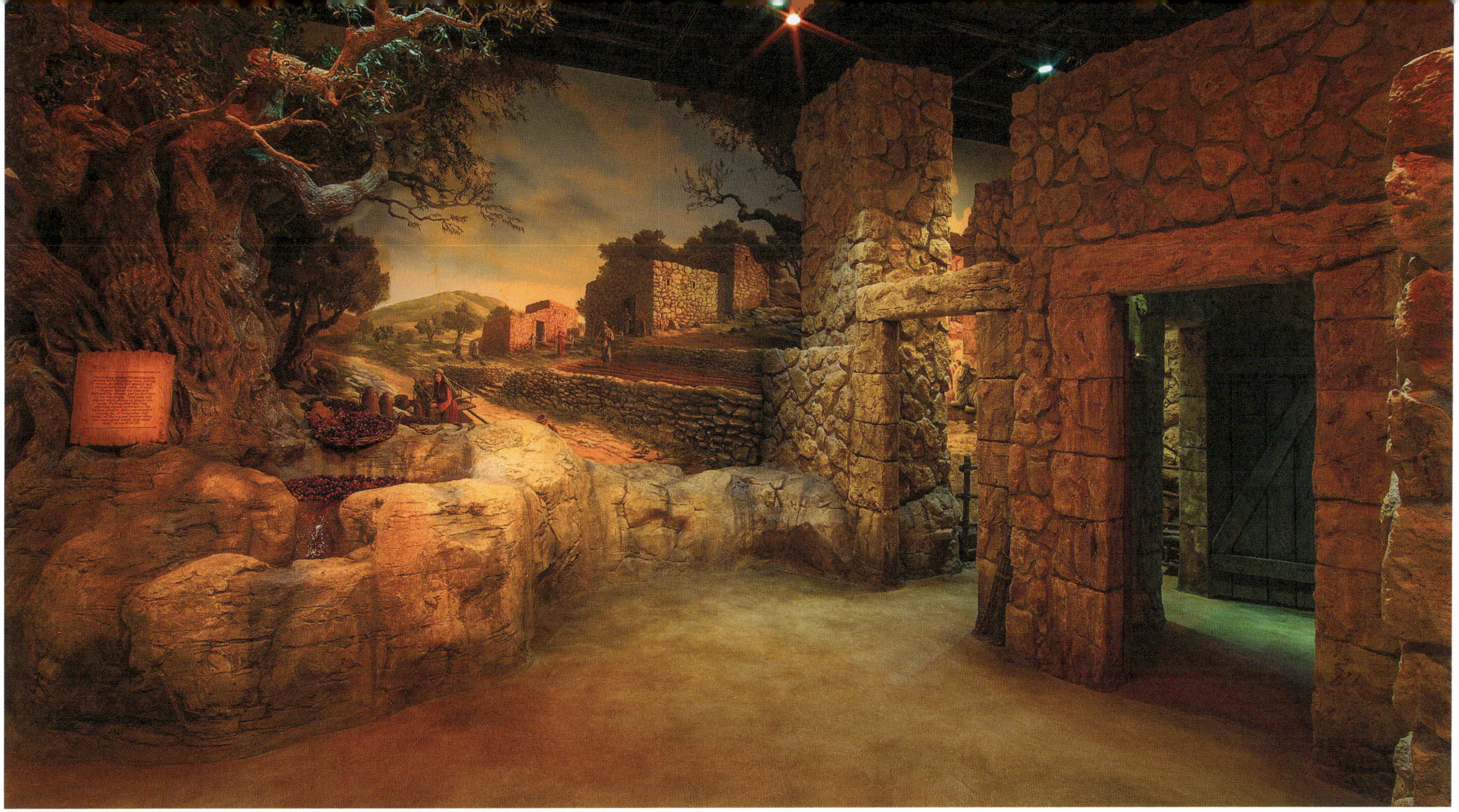

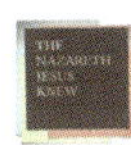

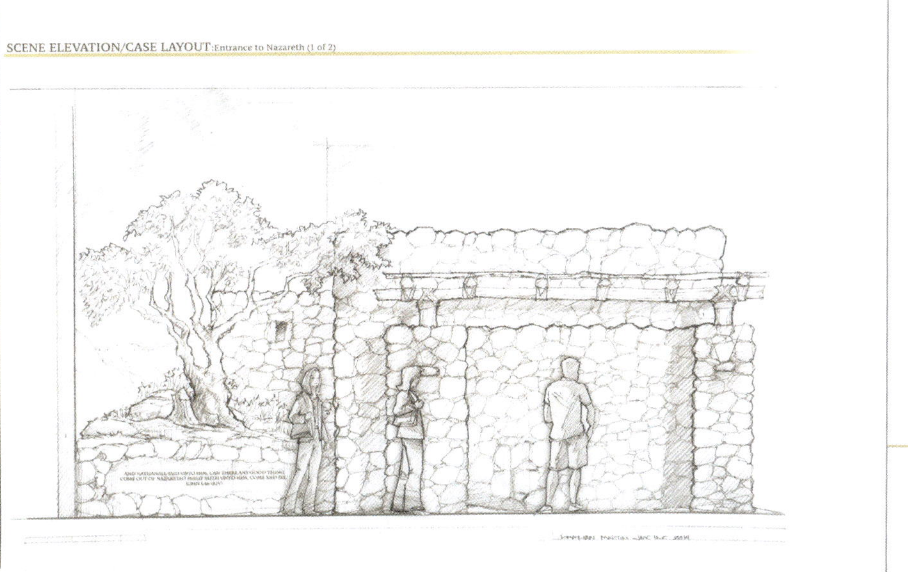

THE WORLD OF Jesus of Nazareth was created by Jonathan Martin Creative Inc. In this interactive experience, you can immerse yourself in first-century Nazareth: walk the streets, see the sights, and chat with the villagers.

2013–2017

Designing a museum—The History of the Bible floor.

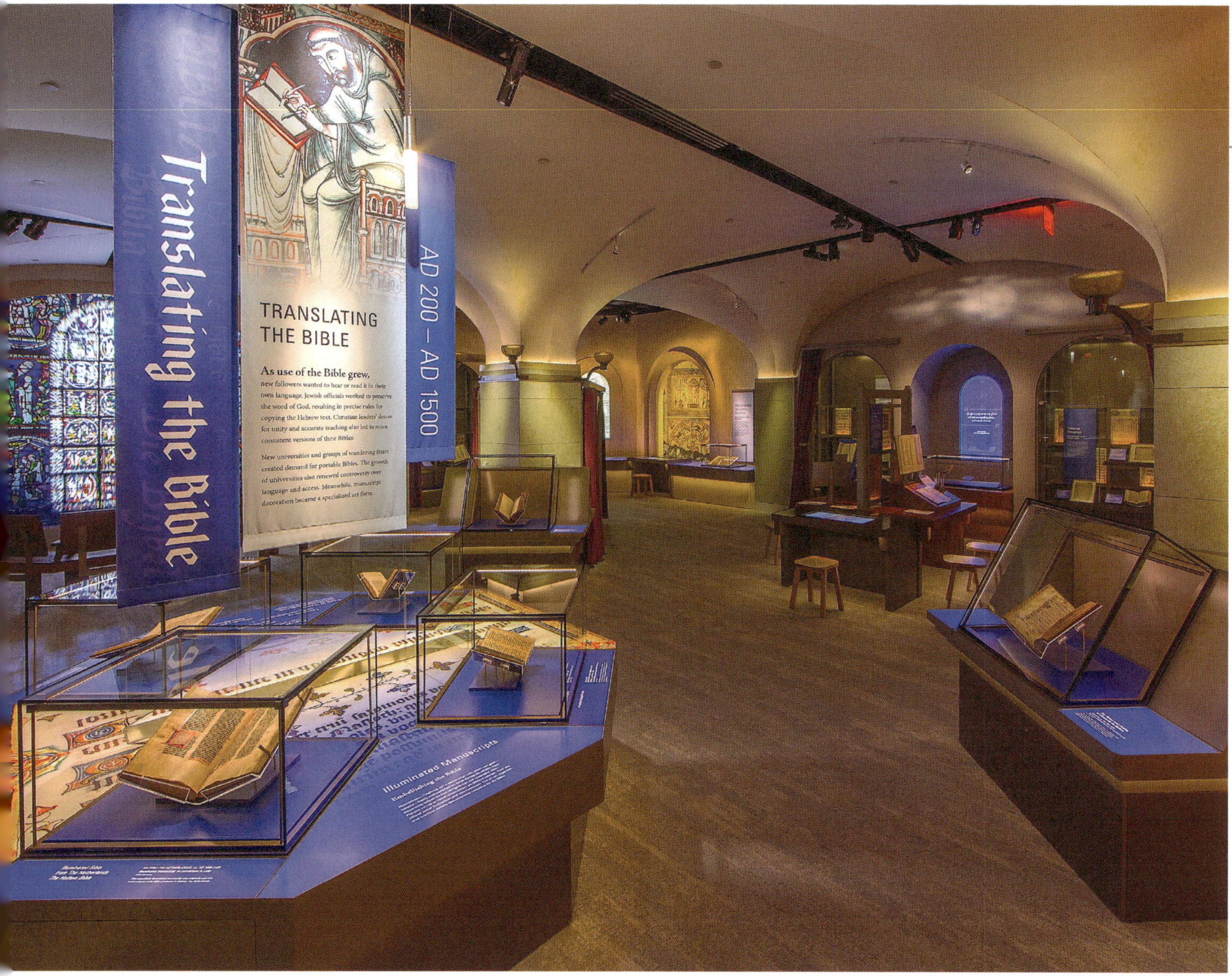

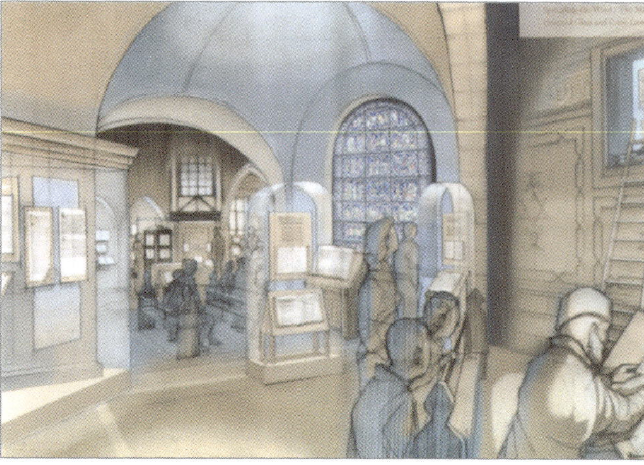

Designed by The PRD Group, Floor 4 of the museum is dedicated entirely to the History of the Bible. With more than 600 fascinating artifacts, including early New Testament manuscripts, ancient coins, Torah scrolls, illuminated manuscripts, and rare printed Bibles, there is plenty to see. Included on this floor is illumiNations Global Bible—an exhibition celebrating the Bible's accessibility. It features Bibles in more than 2,000 different languages.

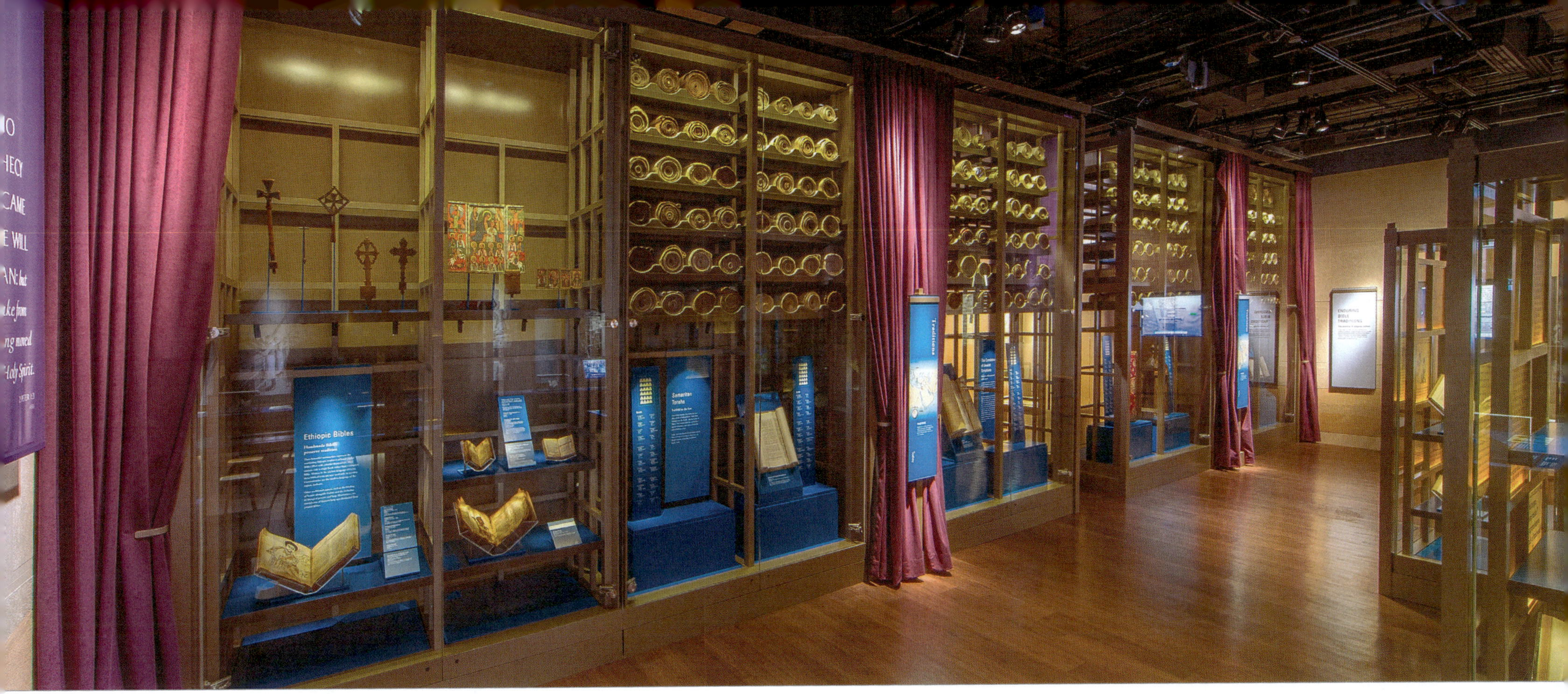

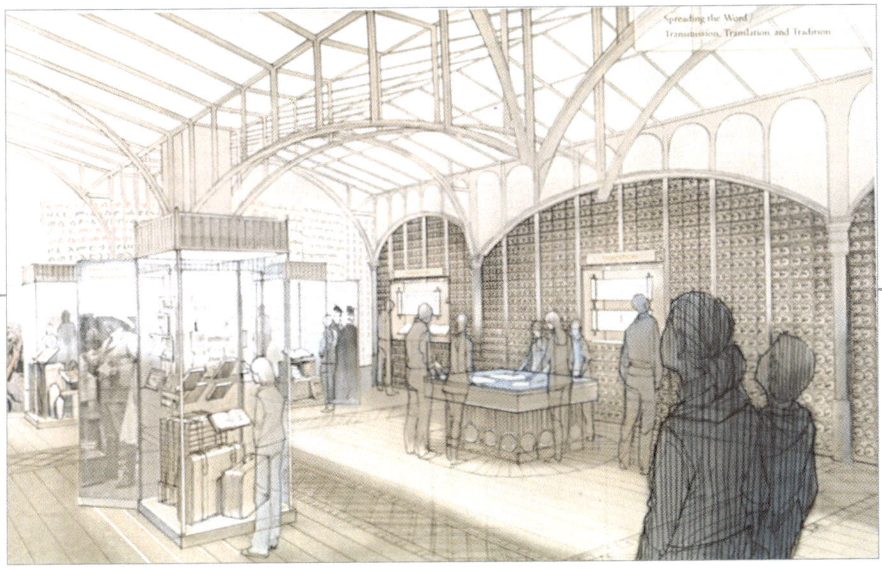

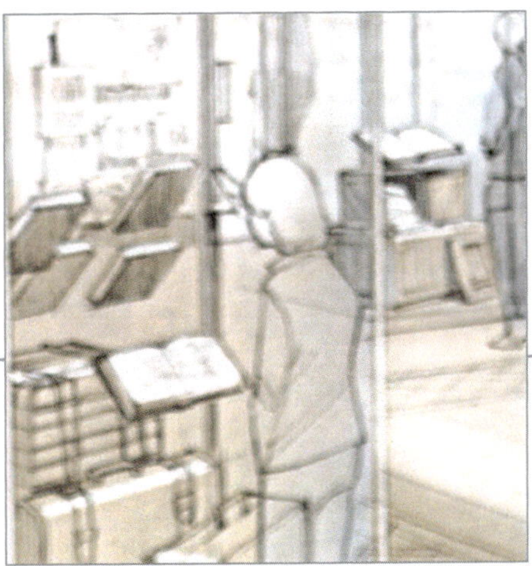

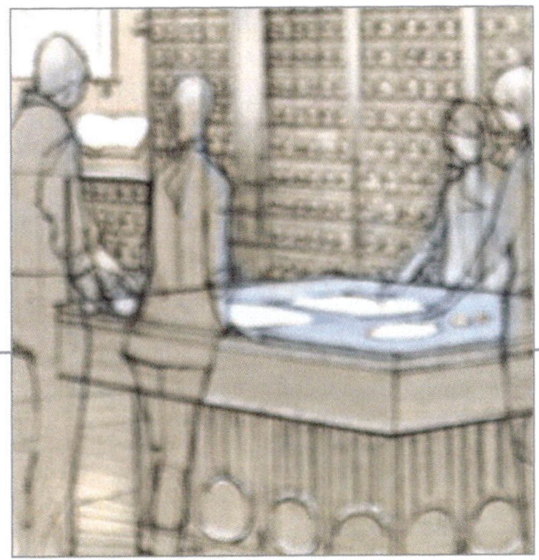

TOP: The Torah Scroll display on the History Floor surveys the broad geographic dispersion of Jews across Europe and the Middle East over the last several centuries.

November 17, 2017

Museum of the Bible opened!

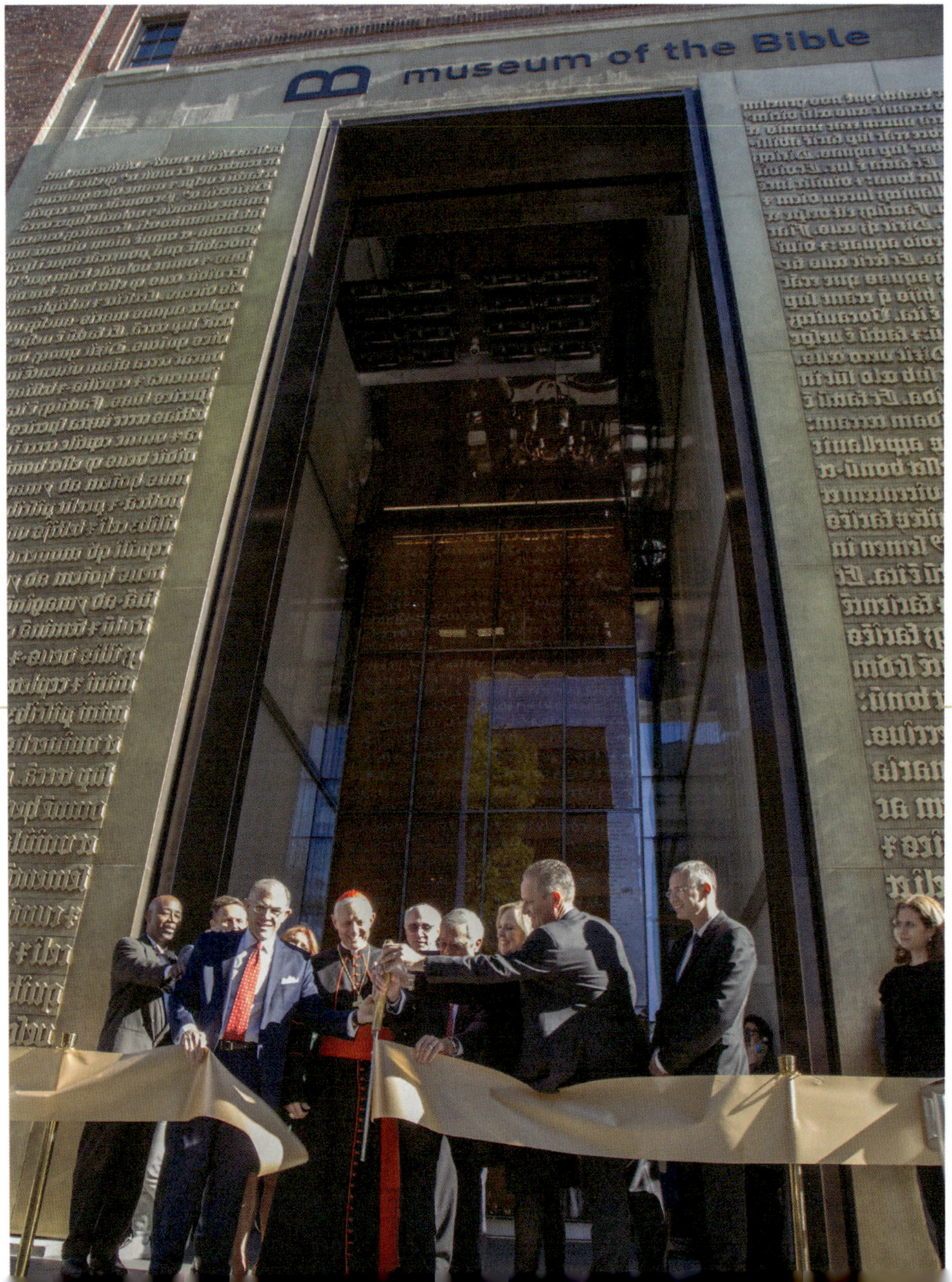

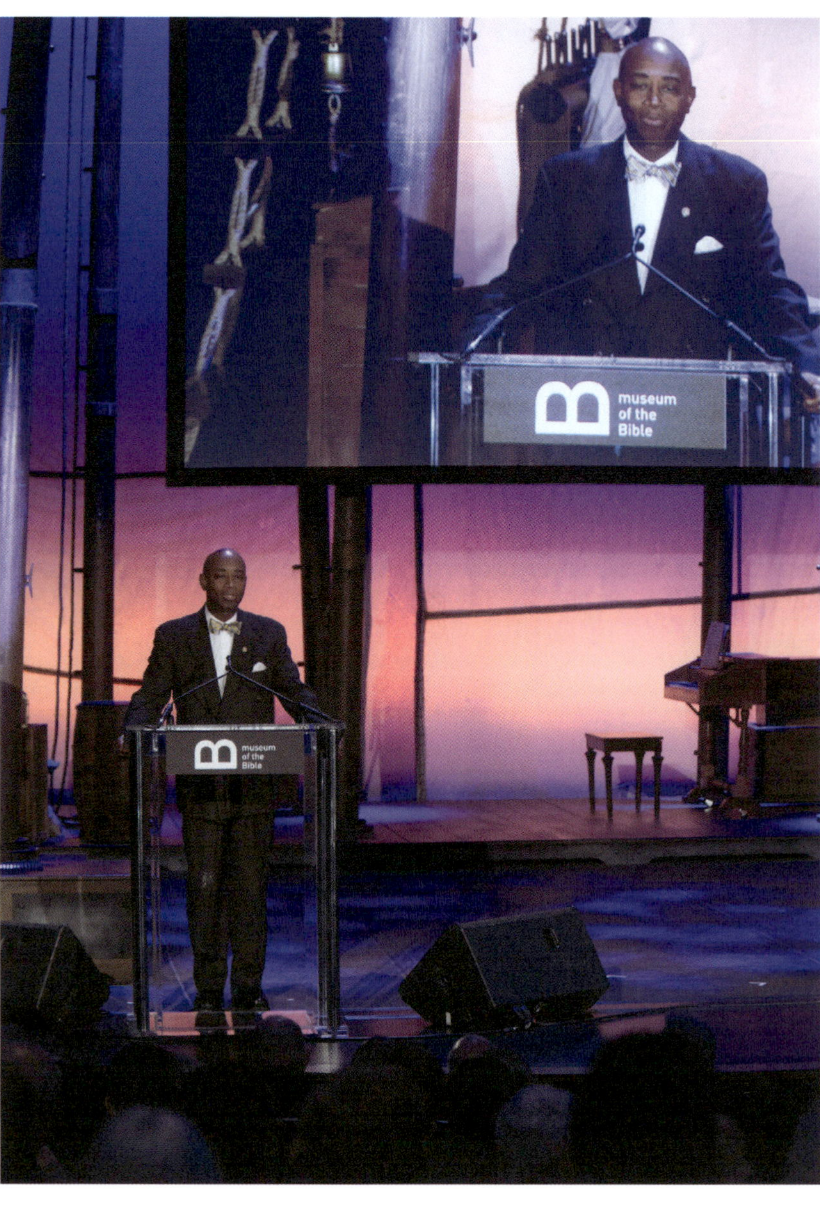

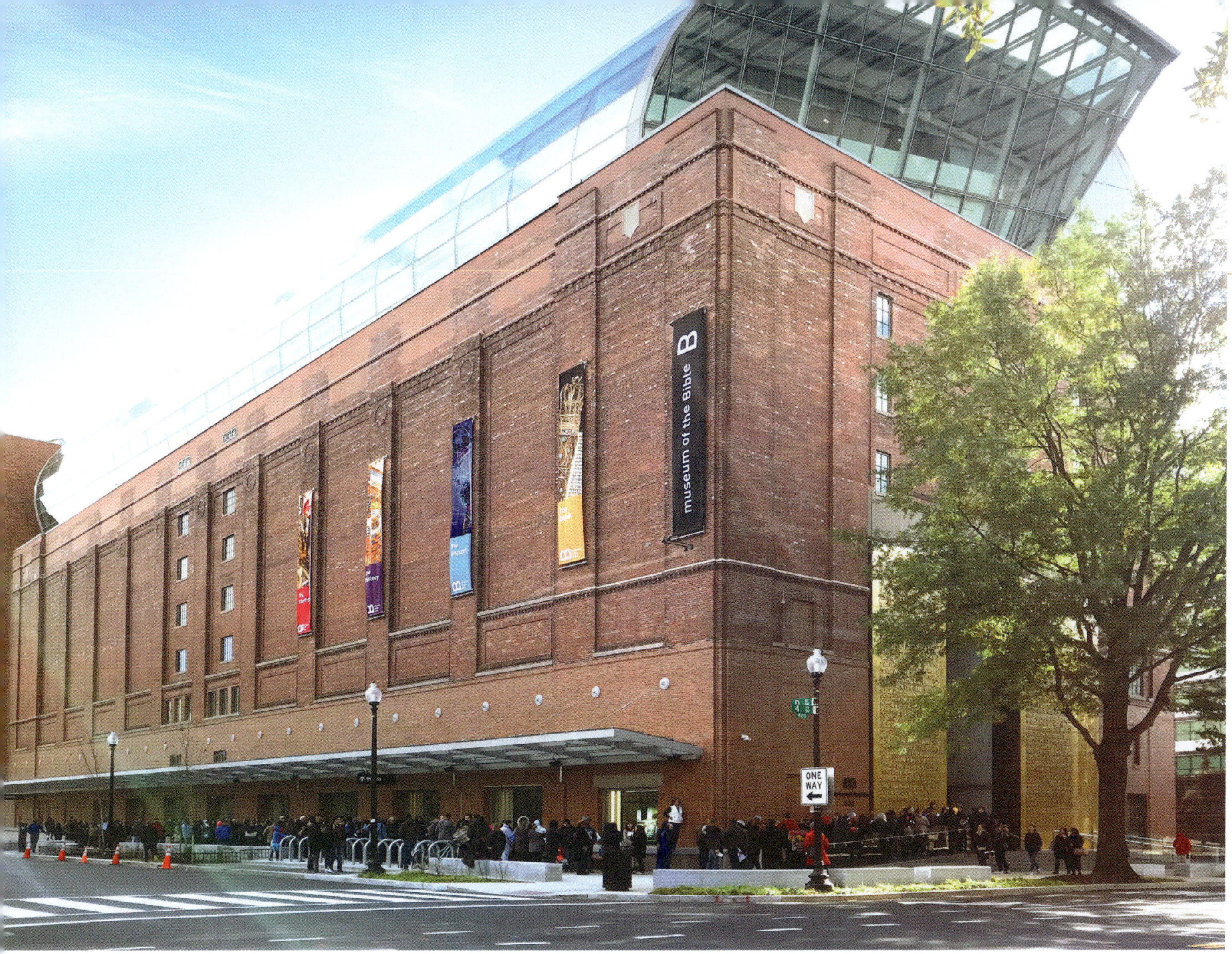

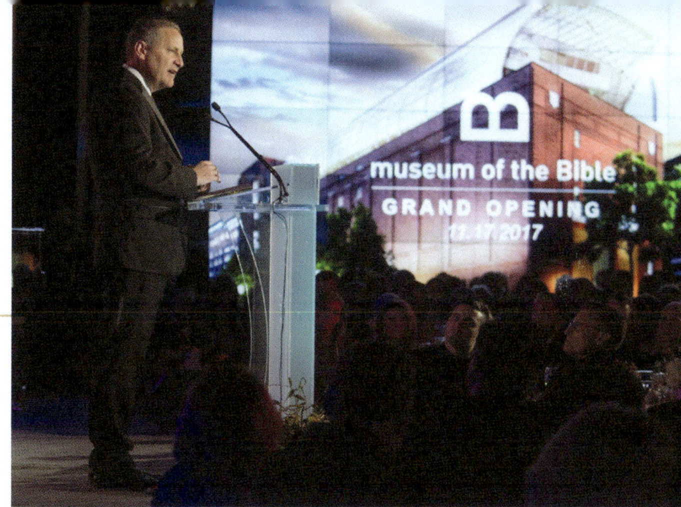

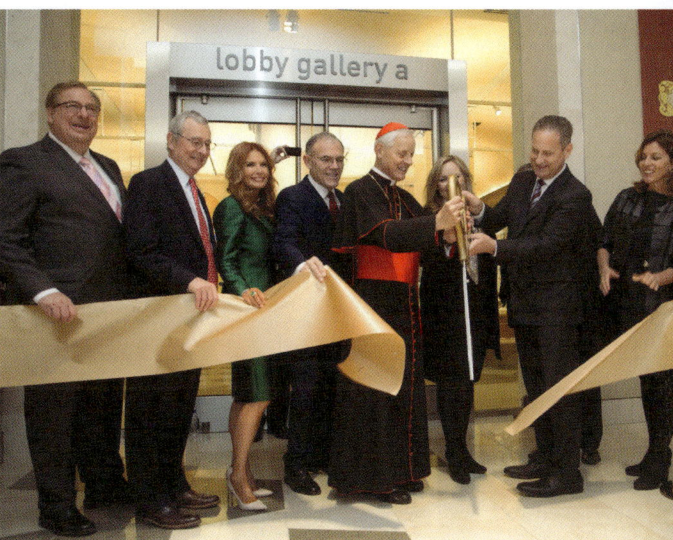

"It is appropriate that in the nation's capital where we have soaring museums and monuments and where people visit us from around the world that the Museum of the Bible would be built here."

MAYOR MURIEL BOWSER
WASHINGTON, DC

November 2017

AMAZING GRACE: The Musical and exhibit Amazing Grace: How Sweet the Sound.

AMAZING GRACE: THE MUSICAL made its first stop on its national tour at Museum of the Bible for an eight-week run. The *Washington Post* proclaimed: "As spectacular as anything on Broadway, AMAZING GRACE tells the story of how the song came to be and elicits widespread gasps and cheering from the audience." To commemorate the musical, the exhibit *Amazing Grace: How Sweet the Sound* opened on November 17, 2017. Museum visitors learned how John Newton's famous hymn, "Amazing Grace," which resonates in the hearts and on the lips of so many, reached depths far beyond any that Newton would have imagined.

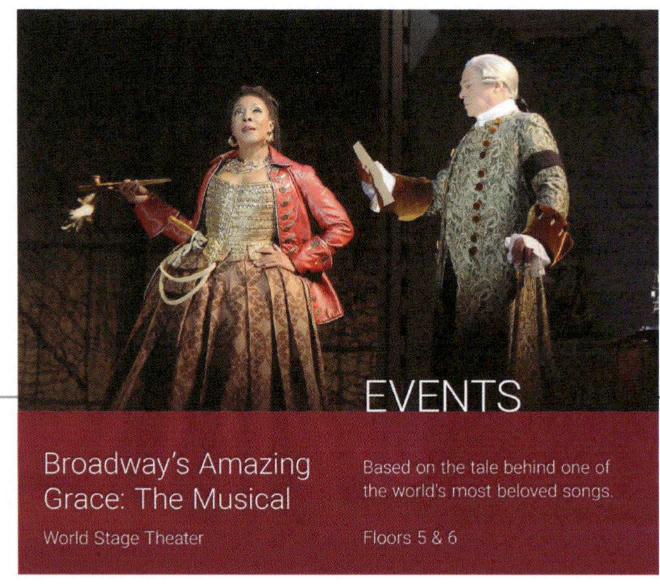

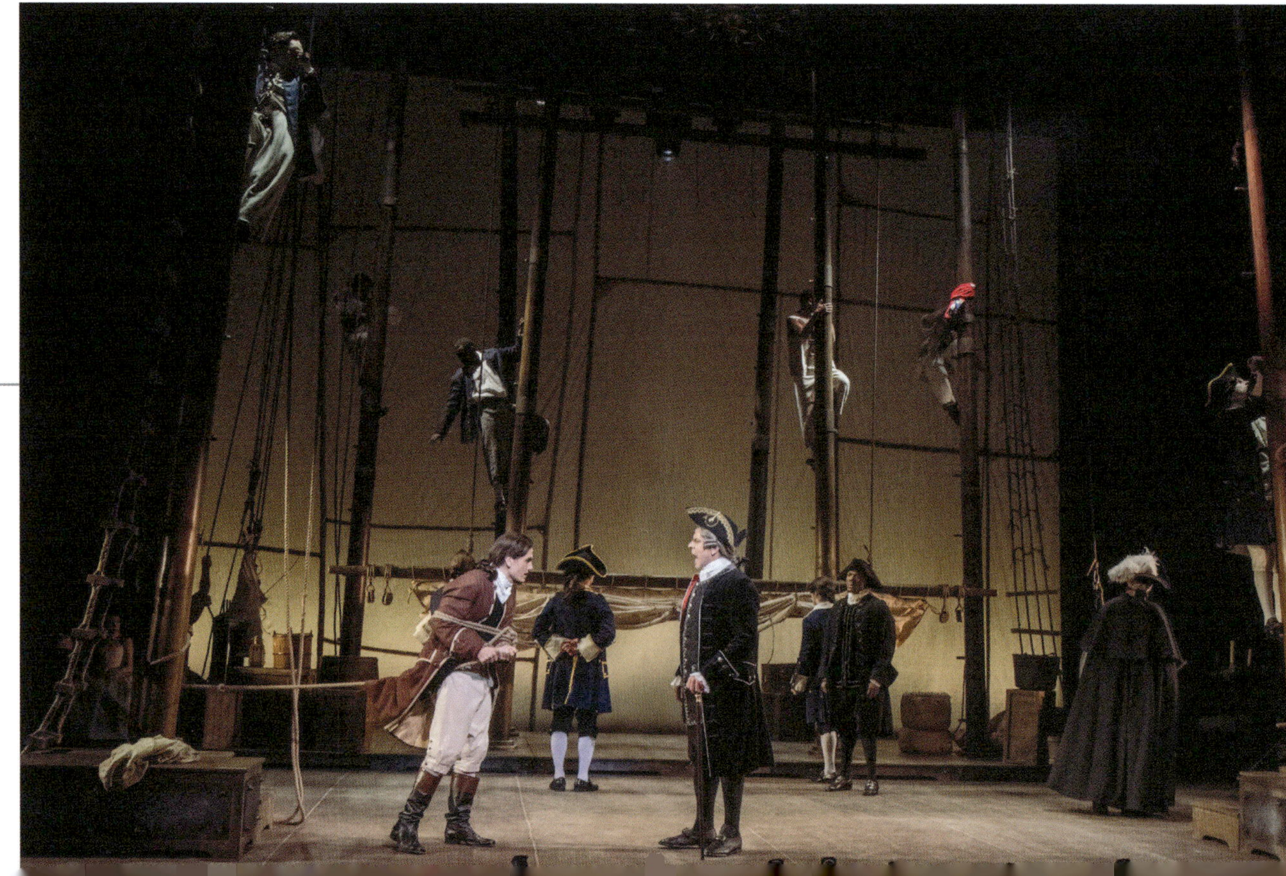

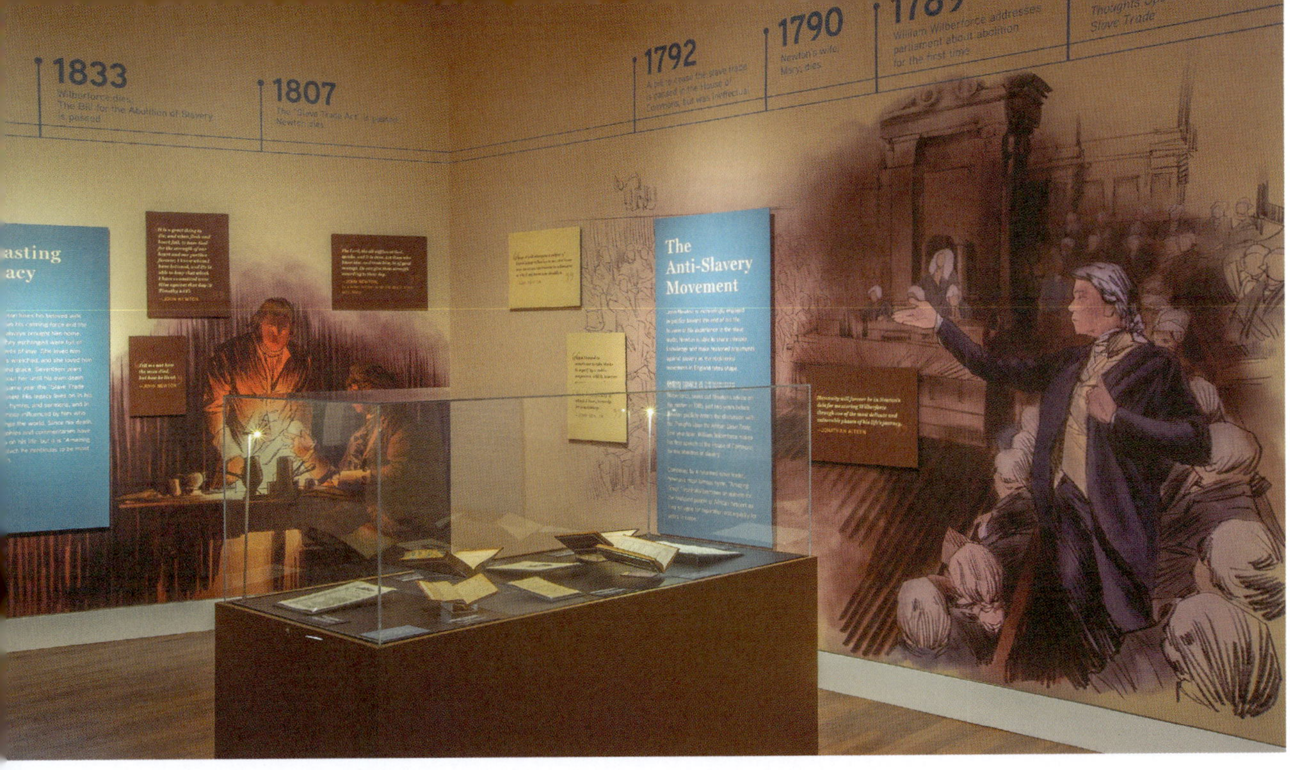
1833
1807
1792
1790
The Anti-Slavery Movement

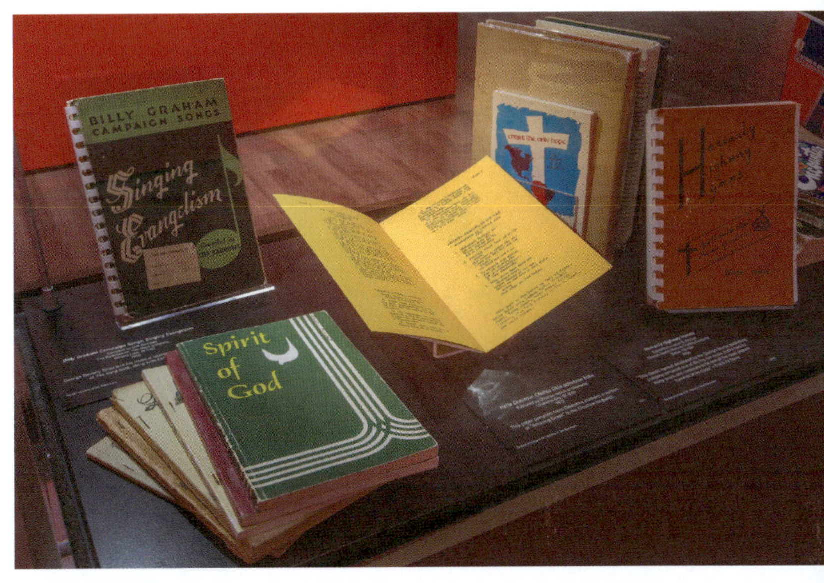
BILLY GRAHAM CAMPAIGN SONGS
Singing Evangelism
Spirit of God

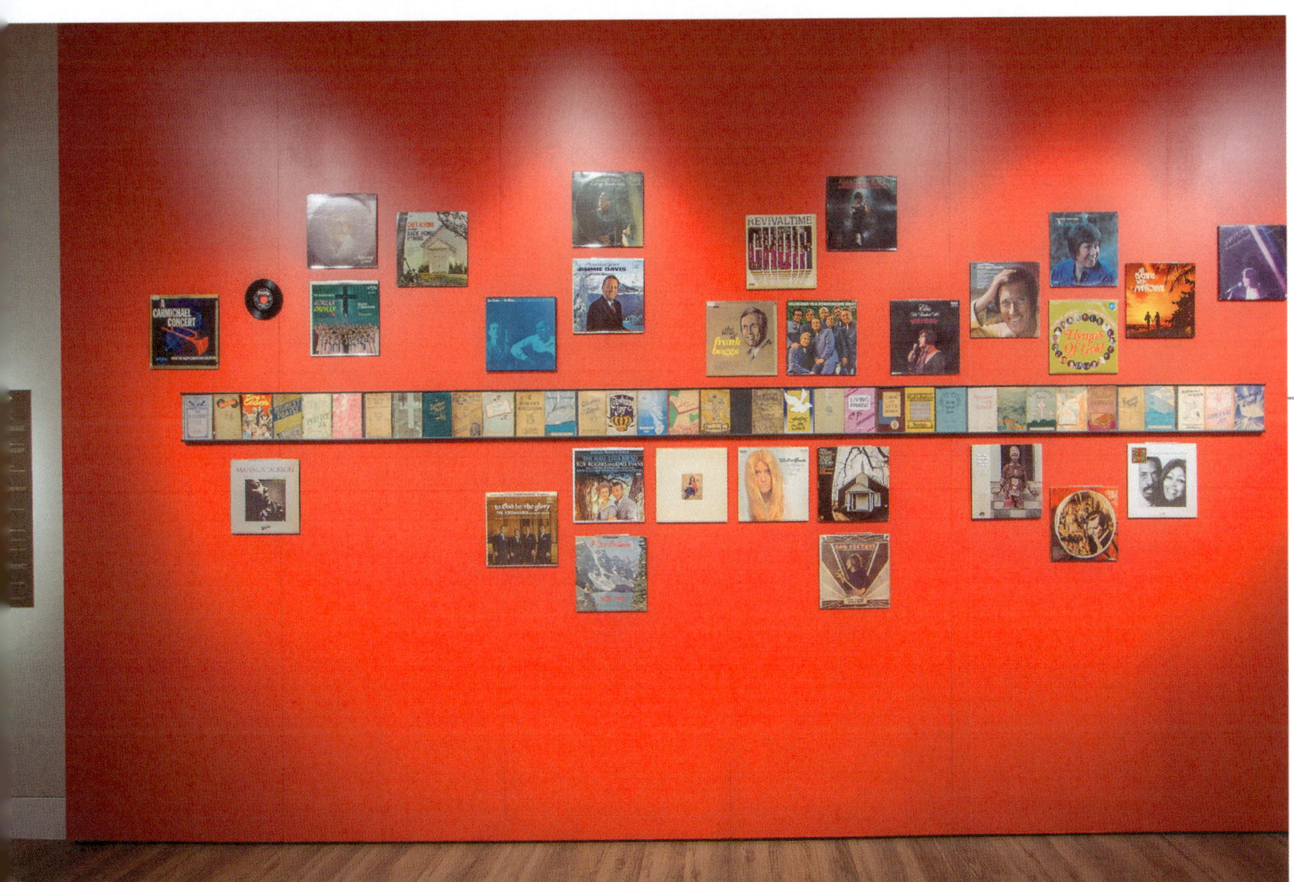
REVIVALTIME

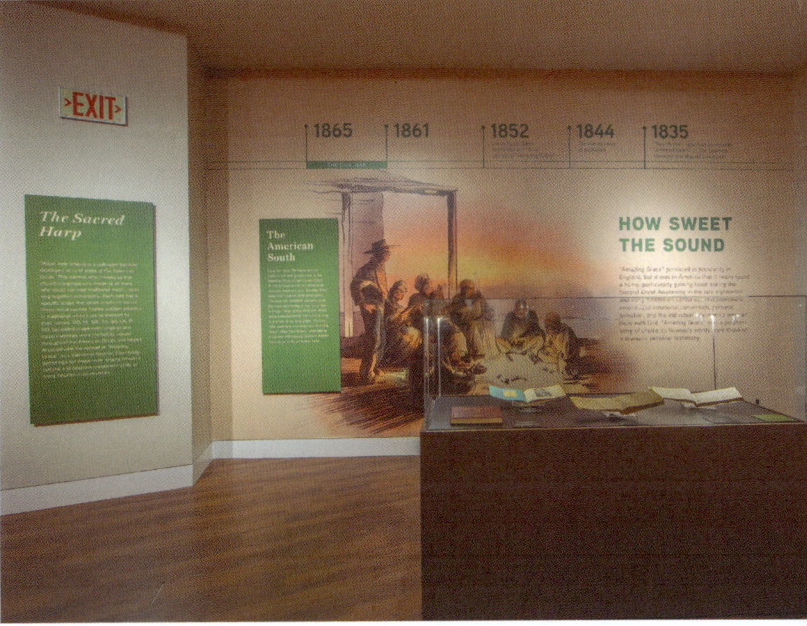
EXIT
1865
1861
1852
1844
1835
The Sacred Harp
The American South
HOW SWEET THE SOUND

August 2018

***Pilgrim Preacher: Billy Graham, the Bible, and the Challenges of the Modern World* exhibited at Museum of the Bible.**

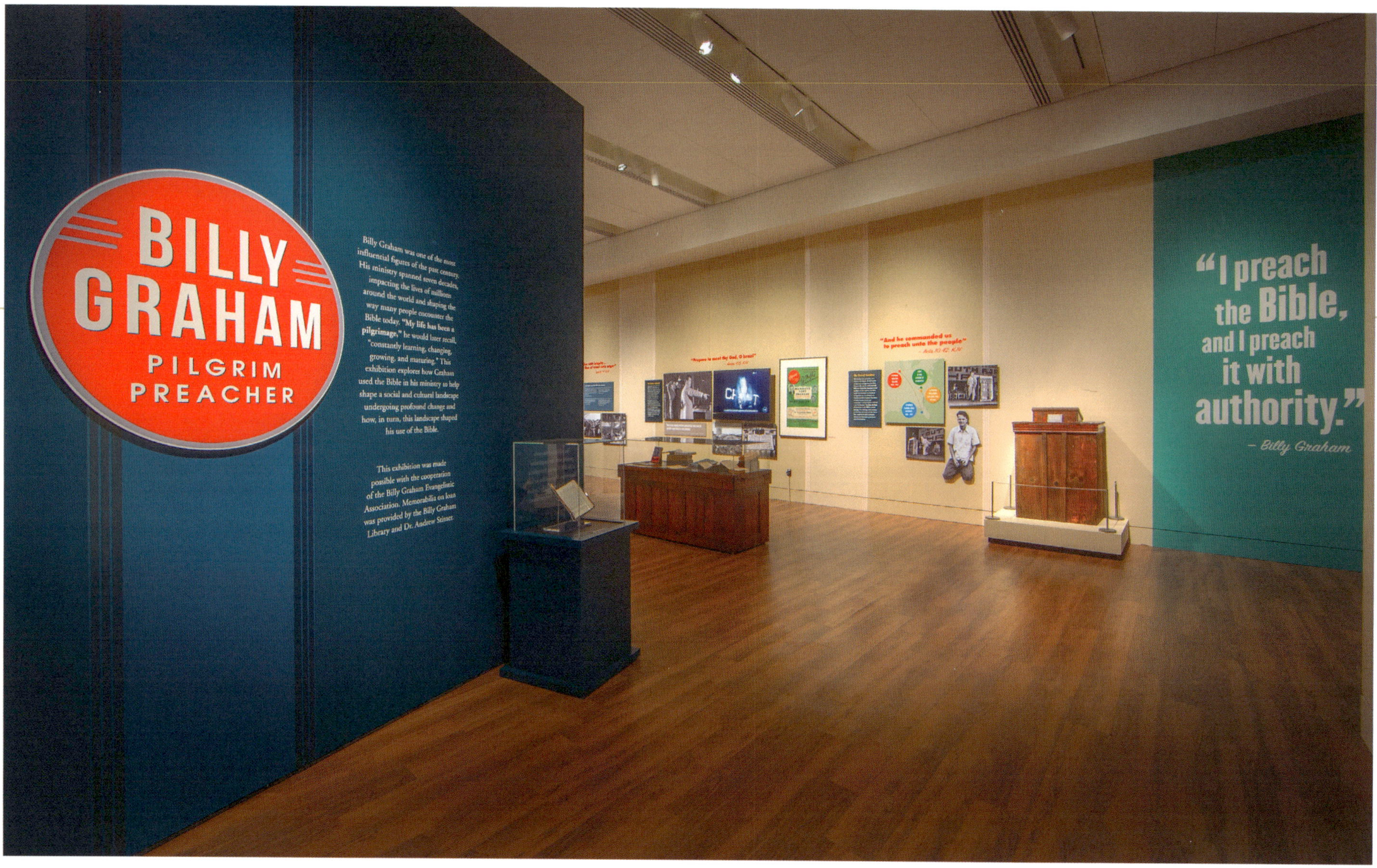

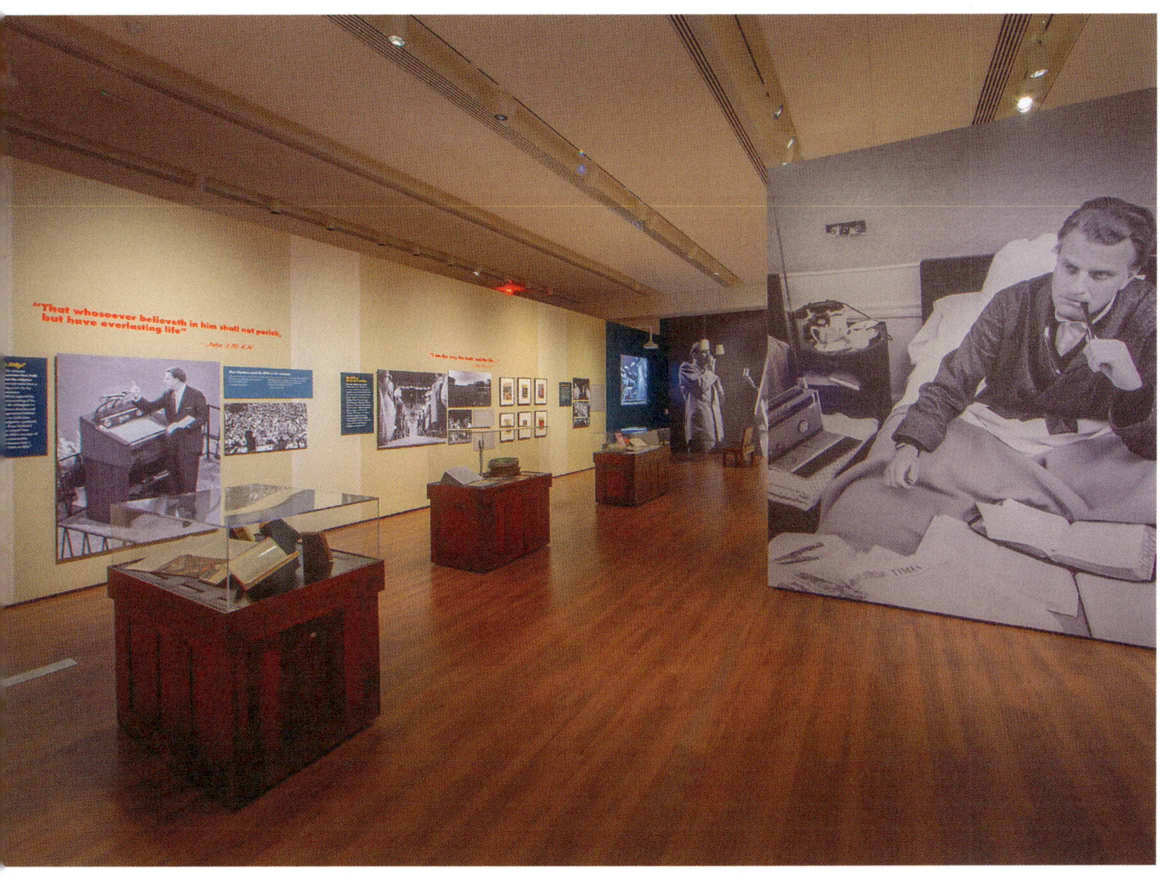

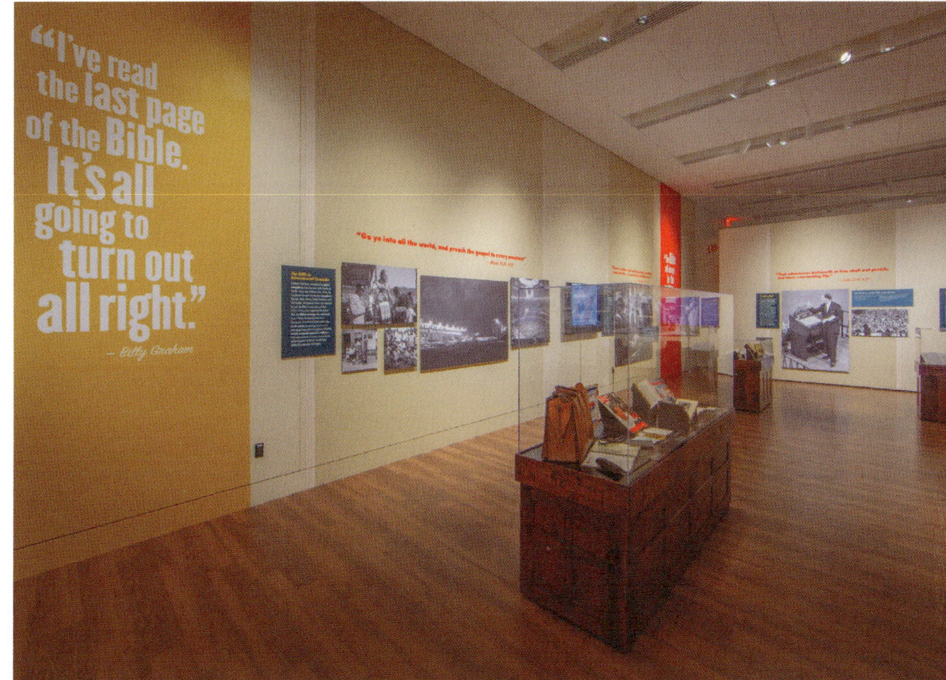

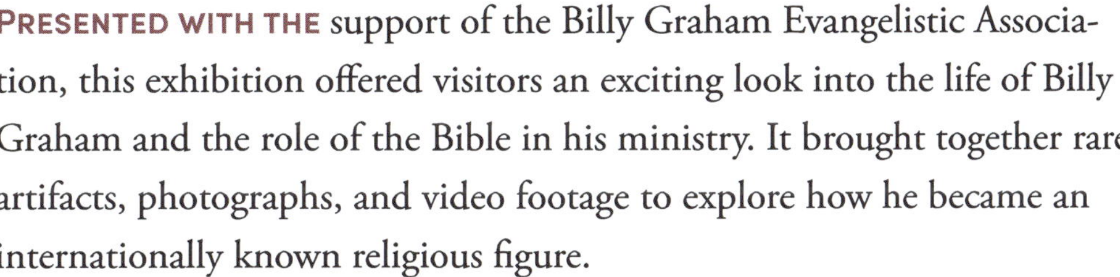

PRESENTED WITH THE support of the Billy Graham Evangelistic Association, this exhibition offered visitors an exciting look into the life of Billy Graham and the role of the Bible in his ministry. It brought together rare artifacts, photographs, and video footage to explore how he became an internationally known religious figure.

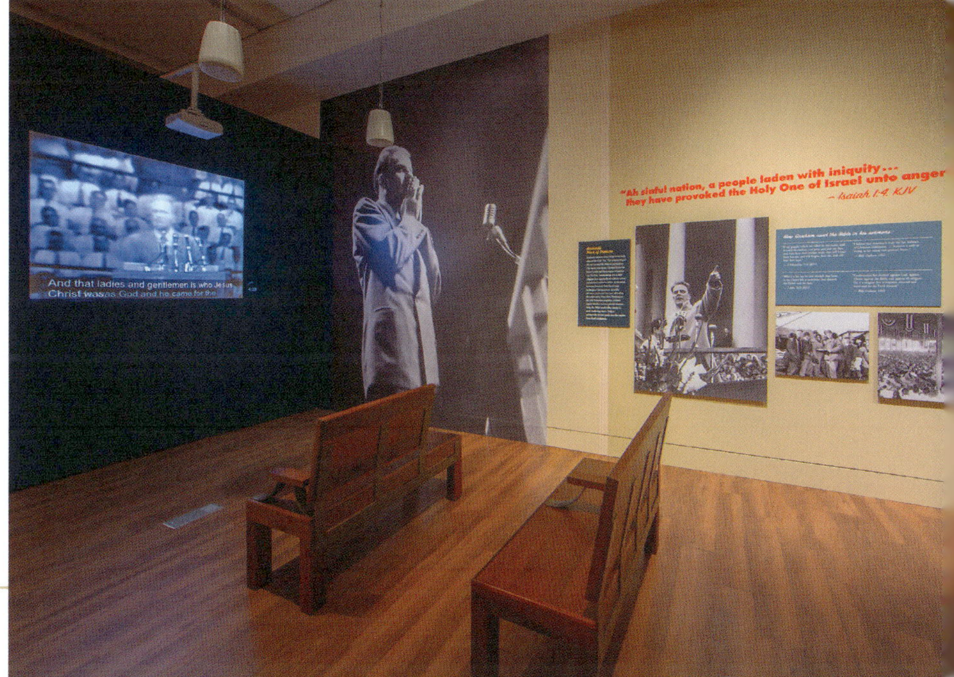

October 2018

The Wiedmann Bible exhibited at Museum of the Bible.

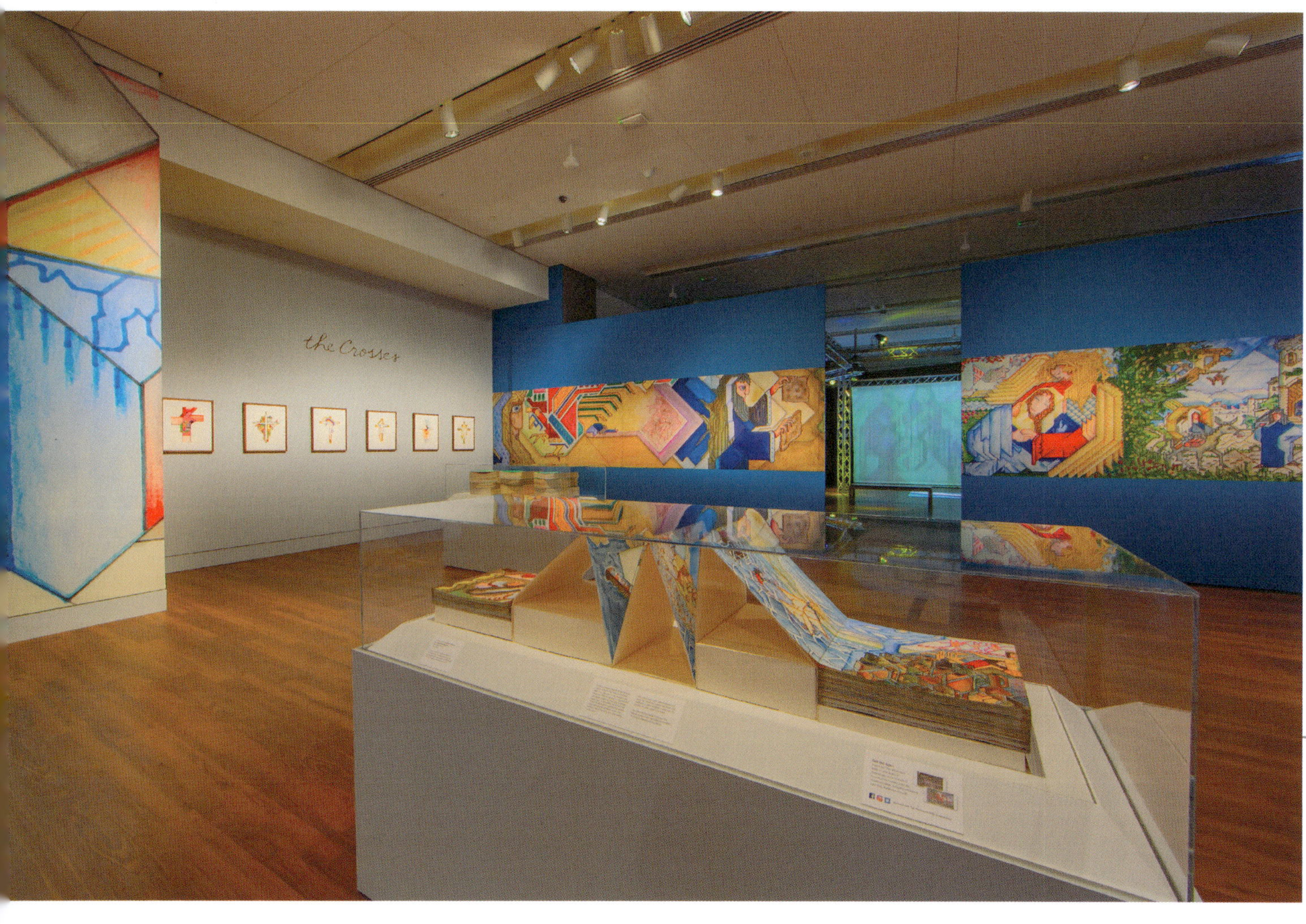

German artist Willy Wiedmann spent sixteen years creating a visual narrative of a Christian Bible in his own unique style, called Polycon. This style was greatly influenced by his lifelong love of music, as well as by some of the major 20th-century European, avant-garde movements such as Surrealism, Dadaism, Cubism, and Abstract Expressionism. Wiedmann's ultimate purpose for his work was simple: to engage people visually with the Bible.

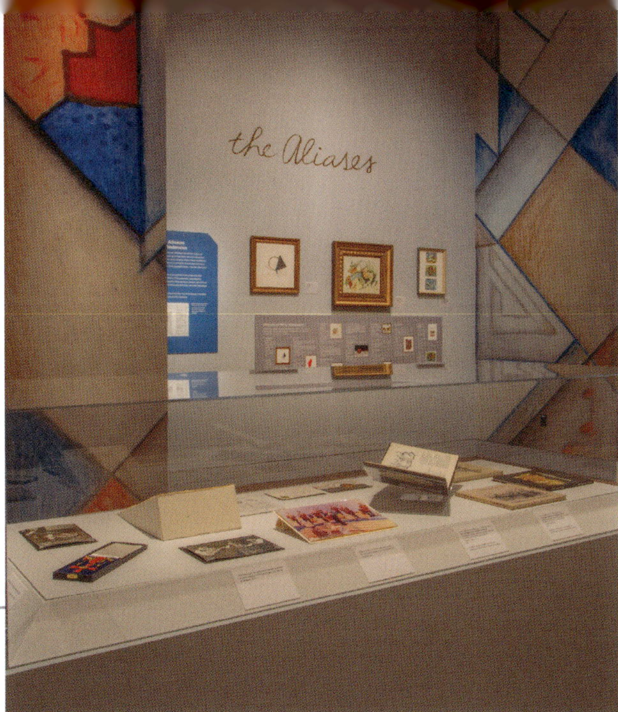

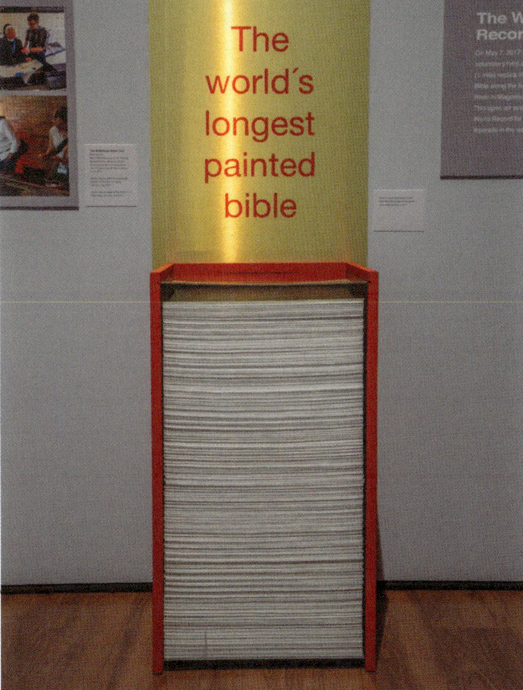

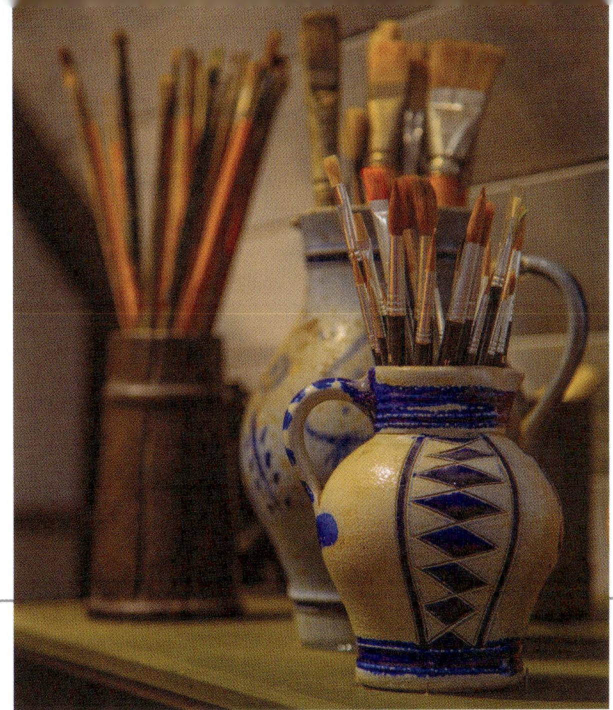

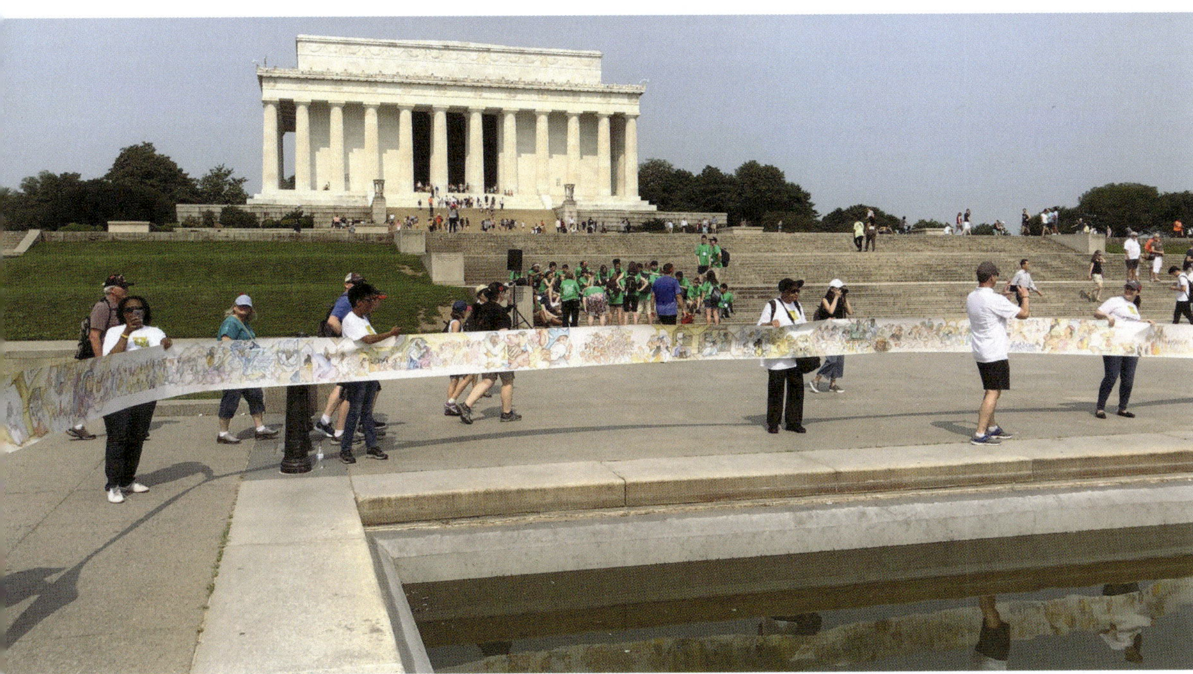

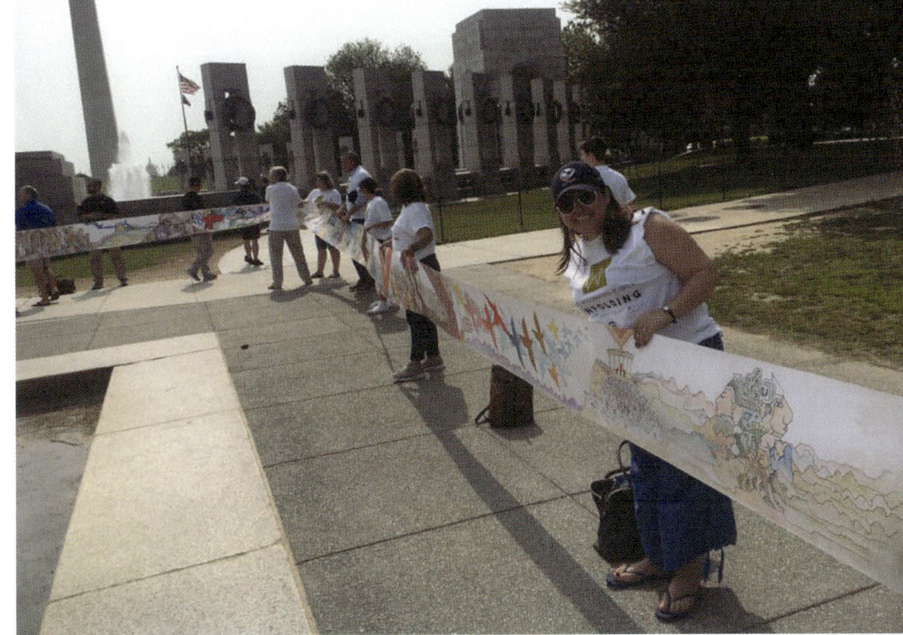

On June 1, 2019, Museum of the Bible and more than 4,000 volunteers unfolded the longest Bible in the world, the Wiedmann Bible, around the Lincoln Memorial Reflecting Pool at the National Mall in Washington, DC.

October 2020

Museum of the Bible acquired the Elisabeth Elliot Collection.

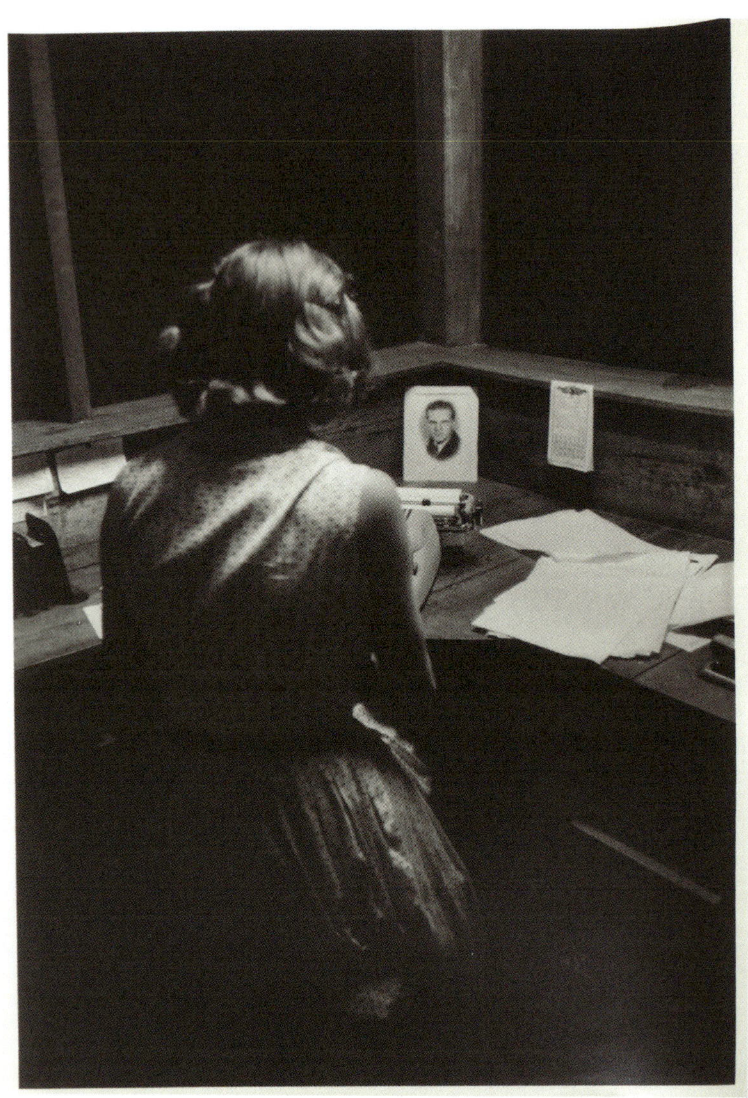

The Elisabeth Elliot Collection at Museum of the Bible includes more than 900 objects from the life and legacy of Elisabeth Elliot, missionary to the Waorani people of Ecuador.

Elisabeth Elliot was a Christian author and speaker most known for her book *Through the Gates of Splendor*, published in 1957. The book details the true account of five families and their attempts to befriend an isolated tribe in the Amazonian rainforest. Tragically, after only a few encounters, five of the missionaries, including Elisabeth's husband Jim, were killed by a group of tribesmen who perceived them as a threat.

Elisabeth and her daughter, Valerie, returned to the United States, but eventually returned to Ecuador in 1958 to live with the tribe that killed her husband. For the next two years, she continued to learn the Waorani language with the help of their translator, Dayume, and was one of the first to work on a written form of the language that would pave the way for a New Testament translation in 1992 by Catherine Peeke and Rosi Jung.

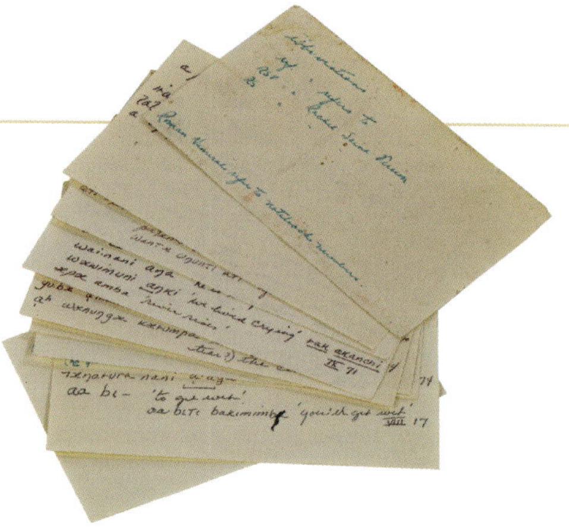

These images are all objects from Museum of the Bible's Elliot Collection. Objects include photographs, letters, books, and objects created by the Waorani people, such as this feathered hat, spear, feathered fan, poison dart holder with darts, and wooden comb.

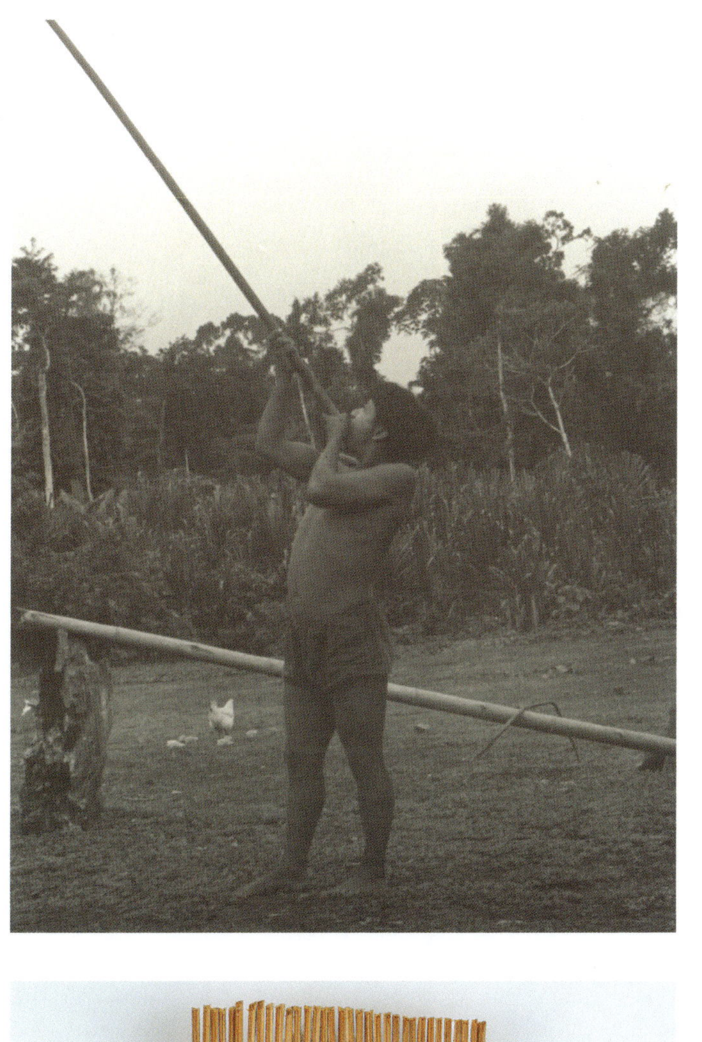

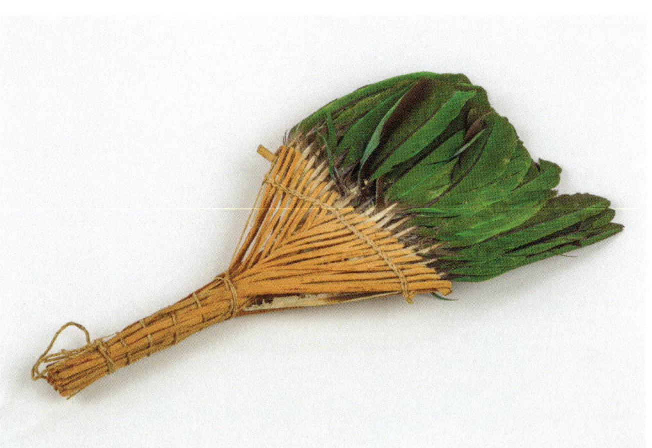

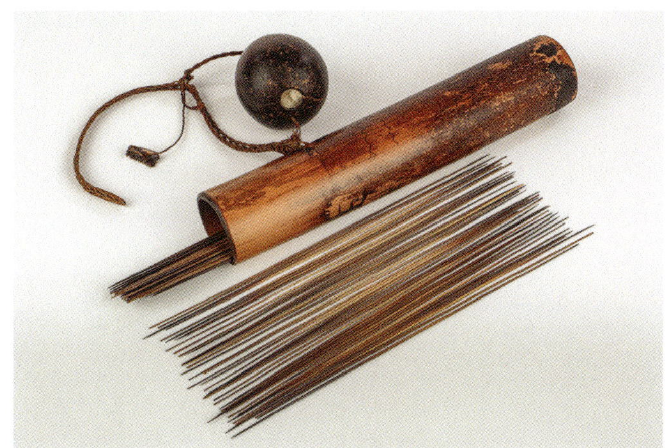

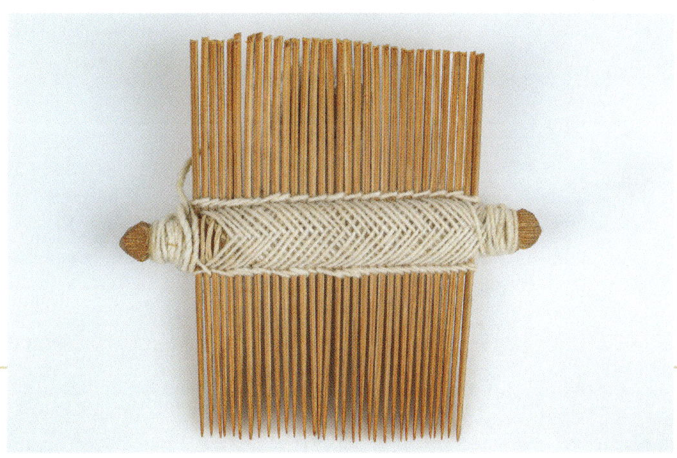

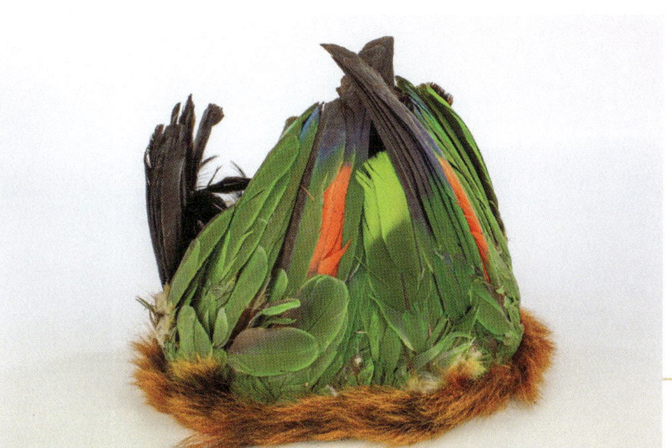

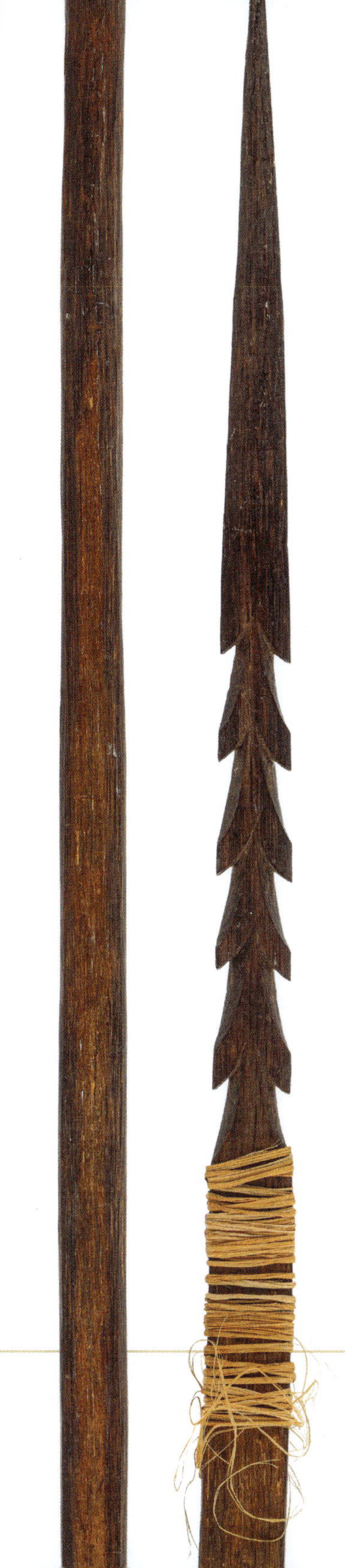

November 2020

Christmas in Malta: Winners of the Nativity Crib Competition **exhibited at Museum of the Bible.**

Constructing handmade Nativity scenes set in elaborate landscapes called “cribs” is a centuries-old tradition that carries strong significance in Maltese culture. In 2020, the nation of Malta, in partnership with the museum, sponsored a crib decorating contest. The top ten entries were featured in the exhibit titled Christmas in Malta and guests voted for their favorites. The winner was Adrian Gatt and Raymond Zammit's crib, with figures by Jesmond Micallef. This Nativity is set in a Maltese house partly demolished during the Second World War. Around the scene, musicians play traditional Maltese instruments, while a woman in traditional dress (għonella) walks with her daughter.

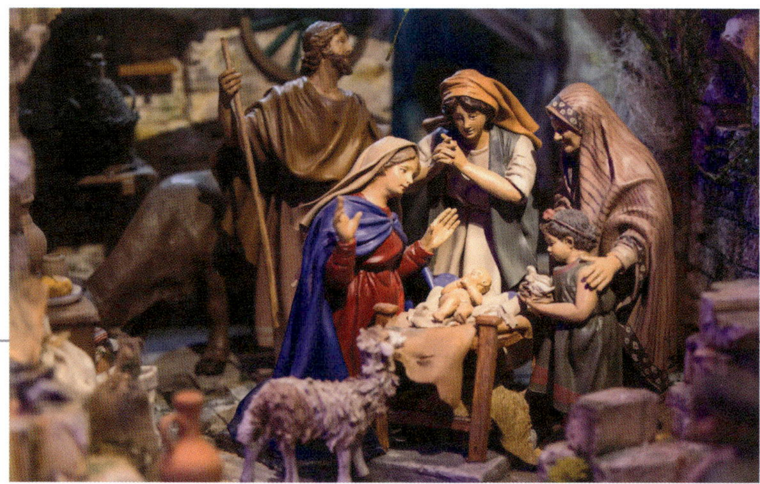

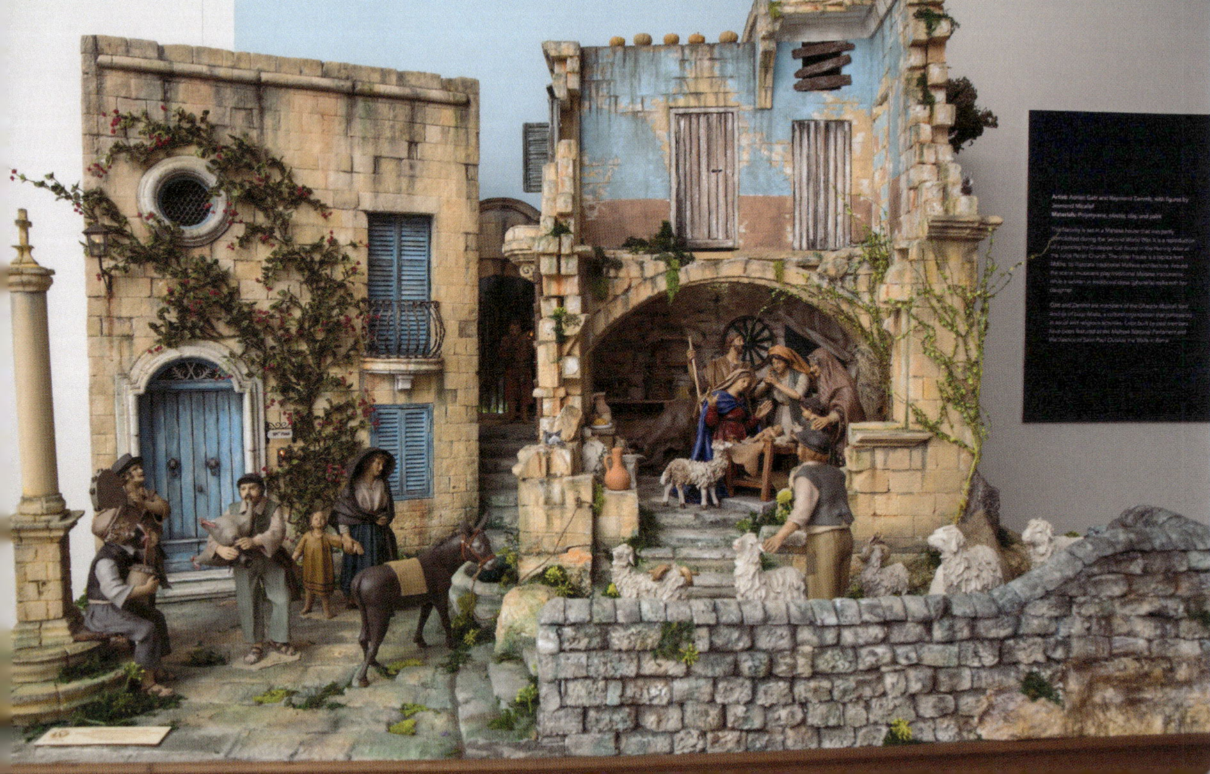

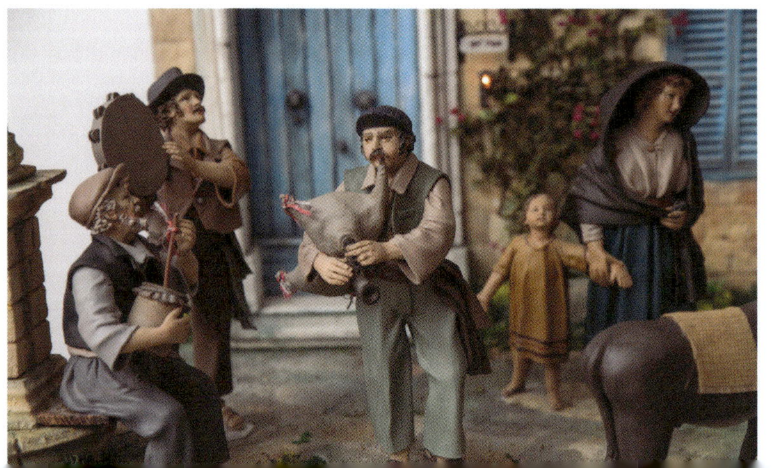

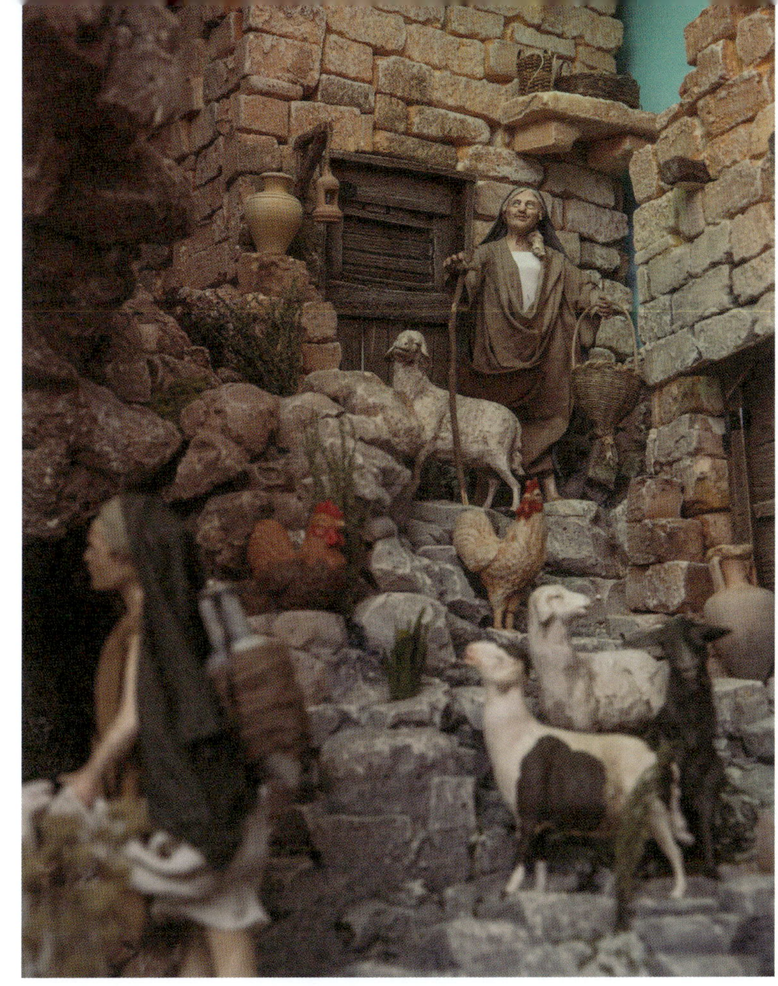

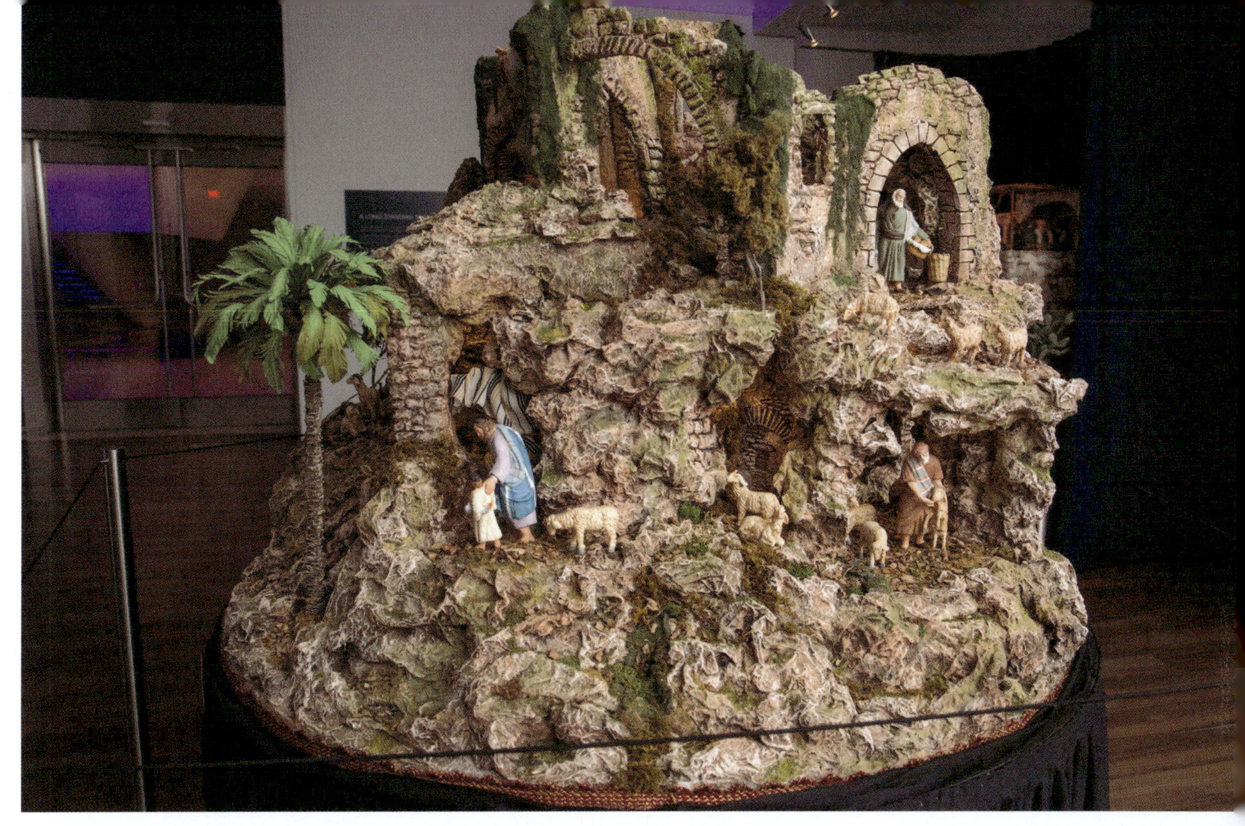

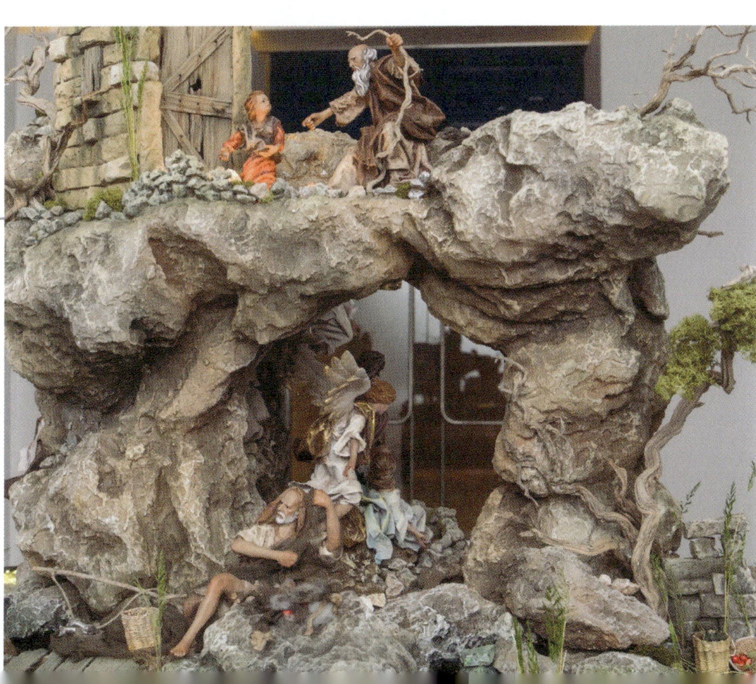

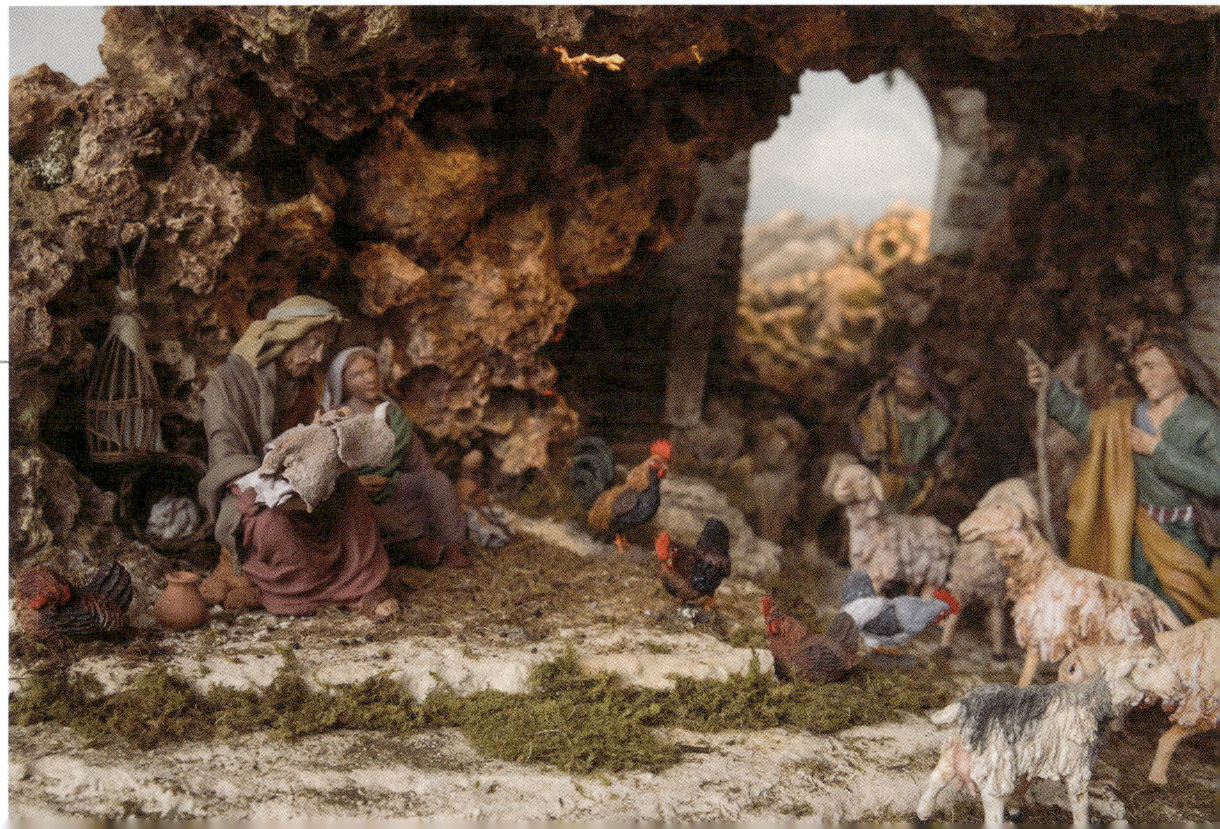

December 2021

Museum of the Bible, for KING & COUNTRY and *The Chosen* teamed up for *A Silent Night at Museum of the Bible* film.

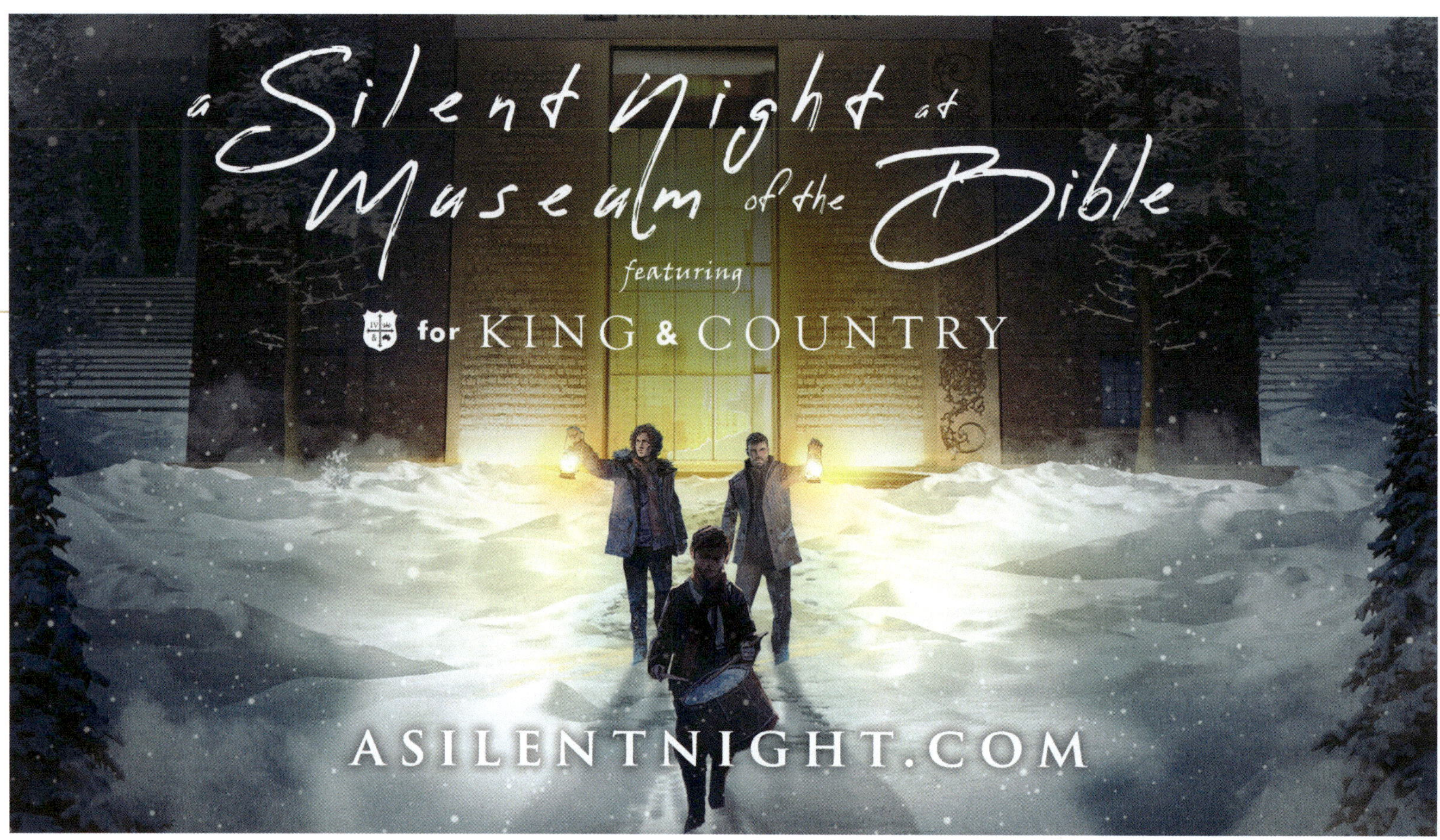

FILMED AT NATIONAL landmarks around Washington, DC, and inside Museum of the Bible, a young drummer boy journeyed to the manger, all synced to the soundtrack of the band's popular album, *A Drummer Boy Christmas*. The film featured classic carols and original hit songs by for KING & COUNTRY, a short clip from the popular *The Chosen* television series, and a performance from Franni Rae Cash Cain of We the Kingdom.

June 2022

Blessing of the Elders awards celebration held at Museum of the Bible.

The Blessing of the Elders awards celebration was held on June 23, 2022, at Museum of the Bible, to honor the rich history of the Black church in America. Seven outstanding pastors whose impact and ministry have been remarkable were recognized. They continue to be examples to all and an inspiration to the generations to come. They have been faithful to the preaching of the Bible and ministering to the souls in their care. By awarding these accomplished leaders, Museum of the Bible upholds their spiritual legacy as they pass the baton to the next generation of preachers, teachers, and pastors who are to come.

The honorees for 2022 were Pastor A. R. Bernard, Bishop Charles E. Blake, Pastor Shirley Caesar, Dr. Tony Evans, Bishop T. D. Jakes, Bishop Vashti McKenzie, and Dr. John M. Perkins.

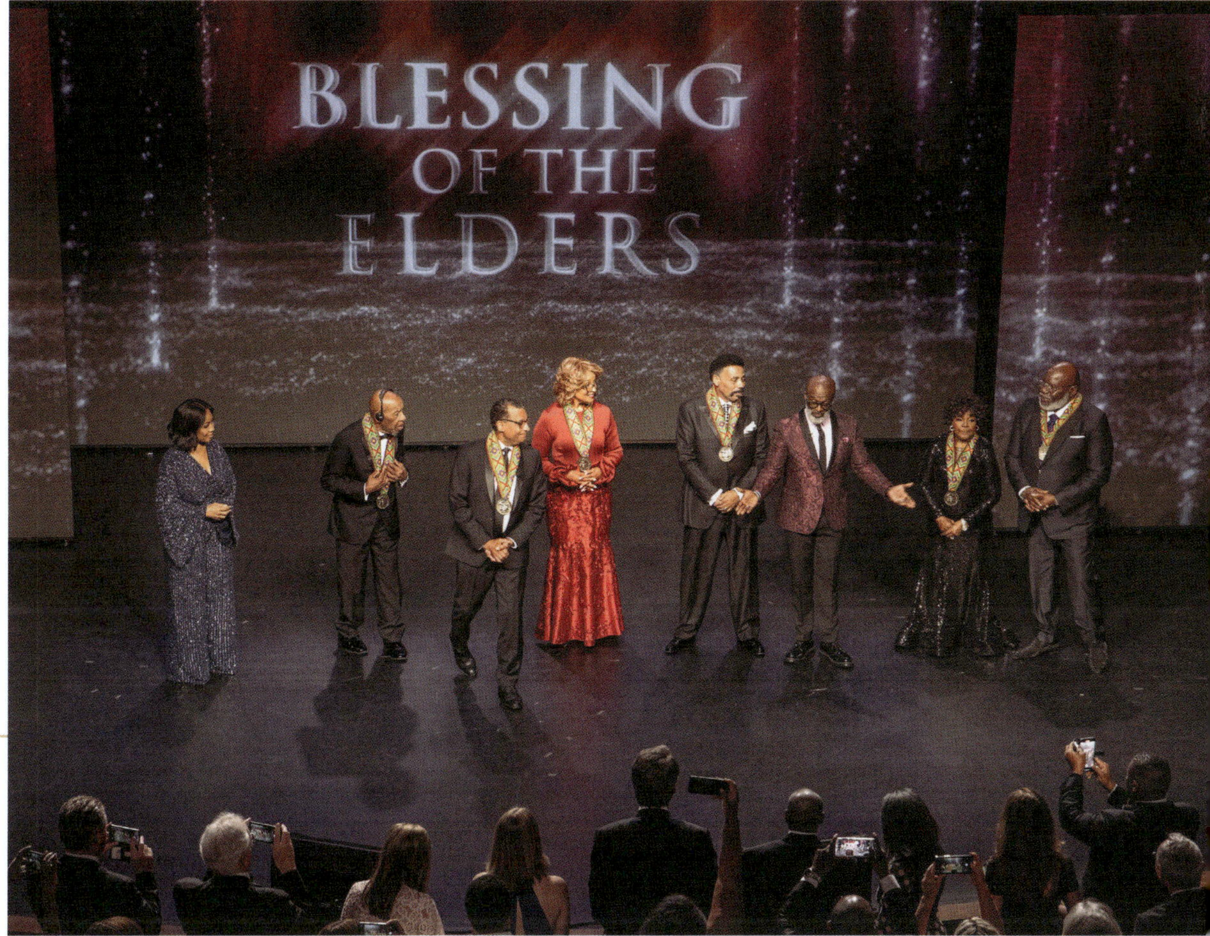

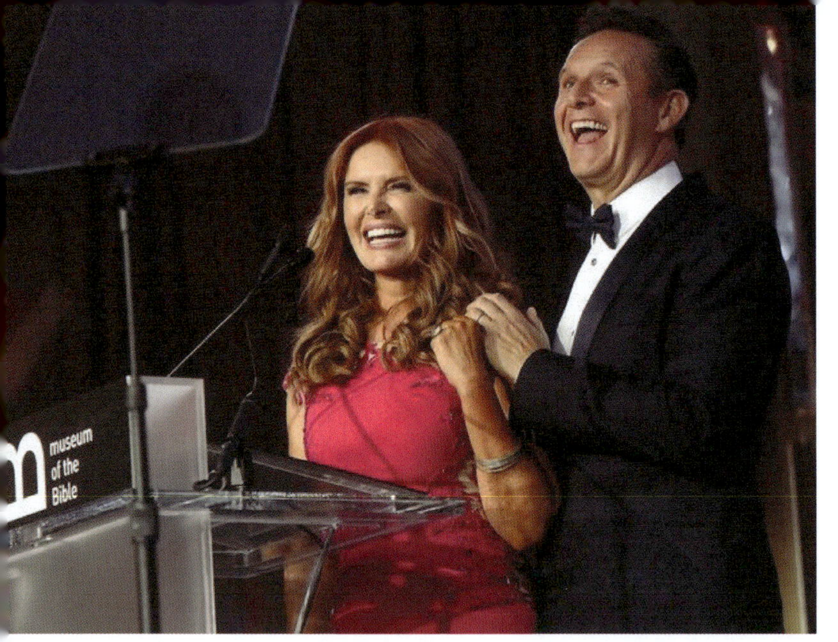

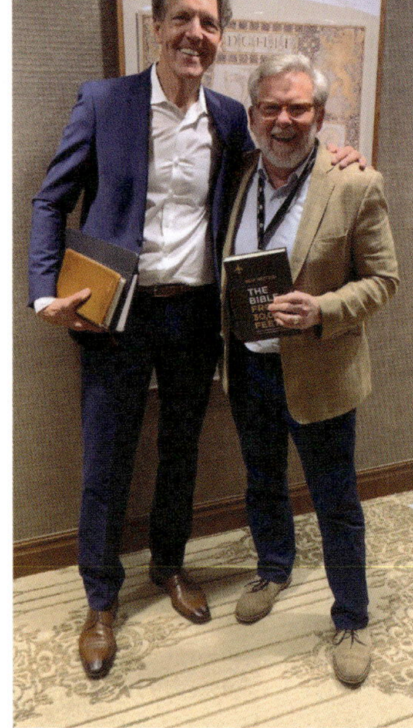

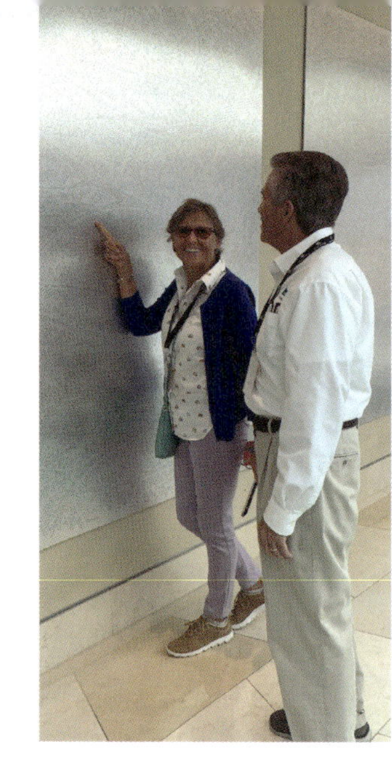

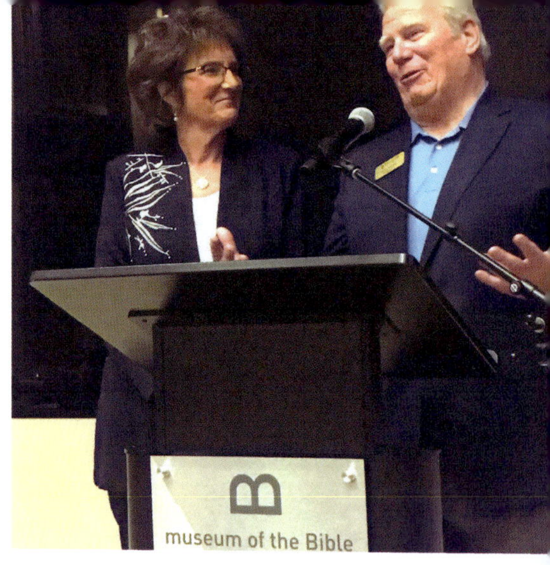

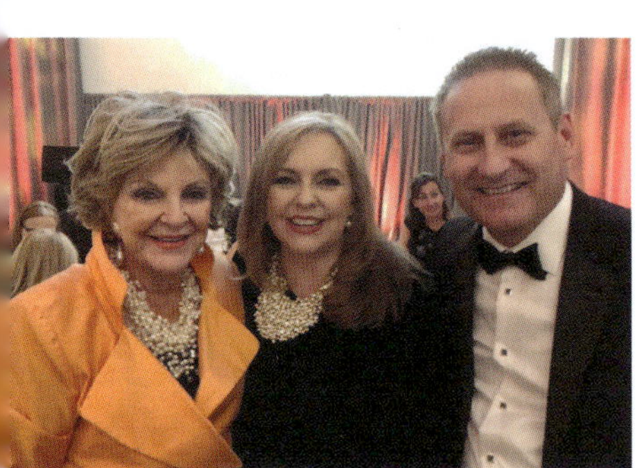

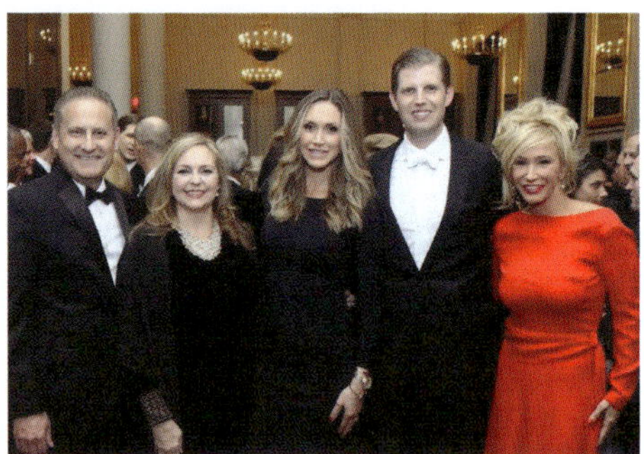

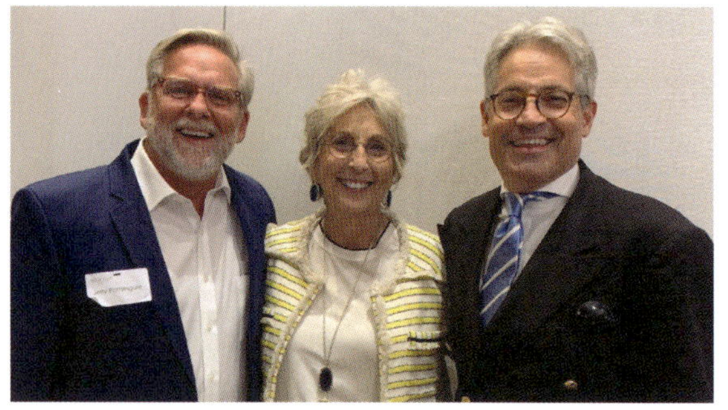

2017- 2022

A Glimpse of Special Faces from a Variety of Places

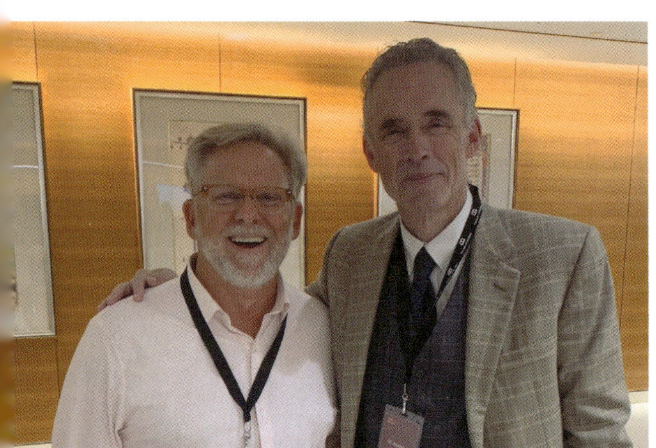

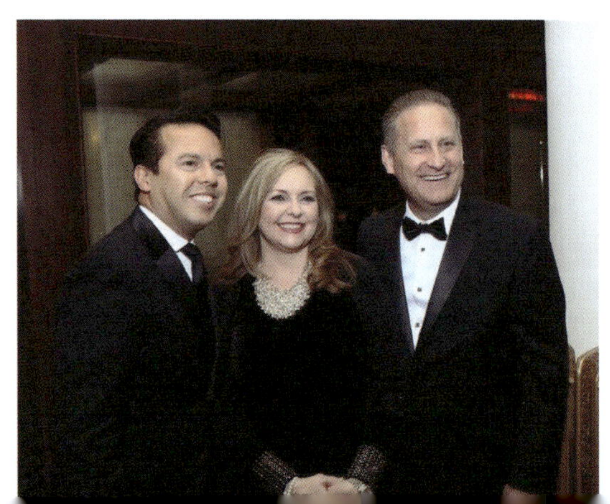

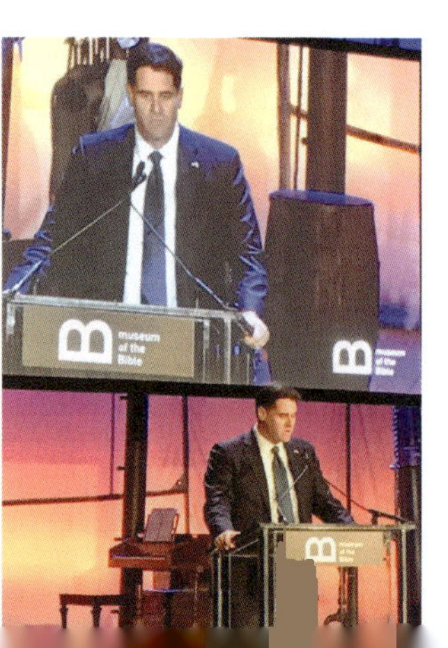

TOP LEFT TO RIGHT:

Roma Downey and Mark Burnett during a festive moment, December 4, 2017.

Skip Heitzig and Jerry Pattengale, March 27, 2022.

Lifetime members Joyce and Bryan Dolan finding their family's names, September 30, 2021.

Congresswoman Jackie Walorski and her good friend P. Eric Turner greeting a large crowd from their alma mater, Taylor University (Upland, Indiana), February 13, 2019.

CENTER LEFT TO RIGHT:

Kay Arthur and Jackie and Steve Green, November 16, 2017.

Steve and Jackie Green with Lara and Eric Trump, and Paula White, December 4, 2017.

Jerry Pattengale, Barbara Green, and Eric Metaxas, August 15, 2019.

BOTTOM LEFT TO RIGHT:

Jerry Pattengale and Jordan Peterson, July 14, 2022.

Samuel Rodriguez and Jackie and Steve Green, December 4, 2017.

Frmr. Israeli Ambassador Ron Dermer, November 17, 2017.

Artifact Highlights

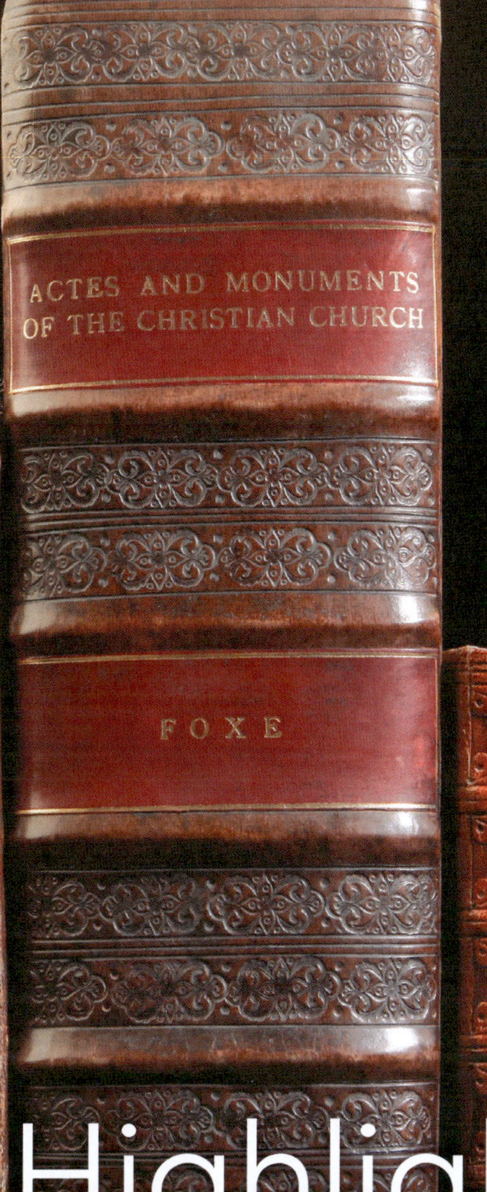

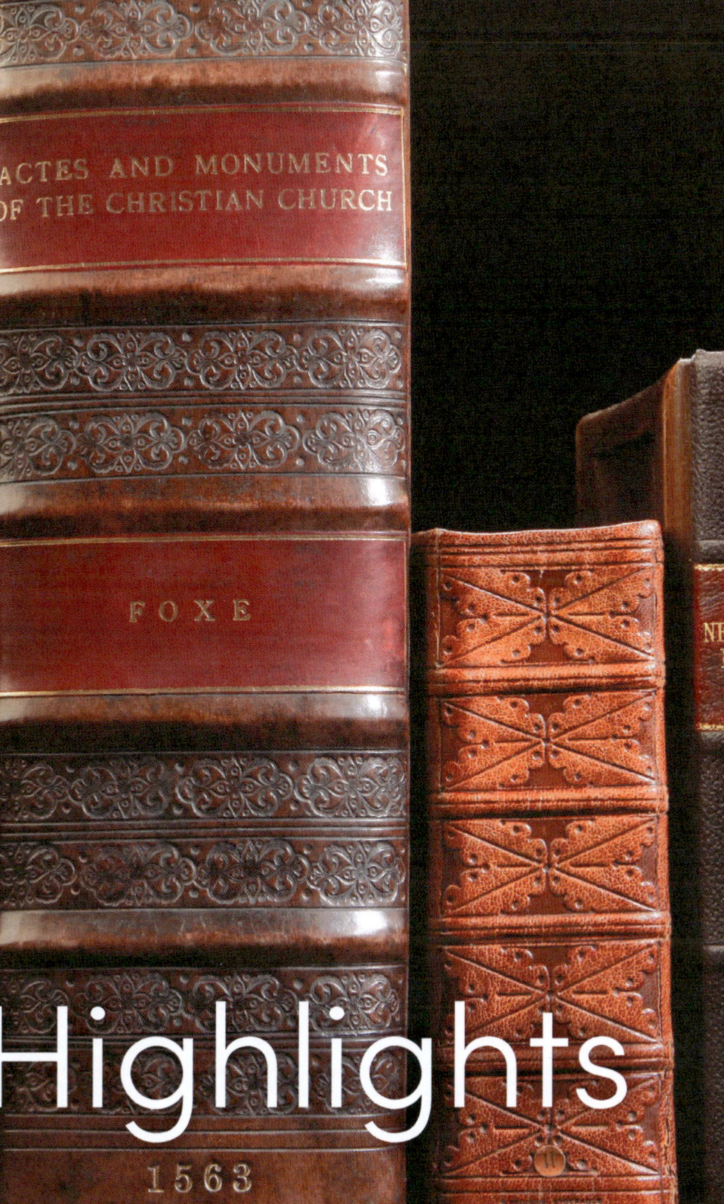

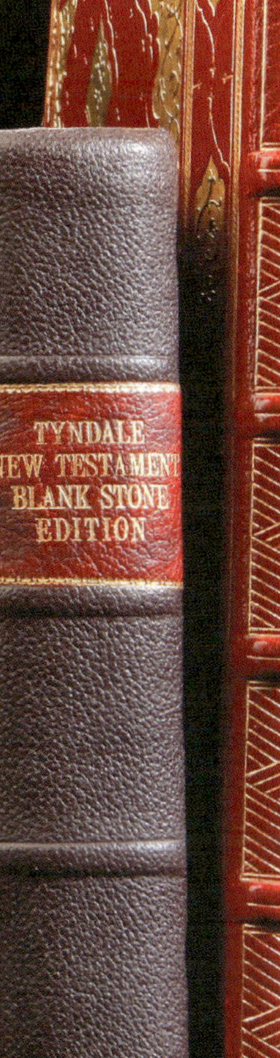

The Rice Psalter, Use of Sarum

MS.000372, parchment codex, ca. 1450–1460

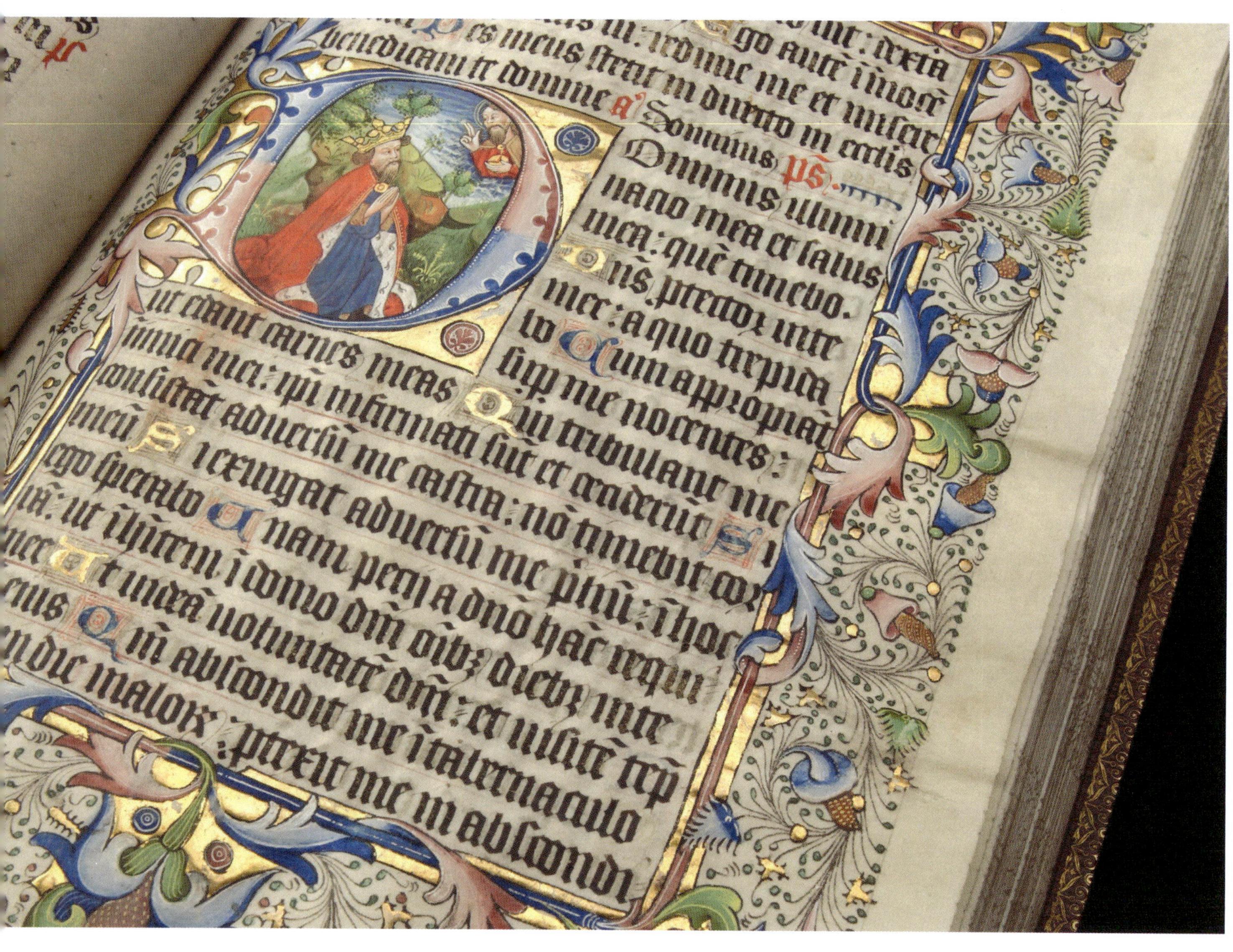

THIS 15TH-CENTURY manuscript takes its name from an inscription at the end of the text which says in part, “Off your charite pray for the soules of Symon Rice and Letyce his wyffe . . .” The inscription likely refers to a known 16th-century London merchant and his wife. The manuscript contains eight fully historiated initials, each on a page framed with a full floral border. The manuscript most likely was made for liturgical, rather than private, use. In the back flyleaves someone in the 16th century kept an account of payments for such things as drinks and spinning.

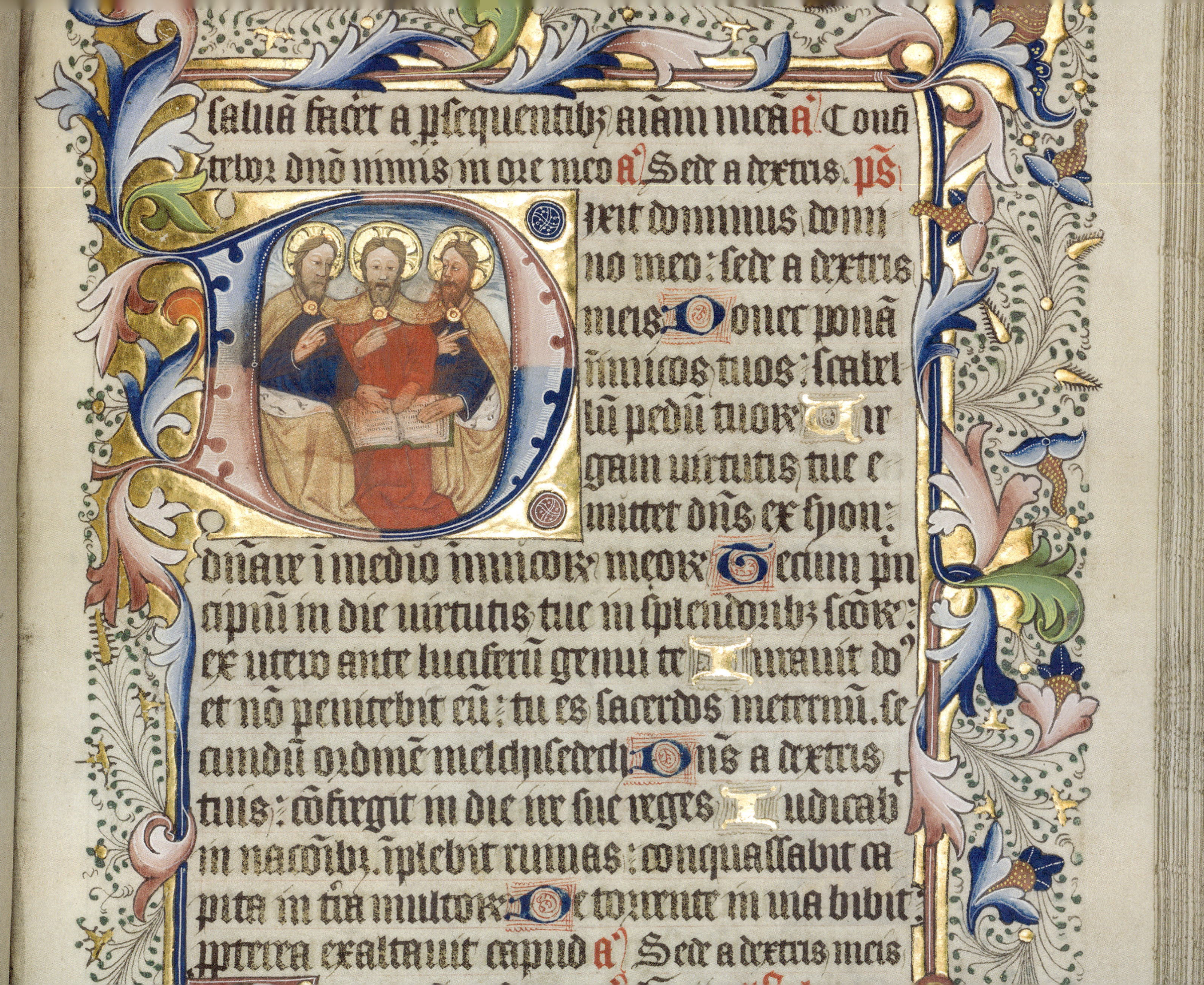

saluã faciet a psequentibꝫ aiam meã A' Confi
tebor dño nimis in ore meo A' Sede a dextris. ps.
Dixit dominus domi
no meo: sede a dextris
meis. Donec ponã
inimicos tuos: scabel
lũ pedũ tuoꝝ. Uir
gam uirtutis tue e
mittet dñs ex syon:
dñare i medio inimicoꝝ meoꝝ. Tecum prin
cipiũ in die uirtutis tue in splendoribꝫ scõꝝ:
ex utero ante luciferũ genui te. Iurauit dñs
et nõ penitebit eũ: tu es sacerdos in eternũ. se
cundũ ordinẽ melchisedech. Dñs a dextris
tuis: cõfregit in die ire sue reges. Iudicabit
in nacõibꝫ. implebit ruinas: conquassabit ca
pita in tra multoꝝ. De torrente in uia bibit:
propterea exaltabit caput. A' Sede a dextris meis

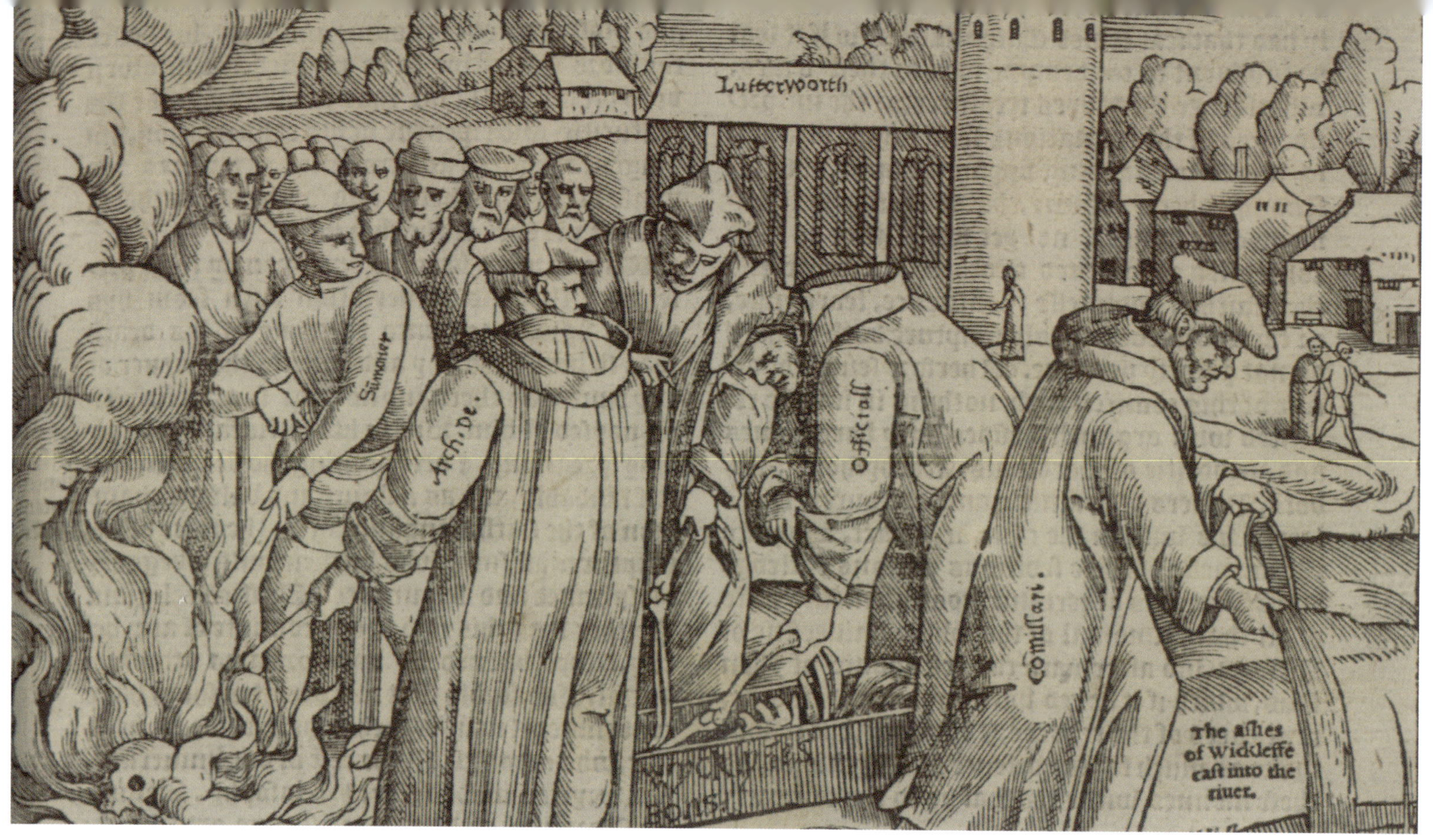

Actes and Monuments of the Christian Church

PBK.000369, printed book, 1563

JOHN FOXE'S *Actes and Monuments of the Christian Church*, often simply called *Foxe's Book of Martyrs*, was one of the most influential publications of the Reformation period. Foxe was an English minister and religious reformer. He began writing the book in the 1550s, shortly before Queen Mary, a devout Catholic, took the throne. The book surveys the history of Christian martyrdom, with special emphasis on the persecution of Protestants in England and Europe. Foxe was hardly an impartial writer, and the popularity of his work helped fan the flame of anti-Catholic sentiment in the English-speaking world for centuries. This is a rare copy of the first English edition, which expanded on the Latin edition published in 1559.

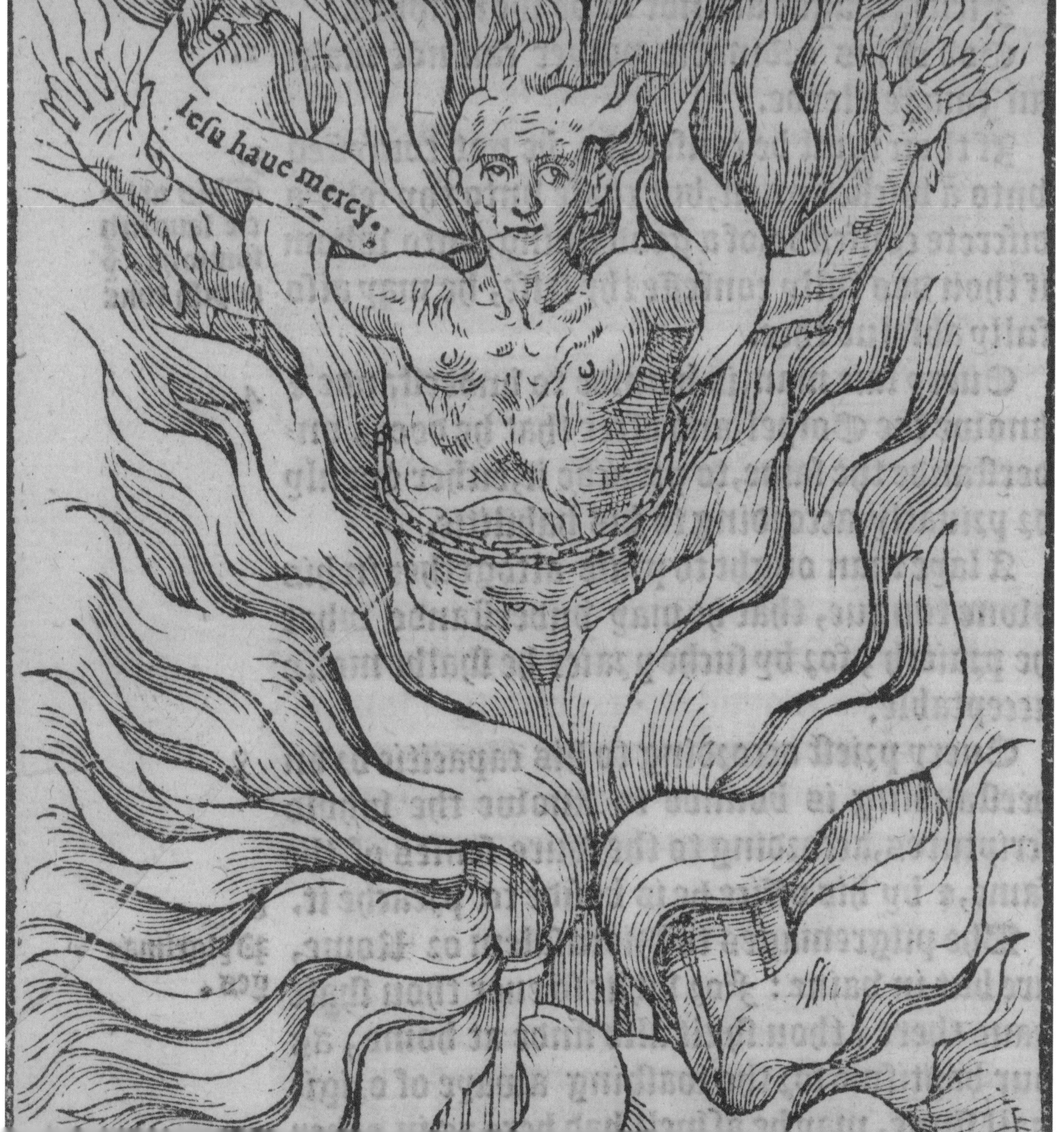

Facing Page: Posthumous burning of John Wycliff's bones.

Left: Martyr, perhaps William Sawtre, burned at the stake.

Almanach pro.xix.annis.

Numerus anni.	Brandones	Pascha.	Aureus numerꝰ	Aduẽtꝰ	Lr̃a do·	Bi sextꝰ
ccccccxij	xxviij februa.	xi apri.	xij	xxviij noue͂.	C	D
ccccccxiij	xiij februa.	xxvij mar.	xiij	xxvij noue͂.	B	
ccccccxiiij	v mar.	xvi apri.	xiiij	iij dece͂b.	A	
ccccccxv	xxv februa.	viij apri.	xv	ij decemb.	G	
ccccccxvi	x februa.	xxij mar.	xvi	xxx noue͂.	E	F
ccccccxvij	i mar.	xij apri.	xvij	xxix noue͂.	D	
ccccccxviij	xxi februa.	iiij apri.	xviij	xxviij noue͂.	C	
ccccccxix	xiij mar.	xxiiij apri.	xix	xxvij noue͂.	B	
ccccccxx	xxv februa.	ij apri.	i	ij dece͂b.	G	A
ccccccxxi	xvij februa	xxxi mar.	ij	i decemb.	F	
ccccccxxij	ix mar.	xx apri.	iij	xxx noue͂.	E	
ccccccxxiij	xxij februa.	v apri.	iiij	xxix noue͂.	D	
ccccccxxiiij	xiij februa.	xxvij mar.	v	xxvij noue͂.	B	C
ccccccxxv	v mar.	xvi apri.	vi	iij dece͂b.	A	
ccccccxxvi	xviij februa.	i apri.	vij	ij decemb.	G	
ccccccxxvij	x mar.	xxi apri.	viij	i decemb.	F	
ccccccxxviij	i mar.	xij apri.	ix	xxix noue͂.	E	D
ccccccxxix	xiiij februa.	xxviij mar.	x	xxviij noue͂.	C	
ccccccxxx	vi mar.	xxvij apri.	xi	xxvij noue͂.	B	

Tabula inueniendi quadragesime principium. Pascha. Aureũ numerũ. Aduentum dñi. Litterã dñicalem: et litterã bissexti. Ab anno salutis. Millesimo. ccccccxii. durans vsq ad annũ domini. Mil. ccccccxxx. inclusiue. quoniã omia

Quant la lune et en aries leo et sagitari' il fait bon saignier au colerique · feu

Quant la lune et en gemini libra et aquariu' il fait bo saigner au sanguin · aer

le colerique tient du feu et du sy on il a perillie ue vin ma le complexion

du singe et de la nt tiet le sanguin qui est large et plaisant et a ioyeuse vin

de leaue et de laiguel tient le flumatique il est simple et doubte da la pratio

melencolique ue du porc tieu et de terre il est pesat et ort doin eux ne luy chault guere

Quant la lune et en cancer scorpio et pisces il fait bo seigner au fleumatique eau

Quant la lune en taurus virgi et capricornus il fait bo saigner au melencoliq te

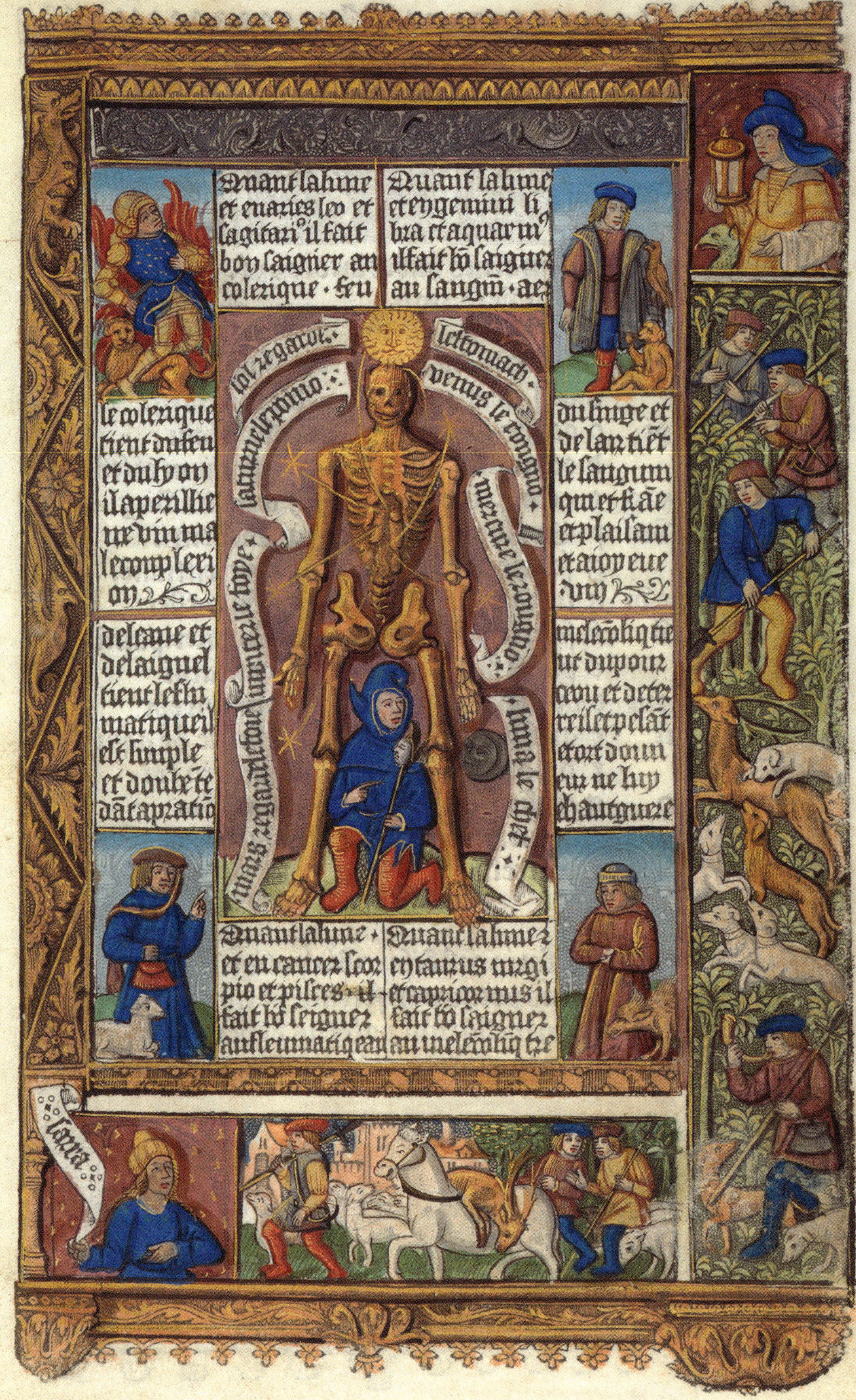

Book of Hours, Use of Salisbury

PBK.002282, parchment, printed book, 1512

THIS BOOK OF HOURS contains a printed text with more than twenty partial and full-page illustrations. Printed in 1512 with wood- or metal-cut illustrations that were then hand illuminated, this devotional work has the rare characteristic of royal provenance. This copy was a gift from King Henry VIII of England to his cousin and features an inscription and his signature below the illustration of the annunciation. The inscription reads: "I pray you pray for me your / lovyng cousin Henry R." While the recipient of the book remains a mystery, Margaret Pole, Henry's cousin once removed and lady-in-waiting to Catherine of Aragon, has been suggested by previous owners of the text.

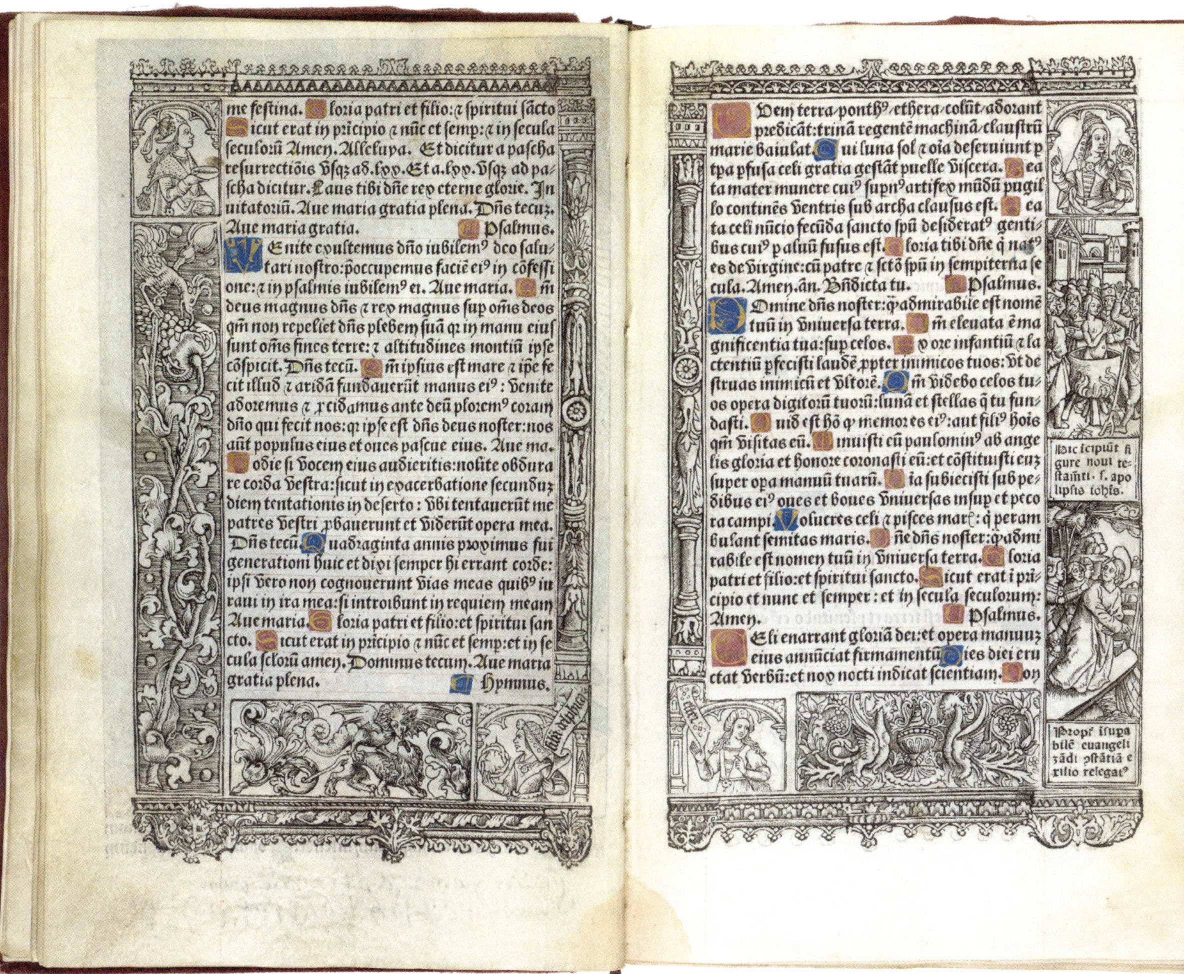

RIGHT: Bifolium with detailed marginalia and colored initials.

FACING PAGE: Bifolium containing a full page, colored illustration with text interspersed amidst local flora and fauna.

Mishnah, with Maimonides's Commentary

INC.000163, printed book, 1492

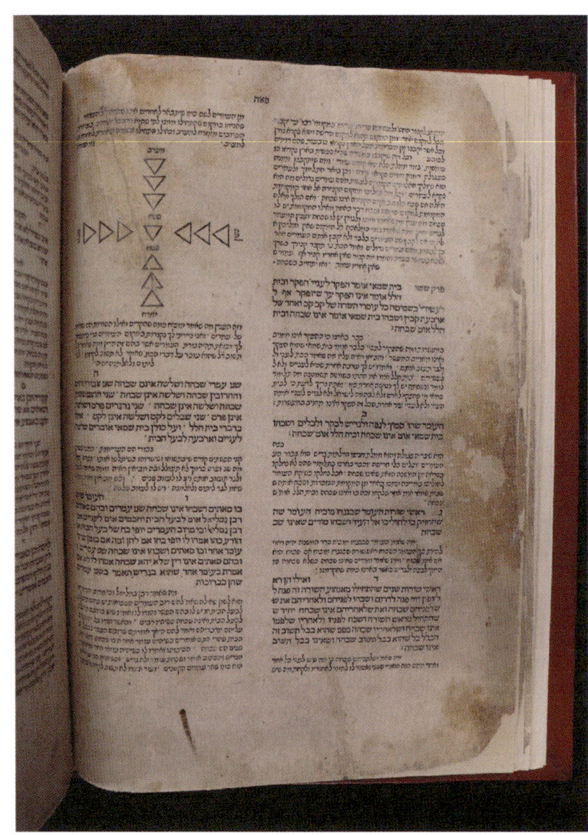

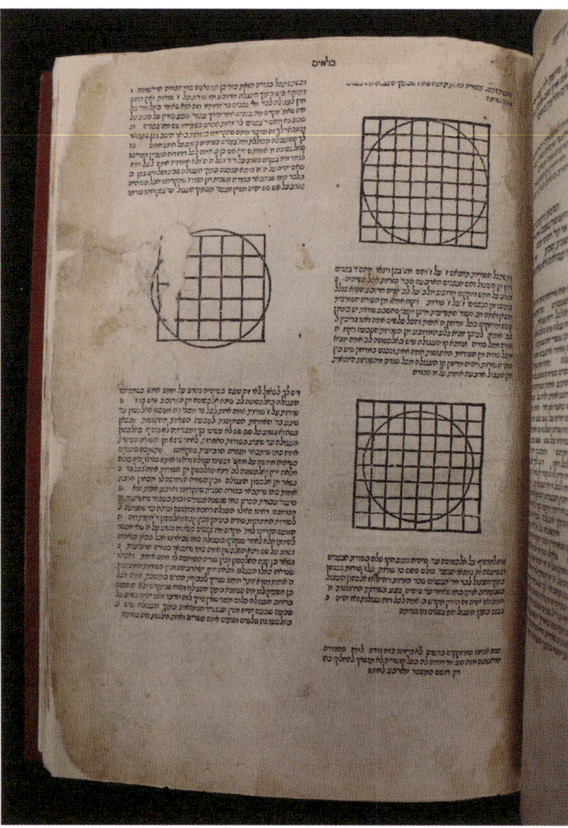

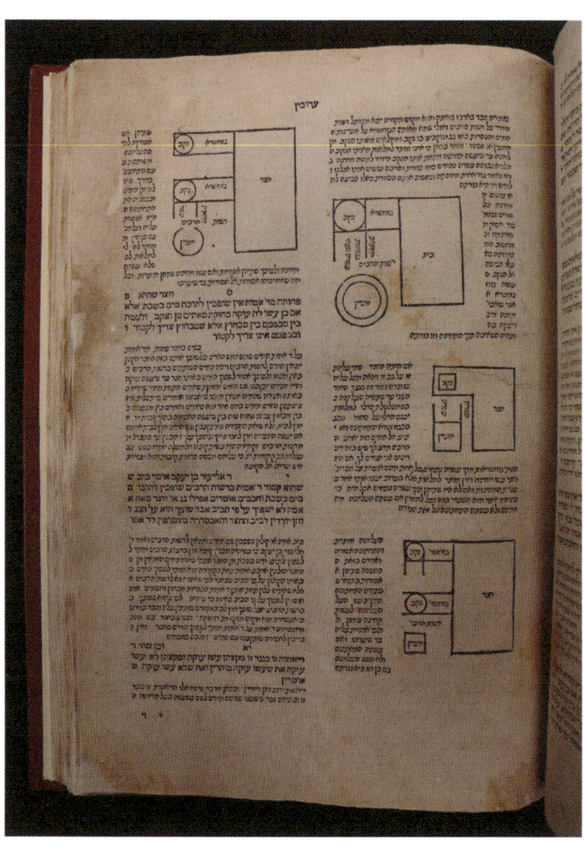

THIS TWO-VOLUME SET is a first-edition, printed Mishnah with commentary by Moses Maimonides. It was completed May 8, 1492, by the well-known Jewish Italian printer Joshua Solomon Soncino, who began printing in 1483 in Soncino, Italy, later moving to Naples where this Mishnah was printed. He completed his first work, a portion of the Talmud, in 1484 and continued printing Jewish texts, including the first complete Hebrew Bible with vowel points, until his death in 1493. His family carried his printing legacy into the mid-1500s, with his nephew Gershom Soncino becoming the most prolific and well-known Soncino printer.

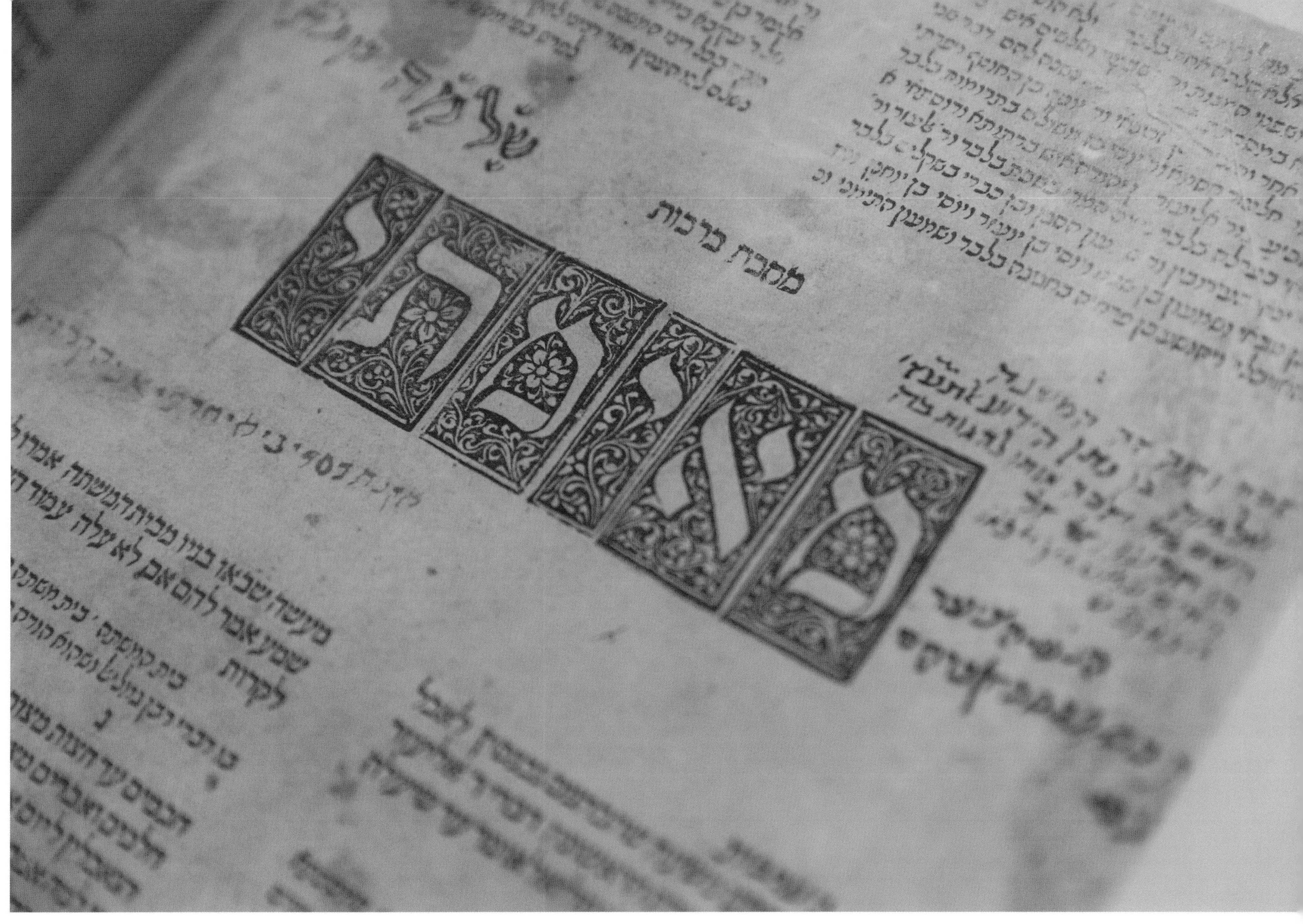

Above: Detail image of a heading with floral motifs.

Facing page: Multiple leaves of the Mishnah containing drawings and diagrams.

Codex Climaci Rescriptus (GA 0250)

MS.000149, parchment codex, ca. 500s (Christian Palestinian Aramaic), ca. 700s (Greek), and ca. 800s–900s (Syriac)

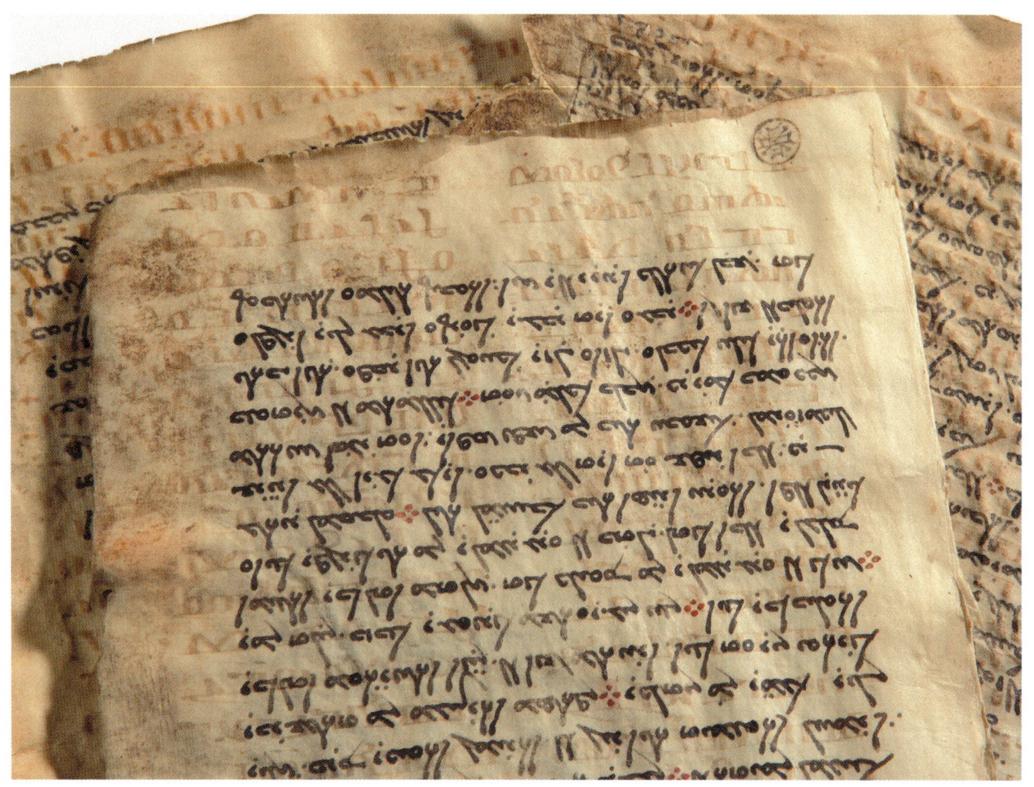

Left: Multiple leaves of Codex Climaci Rescriptus with underlying Christian Palestinian Aramaic text shown upright and Syriac upside down.

Facing page: Detail image of single leaf with Christian Palestinian Aramaic text shown upright and Syriac upside down.

Monks at the monastery of St. Catherine in the Sinai produced this palimpsest manuscript in the ninth or tenth century. They recycled leaves from at least ten different Greek and Christian Palestinian Aramaic manuscripts by erasing the text, and then writing a Syriac translation of John Climacus's works on the reused parchment.

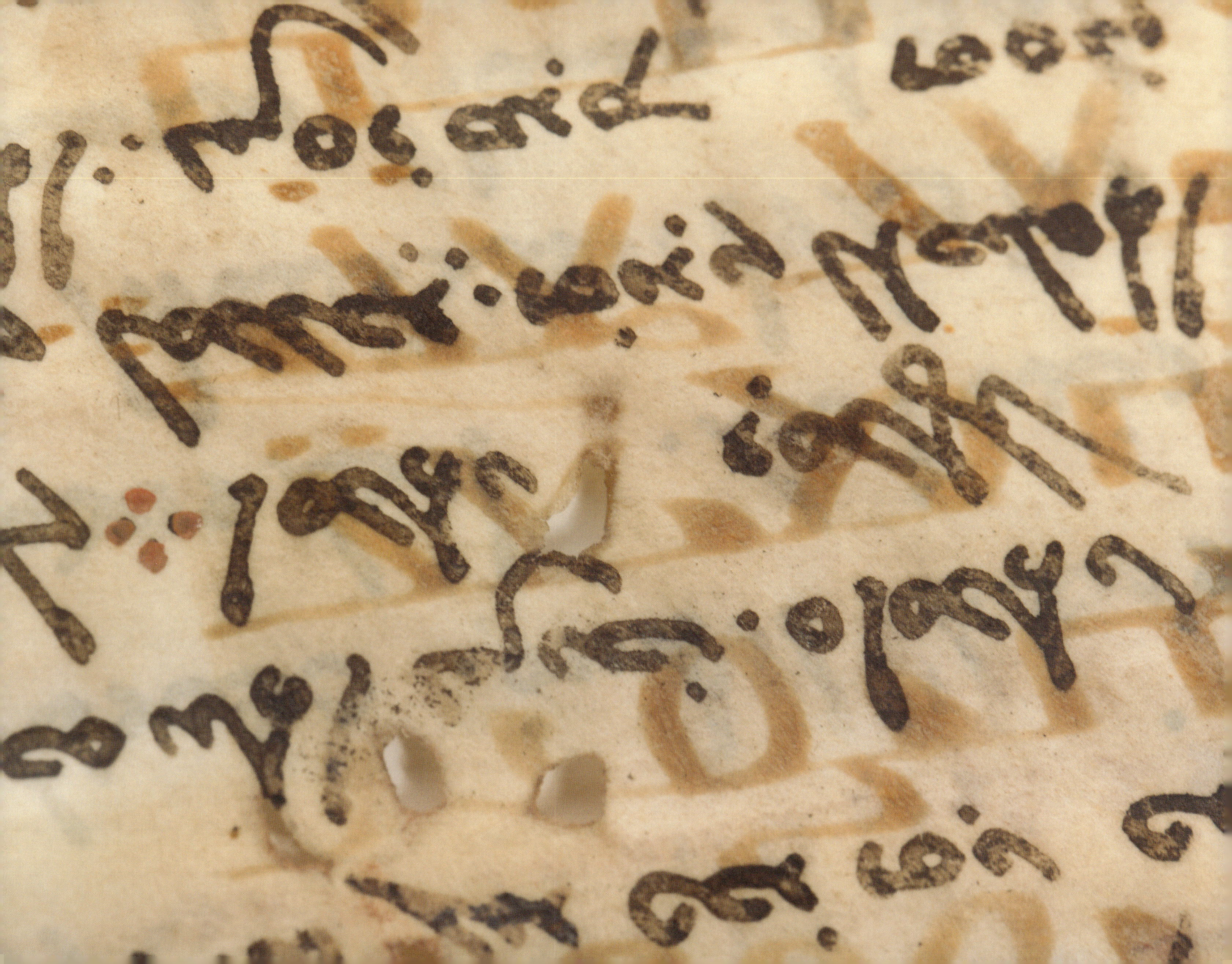

ܐܘ ܚܝܠܐ ܠܡܫܠܡܘ. ܠܡܦܩ ܟܪ ܠܟܠܗ ܘܠܐ ܠܗ ܐܝܟ ܡܪܢܝܬܐ. ܘܟܕ ܠܐ
ܠܡܫܩܠܬܐ ܠܡܬܚܫܒܘ ܠܐ ܢܕܥ ܀ ܡܫܡܠܝܐ ܟܠܗܘܢ ܠܡܫܠܡܘܬܐ ܚܠܠܝܢ:
ܐܦ ܢܣܒܟ ܡܫܠܐ ܠܡܫܝܚܘܬܐ ܀ ܡܫܡܠܝܐ ܡܢܗ ܕܟܠܝܢ ܠܡܪܢܝܬܐ
ܡܫܡܫܢܐ. ܟܕ ܦܘܪܫܢܐ ܠܐ ܡܪܢܝܬܐ ܘܡܫܡܫܢܘܬܐ ܡܫܡܫܢܐ ܠܗܘܢ ܀ ܀ ܀ ܀
ܐܬܚܙܝ ܠܡܫܠܡܘܬܐ ܠܕܪܫܘܬܗ. ܘܟܕ ܗܘ ܟܠ ܐܬ ܟܕ. ܡܫܡܫܢܐ ܐܝܬ
ܫܢܐ ܘܐܬܕܪܫܘܬܐ ܡܫܡܫܢܐ ܢܫܡܗ ܡܢܗ ܐܢܫ ܀ ܕܡܫܡܫ ܘܐܝܟ.

ܥܠ ܣܘܥܪܢܐ ܘܡܫܡܫܢܘܬܐ ܀

ܕܡܫܡܫ ܘܣܥܪܐ ܥܠ ܐܟܪܐ ܕܫܥܬܐ ܘܟܠܗ. ܥܠ ܡܫܡܫܢܘܬܐ ܕܥܕܬܐ
ܡܫܠܡܢܐ: ܕܡܫܡܫܢܘܬܐ ܠܐ ܡܬܚܫܒܢܐ:

ܐܢܐ ܕܡܫܠܡܢܐ ܡܫܡܫܢܐ ܡܢ ܠܡܫܡܠܝܘ: ܥܠ ܡܫܡܫܢܘܬܐ
ܘܡܫܡܫܢܘܬܐ ܕܢܘܚܐ ܕܡܢܐ ܡܕܢܚܐ: ܘܡܫܡܫܢܘܬܐ ܕܢܚܐ ܡܫܡܫܢܐ
ܦܠܛܝܢ: ܘܕܡܫܡܫܢܘܬܐ ܠܗ ܡܫܡܫܢܐ ܡܕܢܚܝܢ: ܘܡܫܡܫܢܘܬܐ ܕܢܘܚܐ ܕܠܗܘܢ
ܚܠܛܝܢ: ܘܕܫܠܡܘ ܠܐ ܕܚܠܛܝܢ: ܘܕܦܫܛܐ ܐܘܟܝܢ ܕܦܠܛܦܘܪܣܝܢ
ܕܟܠ ܡܫܡܫܢܐ: ܘܡܫܡܫܢܐ ܠܡܫܡܫܢܘܬܐ ܡܫܡܫܢܘܬܐ ܕܟܠܐ ܐܝܟ ܗܟܝܠ:
ܠܐ ܠܗ ܕܠܐ ܠܡܫܡܫܢܐ ܐܢܫ. ܘܟܕ ܐܝܬܘܗܝ ...

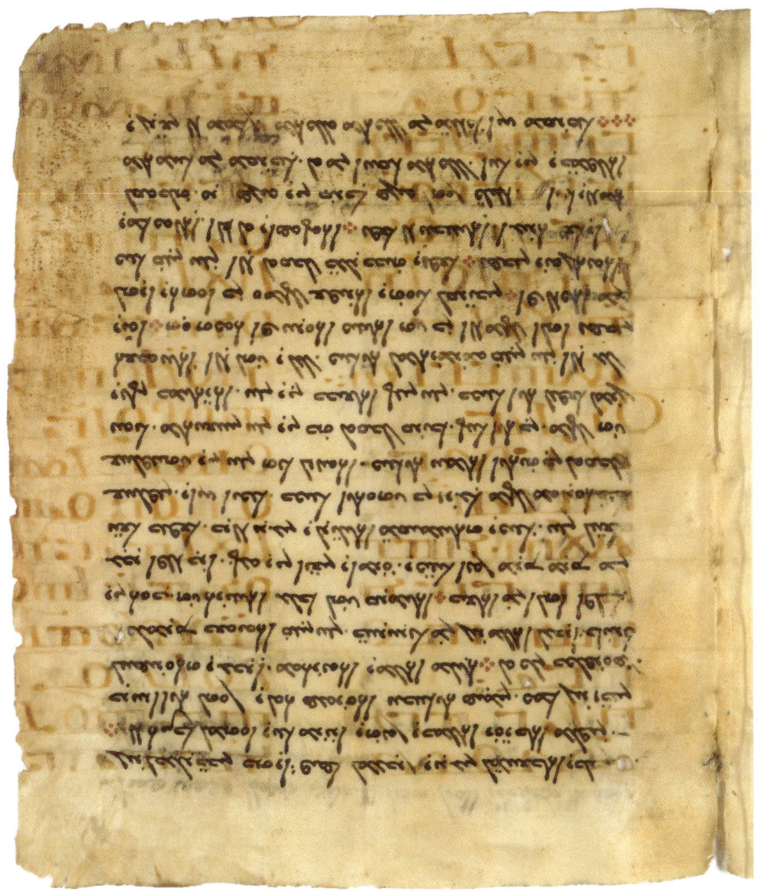

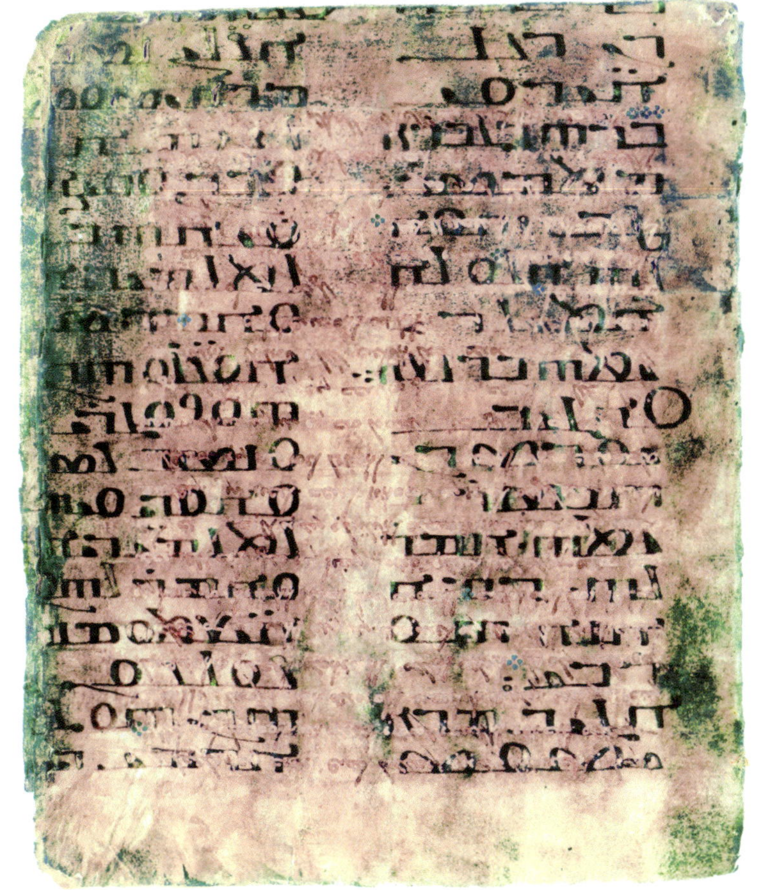

Using multispectral imaging, modern scholars can see and analyze the underlying texts. The original Greek writings are a mixture of classical and biblical texts. All the Christian Palestinian Aramaic texts are biblical. The biblical passages in both languages are a mixture of continuous texts and excerpts for lectionaries or use in homilies. To date, some of the classical texts have not yet been identified.

Above Left: Single leaf using visible light with Syriac text upside down.

Above Right: Single leaf using multispectral imaging with Christian Palestinian Aramaic text of Matthew 26:24–25 upright.

Facing Page: Detail image of the Syriac text of John Climacus's monastic work, *Ladder of Divine Ascent*, showing a drawing of a ladder at the end of one section, and a rubricated section introduction. An erased Greek text is barely legible upside down.

The Ussher Gospels

MS.000474, parchment codex, 1100–1199

THIS IS A small, two-volume copy of the Gospels in Greek. The scribe wrote the text in a careful minuscule hand. The manuscript's small size suggests that it was created for private devotional rather than liturgical or communal use. Later commentary appears in a larger, less regular hand. The manuscript contains fourteen full-page illuminated canon tables. This manuscript takes its nickname from one of its former owners, Archbishop James Ussher, author of the famed 17th-century biblical chronology. The bookplate of the Earl of Moira, Francis Rawdon-Hastings, appears in both volumes. He was a British officer who fought throughout the American Revolution and later became the Governor-General of India.

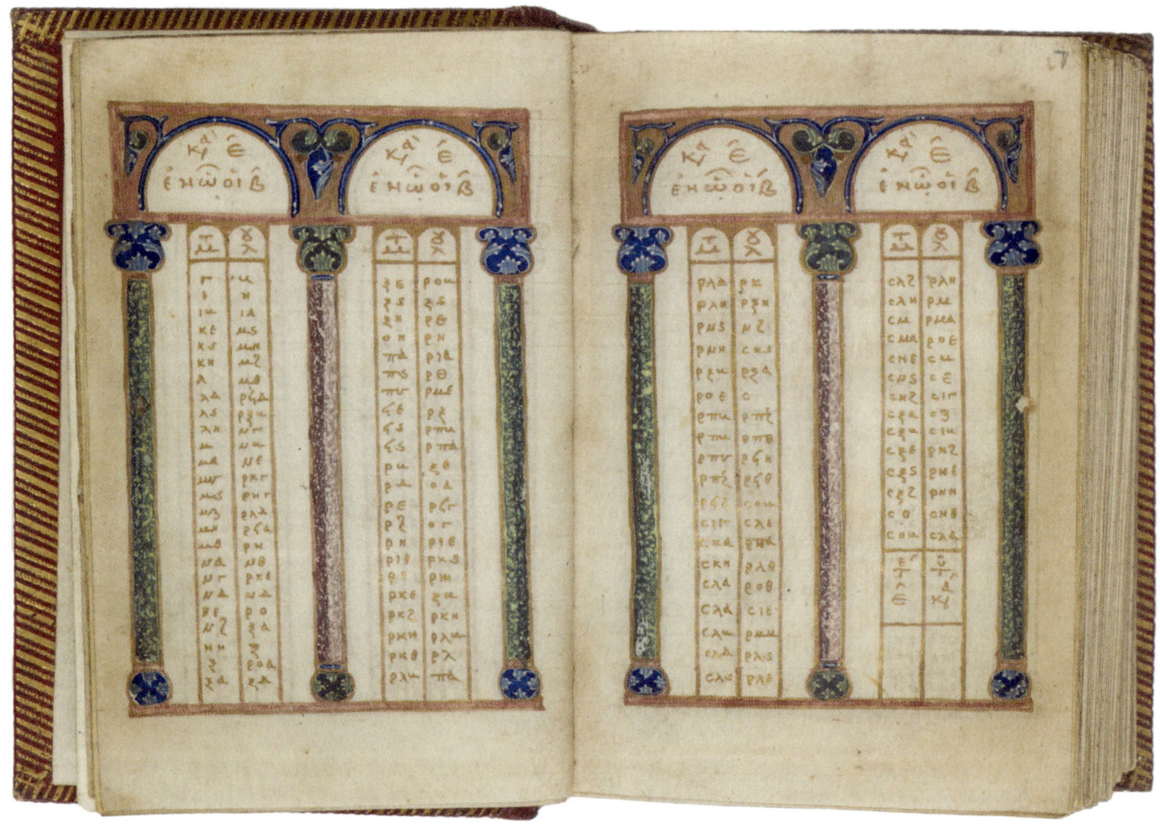

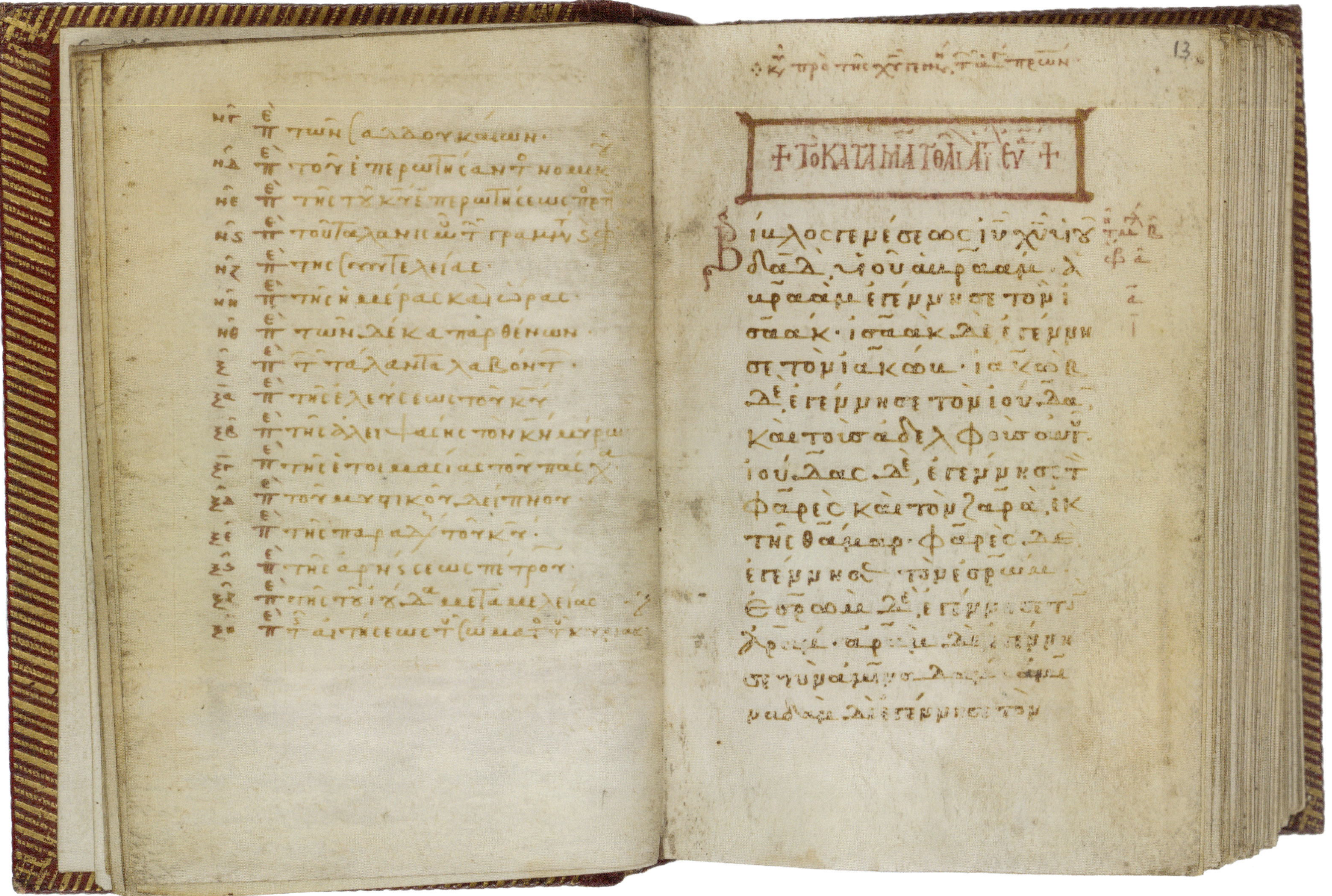

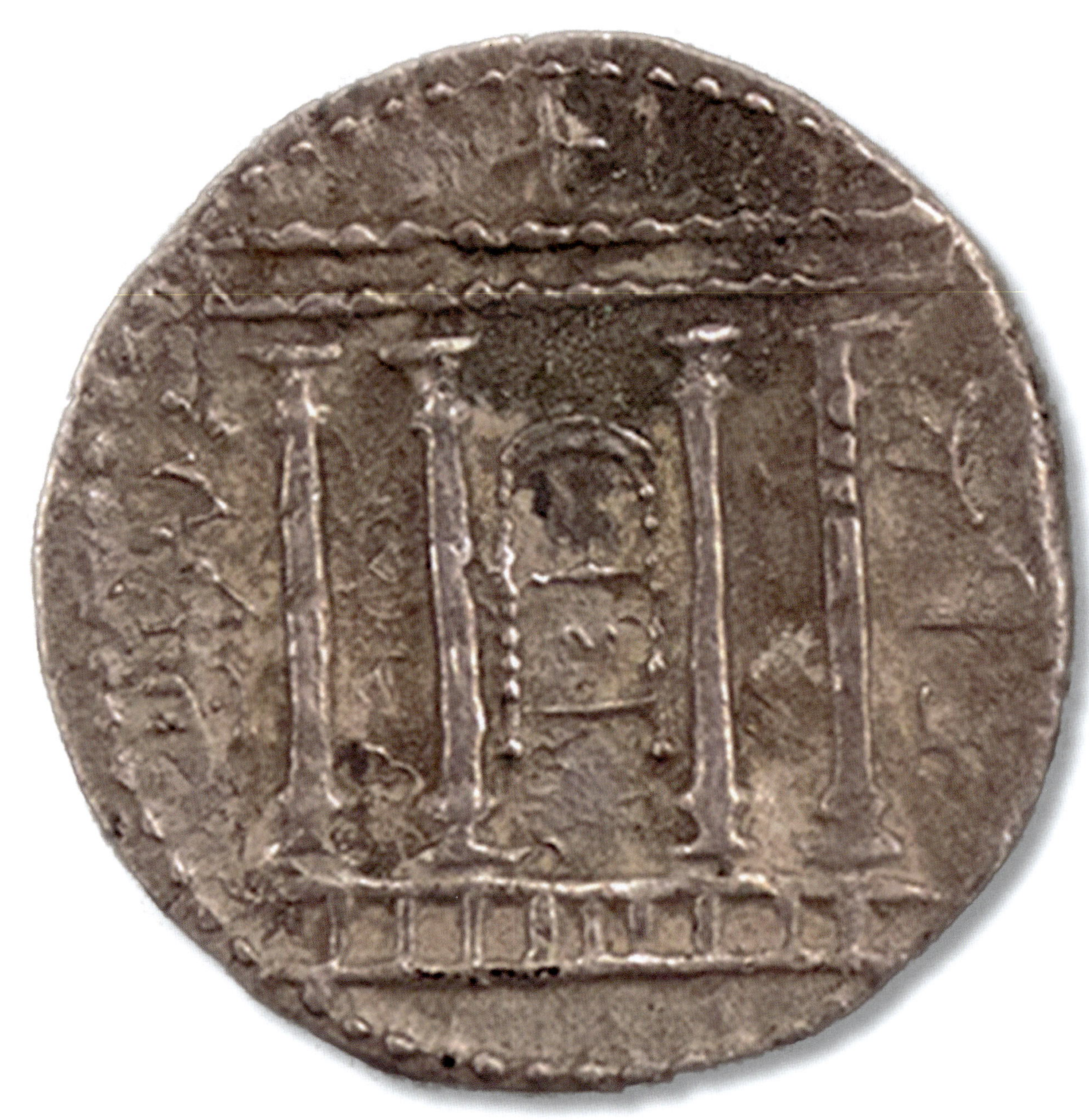

Detail of temple scene,
"Jerusalem" in Hebrew.

Bar Kokhba Year 2 Sela

NUM.000909, silver coin, ca. 133

MINTED WITHIN SEVENTY years of the destruction of Jerusalem, this coin constitutes one of the most significant witnesses to the end of the Second Temple period, preserving a rare depiction of the Jewish Temple. During the Third Jewish Revolt, Jewish patriots re-struck these imperial Roman coins with mottoes of their independence, replacing the iconography of the Roman regent with Jewish patriotic propaganda.

On the front (obverse), a façade of the Second Temple shows a glimpse of the ark of the covenant between two sets of pillars with a star above, representing the holy of holies. The Hebrew inscription reads Yerushalayim, "Jerusalem." The back (reverse) offers agricultural symbols associated with the harvest festival Sukkot. The Hebrew inscription reads L'Herut Yerushalayim—"For the Freedom of Jerusalem."

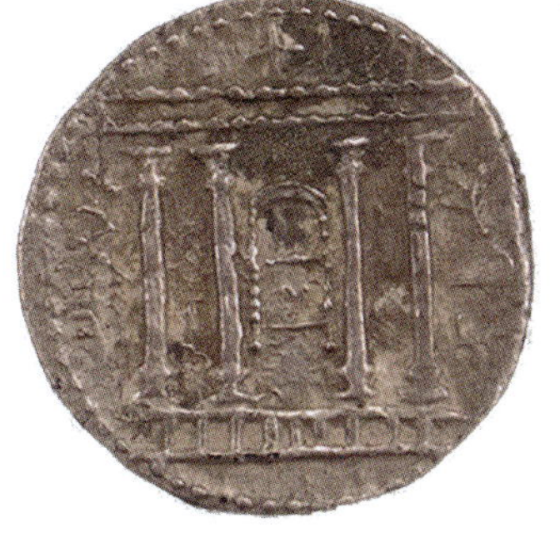

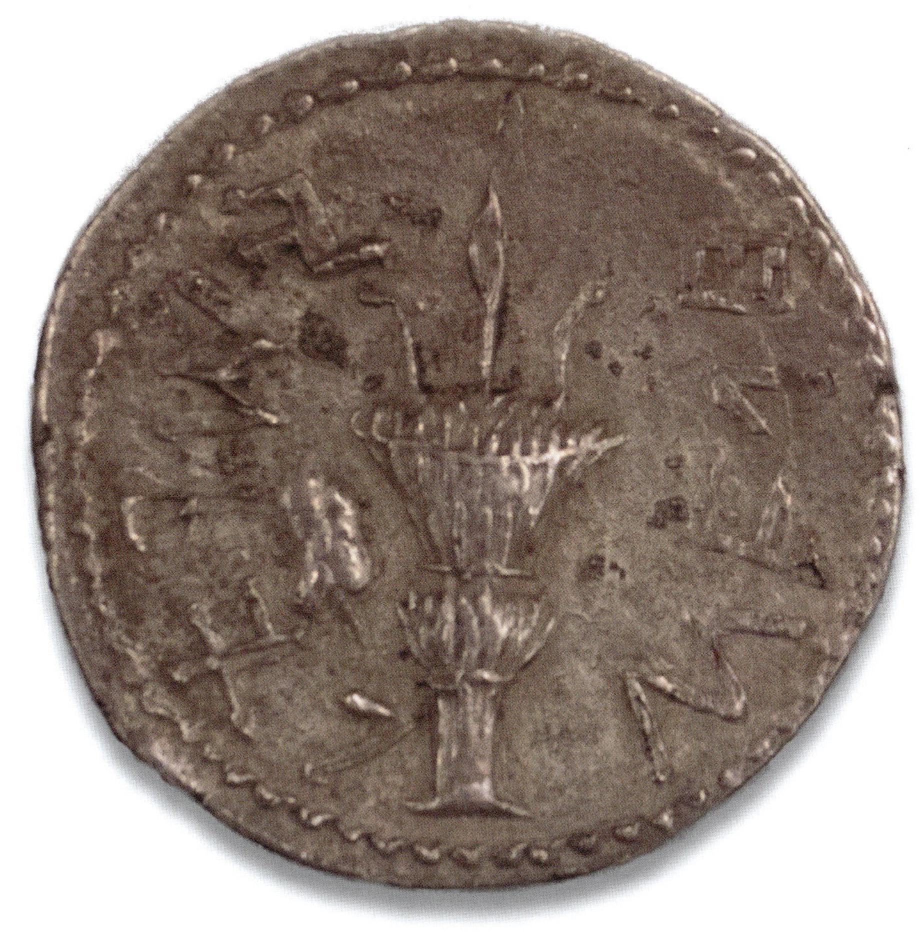

ABOVE LEFT: Temple scene, "Jerusalem" in Paleohebrew.

ABOVE RIGHT: Symbols of the Sukkot festival, "For Jerusalem" in Hebrew.

The Wyman Fragment (GA 0220)

MS.000566, parchment fragment, ca. 300

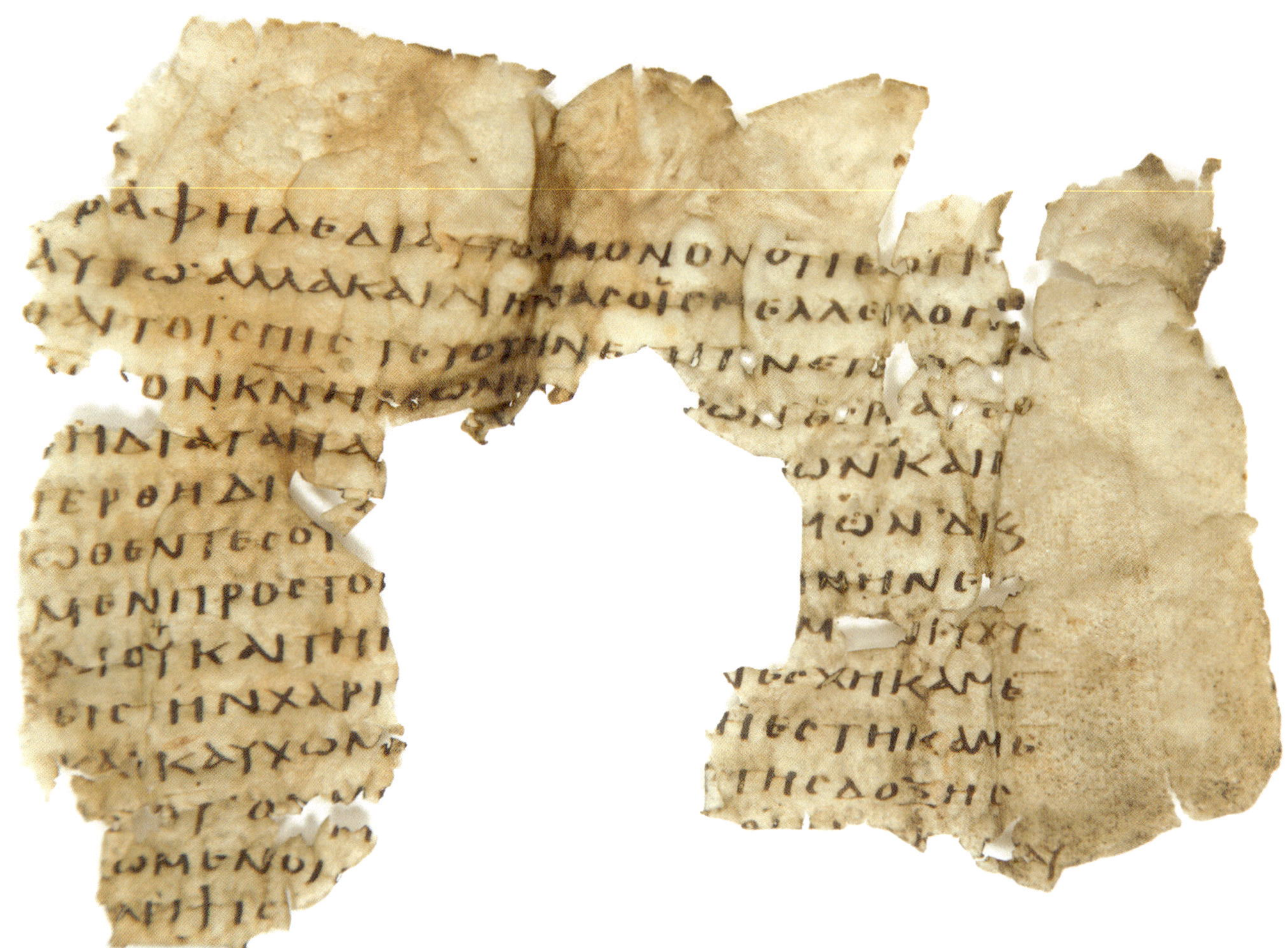

Left: Recto, Romans 4:23–5:3

Facing page: Verso, Romans 5:8–13

The Wyman Fragment (GA 0220) is a leaf from a late third- or early fourth-century Greek codex containing parts of Paul's letter to the Romans, specifically 4:23–5:3 and 5:8–13. It is one of the oldest surviving fragments of these texts. The fragment shows the use of *nomina sacra* (abbreviations of words such as God, Lord, Jesus, Christ), which was a prevalent practice among Christians in their early texts and lasting through the Middle Ages.

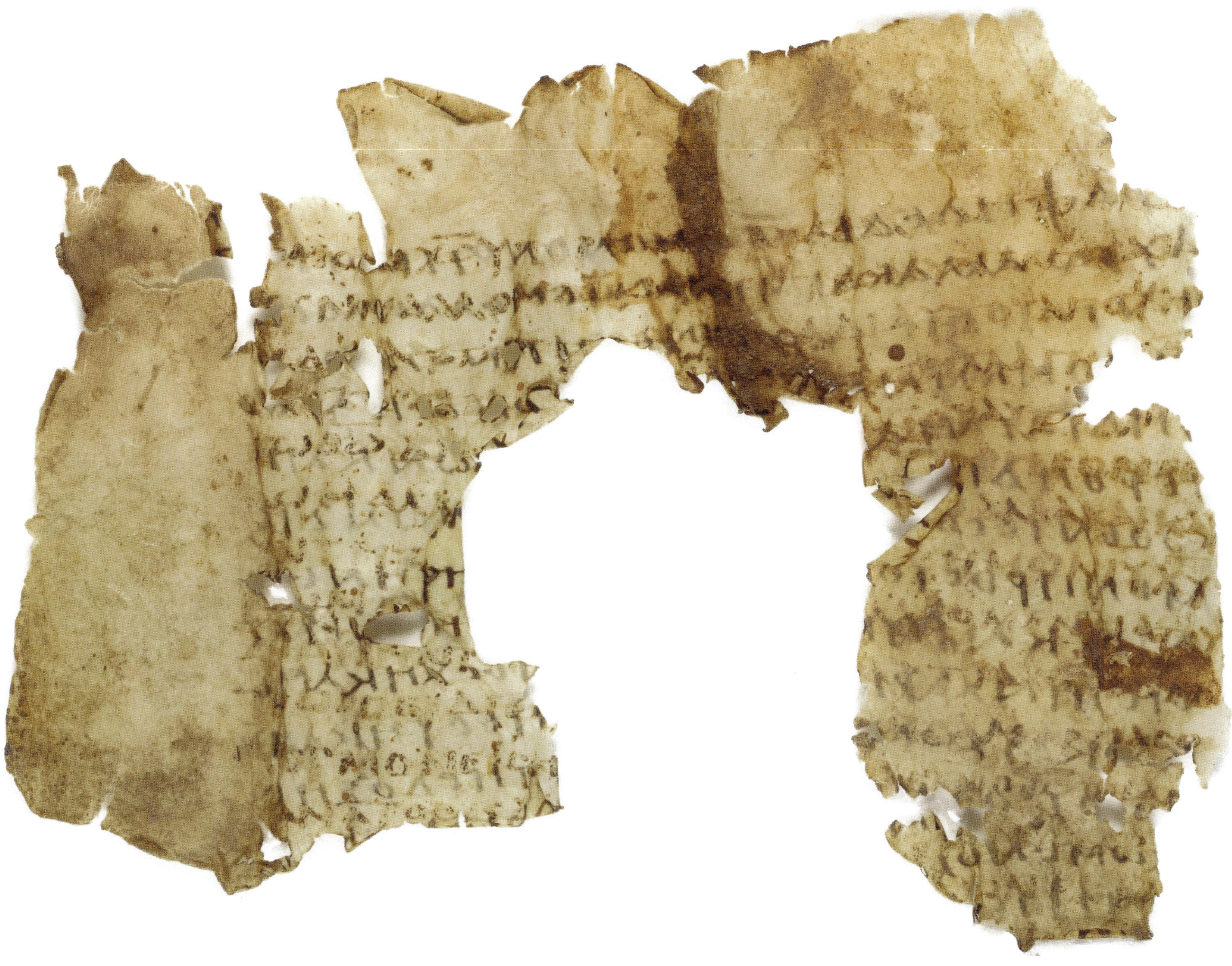

Hours and Psalter of Elizabeth de Bohun

MS.000761, parchment codex, 1330–1340

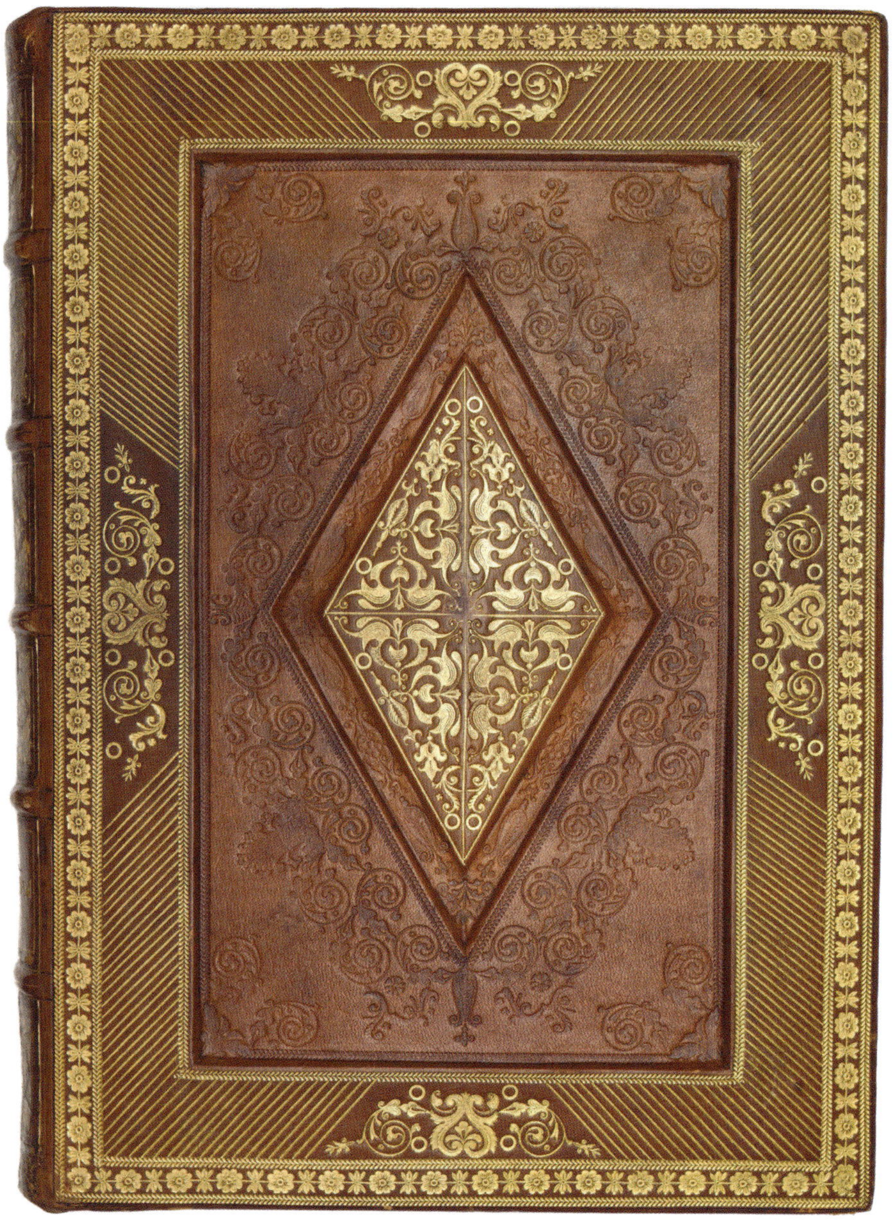

THIS PAIR OF beautiful 14th-century manuscripts that are now bound together belonged to Elizabeth de Bohun, Countess of Northampton (1313–1356). Based on the heraldry present in the manuscripts, she commissioned the Book of Hours while married to her first husband, Sir Edmund Mortimer (d. 1331), and the Psalter while married to her second husband, William de Bohun (d. 1360), first Earl of Northampton and Constable of England.

LEFT: Rebound in 1824 by James Martin for E. Wyndham.

FACING PAGE: Foliated initial from the Book of Psalms

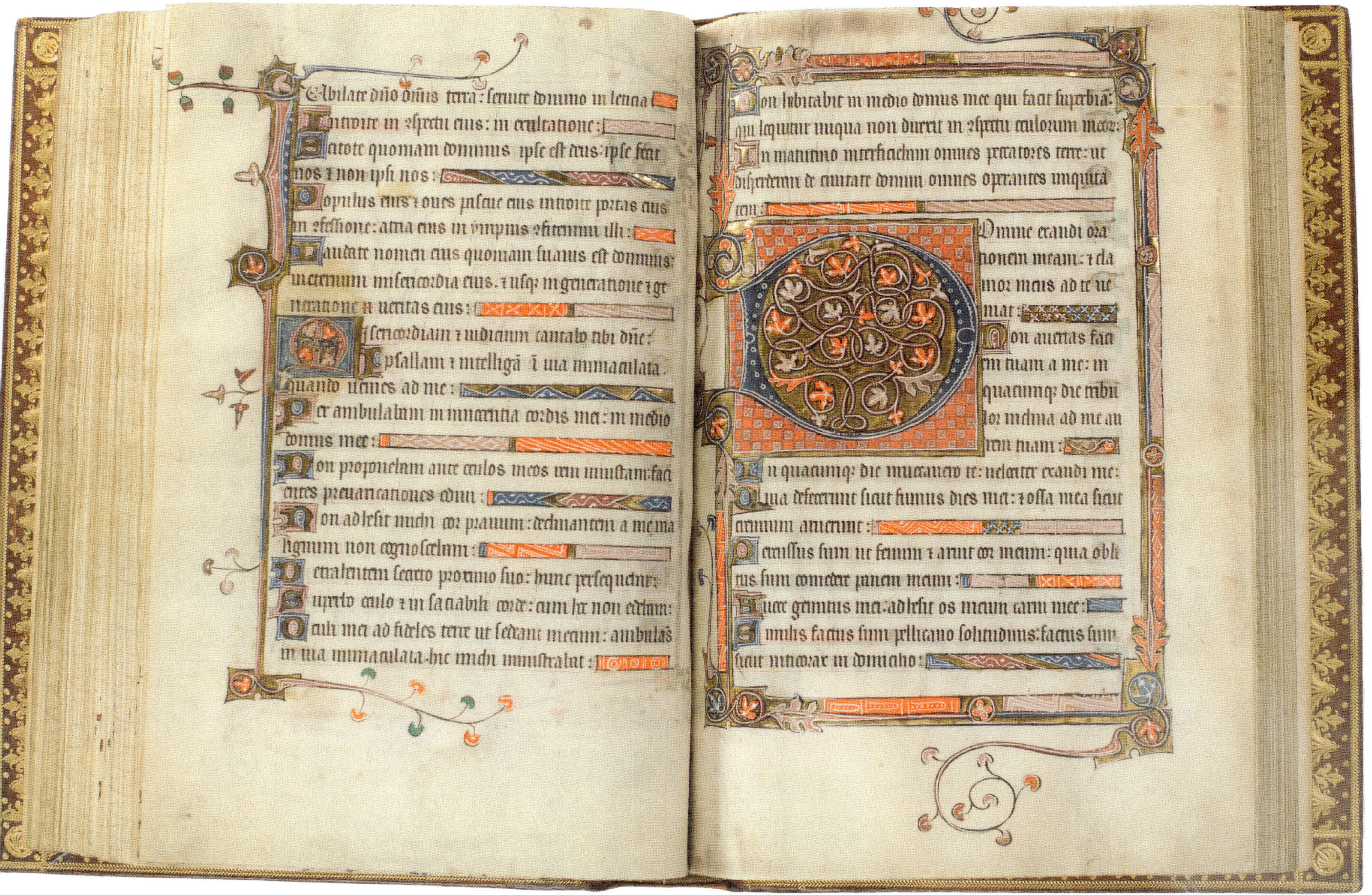

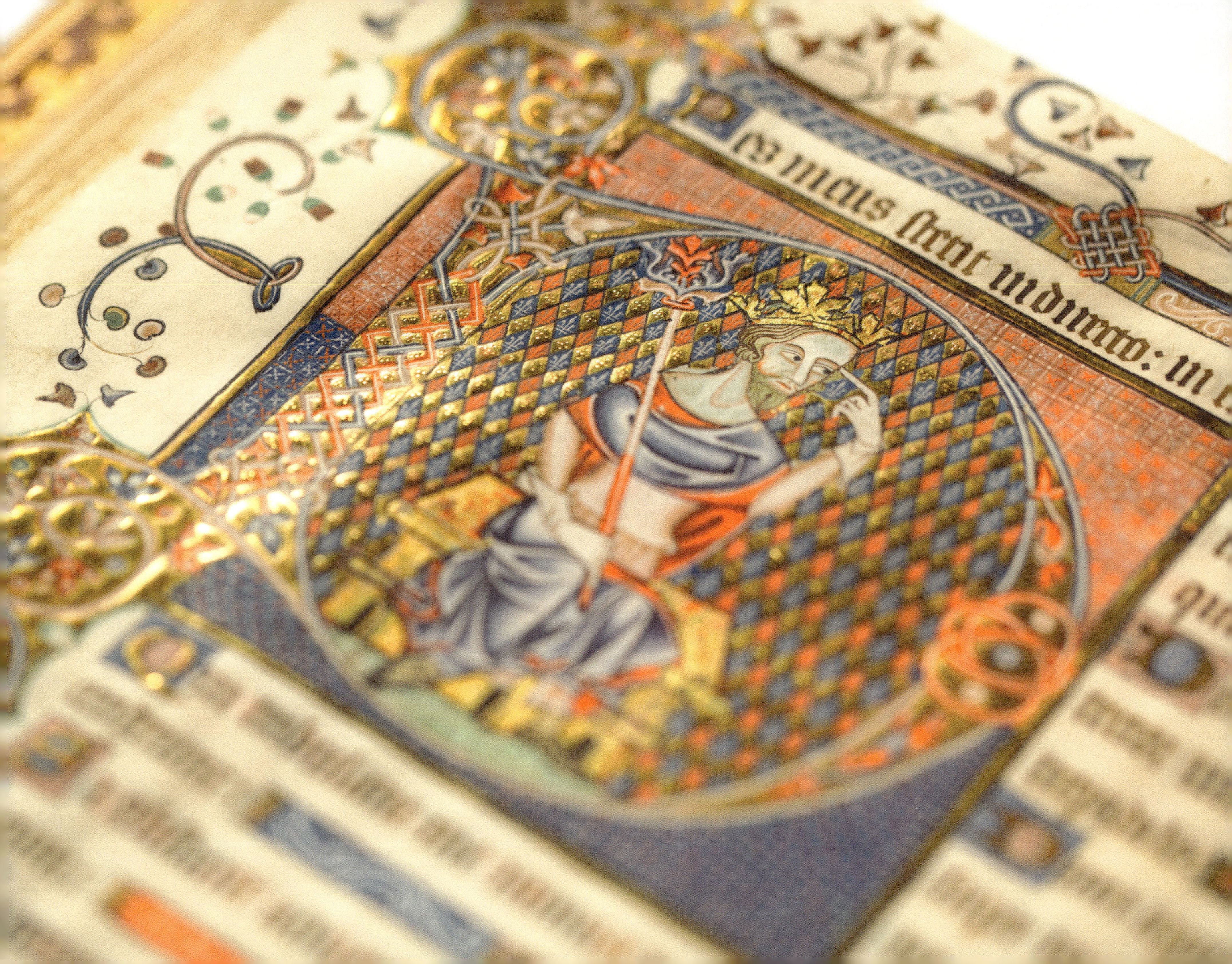

Although there are many similarities in style between the two manuscripts, there are some important differences. The large illuminated initials in the Hours mostly contain floral designs while there are several large historiated initials in the Psalter. The Hours begins with a scene of the annunciation, and the Psalter with the tree of Jesse.

The manuscript was eventually acquired by John Jacob Astor III (1822–1890) who lent it to an exhibition in New York in December 1883 to raise funds for the building of the pedestal of the Statue of Liberty. The number 1209, its exhibit number, is pasted near the bottom of fol. 52v, which indicates that the 1883 exhibit featured the Beatus initial on the facing page.

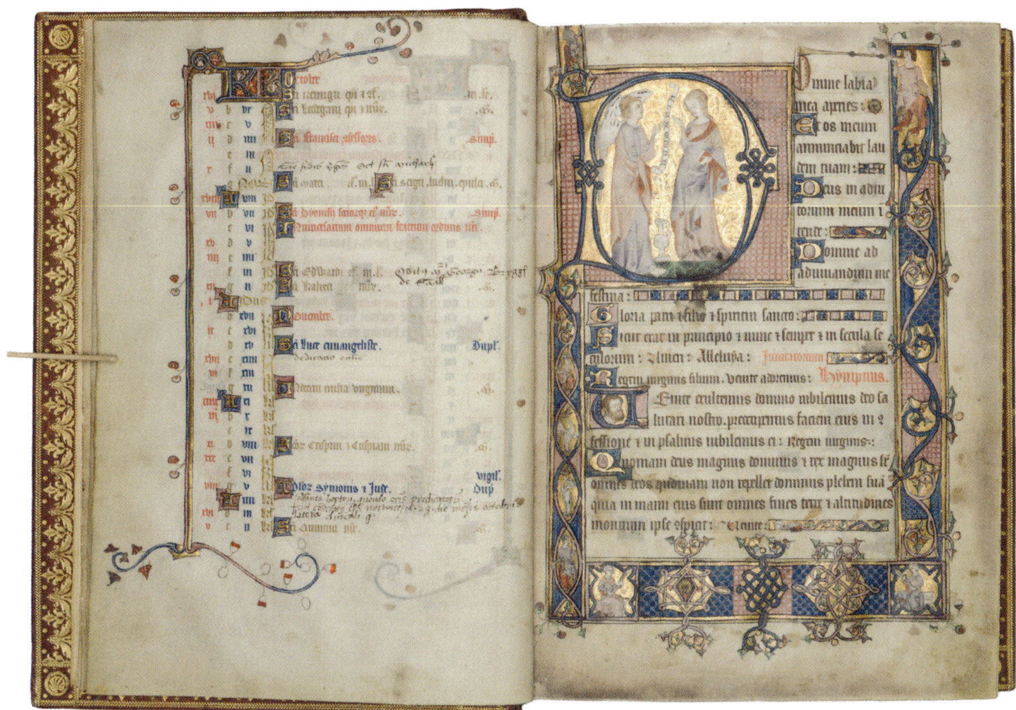

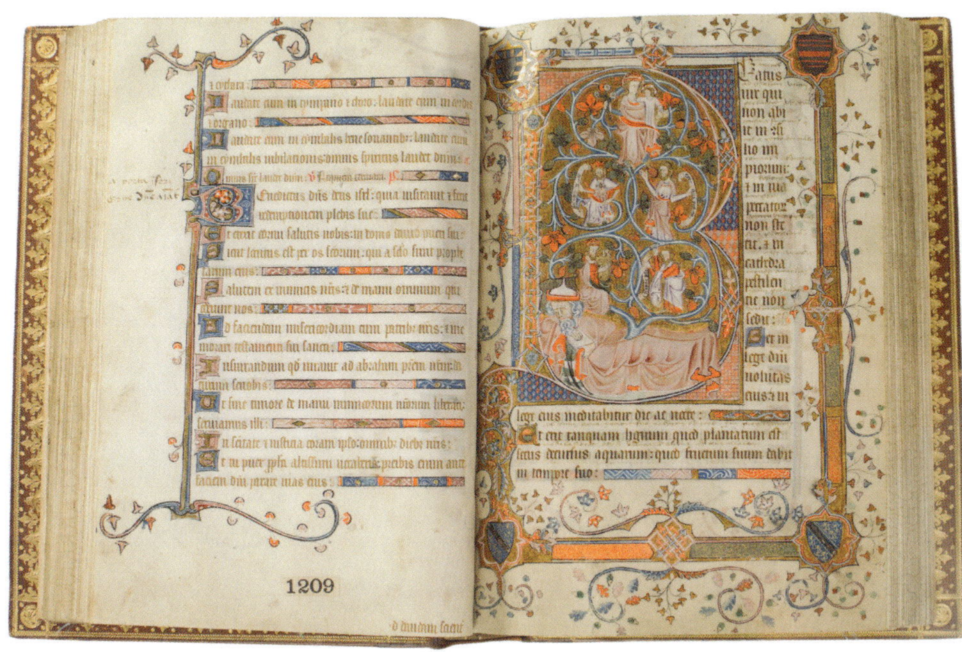

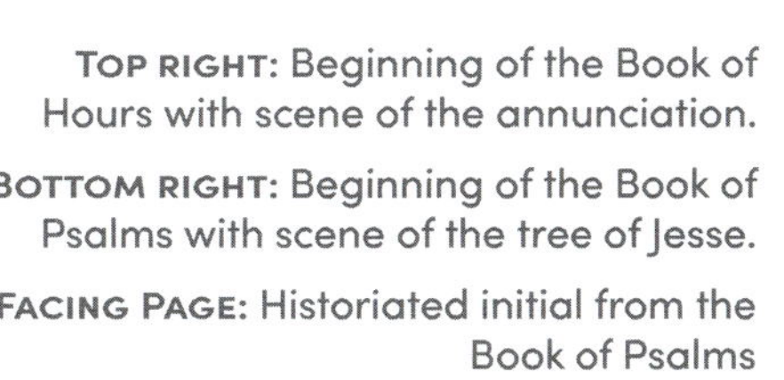

TOP RIGHT: Beginning of the Book of Hours with scene of the annunciation.

BOTTOM RIGHT: Beginning of the Book of Psalms with scene of the tree of Jesse.

FACING PAGE: Historiated initial from the Book of Psalms

"The Wicked Bible"

BIB.002902, printed book, 1631

THIS EDITION OF the King James Bible contains one of the most notorious typographical errors in Bible printing history. One of the Ten Commandments omits the essential command "not," making Exodus 20:14 read "Thou shalt commit adultery" instead of "Thou shalt not." The printer, Robert Barker, was said to have been fined £300 for the error, at that time, a sizable amount. Most copies of the edition were either corrected or destroyed, as 1,000 copies of this Bible were ordered suppressed.

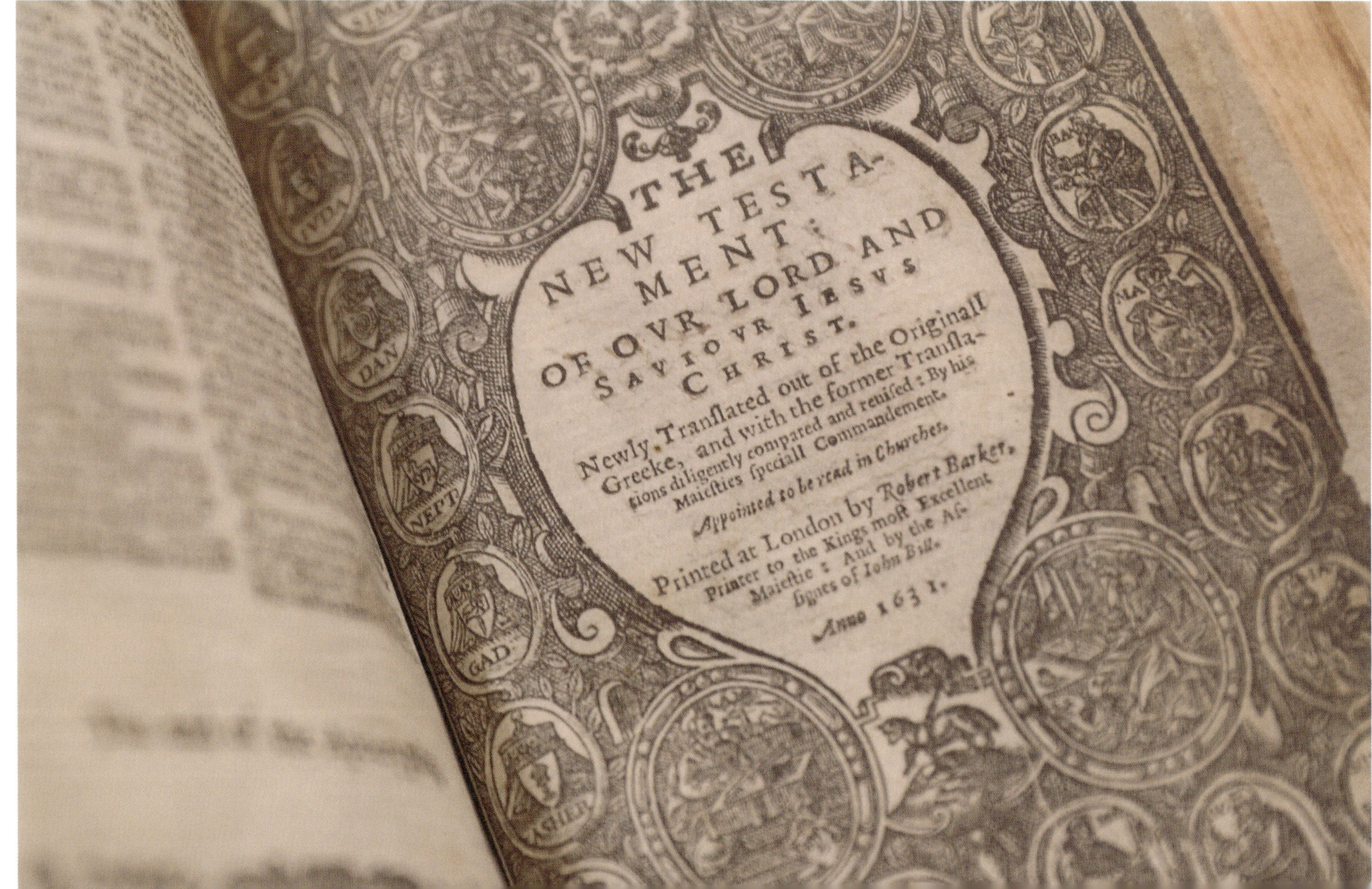

RIGHT: New Testament Incipit

FACING PAGE: Exodus 20:14 ff.

the Sabbath of § LORD
thy God: in it thou shalt not doe any worke, thou
nor thy sonne, nor thy daughter, thy man-seruant, nor
thy maid-seruant, nor thy cattle, nor thy stranger
that is within thy gates:

* Gen.2.2.

11 For in six dayes the LORD made heauen and
earth, the sea and all that in them is, and rested the
seuenth day, wherefore the LORD blessed the Sabbath day, and hallowed it.

* Deut.5. 16. mat. 15.4. ephe 6.2.

12 ¶ * Honour thy father and thy mother, that
thy dayes may bee long vpon the land which the
LORD thy God giueth thee.

* Matth. 5.21.

13 * Thou shalt not kill.
14 Thou shalt commit adultery.
15 Thou shalt not steale.
16 Thou shalt not beare false witnesse against
thy neighbour.

* Rom. 7.7.

17 * Thou shalt not couet thy neighbours house,
thou shalt not couet thy neighbours wife, nor his
man-seruant, nor his maid-seruant, nor his oxe, nor
his asse, nor any thing that is thy neighbours.

* Hebr. 12.18.

18 ¶ And * all the people saw the thunderings,
and the lightnings, and ...

* Deut. 5.24. and 18.16.

6 Then his master shall bring him
he shall also bring him to the doore,
doore post, and his master shall bore
row with an awle, and he shall serue
7 ¶ And if a man sell his daughter
seruant, she shall not go out as the men
8 If shee † please not her master
trothed her to himselfe, then shall he let
deemed: to sell her vnto a strange nation
haue no power, seeing he hath delt deceitfully
9 And if he haue betrothed her vnto
shall deale with her after the manner of
10 If he take him another wife, her food
ment, & her duty of marriage shall he not
11 And if he doe not these three vnto
shall she goe out free without money.
12 ¶ * He that smiteth a man so that he
be surely put to death.

Military Equipment of Pvt. George Rome

BIB.003796/ART.001146/OBJ.000334/OBJ.000336, ca. 1860s

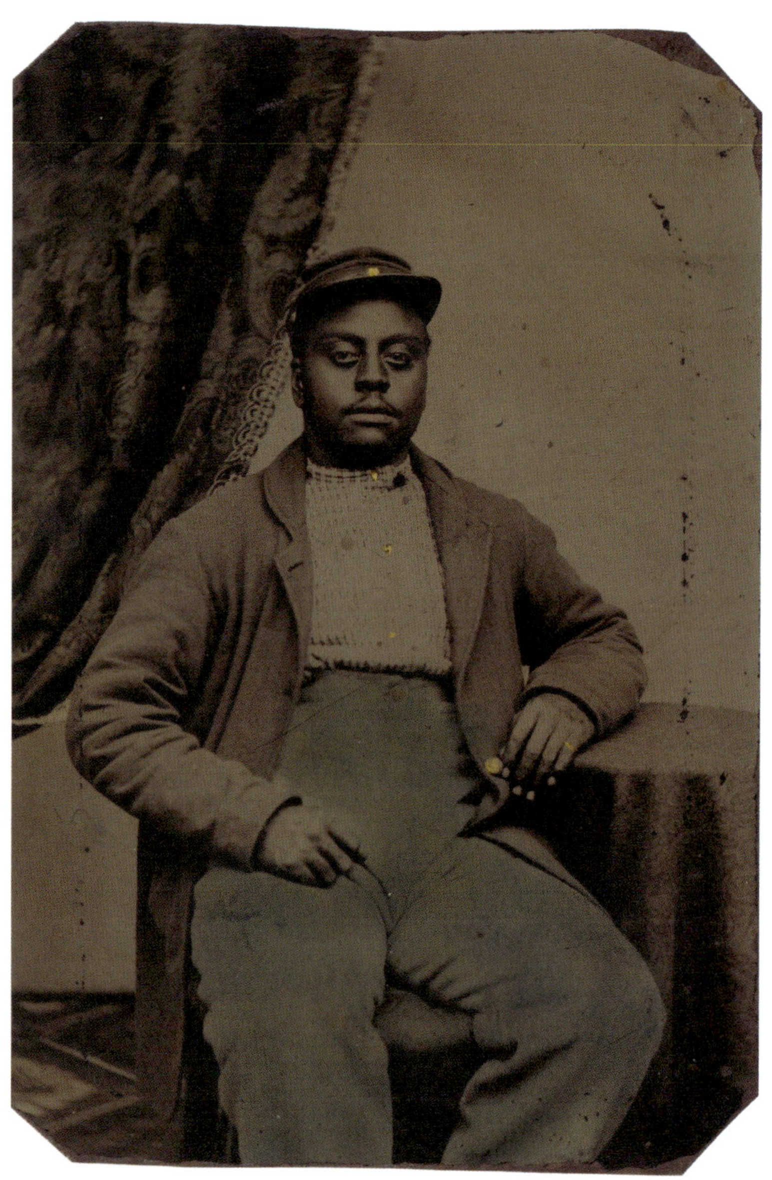

PVT. GEORGE R. ROME (left) was one of nearly 180,000 African Americans who fought for the Union Army during the Civil War. Rome was born in 1835 to free African American parents living in Providence, Rhode Island. He later moved to Worcester, Massachusetts. When the Civil War began in 1861, he and other African Americans were initially denied enlistment. However, the US government reversed its policy in 1863. Rome eventually joined the 55th Massachusetts Infantry Regiment, participating in several campaigns, including Sherman's famous March to the Sea. He survived the war and died in 1900. This equipment is part of a small collection of his items in the museum's care, including his pocket New Testament (below).

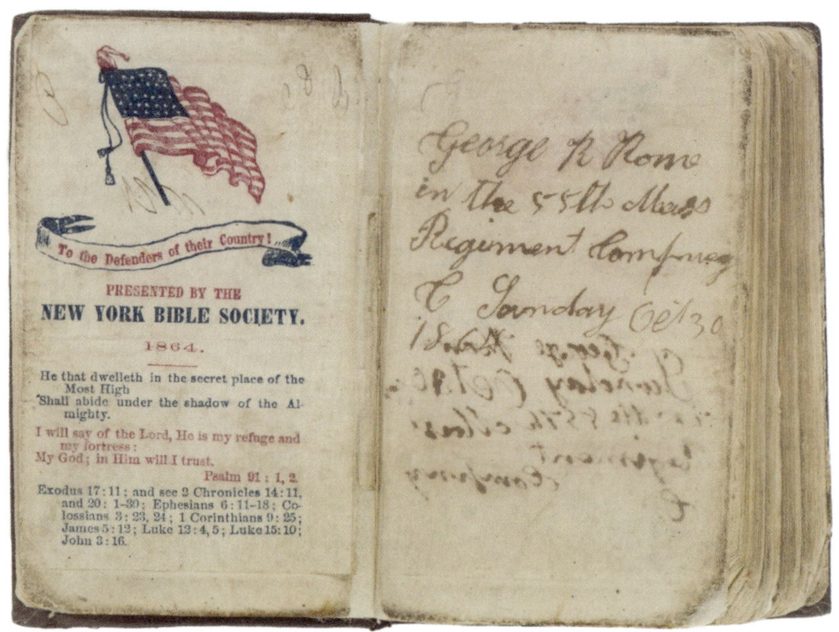

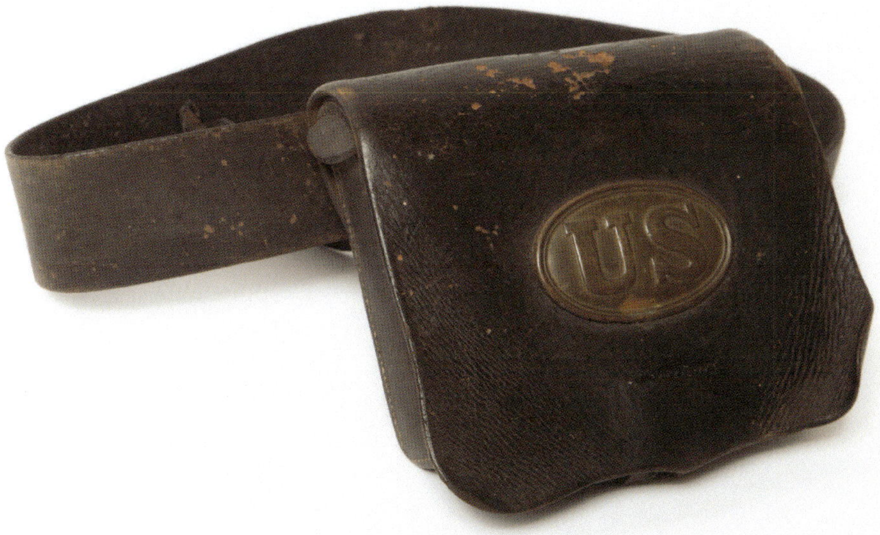

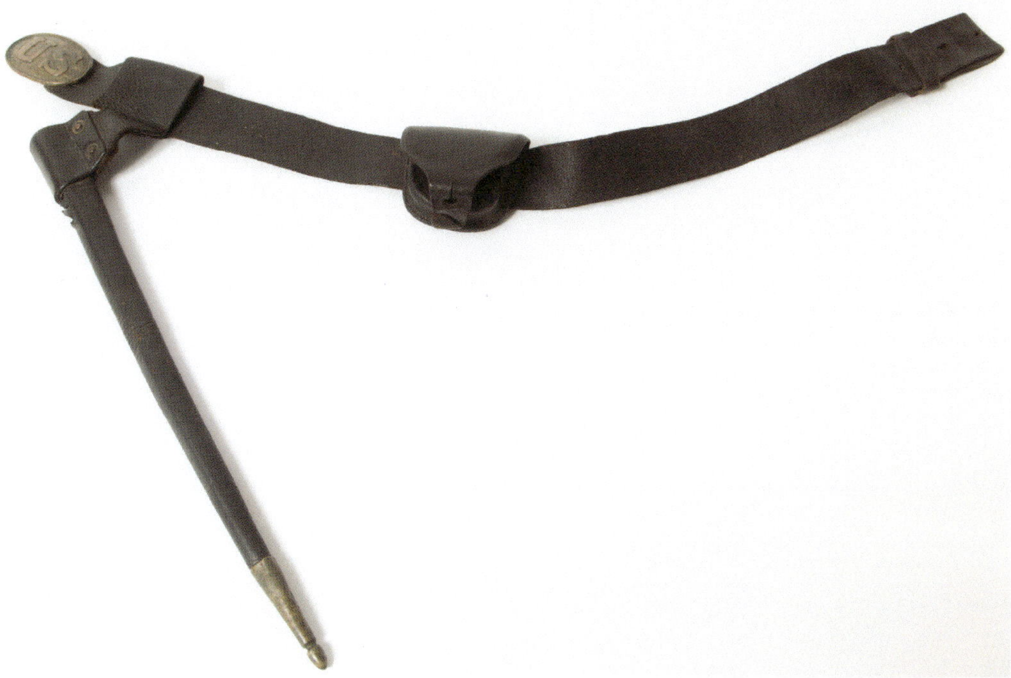

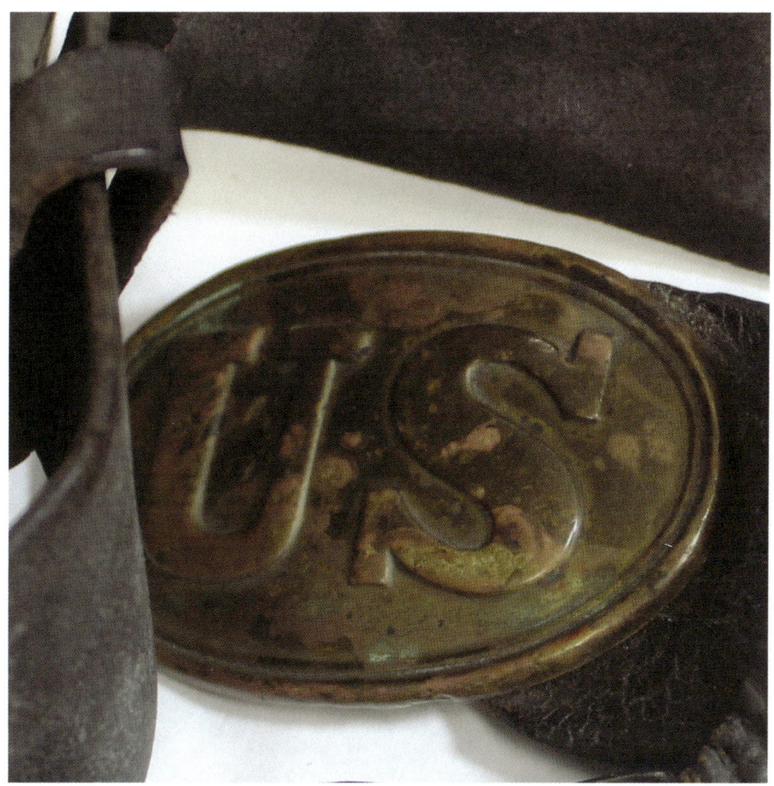

Belt, buckle, scabbard, and percussion cap pouch belonging to Pvt. George Rome, 55th Massachusetts Infantry Regiment.

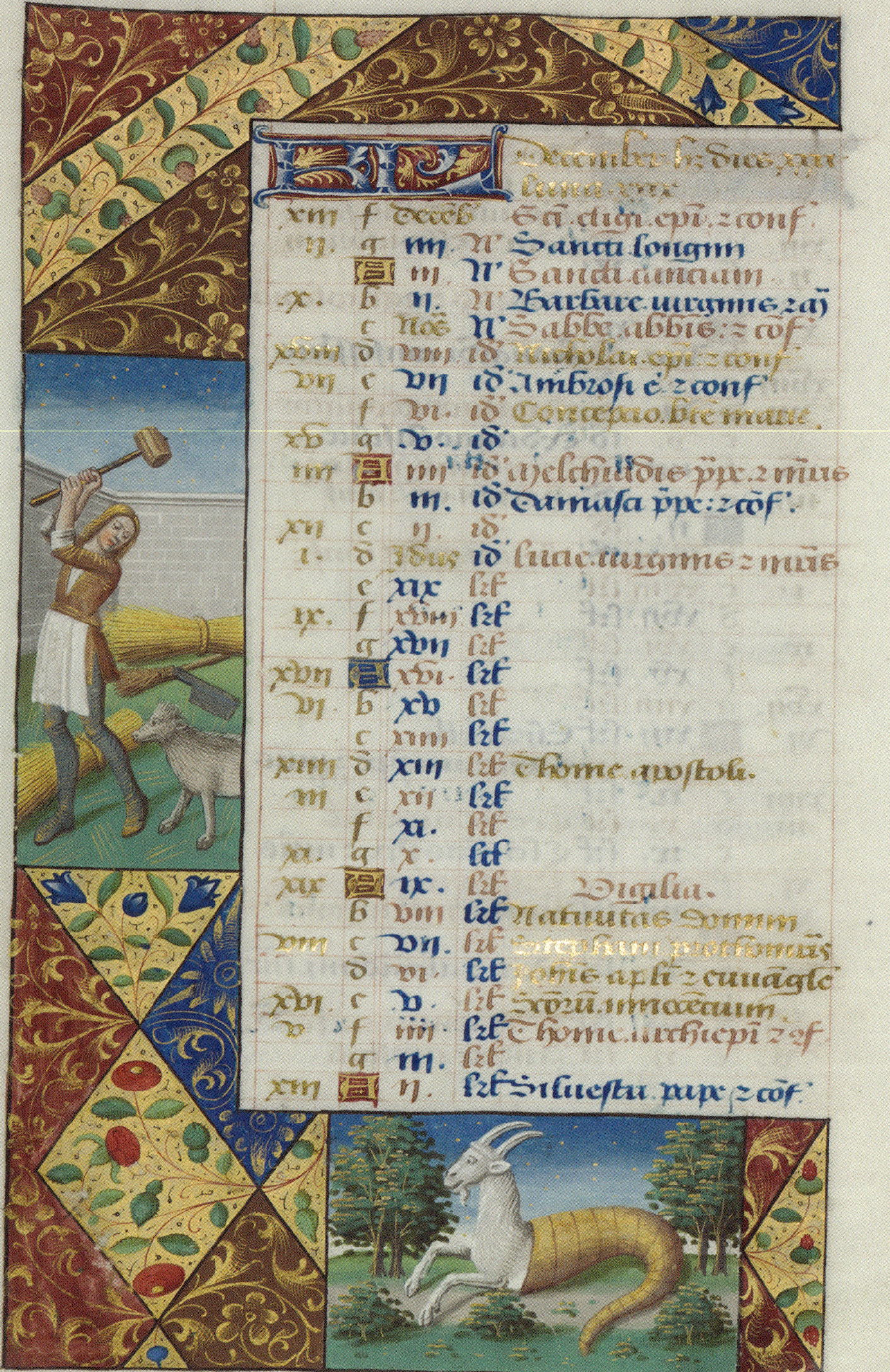

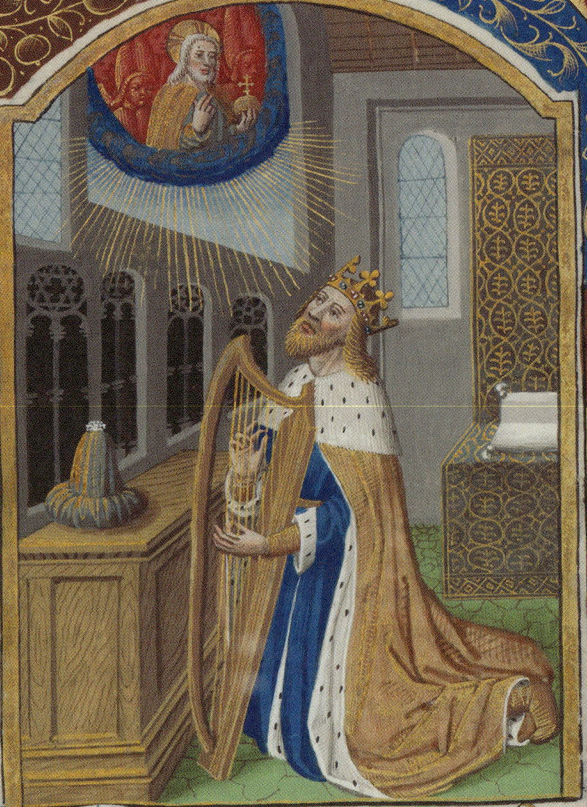

Beatus uir qui non abiit
in consilio impiorum et
in via peccatorum non
stetit: et in cathedra pesti
lencie non sedit.
Sed in lege domini voluntas e
ius: et in lege eius meditabitur

Psalter, Master of Jacques de Besançon

MS.000319, parchment codex, ca. 1490

This Psalter begins with an elaborate calendar containing feast days in gold, red, and blue ink. Each calendar month is surrounded by panels of floral designs that have been subdivided into zones of differing colors and flowers. Miniatures adorn the side and bottom margins of the calendars, depicting scenes from rural life and representations of the zodiac. Seven additional full-page miniatures appear throughout the text. The scribe used a brown ink that harmonizes well with the color scheme of the occasional border pieces that maintain the floral patterns of the calendar throughout the manuscript. The illuminator of the Psalter was the Master of Jacques de Besançon, whose clientele included members of the French royal court, including Kings Charles VIII and Louis XII.

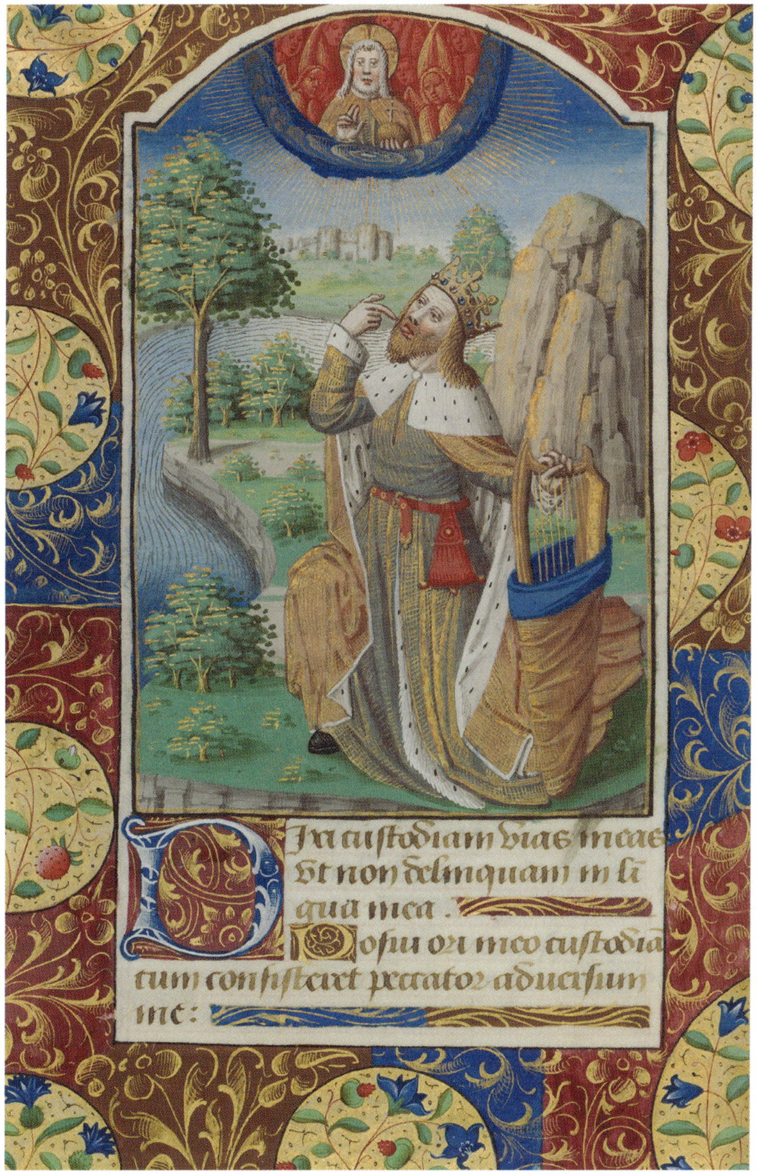

Right: Detail image of a miniature of King David with his harp.

Facing Page: Bifolium showing the beginning of the Psalter with a miniature of King David playing the harp.

King James Bible, The Louis Silver Copy

BIB.003906, printed book, 1611

THIS FIRST EDITION King James Bible was printed in large folio format by Robert Barker. In 1604, King James I approved the work of a new translation, which would be based on the Bishops' Bible of 1602. Over five years, six committees revised the Old Testament, New Testament, and Deuterocanonical books. Considered one of the most influential English texts, this copy contains the frontispiece engraved by Cornelis Boel, the New Testament title page, biblical genealogies, and an engraved map of the Holy Land. Shortly after its printing, this copy belonged to a close friend of King James I, Sir George Moore, and today is the tallest copy known. It is nicknamed the Silver Copy because this copy belonged to a well-known book collector, Louis Silver, in the 1900s.

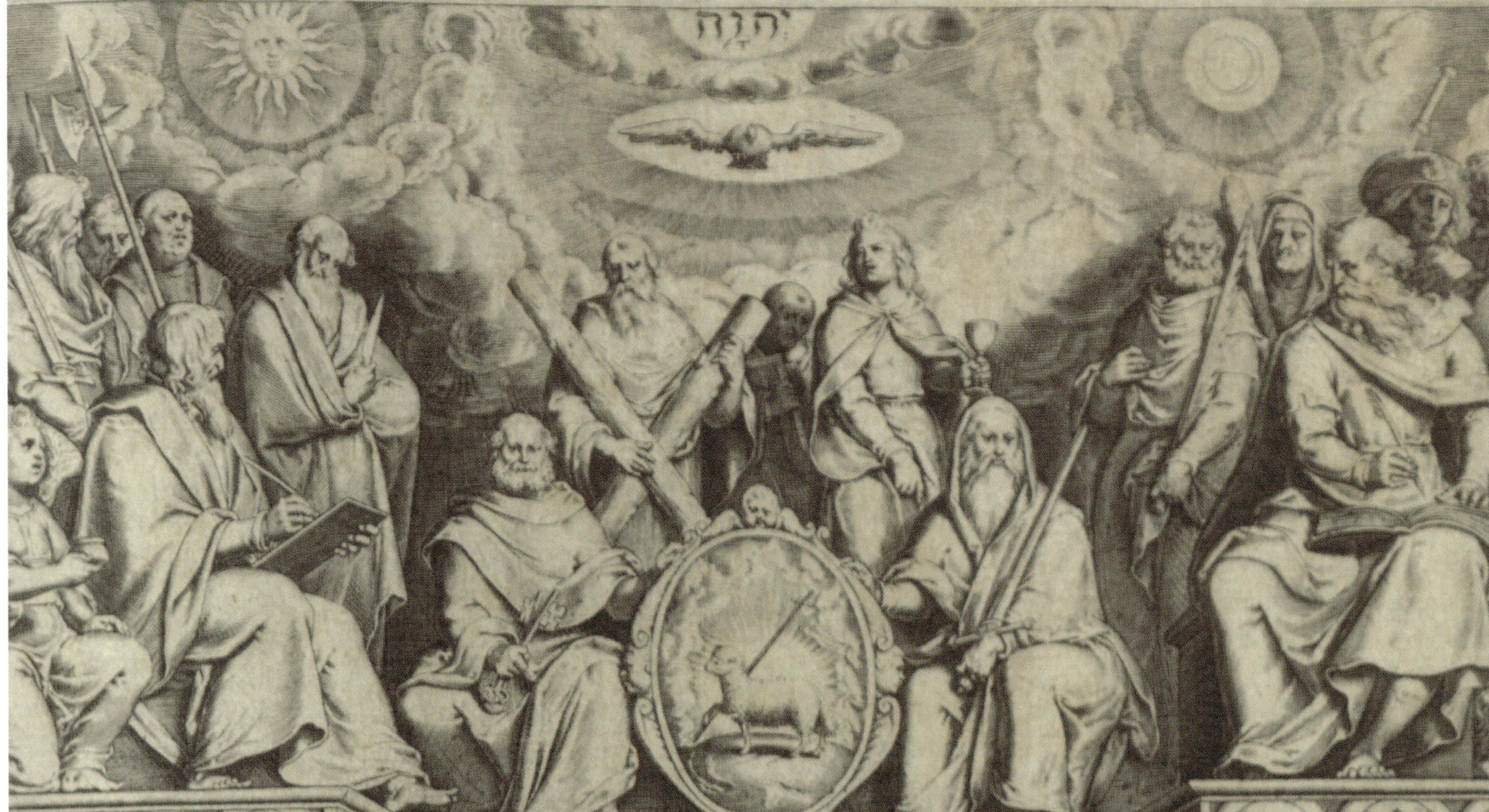

Detail of title page with tetragrammaton.

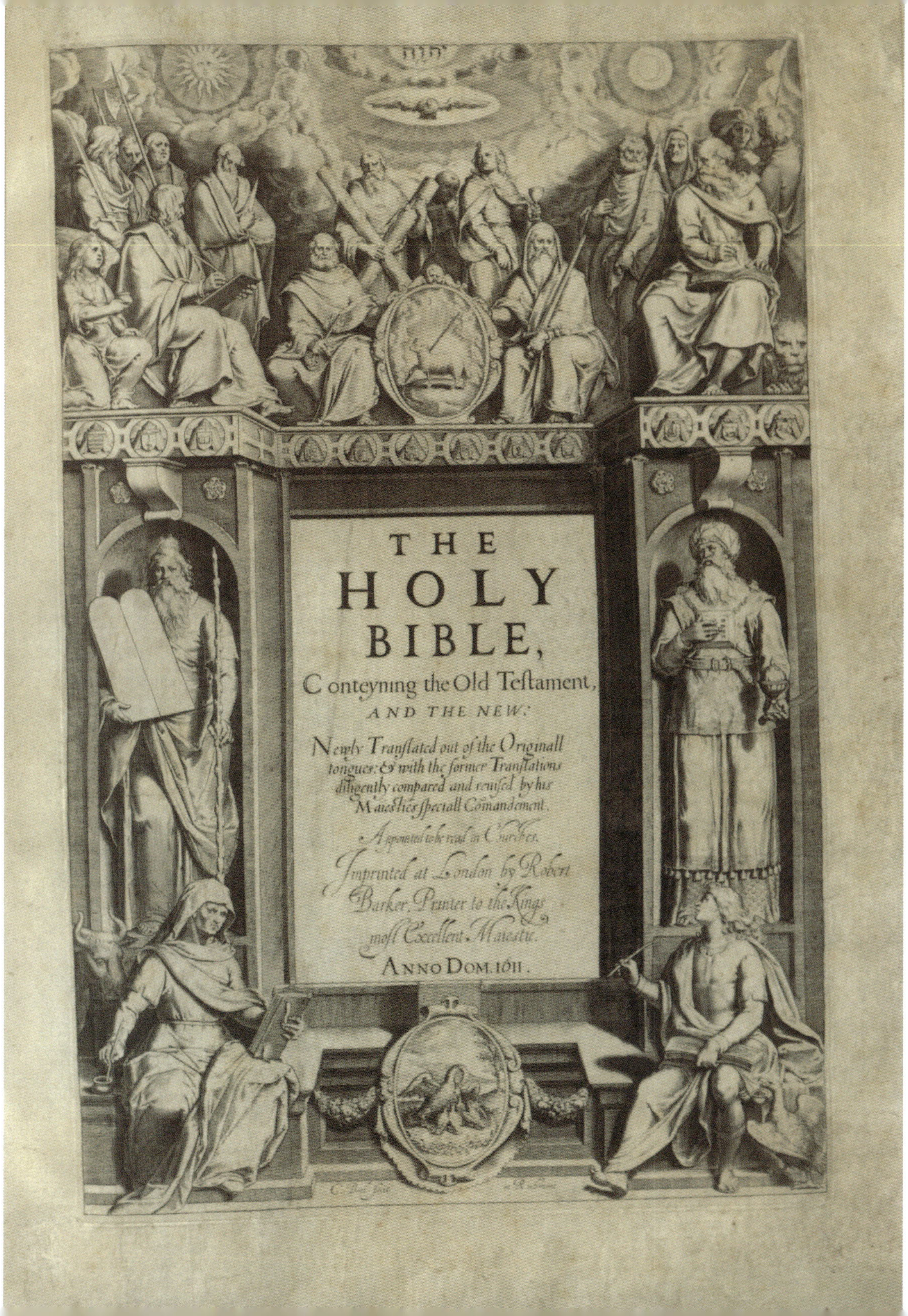

יהוה

THE
HOLY
BIBLE,
Conteyning the Old Teſtament,
AND THE NEW:

Newly Tranſlated out of the Originall
tongues: & with the former Tranſlations
diligently compared and reuiſed by his
Maieſties ſpeciall Comandement.

Appointed to be read in Churches.

Imprinted at London by Robert
Barker, Printer to the Kings
moſt Excellent Maieſtie.

ANNO DOM. 1611.

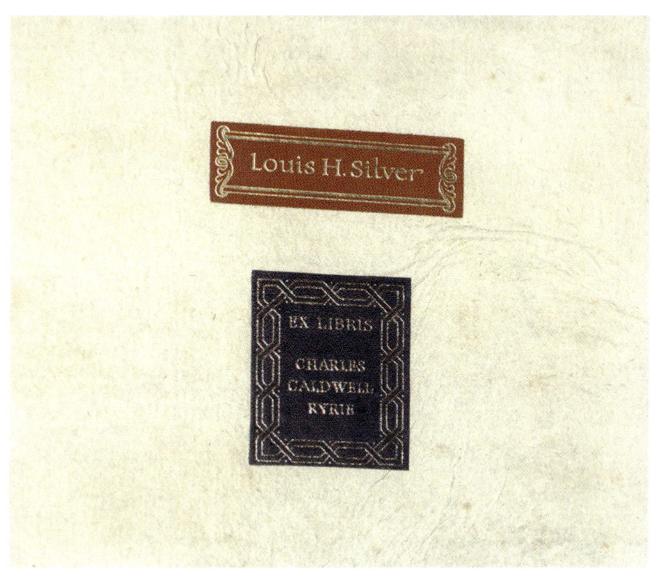

ABOVE: Bookplates of Louis H. Silver and Dr. Charles Ryrie.

LEFT: Title page featuring a woodcut illustration of saints and biblical figures

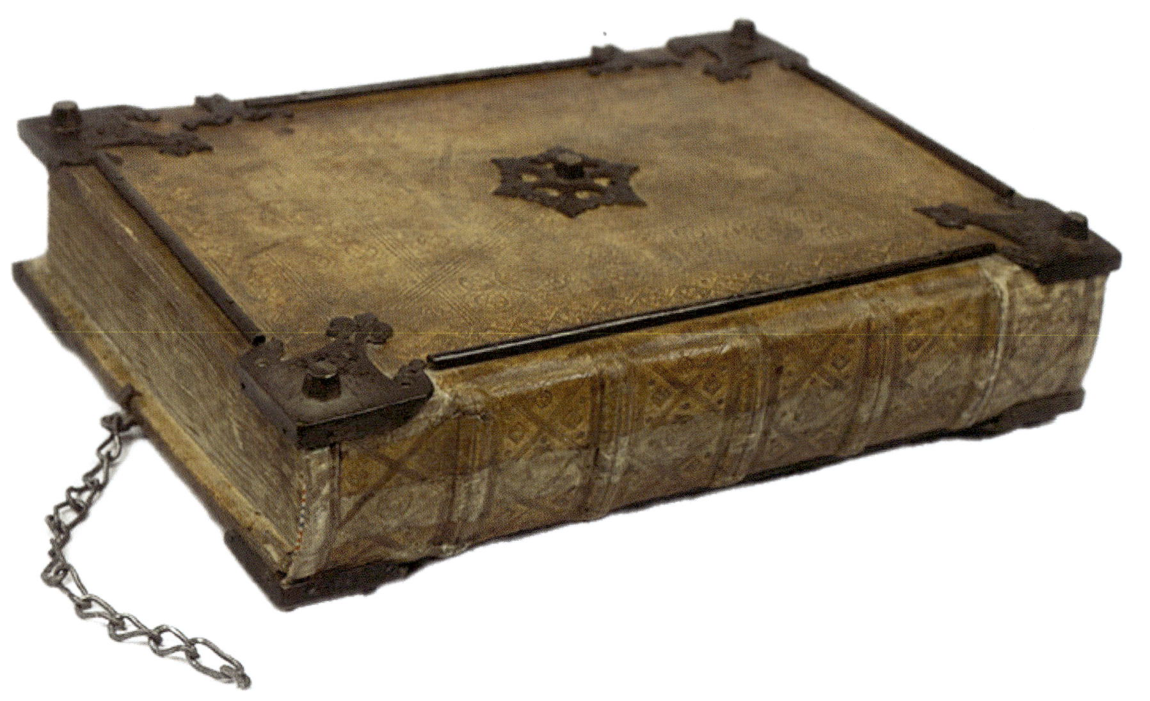

Johann Fust and Peter Schöffer Bible

INC.000140.1–.2, printed book codex, 1462

JOHANN FUST WAS the financier of Gutenberg's famous Bible printed around 1455. After Fust sued Gutenberg in 1455 for the return of his money and won, however, the court ordered Gutenberg's printing equipment and many of his completed Bibles to be turned over to Fust. Fust then partnered with Peter Schöffer, Gutenberg's apprentice, to create their own printing operation. One of the Bibles the new firm produced was this two-volume edition in 1462.

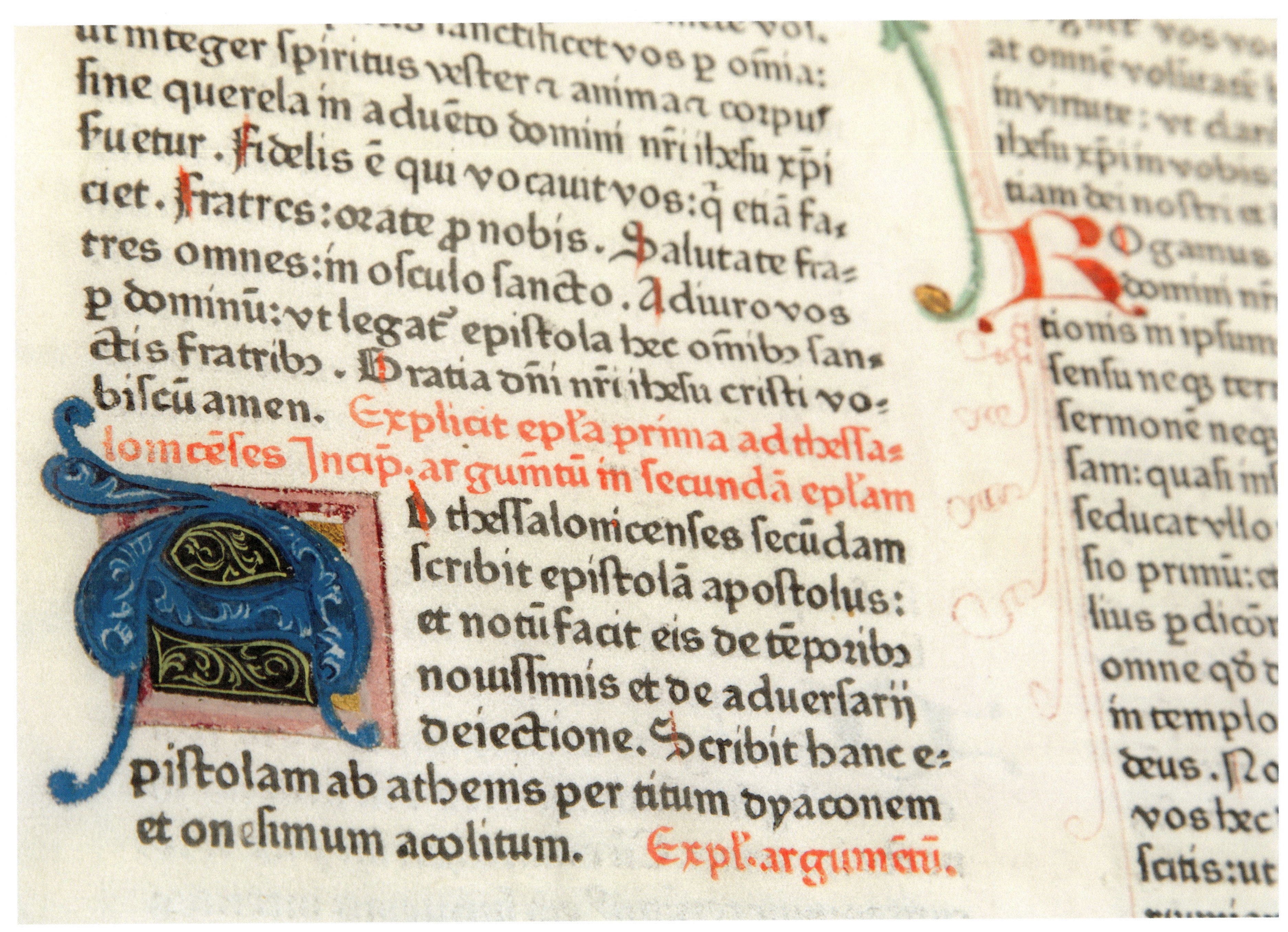

Above: Detail showing a painted initial set within the printed text.

Facing Page: One (of two) Fust volumes showing the original binding, metal details, and chain.

RIGHT: The beginning of Genesis with marginalia depicting exotic flora, fauna, and an image of God creating the world.

FACING PAGE: A painted initial set between the printed text. In 1462 all marginalia was still created by hand.

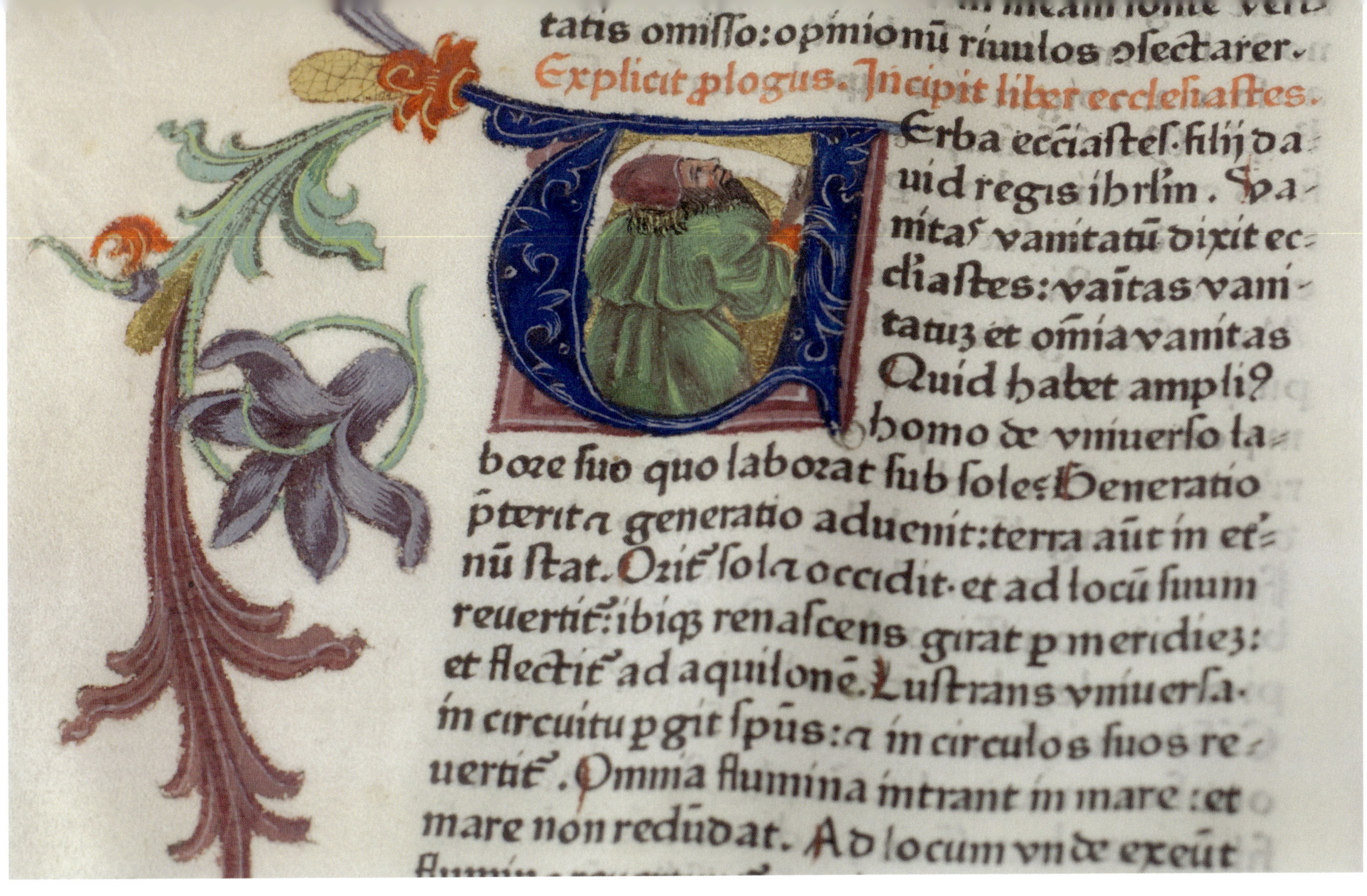
tatis omiſſo: opinionū riuulos ꝯſectarer.
Explicit plogus. Incipit liber eccleſiaſtes.
Verba ecclīaſteſ· filij da-
uid regis ihrlm. Va-
nitas vanitatū dixit ec-
cliaſtes: vaītas vani-
tatū et oīa vanitas
Quid habet ampli?
homo de vniuerſo la-
bore ſuo quo laborat ſub ſole? Generatio
pterit et generatio aduenit: terra aūt in et-
nū ſtat. Orit ſol et occidit. et ad locū ſuum
reuertit: ibiq3 renaſcens girat p meridie3:
et flectit ad aquilonē. Luſtrans vniuerſa.
in circuitu pgit ſpūs: et in circulos ſuos reuertit. Omnia flumina intrant in mare: et
mare non redūdat. Ad locum vnde exeūt

It is printed with 48 lines per page, in contrast to the Gutenberg Bibles, which printed 36 or 42 lines per page. This edition is a beautifully illuminated, iconic early printed Bible. It retains its original leather binding, complete with a metal boss and chain. It is also the first complete Bible to include a printer's mark—two inscribed shields hanging from a branch.

The Aitken Bible

BIB.002615, printed book, 1782

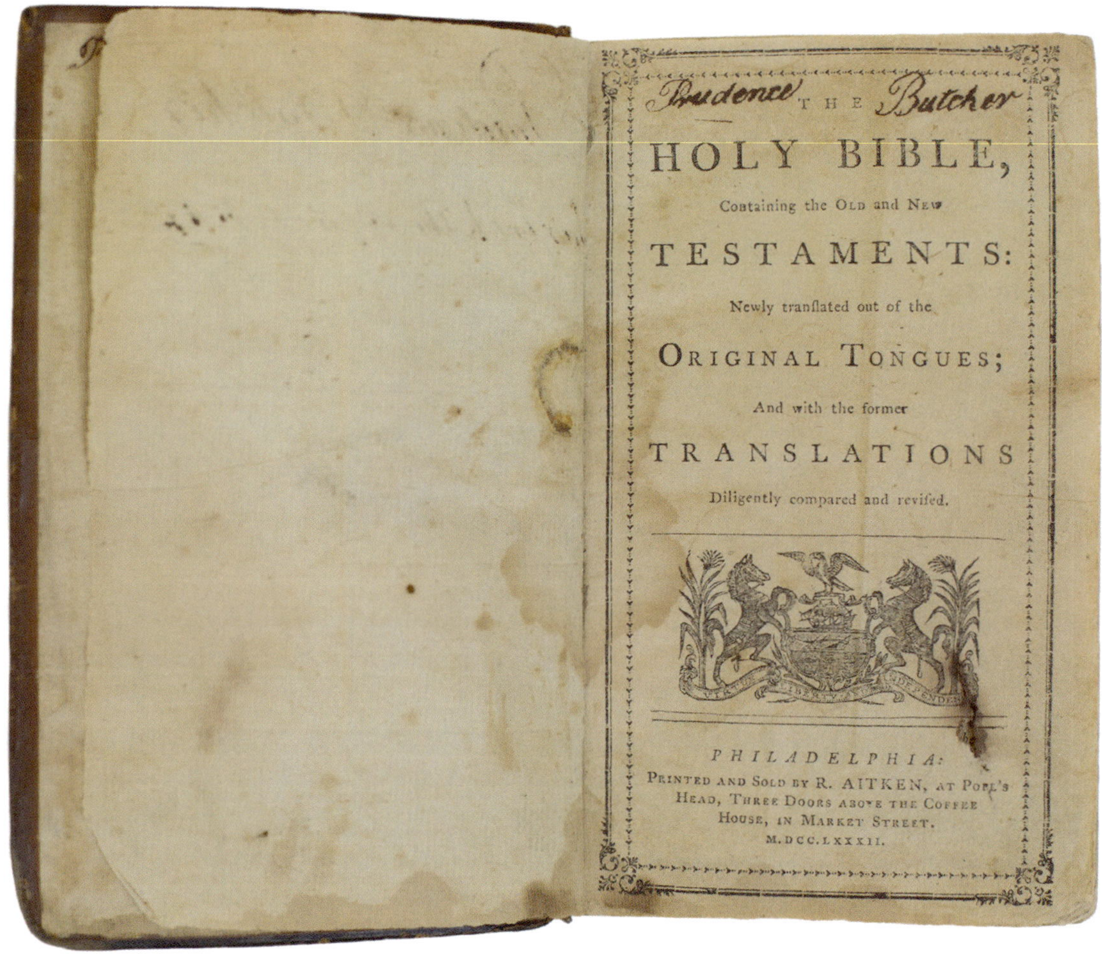

Prudence THE Butcher

HOLY BIBLE,

Containing the OLD and NEW

TESTAMENTS:

Newly tranflated out of the

ORIGINAL TONGUES;

And with the former

TRANSLATIONS

Diligently compared and revifed.

PHILADELPHIA:

PRINTED AND SOLD BY R. AITKEN, AT POPE'S HEAD, THREE DOORS ABOVE THE COFFEE HOUSE, IN MARKET STREET.

M.DCC.LXXXII.

THE AITKEN BIBLE, published by Robert Aitken (1735–1802), was the first Bible printed in English in North America. Aitken was born in Scotland and immigrated to Philadelphia in 1769, where he worked as a bookseller and publisher. In 1781, near the end of the American Revolution, he petitioned congress to support his plans to print a Bible in English. The British government had long regulated the publication of English Bibles, forcing colonists to import them from Britain or Europe. The war subsequently created a shortage in the colonies. Congress endorsed Aitken's Bible when it was completed in 1782. Today, the Aitken Bible is known by many as "the Bible of the Revolution."

LEFT: Title page

FACING PAGE LEFT: Congressional committee report commending the imprint.

FACING PAGE RIGHT: Congressional resolution authorizing sale of the Aitken Bible.

By the UNITED STATES in CONGRESS assembled:

September 12th, 1782.

THE *Committee to whom was referred a Memorial of* Robert Aitken, *Printer, dated 21st January, 1781, respecting an edition of the Holy Scriptures, report,* "*That Mr.* Aitken *has, at a great expence, now finished an American edition of the Holy Scriptures in English; that the Committee have from time to time attended to his progress in the work; that they also recommended it to the two Chaplains of Congress to examine and give their opinion of the execution, who have accordingly reported thereon; the recommendation and report being as follows:*

"*Philadelphia, 1st September, 1782.*

"*Reverend Gentlemen,*

"*OUR knowledge of your piety and public spirit leads us without apology to recommend to your particular attention the edition of the Holy Scriptures publishing by Mr.* Aitken. *He undertook this expensive work at a time when, from the circumstances of the war, an English edition of the Bible could not be imported, nor any opinion formed how long the obstruction might continue. On this account particularly he deserves applause and encouragement. We therefore wish you, Reverend Gentlemen, to examine the execution of the work, and if approved, to give it the sanction of your judgment, and the weight of your recommendation.*

We are, with very great respect,
Your most obedient humble servants.

(*Sign'd*) *JAMES DUANE, Chairman in behalf of a Committee of Congress on Mr.* Aitken's *Memorial.*

Reverend Doct. White *and Revd. Mr.* Duffield,
Chaplains of the United States in Congress assembled.

Report.

Gentlemen,

AGREEABLY to your desire we have paid attention to Mr. Robert Aitken's *impression of the Holy Scriptures of the Old and New Testament. Having selected and examined a variety of passages through-*
...h bring *work, we are of opinion that it is executed with great accuracy*
yielding seed, *...ense, and with as few grammatical and typographical errors*
yielding fruit *...be expected in an undertaking of such magnitude. Being our-*
whose seed is *...itnesses of the demand for this invaluable book, we rejoice in the*
12 And the earth brought forth *...oping that it will prove as advantageous*
grass, and herb yielding seed after e... *as*

as it is honorable to the Gentleman, who has exerted himself to furnish it, at the evident risque of private fortune. We are, Gentlemen,
Your very respectful and humble servants,

(*Sign'd*) *WILLIAM WHITE,*
GEORGE DUFFIELD.

Philadelphia, September 10th, 1782.

Honble James Duane, *Esq. Chairman, and the other Honble Gentlemen of the Committee of Congress on Mr.* Aitken's *Memorial.*"

Whereupon,
RESOLVED,

THAT the United States in Congress assembled highly approve the pious and laudable undertaking of Mr. Aitken, *as subservient to the interest of religion, as well as an instance of the progress of arts in this country, and being satisfied from the above report of his care and accuracy in the execution of the work, they recommend this edition of the Bible to the inhabitants of the United States, and hereby authorise him to publish this Recommendation in the manner he shall think proper.*

CHA. THOMSON, Sec'ry.

¶ The Names and Order of all the Books of the Old and New Testament, with the Number of their Chapters.

Genesis hath Chapters	50	II. Chronicles hath Chapters	36	Daniel hath Chapters	12
Exodus	42	Ezra	10	Hosea	14
Leviticus	27	Nehemiah	13	Joel	3
Numbers	36	Esther	10	Amos	9
Deuteronomy	34	Job	42	Obadiah	1
Joshua	24	Psalms	150	Jonah	4
Judges	21	Proverbs	31	Micah	7
Ruth	4	Ecclesiastes	12	Nahum	3
I. Samuel	31	The song of Solomon	8	Habakkuk	3
II. Samuel	24	Isaiah	66	Zephaniah	3
I. Kings	22	Jeremiah	52	Haggai	2
II. Kings	25	Lamentations	5	Zechariah	14
I. Chronicles	29	Ezekiel	48	Malachi	4

Matthew hath Chapters	28	Galatians hath Chapters	6	To the Hebrews hath Chapters	13
Mark	16	Ephesians	6	Epistle of James	5
Luke	24	Philippians	4	I. Peter	[illegible]
John	21	Colossians	4	II. Peter	[illegible]
The Acts	28	I. Thessalonians	5	I. John	[illegible]
The Epistle to the Romans	16	II. Thessalonians	3	II. John	[illegible]
I. Corinthians	16	I. Timothy	6	III. John	[illegible]
II. Corinthians	13	II. Timothy	4		
		Titus	[illegible]		
		Philemon	[illegible]		

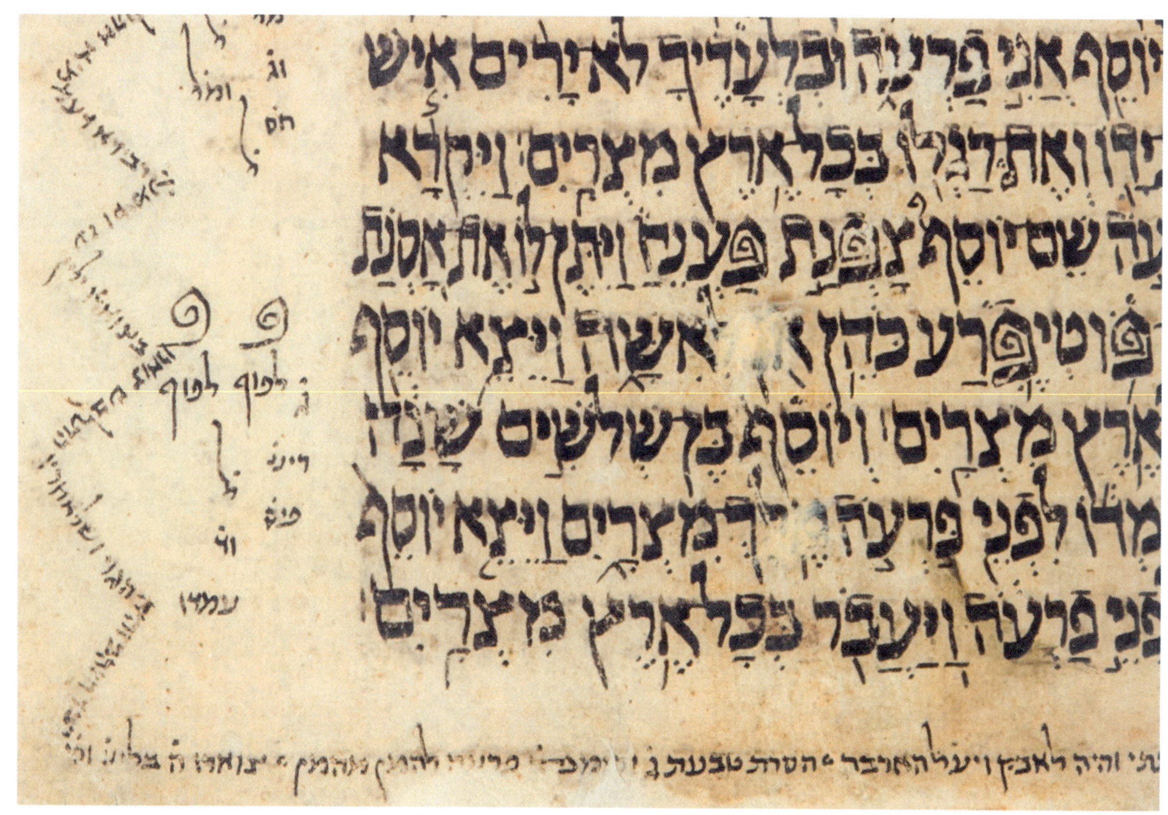

Left: Detail of micrography.

Facing Page: Bifolium of the Torah Codex with micrographic commentary surrounding the biblical text.

Torah Codex by Benayah ben Sa'adyah

MS.000884, paper codex, 1469–1470

Benayah ben Sa'adyah ben Zechariah and his descendants are widely known as the most prominent scribal family in Yemenite Jewish tradition. Unfortunately, of the hundreds of texts written by them, only a few dozen have survived. Benayah ben Sa'adyah himself wrote this beautiful codex in Yemen in 1469–1470. It contains all the books of the Torah from Genesis to Deuteronomy with masorah, a Masoretic introduction to the Bible, and a poem. As with all Benayah codices, its text adheres precisely to the scribal guidelines established in Maimonides's "Mishnah Torah."

הנה ושבע השבלים הטבת שבע שנים
הנה חלום אחד הוא: ושבע הפרות הרקות
והרעת העלת אחריהן שבע שנים הנה
ושבע השבלים הרקות שדפות הקדים
יהיו שבע שני רעב: הוא הדבר אשר
דברתי אל פרעה אשר האלהים עשה
הראה את פרעה: הנה שבע שנים באות
שבע גדול בכל ארץ מצרים: וקמו שבע
שני רעב אחריהן ונשכח כל השבע
בארץ מצרים וכלה הרעב את הארץ:
ולא יודע השבע בארץ מפני הרעב ההוא
אחרי כן כי כבד הוא מאד: ועל השנות החלום
אל פרעה פעמים כי נכון הדבר מעם האלהים
וממהר האלהים לעשתו: ועתה ירא פרעה
איש נבון וחכם וישיתהו על ארץ מצרים:
יעשה פרעה ויפקד פקדים על הארץ וחמש
את ארץ מצרים בשבע שני השבע: ויקבצו
את כל אכל השנים הטבות הבאת האלה ויצברו
בר תחת יד פרעה אכל בערים ושמרו: והיה

תהיין בארץ מצרים ולא תכרת הארץ ברעב:
וייטב הדבר בעיני פרעה ובעיני כל עבדיו:
ויאמר פרעה אל עבדיו הנמצא כזה איש
אשר רוח אלהים בו: ויאמר פרעה אל יוסף
אחרי הודיע אלהים אותך את כל זאת אין
נבון וחכם כמוך: אתה תהיה על ביתי ועל
פיך ישק כל עמי רק הכסא אגדל ממך: ויאמר
פרעה אל יוסף ראה נתתי אתך על כל ארץ
מצרים: ויסר פרעה את טבעתו מעל ידו ויתן
אתה על יד יוסף וילבש אתו בגדי שש
וישם רבד הזהב על צוארו: וירכב אתו
במרכבת המשנה אשר לו ויקראו לפניו אברך
ונתון אתו על כל ארץ מצרים: ויאמר פרעה
אל יוסף אני פרעה ובלעדיך לא ירים איש
את ידו ואת רגלו בכל ארץ מצרים: ויקרא
פרעה שם יוסף צפנת פענח ויתן לו את אסנת
בת פוטי פרע כהן און לאשה ויצא יוסף
על ארץ מצרים: ויוסף בן שלשים שנה
בעמדו לפני פרעה מלך מצרים ויצא יוסף

The Bute Hours

MS.000893, parchment codex, ca. 1500-1520

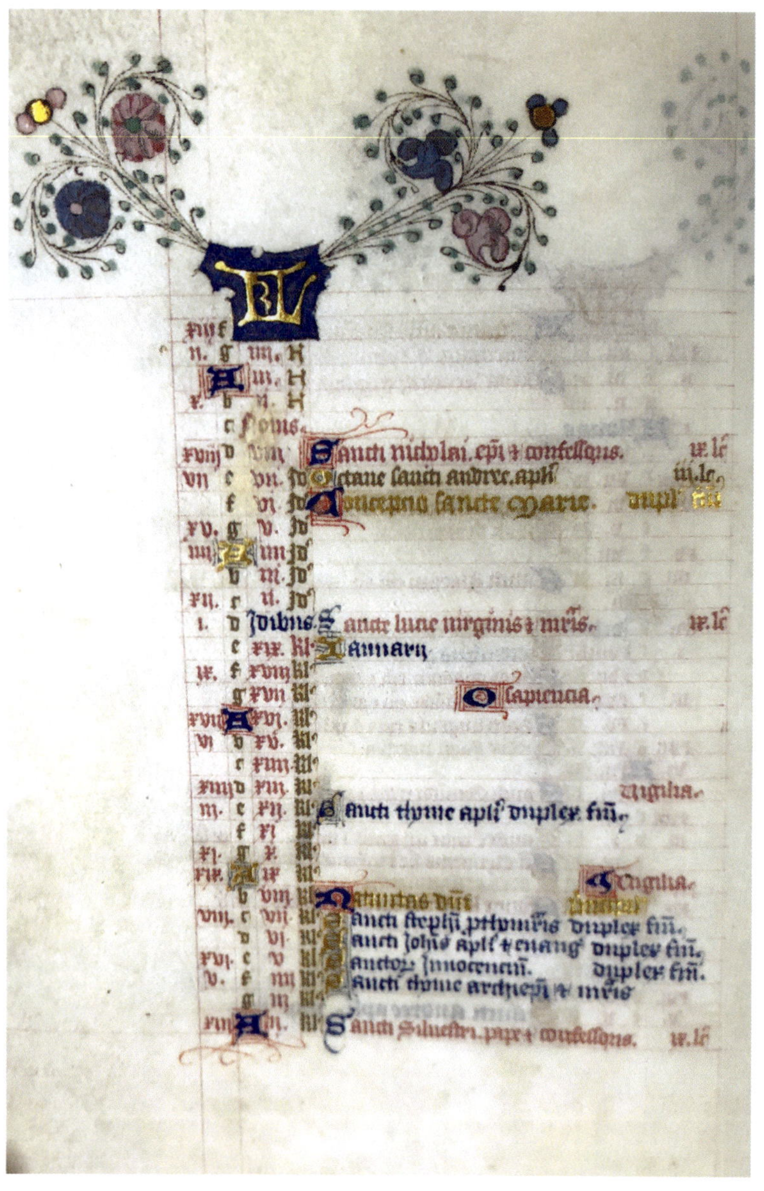

The Bute Book of Hours is a richly decorated manuscript made in England in the early 16th century for an influential patron. Miniatures attest to the patron's support of the Tudor dynasty; Lancastrian roses abound, and one miniature depicts King Henry VI, who died in the Tower of London in 1471 and was popularly considered to be a miracle worker, saint, and martyr. Henry VII proposed his canonization around 1492. Another miniature portraying St. Thomas Becket with devotional prayers survived the suppression of Becket's cult by Henry VIII.

Left: Decorated tables showing fine, thin parchment very white in color. This type of material was strong and expensive.

Facing page: Bifolium showing rich illumination using gold leaf throughout.

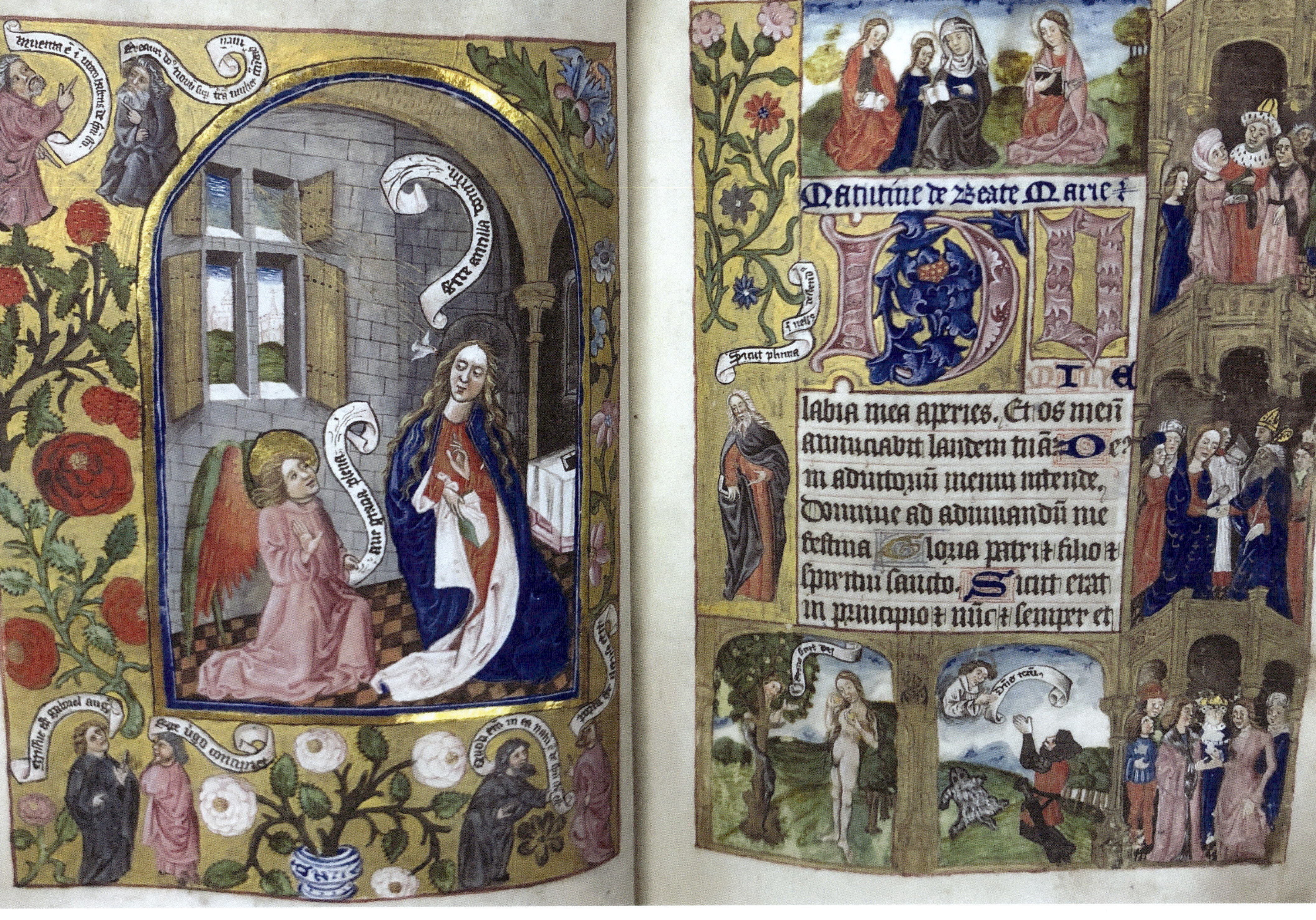

Ecce ancilla domini
Aue gratia plena
Matutine de beate Marie
labia mea aperies. Et os meu[m]
annunciabit laudem tuam. Deus
in adiutoriu[m] meum intende.
Domine ad adiuvandu[m] me
festina. Gloria patri et filio et
spiritui sancto. Sicut erat
in principio et nunc et semper et

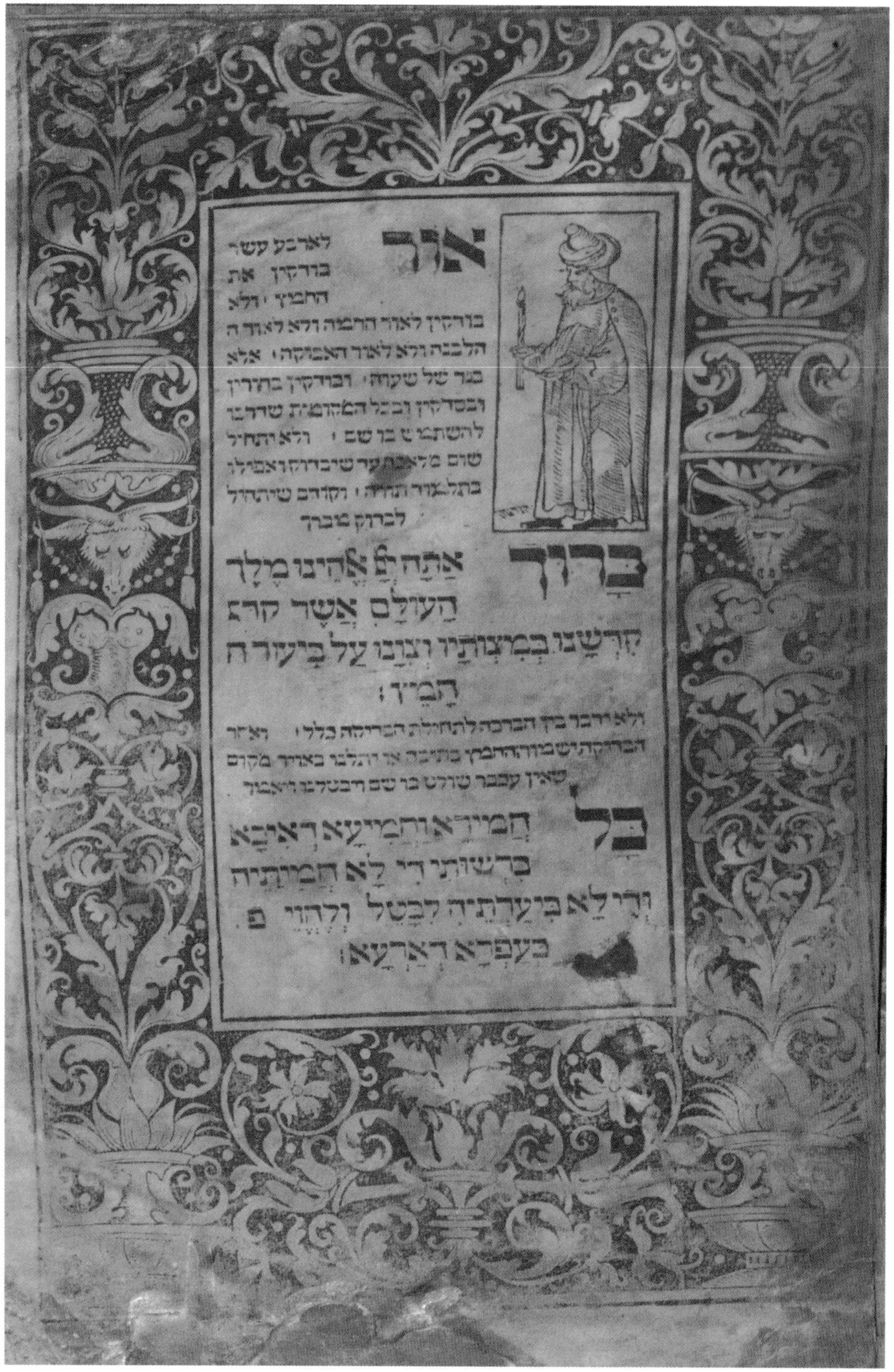

אור לארבעה עשר בודקין את החמץ ולא בודקין לאור החמה ולא לאור הלבנה ולא לאור האבוקה אלא בנר של שעוה ובודקין בחורין ובסדקין ובכל המקומות שדרכו להשתמש בו חמץ ולא יתחיל שום מלאכה עד שיבדוק ואפילו בתלמוד תורה וקודם שיתחיל לבדוק מברך

ברוך אתה יי אלהינו מלך העולם אשר קדשנו במצותיו וצונו על ביעור חמץ:

ולא ידבר בין הברכה לתחלת הבדיקה כלל ואחר הבדיקה ישמור החמץ [illegible] שאין עכבר [illegible] ויאמר

כל חמירא וחמיעא דאיכא ברשותי די לא חמיתיה ודי לא ביערתיה לבטל ולהוי כעפרא דארעא:

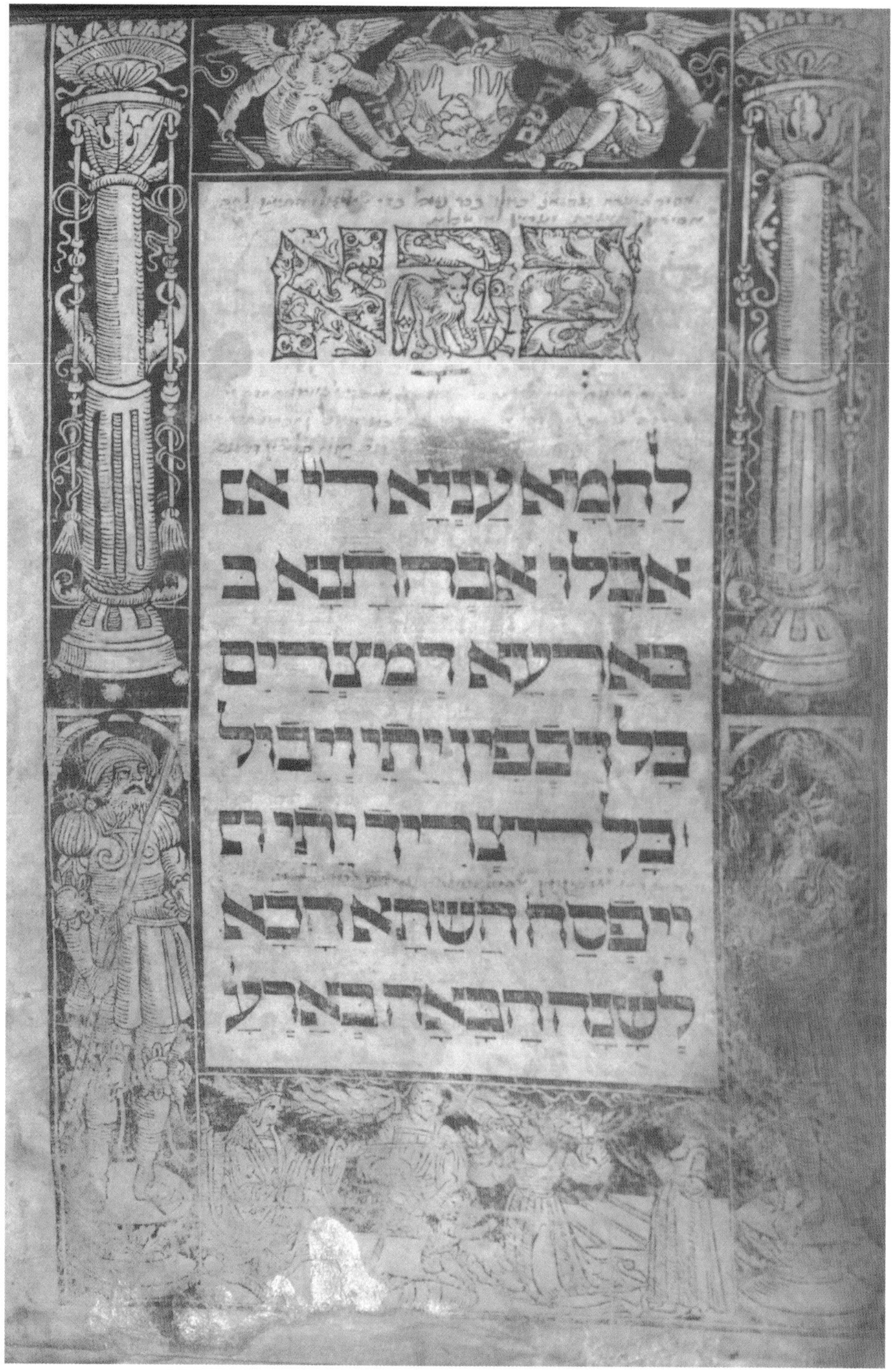

הא

לחמא עניא די א
אכלו אבהתנא ב
בארעא דמצרים
כל דכפין ייתי ויכול
כל דצריך ייתי ו
ויפסח השתא הכא
לשנה הבאה בארע

Haggadah shel Pesah (Prague Haggadah)

PBK.003090, parchment, printed book, 1526

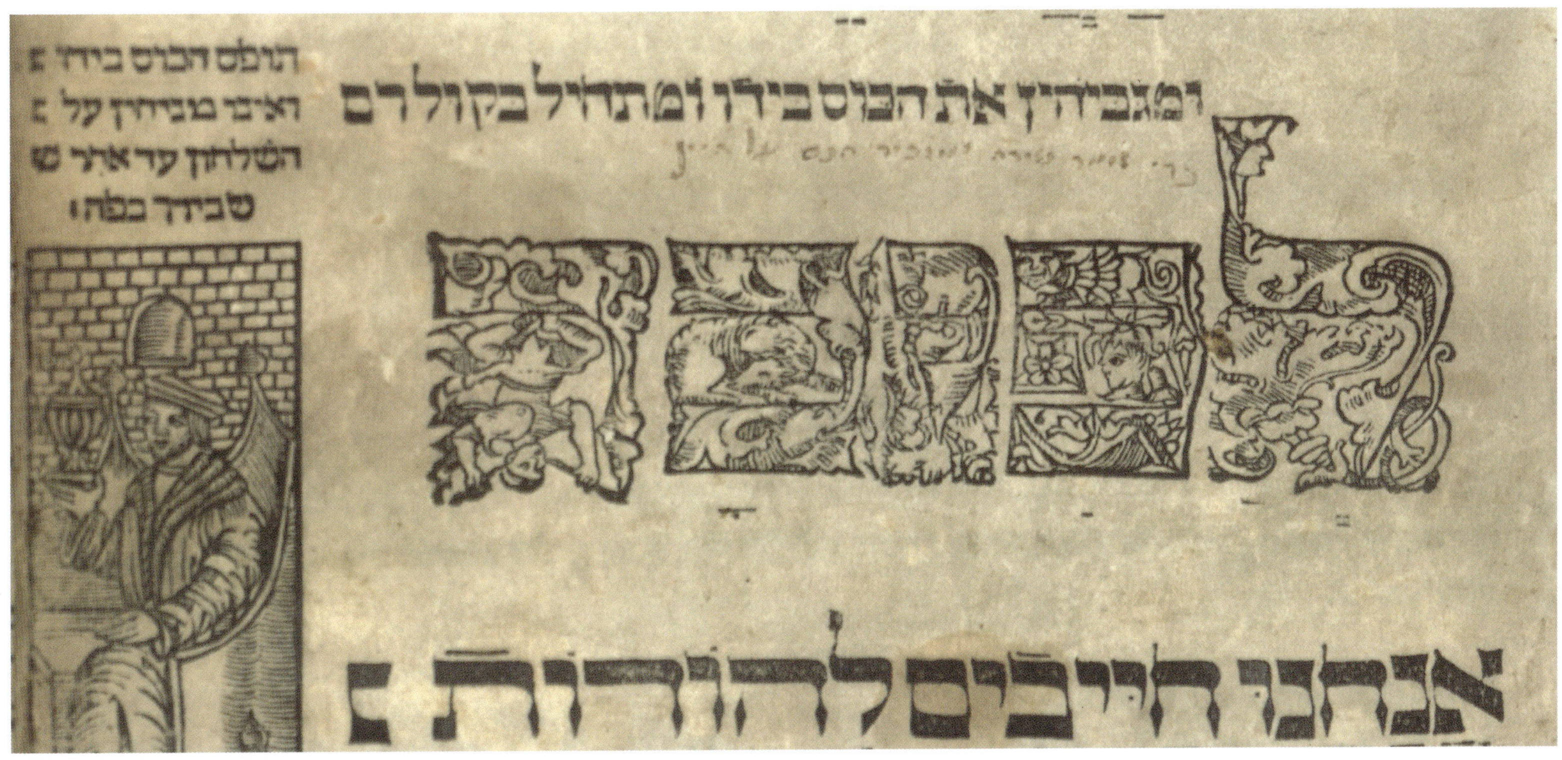

LEFT: Detail of anthropomorphic Hebrew script.

FACING PAGE: Pages from the Prague Haggadah written in Hebrew and Aramaic, with marginal notes in Hebrew, Yiddish, and English.

THE HAGGADAH IS the central text of the Seder ritual meal that takes place at the beginning of Passover. It is one of the most printed Hebrew books. The Prague Haggadah of 1526 is the earliest fully illustrated printed Haggadah, and its woodcuts had an enormous influence on the history of Haggadah illustration. This copy is important to the history of Jews in America, as it was owned by the Lewith family of Charleston, South Carolina, for a large part of the 19th century, before being donated to Congregation Kahal Kadosh Beth Elohim of Charleston. It contains birth and death announcements for family members noted in the margins, which shows how central it was to the Lewith family, similar to family Bibles that many other American families have cherished.

Tiffany Stained Glass Windows

ART.001166/1168/1171, glass with lead and aluminum frames, 1905/1909

On display at Museum of the Bible are five beautiful stained glass windows designed by Louis Comfort Tiffany, founder of Tiffany Studios, and son of the famous Charles Tiffany, who founded the jewlery brand, Tiffany & Co. Tiffany's innovative techniques include mottled glass, favrile glass, opalescent glass, and drapery glass.

Louis Tiffany was commissioned by Grace Episcopal Church (later Church of the Epiphany) in Orange, New Jersey, to create four windows of the Evangelists in 1905 for Mr. Alexander Mann. Then, in 1909, Tiffany was commissioned again to create a larger window depicting Jesus on Easter morning, in honor of Frank and Lois Barstow.

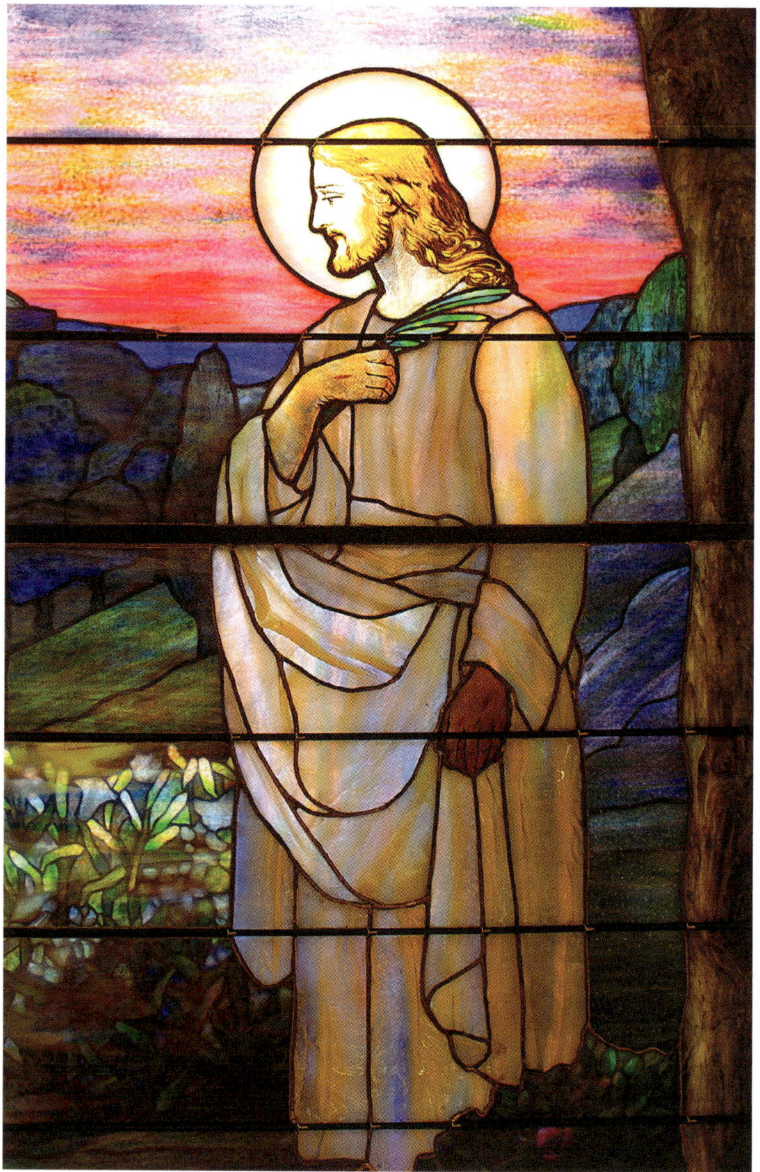

Right: Central panel of *Easter Morning* depicting a resurrected Jesus.

Facing page: All five windows on display at the brand launch event in Oklahoma City.

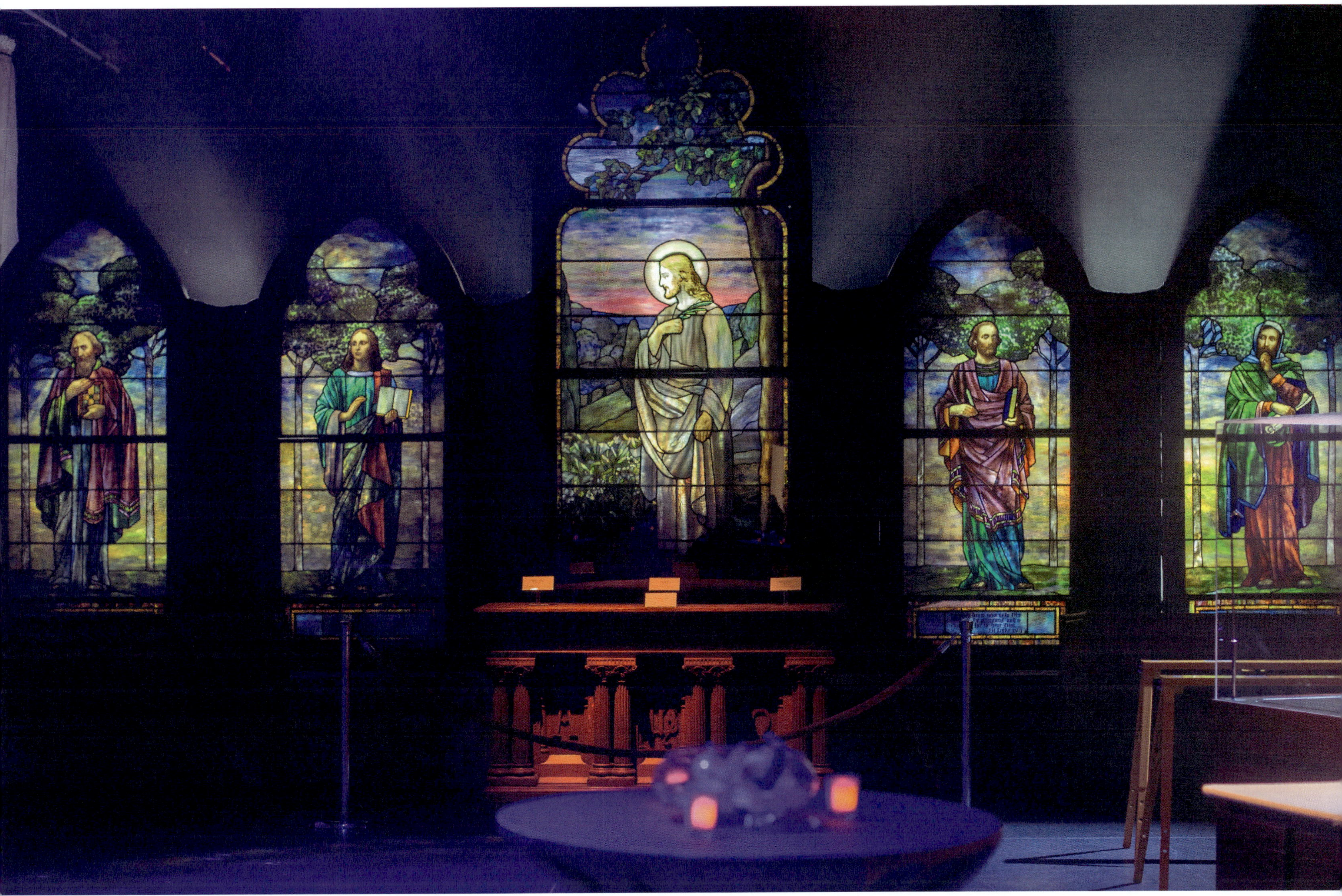

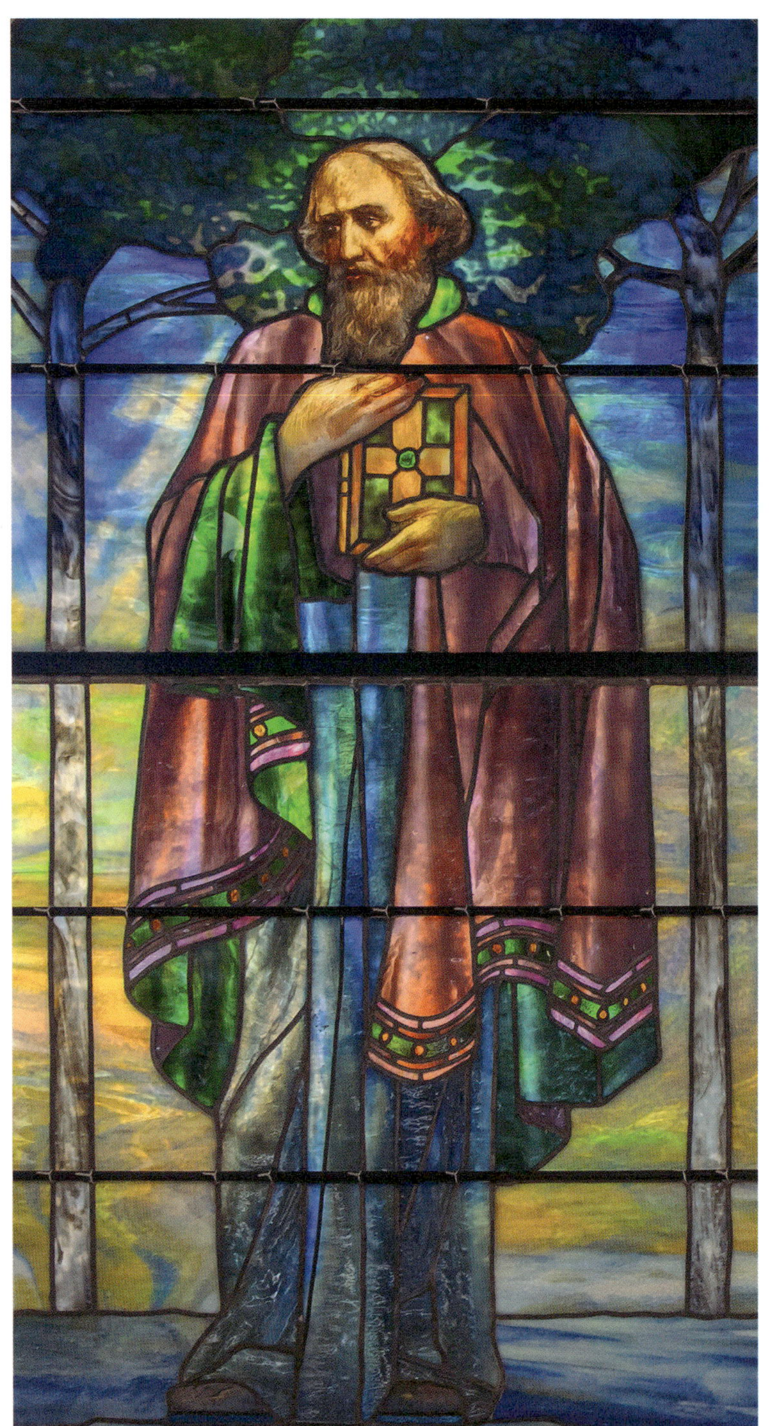

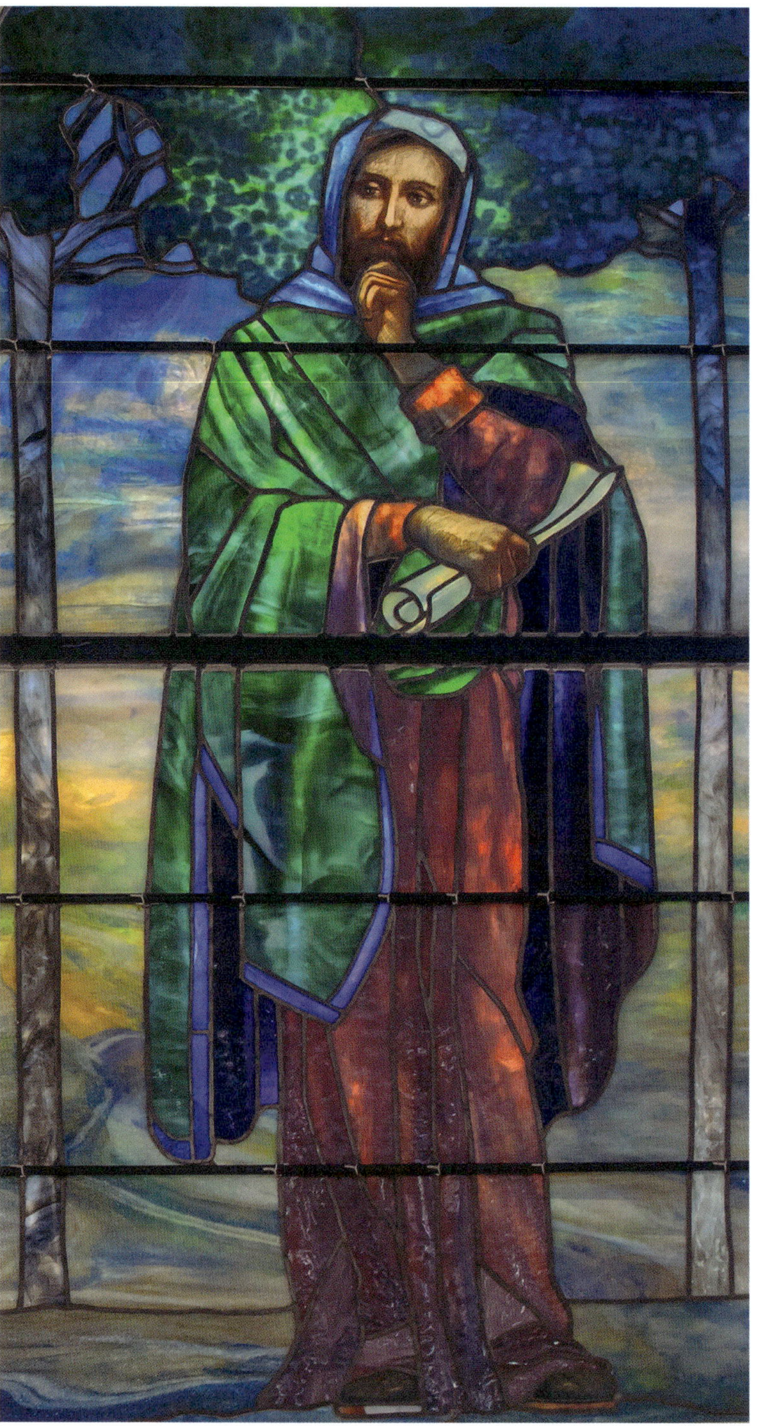

Left: "Matthew" from *The Four Evangelists.*

Right: "Mark" from *The Four Evangelists.*

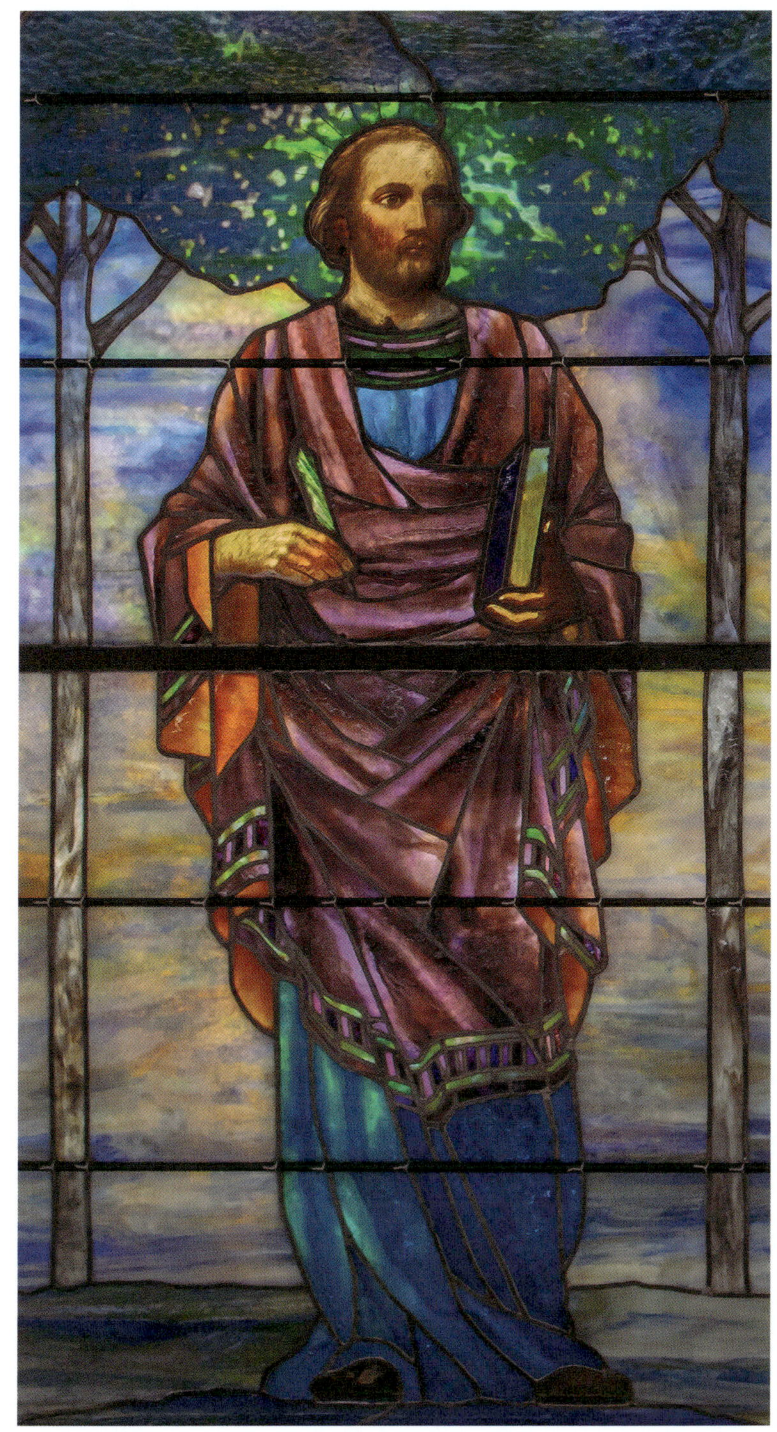

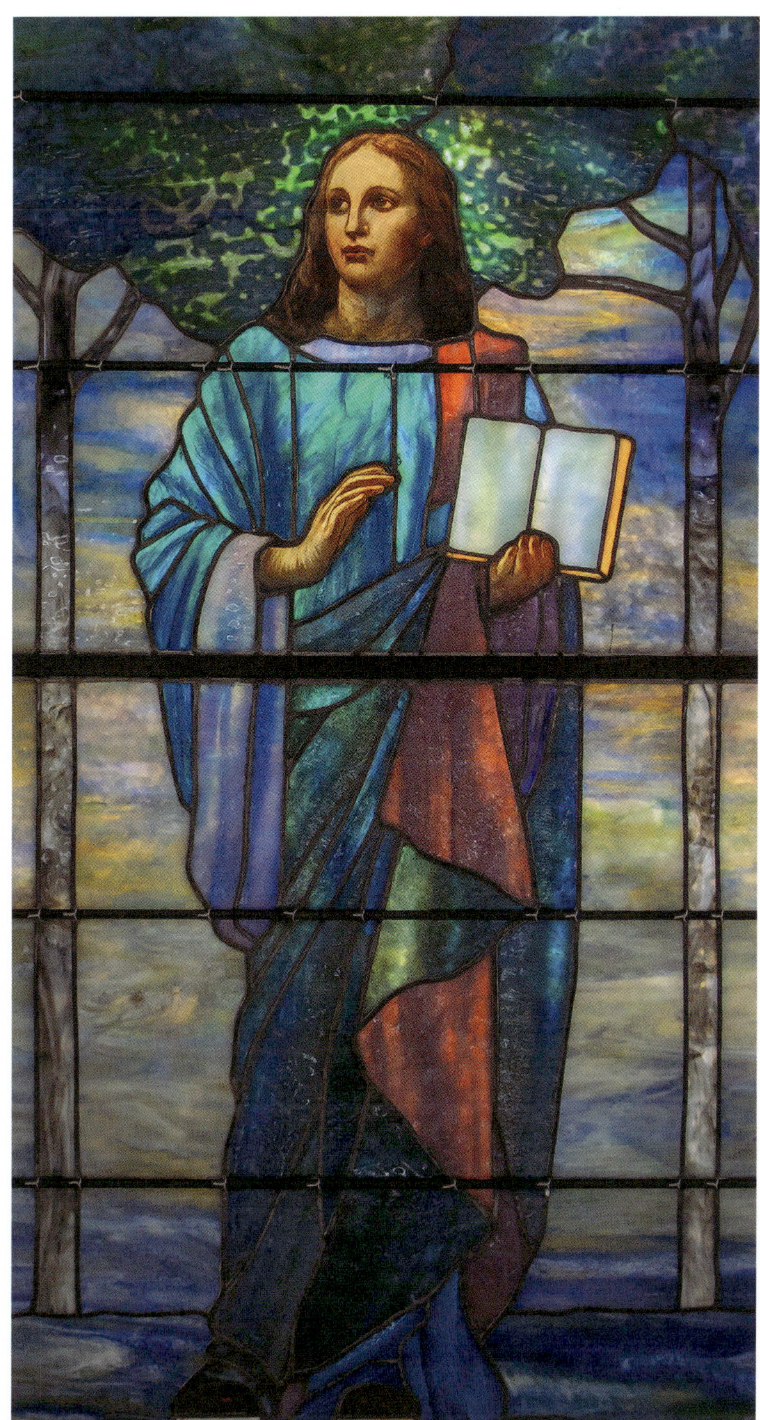

Left: "Luke" from *The Four Evangelists.*

Right: "John" from *The Four Evangelists.*

Thomas Jefferson Letter

PPR.0010217, paper, 1809

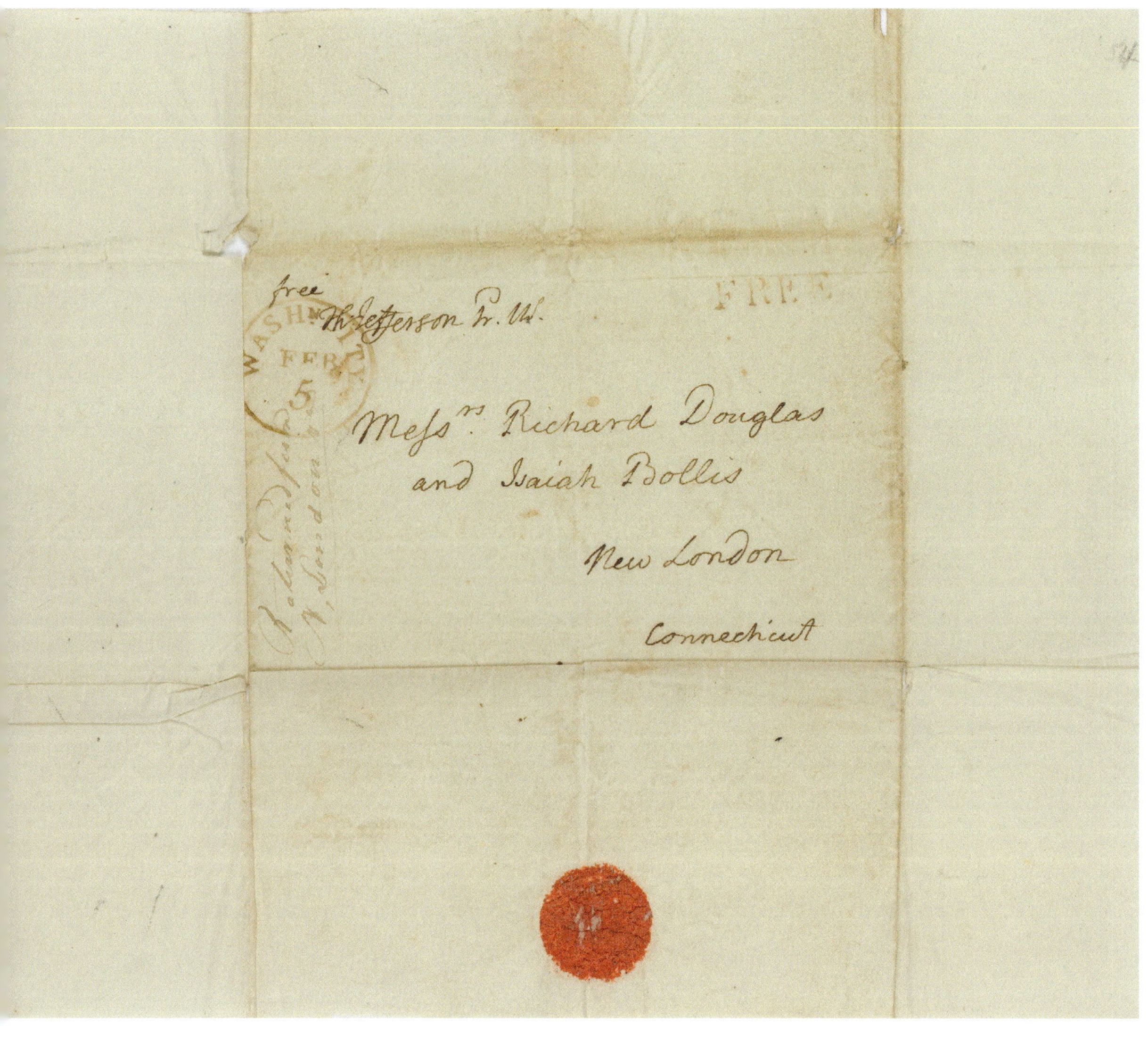

free Th:Jefferson Pr. U.S.

FREE

Messrs. Richard Douglas
and Isaiah Bollis
New London
Connecticut

THOMAS JEFFERSON WAS a towering figure among America's founding generation, serving as the nation's third president from 1801 to 1809. Influenced by Enlightenment philosophers such as John Locke, Jefferson was a fierce advocate of religious freedom. Indeed, he authored the Virginia Statute for Religious Freedom in 1777, which later served as a model for the First Amendment. Religious freedom in America enabled religious diversity to flourish, heavily influencing the way people used and encountered the Bible. Jefferson reflected on religious freedom in this letter, which he wrote at the end of his presidency, to a Methodist church in Connecticut. He wrote, "No provision in our constitution ought to be dearer to man than that which protects the rights of conscience against the enterprises of the civil authority . . . I trust that the whole course of my life has proved me a sincere friend to religious, as well as civil liberty."

FACING PAGE: Front of envelope addressed to Richard Douglas and Isaiah Bollis.

RIGHT: Letter addressed "To the Society of the Methodist Episcopal Church at New London, Connecticutt," signed by Thomas Jefferson, Feb. 4, 1809.

To the Society of the Methodist Episcopal church at New London. Connecticut

The approbation you are so good as to express of the measures which have been recommended & pursued during the course of my administration of the National concerns, is highly acceptable. the approving voice of our fellow citizens, for endeavors to be useful, is the greatest of all earthly rewards.

No provision in our constitution ought to be dearer to man, than that which protects the rights of conscience, against the enterprizes of the civil authority. it has not left the religion of it's citizens under the power of it's public functionaries, were it possible that any of these should consider a conquest over the consciences of men either attainable, or applicable to any desirable purpose. to me, no information could be more welcome than that the minutes of the several religious societies should prove, of late, larger additions, than have been usual, to their several associations: and I trust that the whole course of my life has proved me a sincere friend to religious, as well as civil liberty.

I thank you for your affectionate good wishes for my future happiness. retirement is become essential to it: and one of it's best consolations will be to witness the advancement of my country in all those pursuits & acquisitions which constitute the character of a wise & virtuous nation: and I offer sincere prayers to heaven that it's benedictions may attend yourselves, our country, & all it's sons.

Th: Jefferson

Feb. 4. 1809.

The Rosebery Richard Rolle

MS.000148, parchment codex, late 1300s–early 1400s

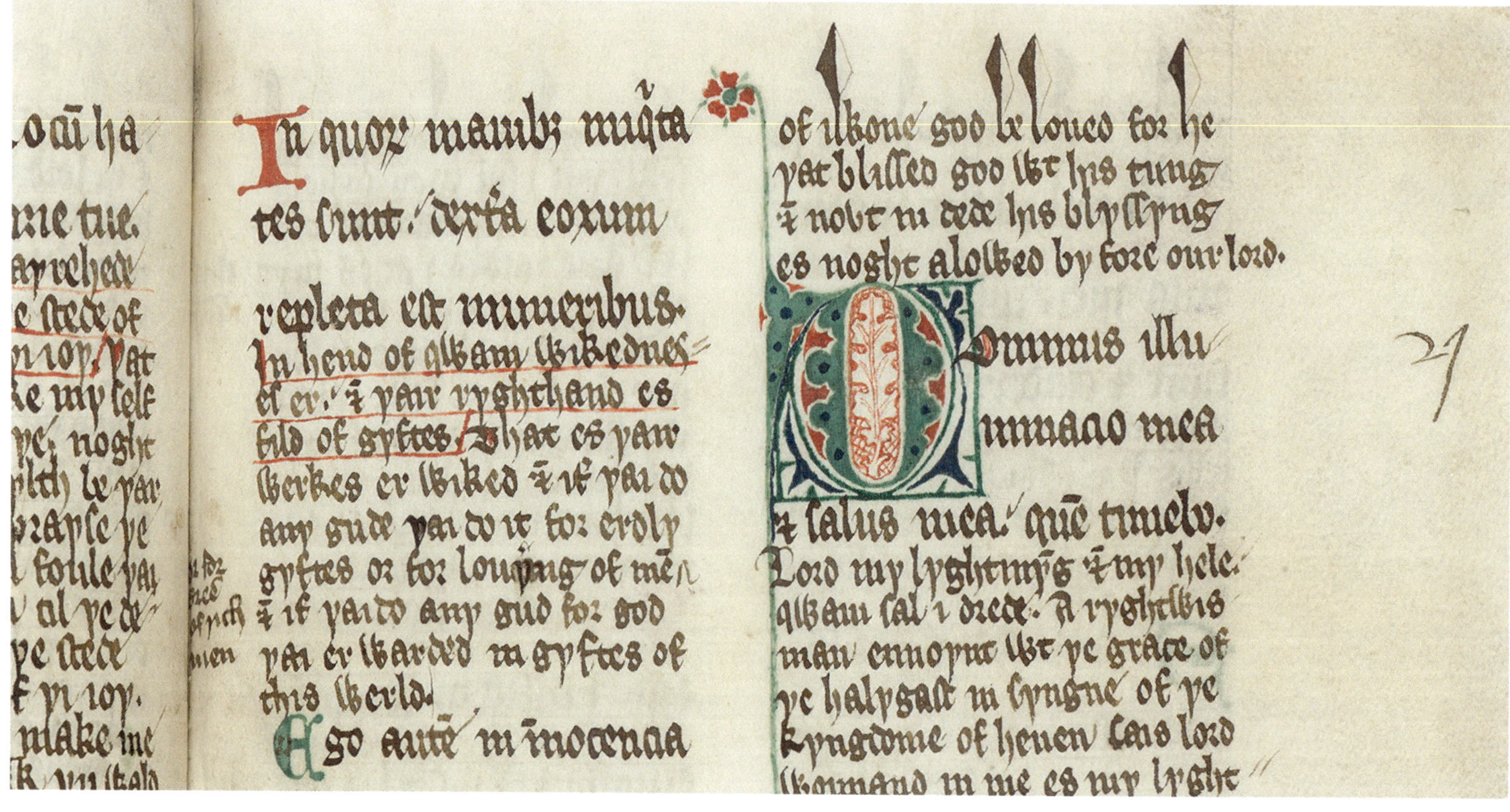

The English mystic Richard Rolle (d. 1349) translated the Psalms and canticles into Middle English. This copy of his work was probably made at a convent in Yorkshire, England, about fifty years after his death. Rolle broke up each psalm into short Latin passages that are not the same as modern verses. Next, he translated each passage. Rolle added commentary in Middle English, perhaps to guide the hermit Margaret Kirkby. This manuscript begins with the end of his commentary on Psalm 7 and is almost complete. One quire is missing. The manuscript once belonged to the family of the Earl of Rosebery.

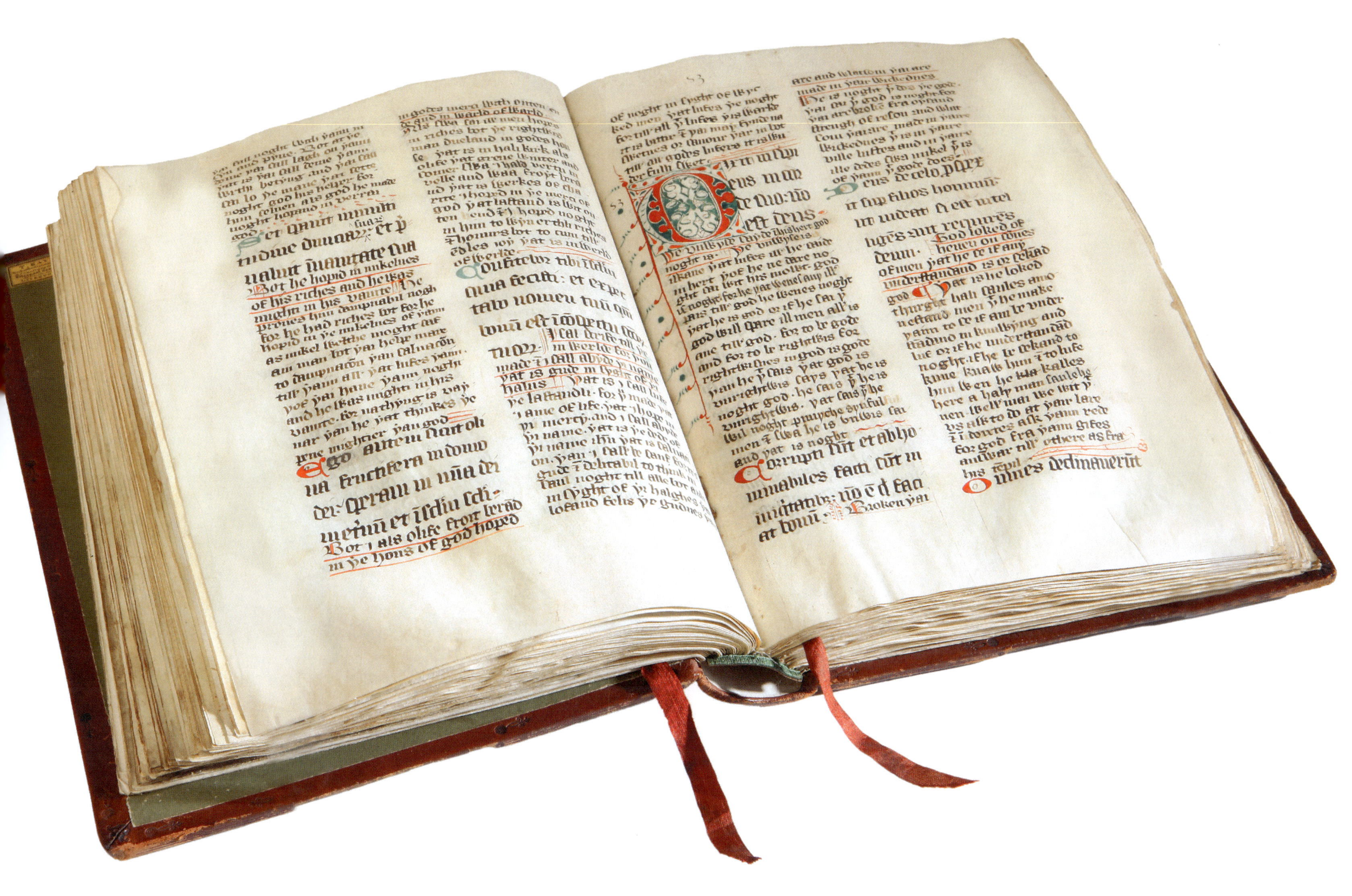

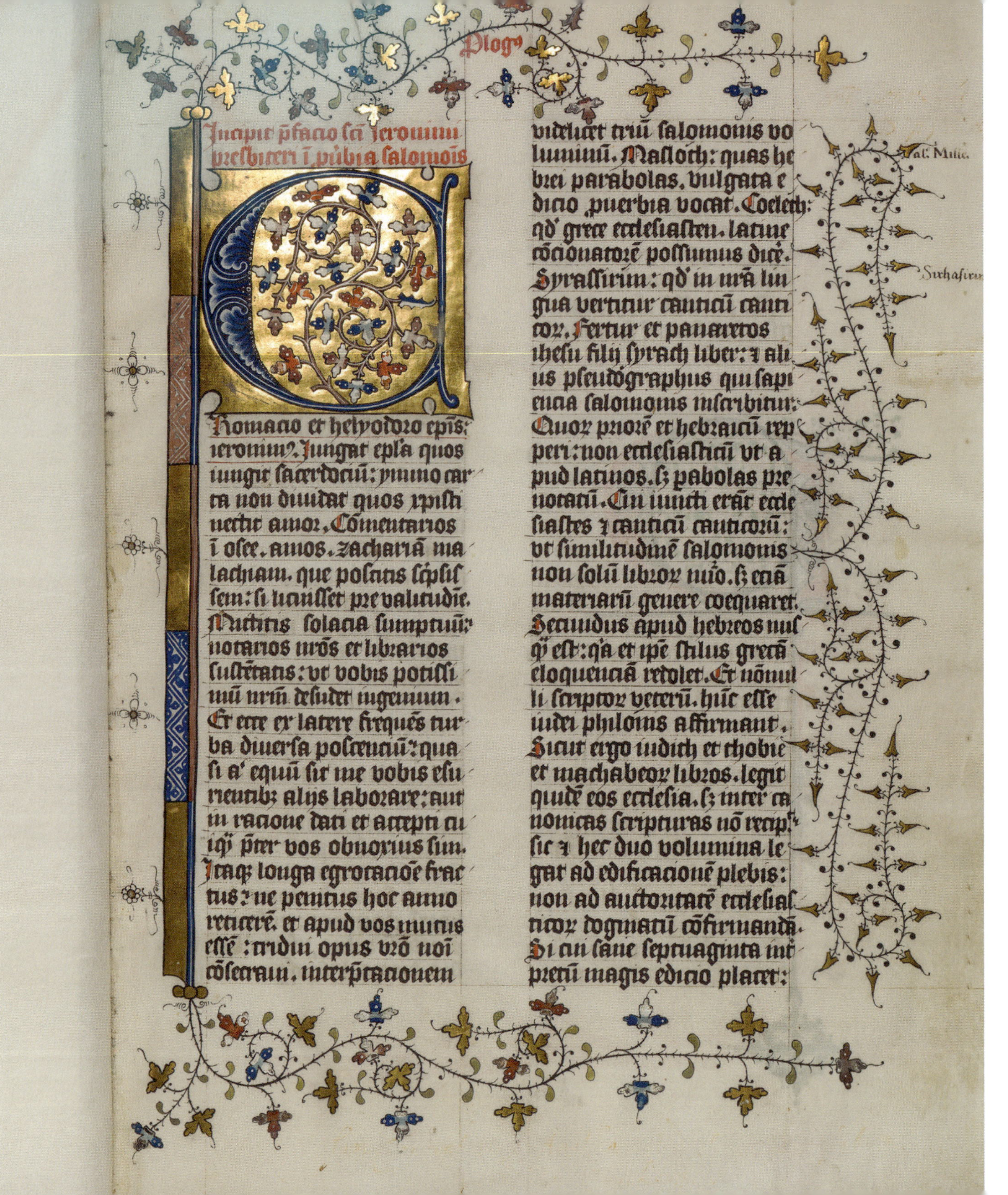

Hattem Vulgate

MS.000159, parchment codex, ca. 1420–1430

The Brethren of the Common Life sought to produce a version of the Vulgate that accurately reflected Jerome's translation, purged of Vetus Latina additions. This manuscript, containing eleven books from the Old Testament, is part of a multivolume set likely produced by the Brethren in the early 15th century in Hattem, the Netherlands. The volume begins with an illuminated initial C with an attached, page-long border in gold, red, and blue from which leafy tendrils sprout. Elaborate red and blue initials at the start of each prologue and book extend from 7 to 12 lines. The scribe copied the text in two columns of 35 lines each.

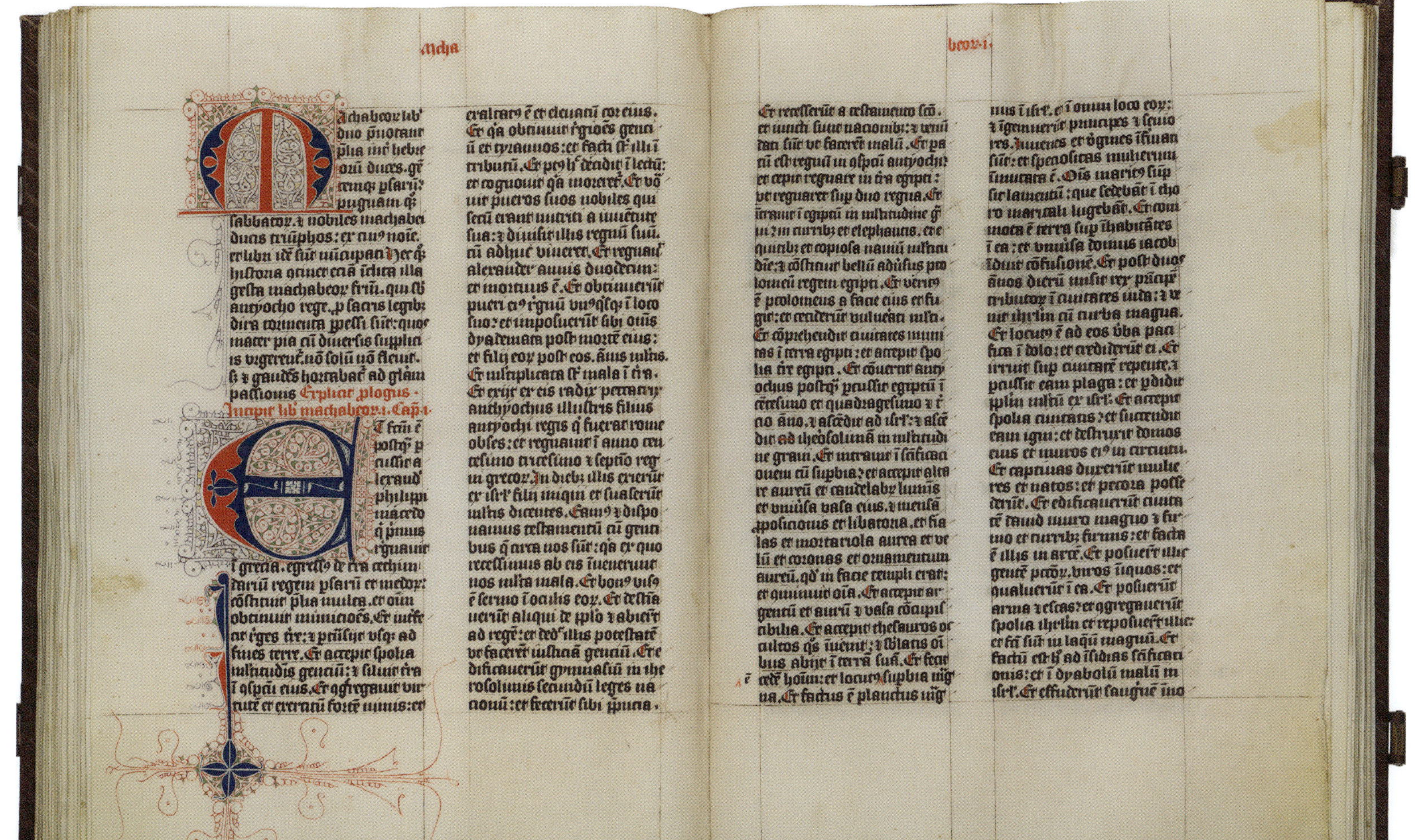

The Lunar Bible

BIB.005001, microfiche, 1964

PRIOR TO HIS death in 1967, Astronaut Edward White II (Apollo 1) told a reporter he hoped to carry a Bible to the moon. In his memory, the Apollo Prayer League formed in 1968, in part to fulfill that desire. Several missions attempted to land the Bible on the moon. Alan Bean (Apollo 12) was the first, but due to a mix-up the Bible only orbited the moon. Apollo 13 carried 512 copies, but an explosion prevented a lunar landing. Finally, in 1971, Apollo 14 astronaut Edgar Mitchell carried 300 copies of the Bible with him (100 in the lunar module, 200 in the command module, and 212 also secretly stowed in the command module). On February 5, 1971, Antares, Apollo 14's lunar module, touched down on the moon, bringing with it the Bible.

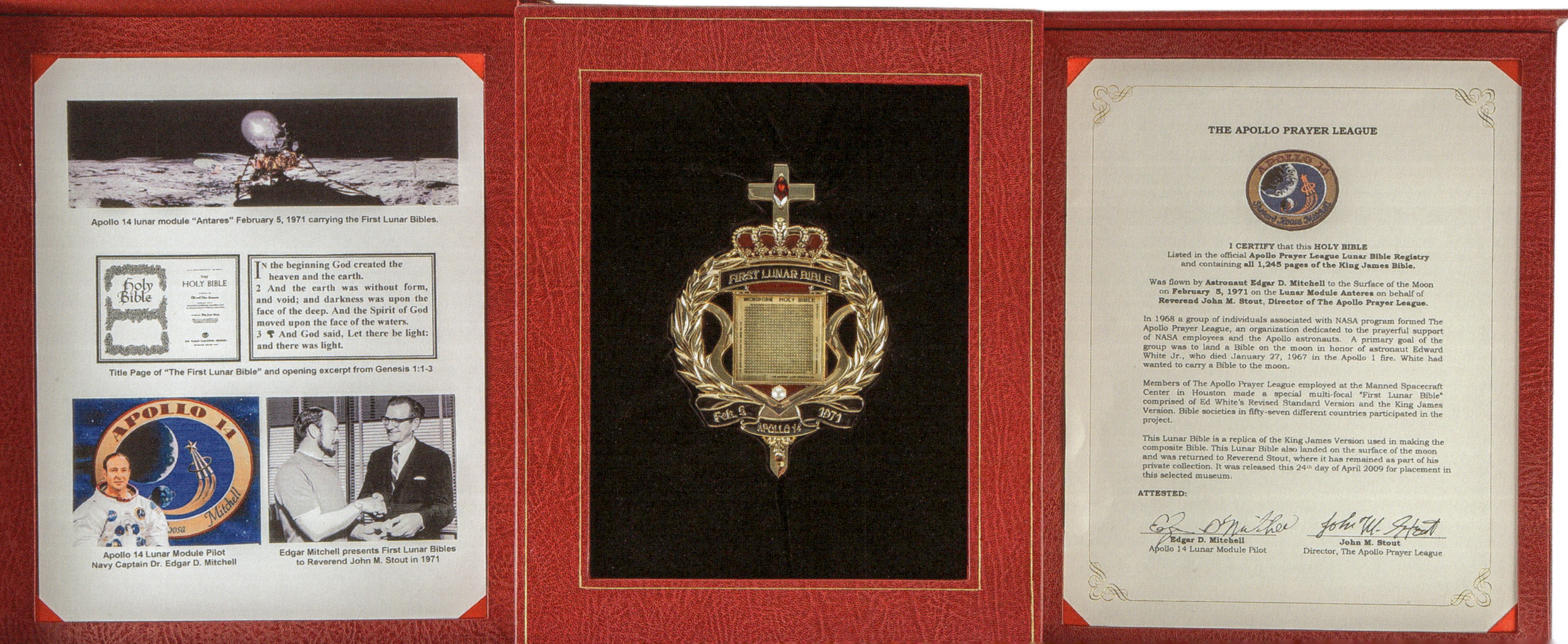

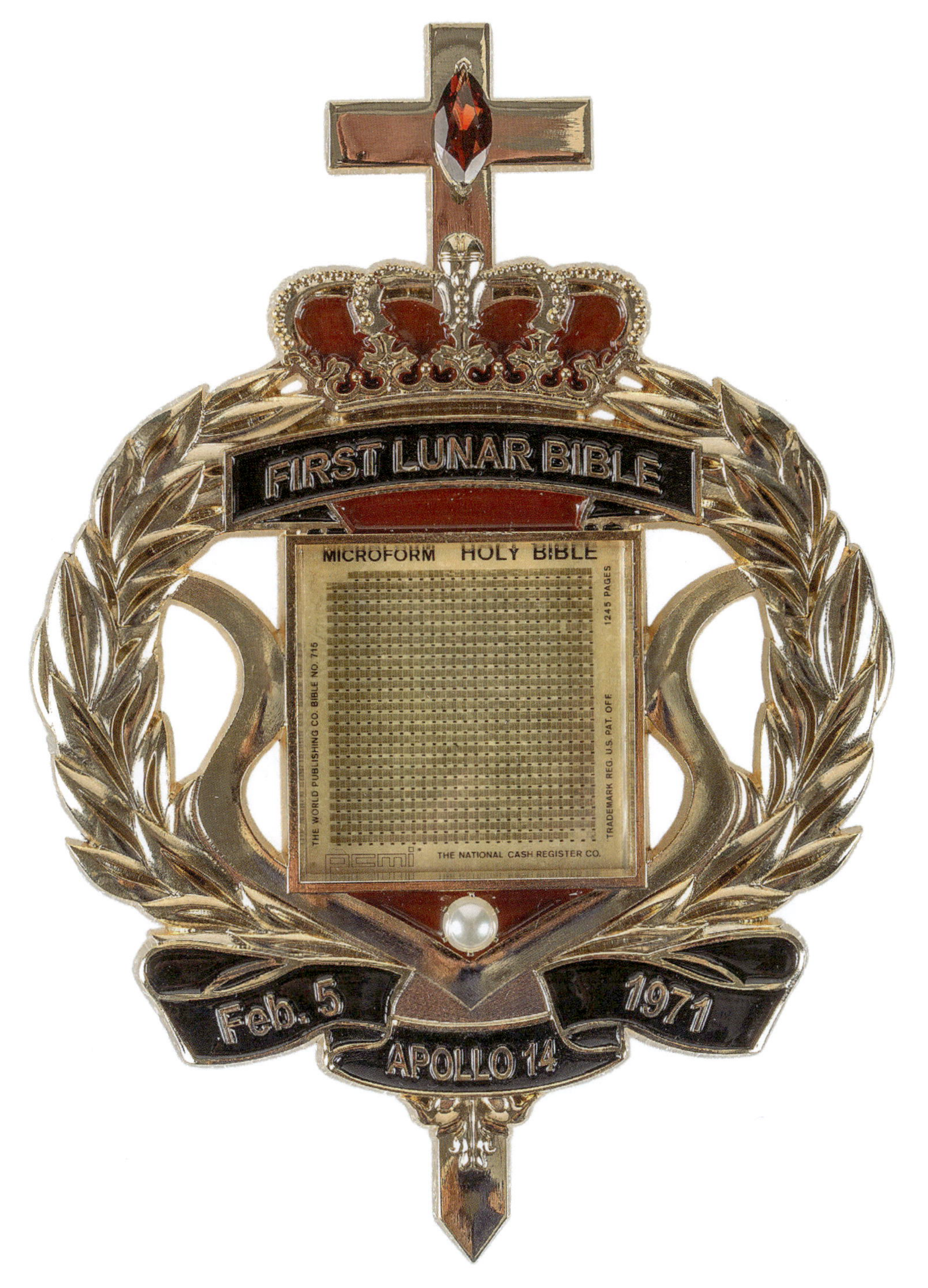
FIRST LUNAR BIBLE
MICROFORM HOLY BIBLE
THE WORLD PUBLISHING CO. BIBLE NO. 715
1245 PAGES
TRADEMARK REG. U.S. PAT OFF
THE NATIONAL CASH REGISTER CO.
Feb. 5
1971
APOLLO 14

Sha'ar Hashem He-Chadash

Daniel Bomberg's "Miqra'ot Gedolot," BIB.003057, printed book, 1525–1526

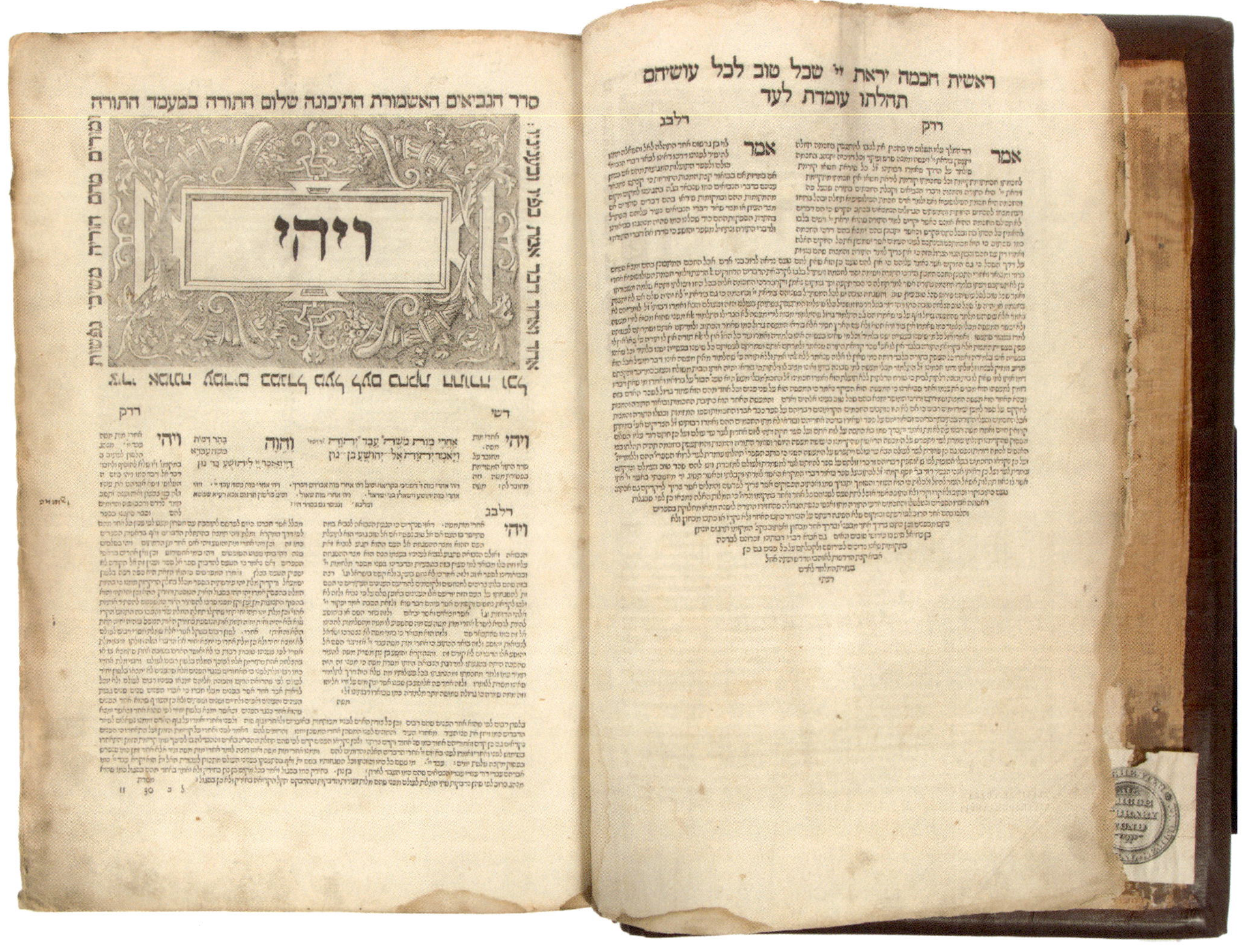

ABOVE: Joshua 1:1

FACING PAGE: Genesis 1:1

DANIEL BOMBERG WAS a Christian publisher from Antwerp who is best known for printing Hebrew texts. He established the first Hebrew press in Venice, where, in 1517, he published his first rabbinic Bible—a Bible with rabbinic commentaries printed around the biblical text. It was criticized for containing numerous errors. In response, Bomberg hired Jacob ben Chayyim, a Jewish scholar of the Masorah, to edit a second rabbinic Bible, represented here. Due to the efforts of Jacob ben Chayyim, this edition, known as a Miqra'ot Gedolot (Large Scriptures) because of the large size of the folio, became the first printed version of the Hebrew Bible to contain the entire Masorah along with the Tanakh, targumim, and rabbinic commentaries.

בית רבתי מאותיות גדולות דמשתמשי בהו דאינון א׳ אדם שת · ב׳ בראשית ברא · ג׳ והתגלח · ד׳ ״אחד · ה׳ הל״הגמלו · ו׳ של ויזתא · ז׳ זכרו תורת

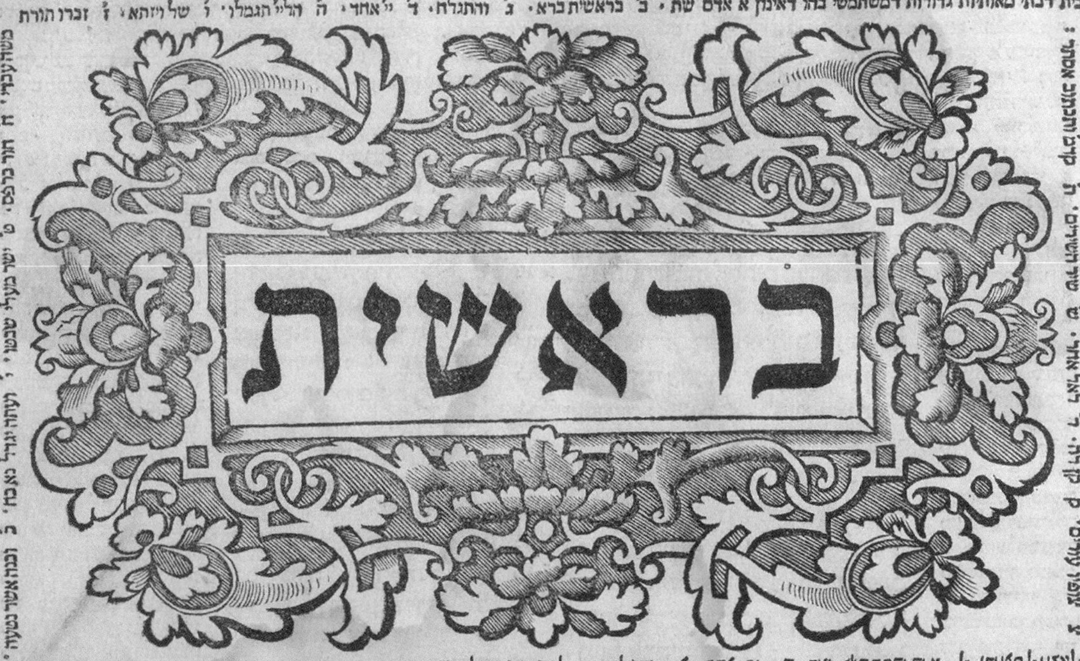

אמר ר׳ יצחק לא היה צריך להתחיל את התורה אלא מהחדש הזה לכם שהיא מצוה ראשונה שנצטוו ישראל ומה טעם פתח בבראשית משום כח

בְּרֵאשִׁית בָּרָא אֱלֹהִים אֵת הַשָּׁמַיִם וְאֵת הָאָרֶץ׃

בְּקַדְמִין בְּרָא יְיָ יָת שְׁמַיָּא וְיָת אַרְעָא׃

בראשית ה׳ ג׳ מנהון ר״פ וב׳ במצעו׳ וסי׳ בראשית ברא · בראשית ממלכו׳ יהויקים · בראשית ממלכת יהויקים · בראשית ממלכת צדקיה · בראשית מלכות צדקיה ׃ ברא אלהים ג׳ וסי׳ בראשית ברא אלהים · אשר ברא אלהים לעשות · למן היום אשר ברא · ואינון באורי׳ ׃ הארץ ג׳ ס״פ וכתריהון והארץ וסי׳ בראשית ברא · והארץ היתה תהו · אבלה נבלה הארץ · והארץ חנפה · והם יענו את הארץ · והארץ תענה׃

חכמינו אמרו שהב״ית כוסף

כב״ית בראשונה כי כמנהג ראשונה יקנו ולו היה טעמו כן היה הב״ית קמוץ בקמץ גדול ויש אומרים כי בראשית לעולם סמוך והטעם בראשית הערב או הלילה או החשך והנה

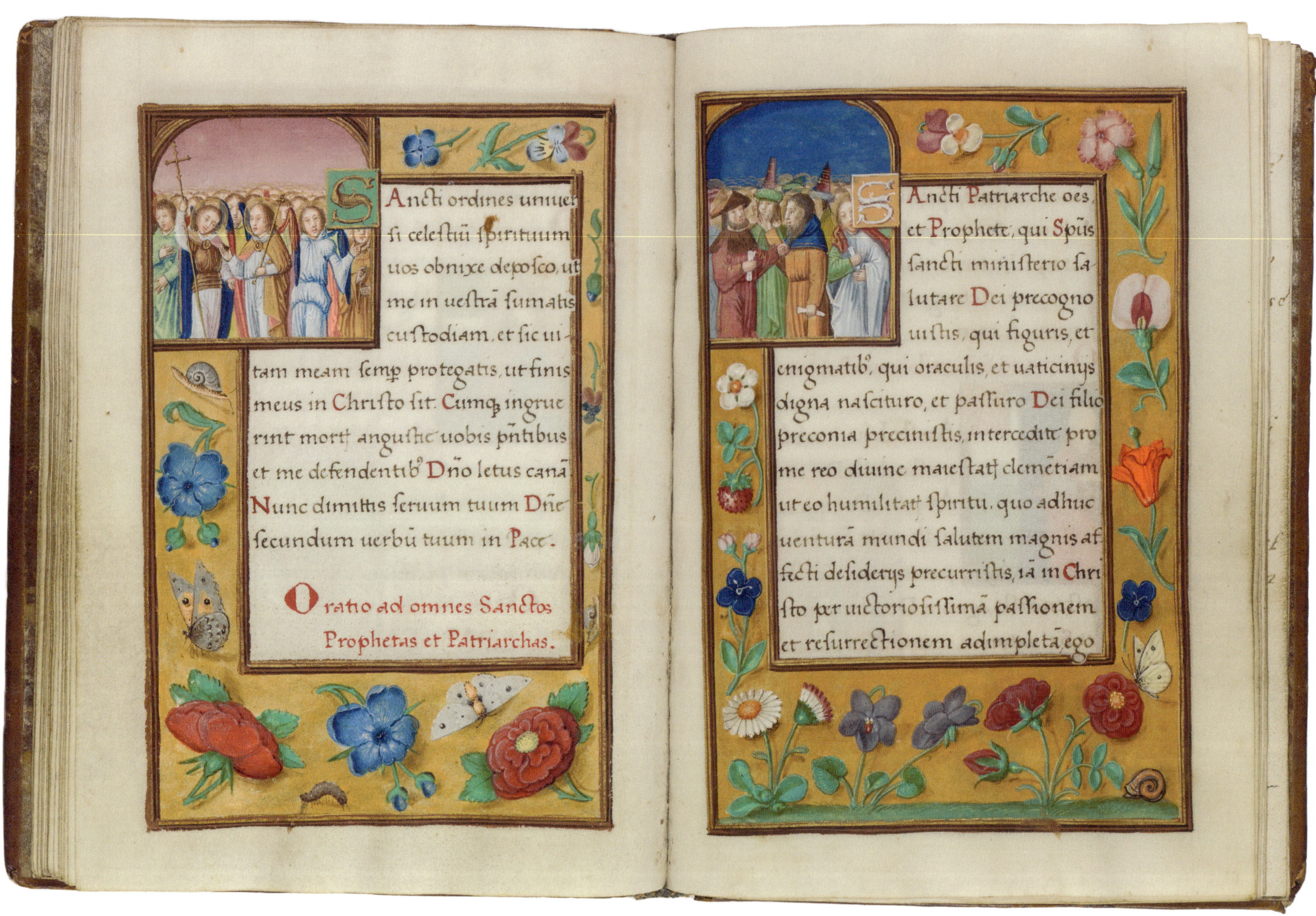
Sancti ordines uniuer
si celestiũ spirituum
uos obnixe deposco, ut
me in uestrã sumatis
custodiam, et sic ui
tam meam semp protegatis, ut finis
meus in Christo sit. Cumq; ingrue
rint mort angustie uobis p̃ntibus
et me defendentib Dño letus canã.
Nunc dimittis seruum tuum Dñe
secundum uerbũ tuum in Pace.

Oratio ad omnes Sanctos
Prophetas et Patriarchas.

Sancti Patriarche oes,
et Prophete, qui Spũs
sancti ministerio sa
lutare Dei precogno
uistis, qui figuris, et
enigmatib, qui oraculis, et uaticinijs
digna nascituro, et passuro Dei filio
preconia precinistis, intercedite pro
me reo diuine maiestat clemẽtiam
ut eo humilitat spiritu, quo adhuc
uenturã mundi salutem magnis af
fecti desiderijs precurristis, iã in Chri
sto per uictoriosissimã passionem
et resurrectionem adimpletã, ego

Prayer Book for Young Charles V

MS.000788, parchment codex, 1516–1519

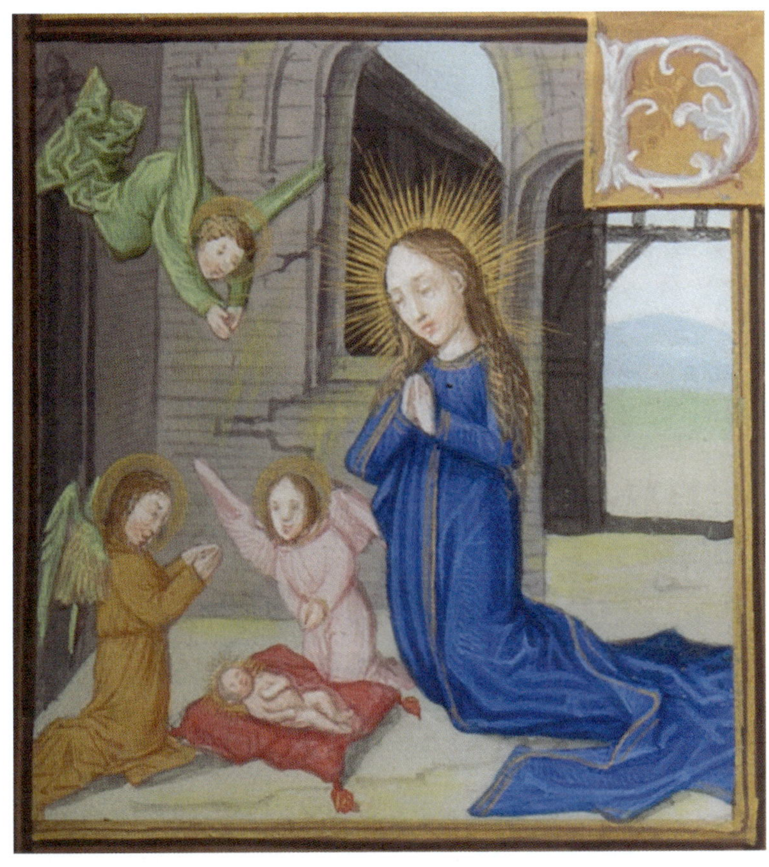

BASED ON THE coat of arms at the beginning of this small manuscript, it was made for the young Charles V (1500–1558) after he became king of Spain (1516) and shortly before his election as Holy Roman Emperor (1519). The Latin text contains common prayers in simple language written in two easy-to-read humanistic scripts suitable for a younger reader. The illuminations are in the style of Simon Bening (ca. 1483–1561), the Flemish master who shaped artistic tastes in the region surrounding Ghent and Bruges in the 16th century. The manuscript contains 36 pages decorated with images that stress self-sacrifice, humility, and devotion to the Catholic sacraments.

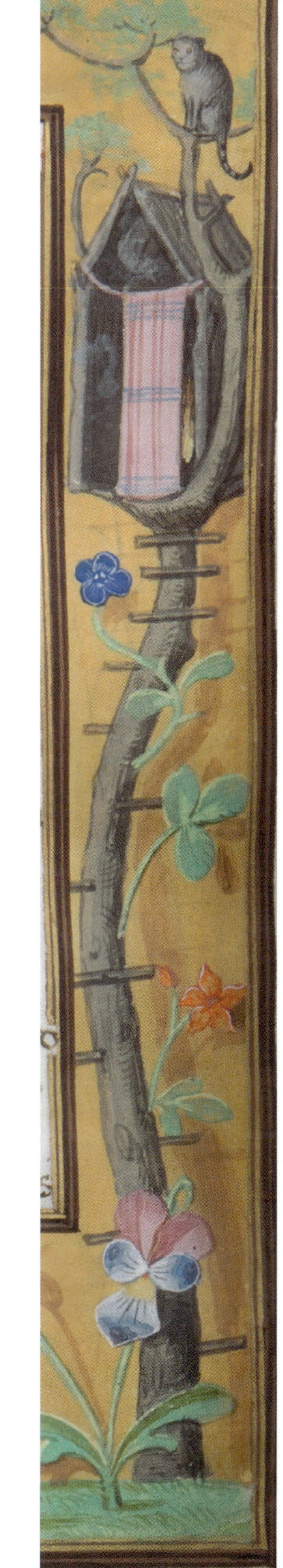

ABOVE: A miniature of the birth of Jesus.

RIGHT: Detail of a treehouse.

FACING PAGE: Bifolium with elaborate marginalia depicting flora and fauna in a style of art that was typical of the northern area of Brughes/Ghent.

The Washington Pentateuch

MS.000882, parchment codex, ca. 1000

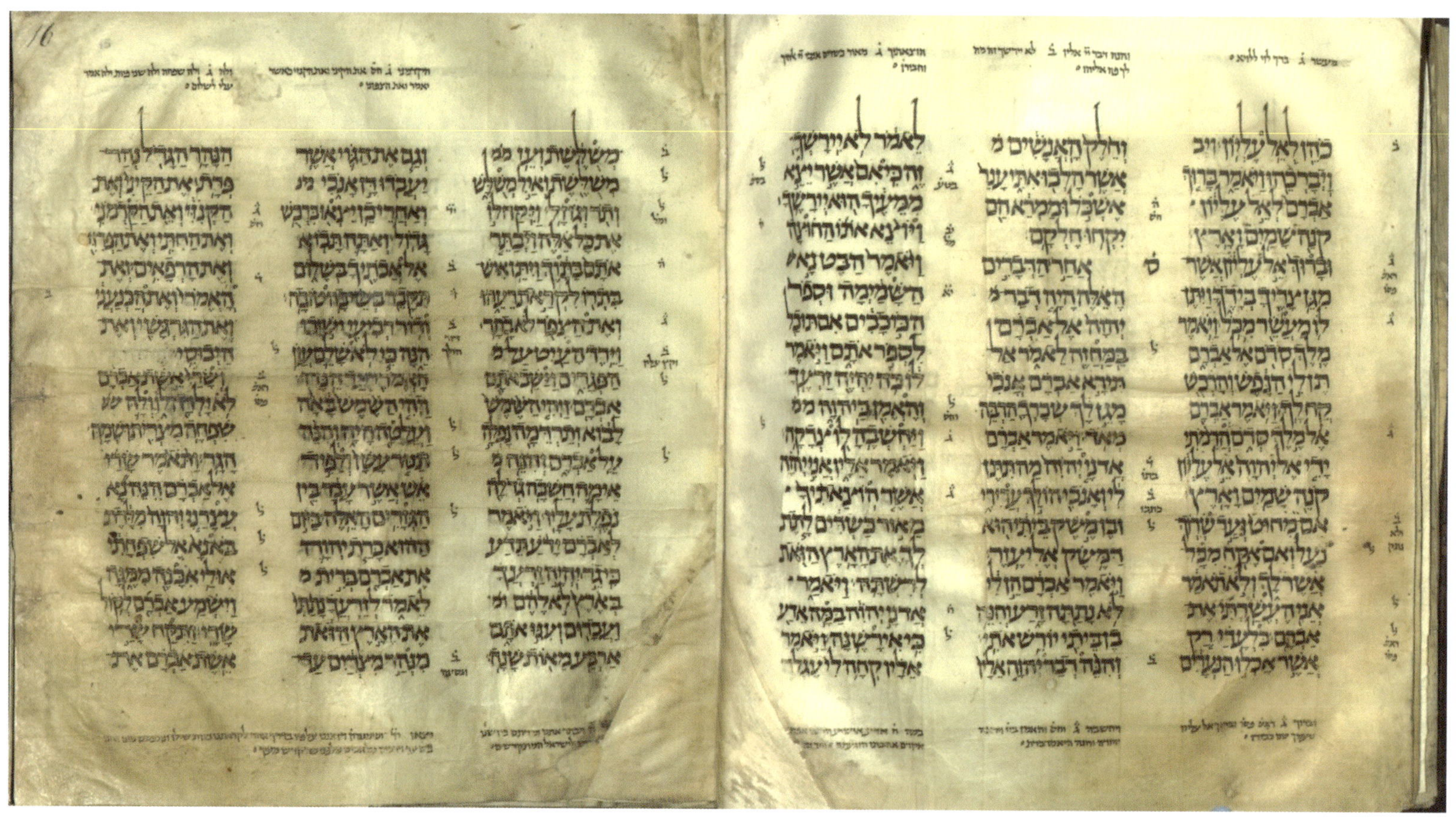

The Washington Pentateuch (WP) is one of the oldest, most-complete, Jewish Bible manuscripts in the United States. The manuscript was created around the year 1000, and it contains the entire Pentateuch—the "five books" from Genesis through Deuteronomy.

At some point, the final 10 folios were lost and replaced with folios from a different manuscript written in 1141 by the scribe Joseph ben Jacob, according to his colophon on f. 245r. Though these few pages connect to medieval Egypt, the majority of the manuscript may be associated with Tiberias, based on its writing style and use of the Tiberian Masoretic system.

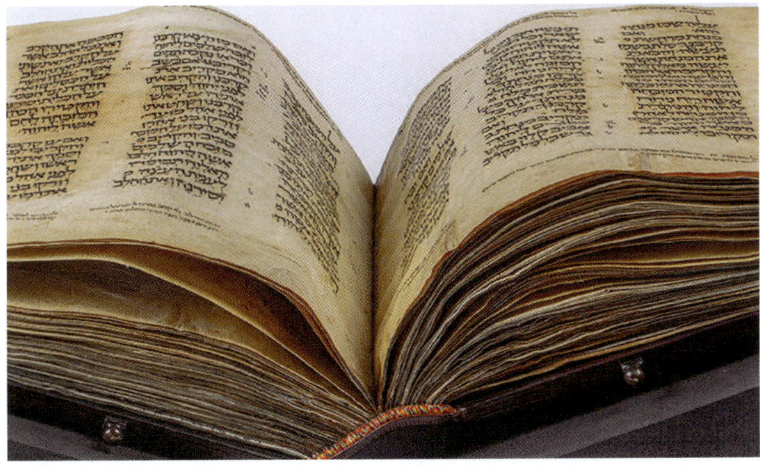

Iconic manuscripts like the WP are often called Masoretic Bibles because they contain the masorah (a vast system of annotations) and were created during or near the Masoretic era (AD 700–1000). Indeed, some scholars suggest that the WP might have a direct link to another famous Masoretic manuscript—Codex Cairo of the Prophets. Further research is needed, however, to confirm or deny this proposition.

Above: Detail of the Washington Pentateuch.

Facing Page: Bifolium containing the masorah and six columns of text.

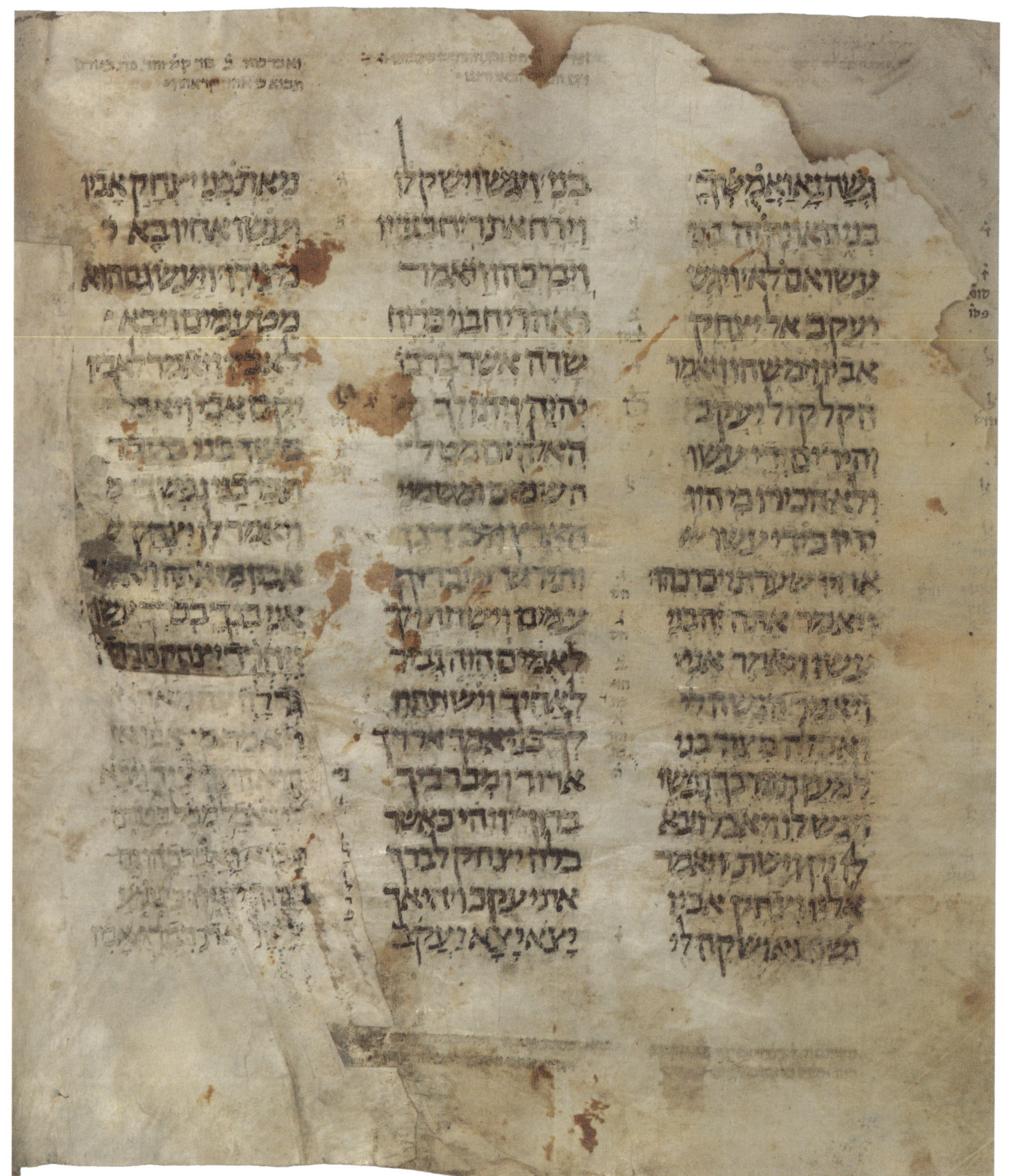

Single page of the Washington Pentateuch imaged with visible light and two forms of multispectral light.

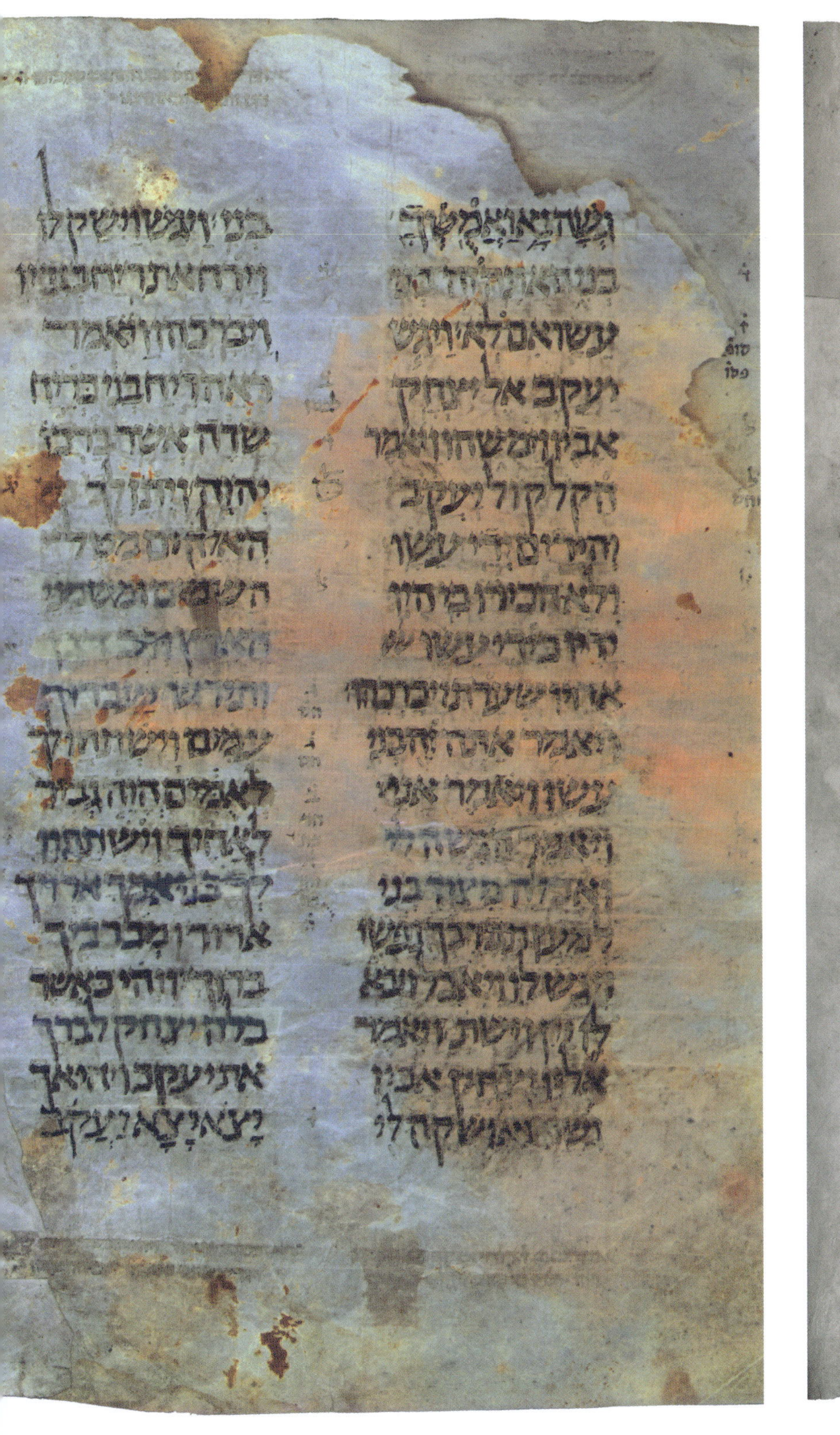

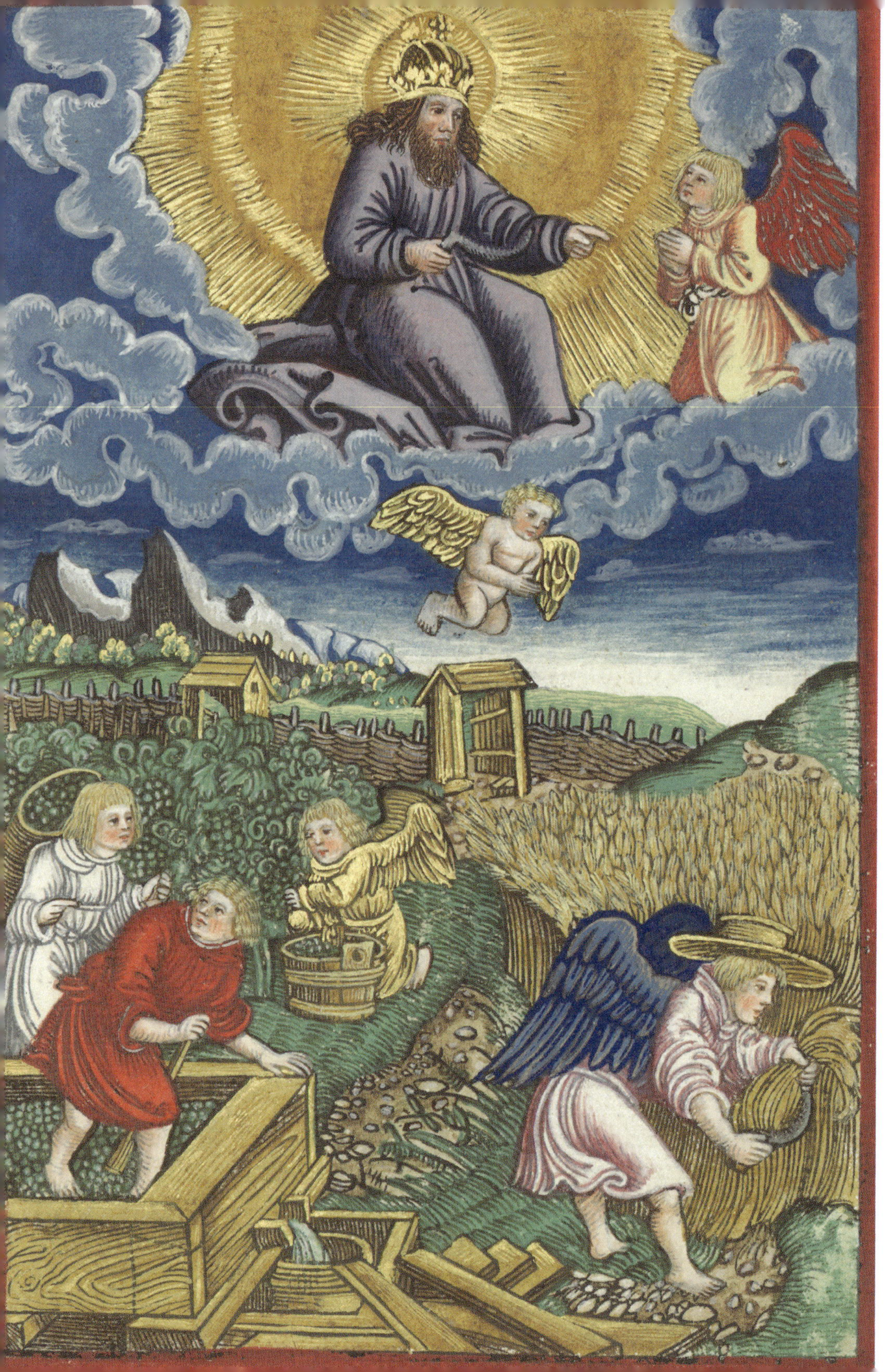

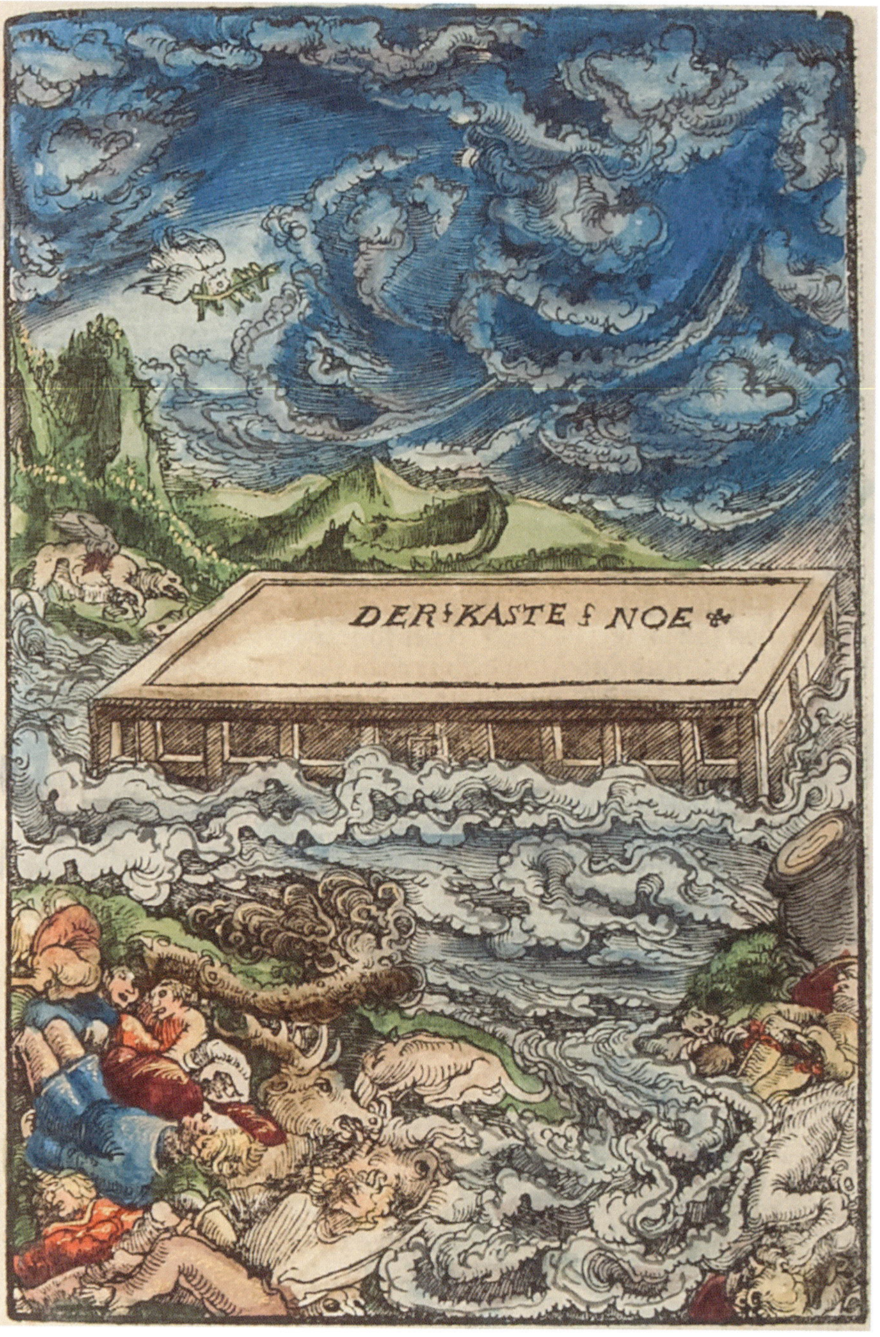

Above: 'Noah's Ark,' woodcut by Georg Lotter.

Left: 'Angels Tending the Fields,' woodcut by Georg Lotter.

Luther's Pentateuch

BIB.003838, printed book, 1524

MARTIN LUTHER PUBLISHED his initial Old Testament translation in parts. He completed the first portion, consisting of the first five books of the Bible, in 1523 under the title Das Alte Testament Deutsch. This 1524 edition was printed by Melchior Lotter in Wittenberg, Germany. It contains thirteen brilliantly colored illustrations made from woodcuts by Georg Lemberger, some in what is known as Fürstenkolorit. In this type of illumination, the woodcuts are colored and heightened with gold, suggesting this Bible was created for an aristocrat. Only ten copies of this edition are known to exist. Moreover, 16th-century prints showing Fürstenkolorit are extremely rare.

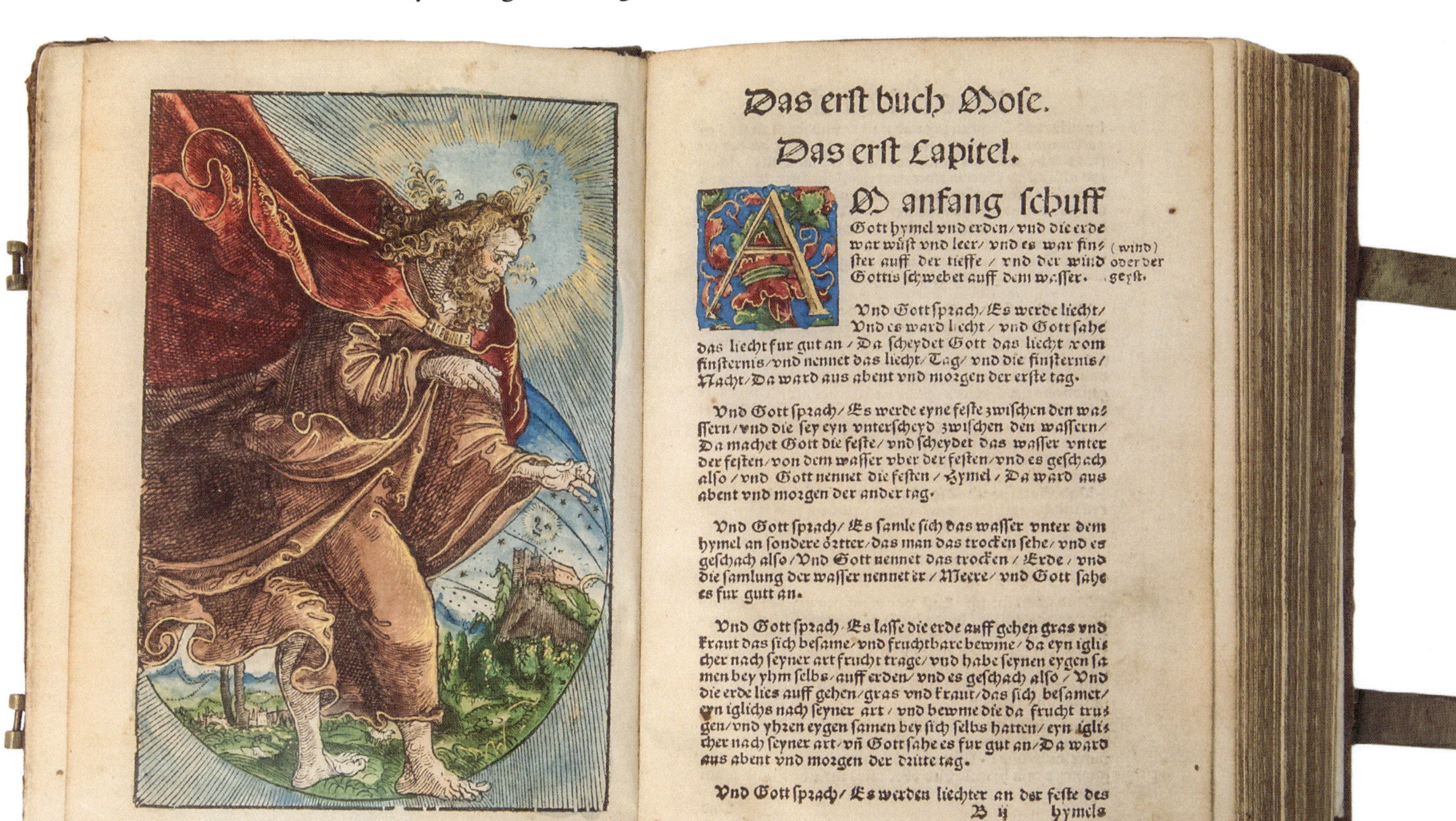

'Creation' woodcut by Georg Lotter, Genesis 1:1.

The Lipnice Bible

MS.000486, parchment codex, 1421

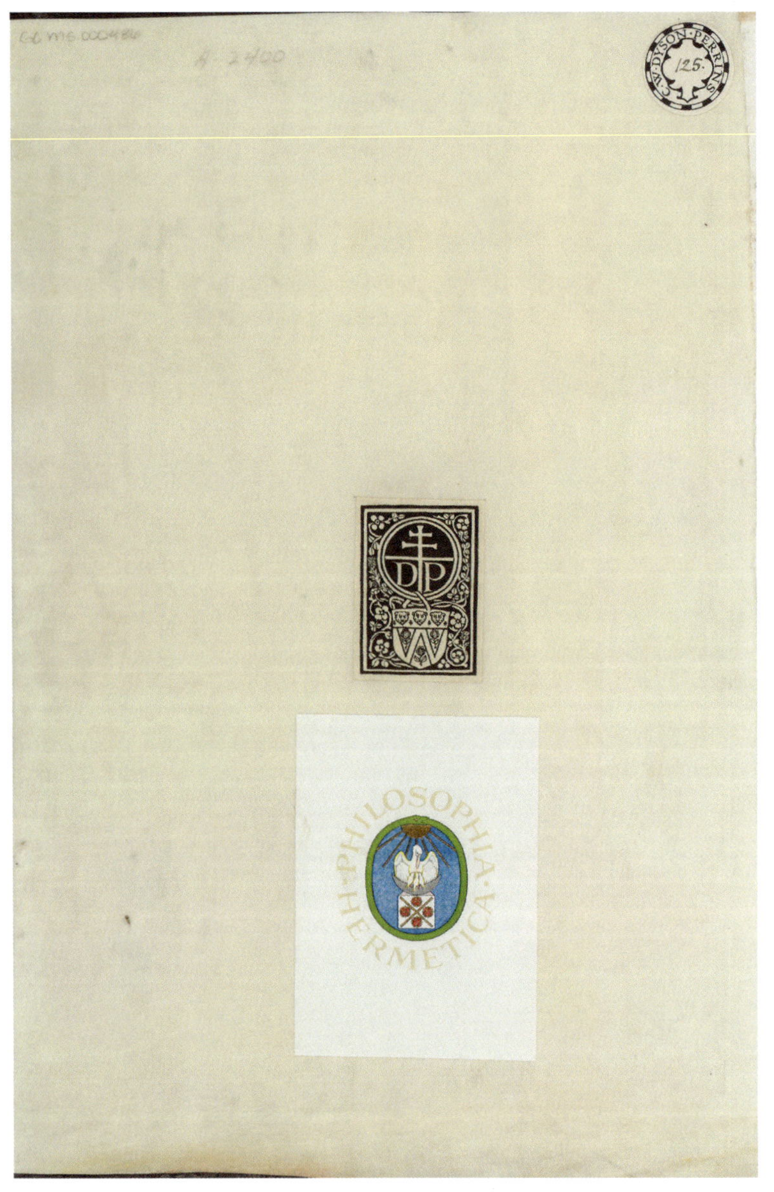

THE SCRIBE MATTHIAS of Raudnitz produced this Bible during the early chaos of the Hussite wars in Bohemia, completing it in 1421 according to the colophons. The manuscript's text is written in a single, clear hand with capitals highlighted in red or yellow. There are red annotations in the margins throughout, citing parallel passages and sources for quotations. Matthias wrote his first colophon in burnished gold. The manuscript contains ninety large initials in a variety of colors, including the capital I at the beginning of Genesis, which contains a cameo-like painting of God holding the world. The manuscript retains its original binding.

LEFT: Front pastedown with Dyson Perrins and Bibliotheca Philosophia Hermetica bookplates.

FACING PAGE: Bifolium with extensive rubrication and illustrated capitals.

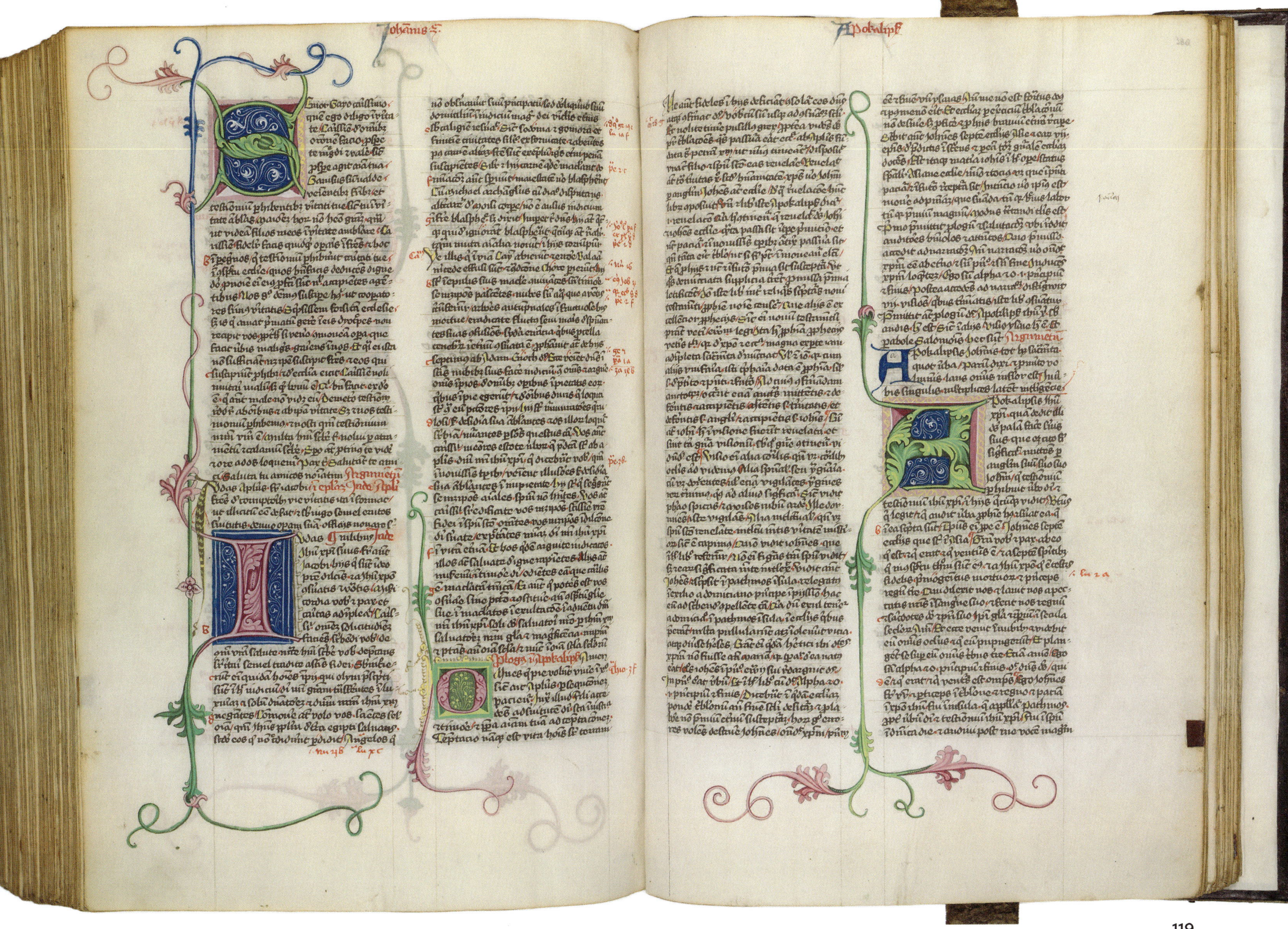

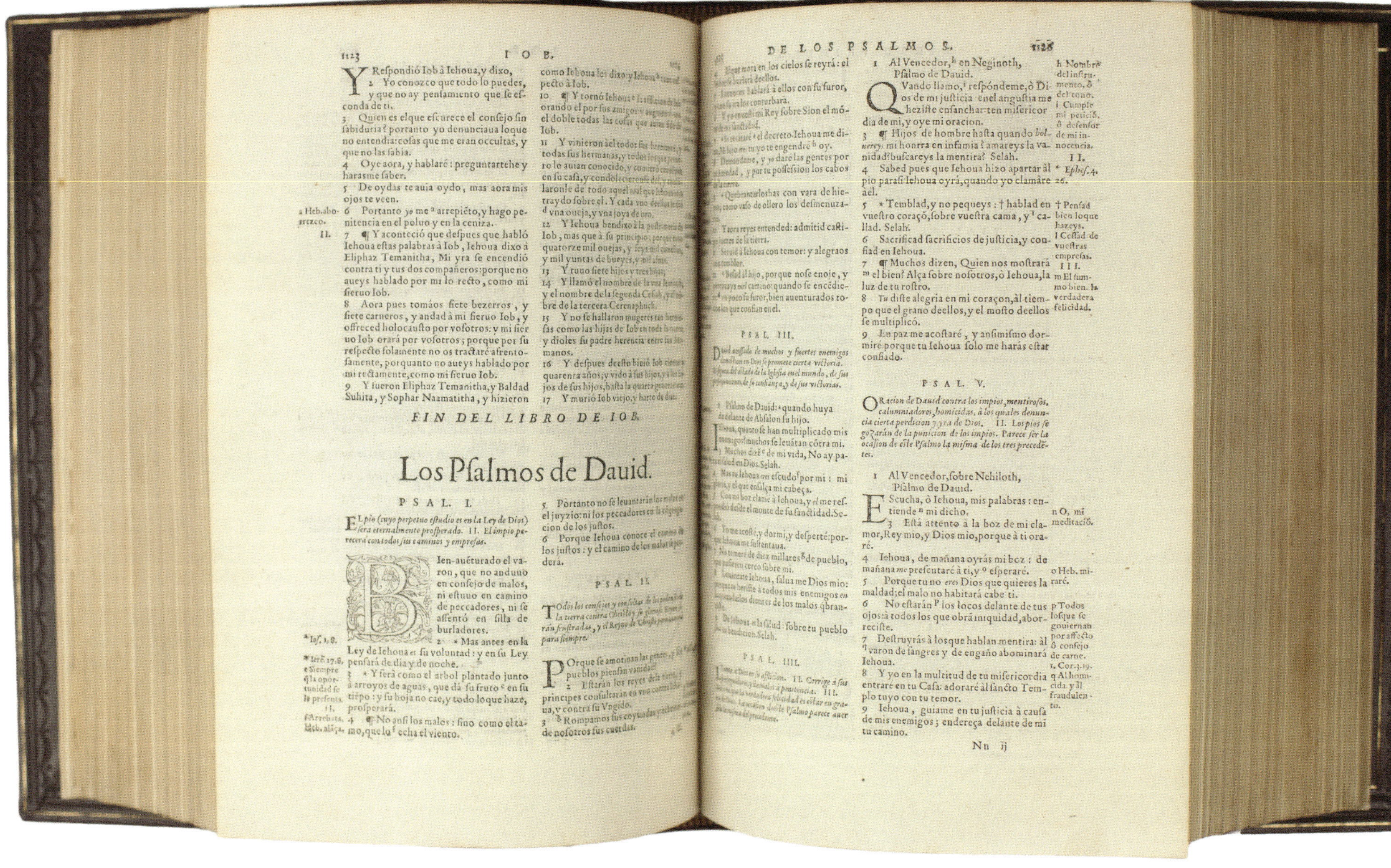
1123 IOB.

Y Respondió Iob à Iehoua, y dixo,
2 Yo conozco que todo lo puedes, y que no ay pensamiento que se esconda de ti.
3 Quien es el que escurece el consejo sin sabiduria? portanto yo denunciaua lo que no entendia: cosas que me eran occultas, y que no las sabia.
4 Oye aora, y hablaré: preguntartehe y harasme saber.
5 De oydas te auia oydo, mas aora mis ojos te veen.
6 Portanto yo me a arrepiéto, y hago penitencia en el poluo y en la ceniza.
7 ¶ Y aconteció que despues que habló Iehoua estas palabras à Iob, Iehoua dixo à Eliphaz Temanitha, Mi yra se encendió contra ti y tus dos compañeros: porque no aueys hablado por mi lo recto, como mi sieruo Iob.
8 Aora pues tomáos siete bezerros, y siete carneros, y andad à mi sieruo Iob, y offreced holocausto por vosotros: y mi sieruo Iob orará por vosotros; porque por su respecto solamente no os tractaré afrentosamente, porquanto no aueys hablado por mi rectamente, como mi sieruo Iob.
9 Y fueron Eliphaz Temanitha, y Baldad Suhita, y Sophar Naamatitha, y hizieron

FIN DEL LIBRO DE IOB.

Los Psalmos de Dauid.

PSAL. I.

El pio (cuyo perpetuo estudio es en la Ley de Dios) será eternalmente prosperado. II. El impio perecerá con todos sus caminos y empresas.

Bien-auéturado el varon, que no anduuo en consejo de malos, ni estuuo en camino de peccadores, ni se assentó en silla de burladores.
2 * Mas antes en la Ley de Iehoua es su voluntad: y en su Ley pensará de dia y de noche.
3 * Y será como el arbol plantado junto à arroyos de aguas, que dá su fruto en su tiépo: y su hoja no cae, y todo lo que haze, prosperará.
4 ¶ No ansi los malos: sino como el tamo, que lo echa el viento.

DE LOS PSALMOS. 1128

1 Al Vencedor, en Neginoth, Psalmo de Dauid.
Quando llamo, respóndeme, ô Dios de mi justicia: en el angustia me heziste ensanchar: ten misericor dia de mi, y oye mi oracion.
3 ¶ Hijos de hombre hasta quando boluereys mi honrra en infamia? amareys la vanidad? buscareys la mentira? Selah.
4 Sabed pues que Iehoua hizo apartar al pio para si: Iehoua oyrá, quando yo clamáre à él.
5 * Temblad, y no pequeys: † hablad en vuestro coraço, sobre vuestra cama, y callad. Selah.
6 Sacrificad sacrificios de justicia, y confiad en Iehoua.
7 ¶ Muchos dizen, Quien nos mostrará el bien? Alça sobre nosotros, ô Iehoua, la luz de tu rostro.
8 Tu diste alegria en mi coraçon, al tiempo que el grano dellos, y el mosto dellos se multiplicó.
9 En paz me acostaré, y ansimismo dormiré: porque tu Iehoua solo me harás estar confiado.

PSAL. V.

Oracion de Dauid contra los impios, mentirosos, calumniadores, homicidas, à los quales denuncia cierta perdicion y yra de Dios. II. Los pios se gozarán de la punicion de los impios.

1 Al Vencedor, sobre Nehiloth, Psalmo de Dauid.
Escucha, ô Iehoua, mis palabras: entiende mi dicho.
3 Está attento à la boz de mi clamor, Rey mio, y Dios mio, porque à ti oraré.
4 Iehoua, de mañana oyrás mi boz: de mañana me presentaré à ti, y esperaré.
5 Porque tu no eres Dios que quieres la maldad; el malo no habitará cabe ti.
6 No estarán los locos delante de tus ojos: à todos los que obrá iniquidad, aborreciste.
7 Destruyrás à los que hablan mentira: al varon de sangres y de engaño abominará Iehoua.
8 Y yo en la multitud de tu misericordia entraré en tu Casa: adoraré al sancto Templo tuyo con tu temor.
9 Iehoua, guiame en tu justicia à causa de mis enemigos; endereça delante de mi tu camino.

Nn ij

End of Job, Psalms 1–5.

Bible of the Bear

BIB.001153, printed book, 1569

IN 1569, PRINTER Thomas Guarinus published the first complete Spanish Bible in Basel, Switzerland. It's often called the Biblia del Oso, or "Bible of the Bear," because of the printer's emblem on the title page, which shows a bear grasping for honey in the trunk of a tree. It was translated by the Spanish Reformer Casiodoro de Reina (1520–1594). For the Old Testament, he may have used earlier translations, but he compared them against Hebrew and Latin editions. The New Testament is based on Erasmus's editions of the Greek texts. De Reina's Bible was eventually revised by another Protestant Reformer, Cipriano de Valera, and published in 1602.

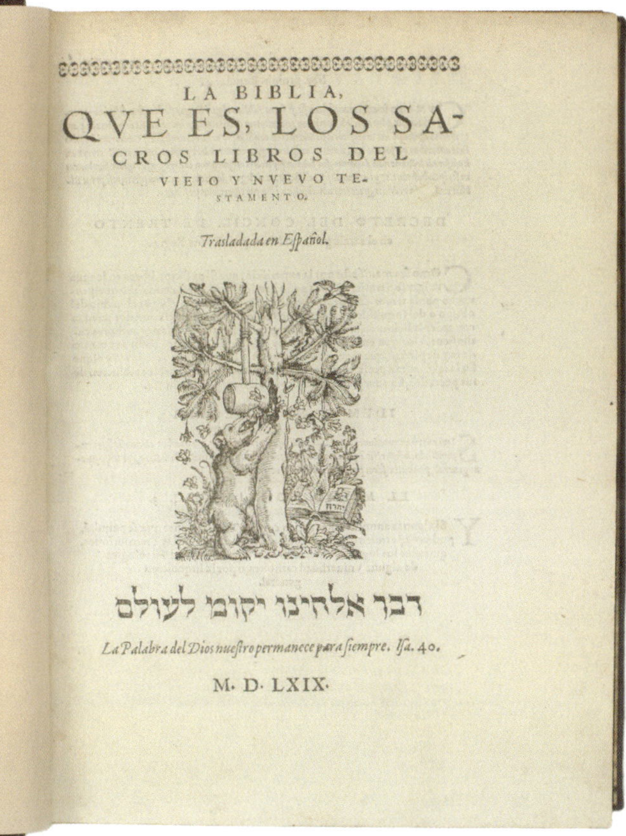

LA BIBLIA,
QVE ES, LOS SA-
CROS LIBROS DEL
VIEIO Y NVEVO TE-
STAMENTO.
Trasladada en Español.

דבר אלהינו יקום לעולם
La Palabra del Dios nuestro permanece para siempre. Isa. 40.
M. D. LXIX.

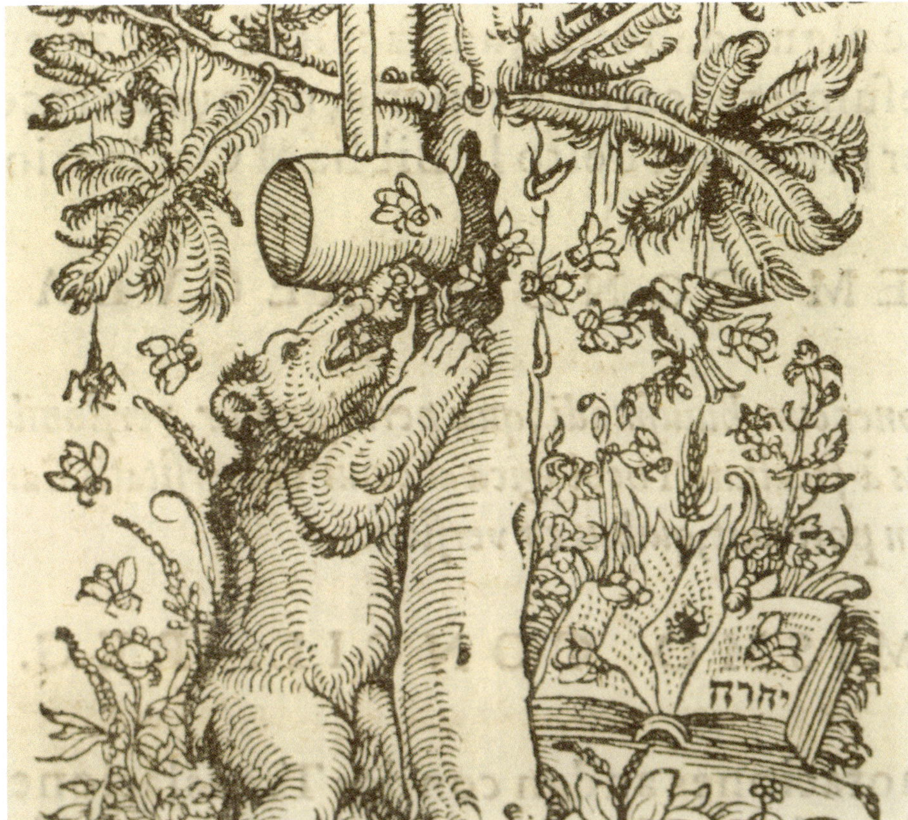

LEFT: Title page with bear woodcut.

RIGHT: Enlargement of title page woodcut featuring a bear.

Bodmer Psalms (P.Bodmer XXIV, Rahlfs 2110)

MS.000170.1-.49, papyrus codex, ca. 225–325

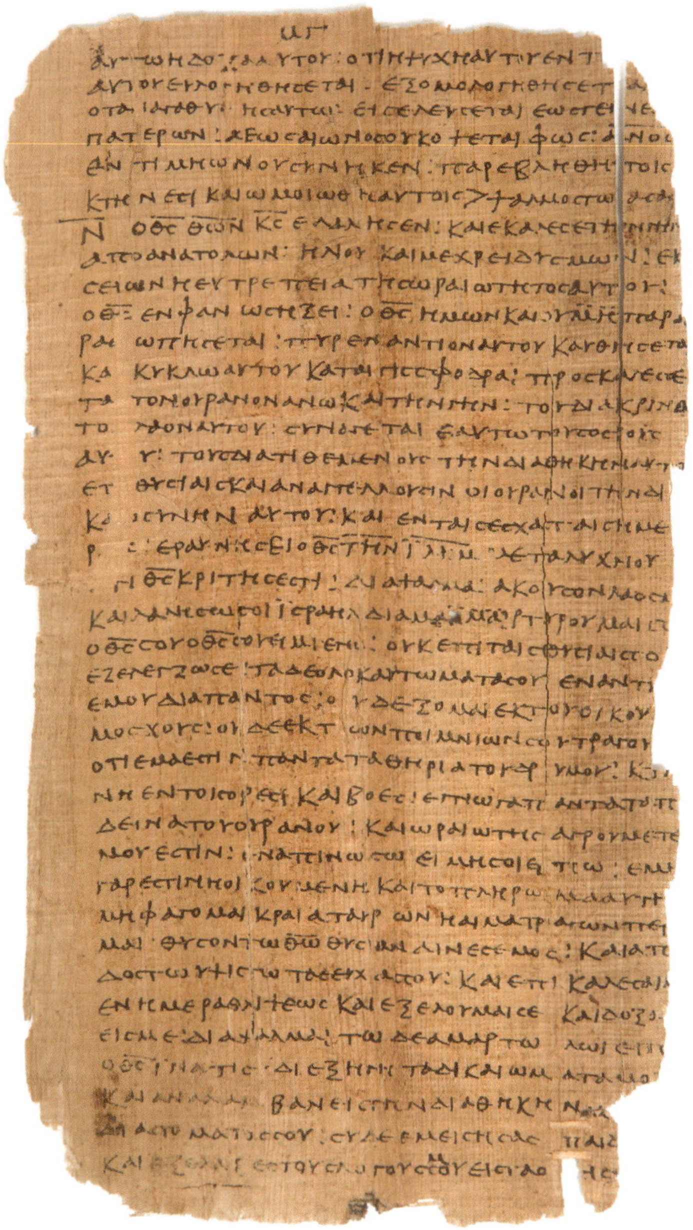

This papyrus codex originally contained approximately 84 leaves (168 pages) of an ancient Psalter. More than half of the codex survives, preserving most of Psalms 17:45–118:44 in Greek (18:44–119:44 in most English versions). All 49 surviving leaves (98 pages) are in Museum of the Bible's collection. The text was written by two different scribes whose handwriting differed noticeably in size, so the amount of text varies from 33 to 44 lines per page. This manuscript takes its name from Martin Bodmer, a Swiss collector, who purchased the manuscript in the 1950s.

Left: Recto (or front) side of a single leaf with page number 43 (Mu Gamma) and the beginning of Psalm 50 (Greek Nu).

Facing Page: Codex (or book) inspired display of 5 pages of the Bodmer Psalms on Museum of the Bible's History Floor.

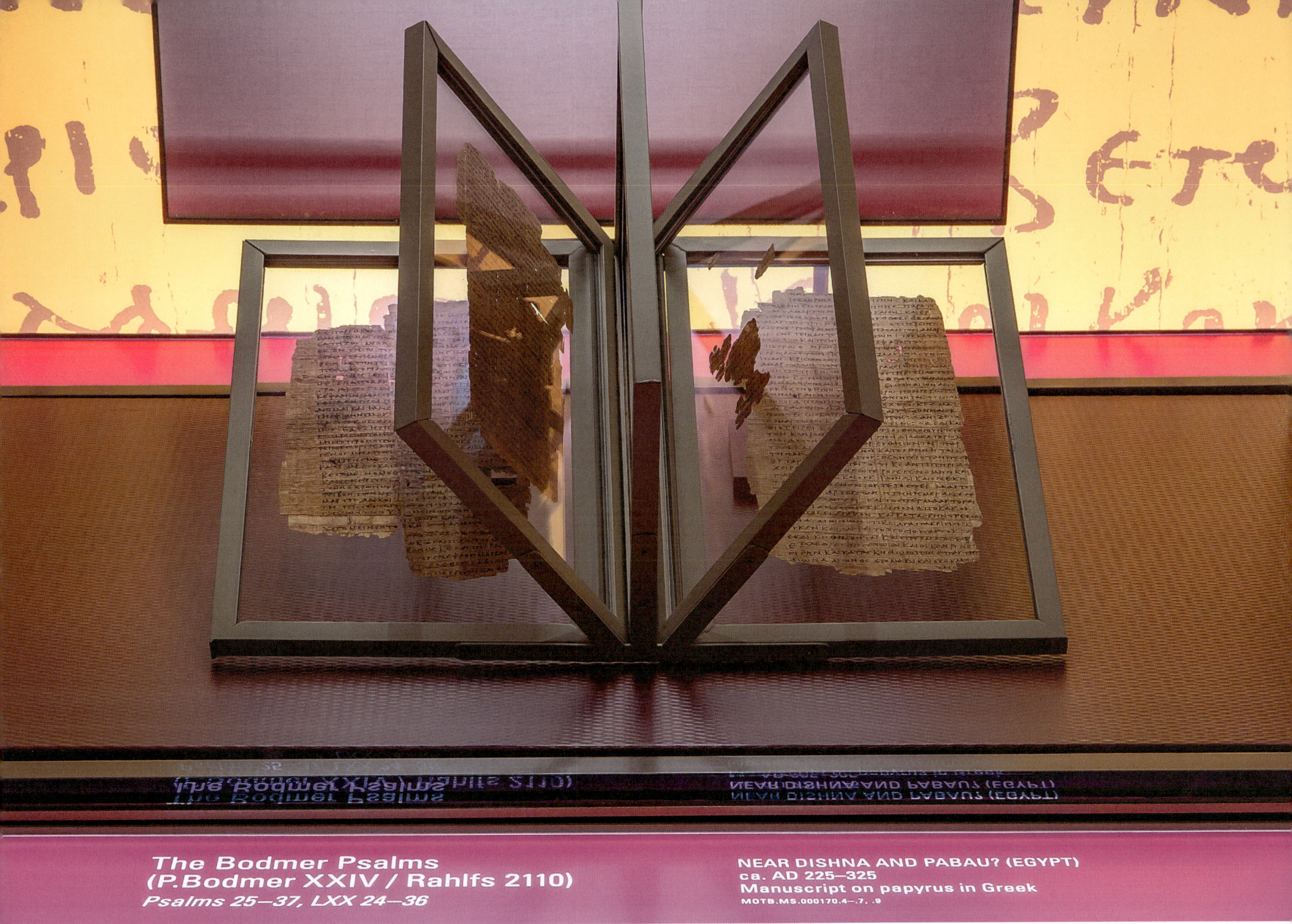
The Bodmer Psalms
(P.Bodmer XXIV / Rahlfs 2110)
Psalms 25–37, LXX 24–36
NEAR DISHNA AND PABAU? (EGYPT)
ca. AD 225–325
Manuscript on papyrus in Greek
MOTB.MS.000170.4–.7, .9

The manuscript was created around the third- to fourth centuries AD in Egypt and later discovered in 1952. Albert Pietersma states in his article, "Bodmer Papyri," in *The Anchor Bible Dictionary* (Doubleday, 1992), that the place of discovery is believed to have been "Pabau, (near Dishna), the ancient headquarters of the Pachomian order of monks."

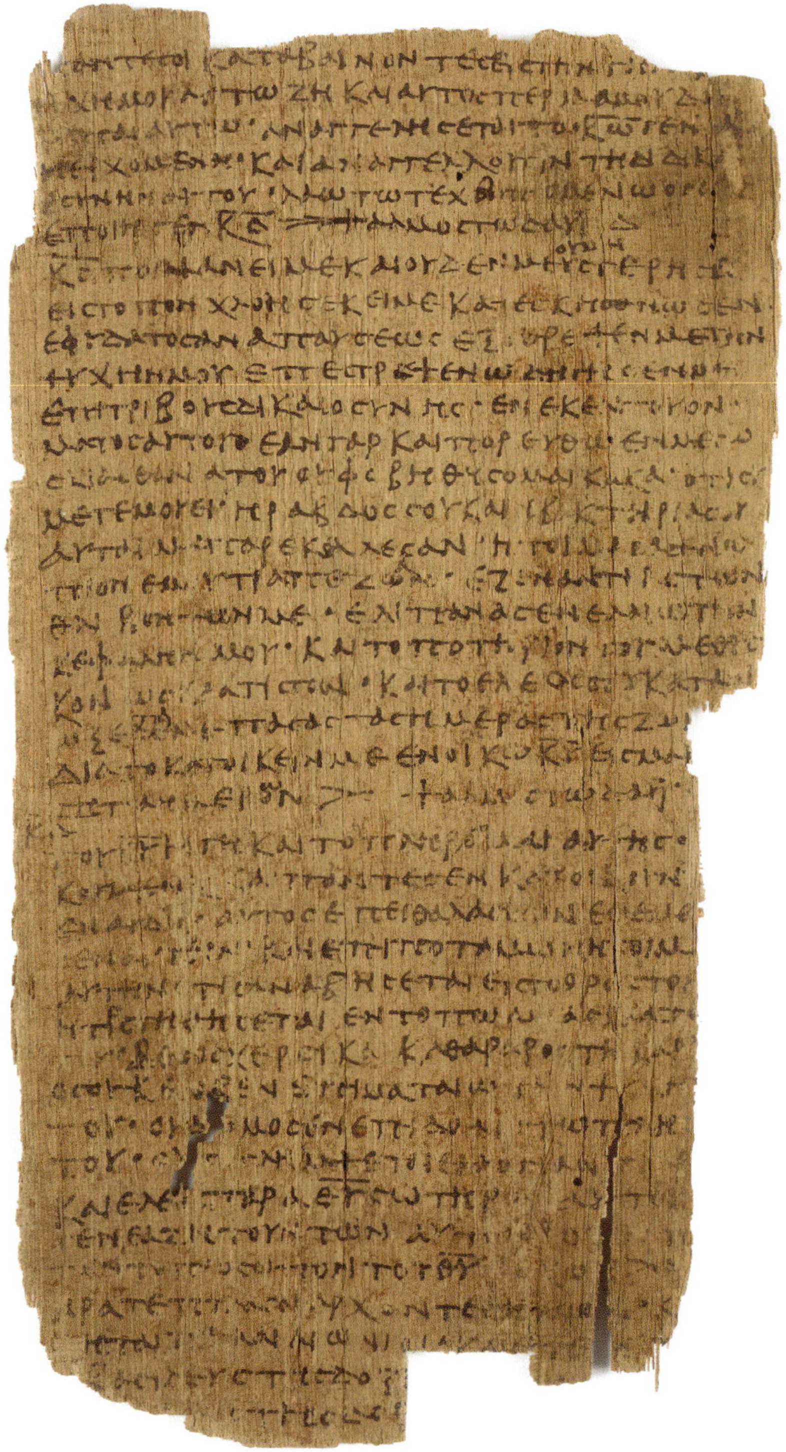

Recto (or front) side of a single leaf containing the beginning of Psalm 24.

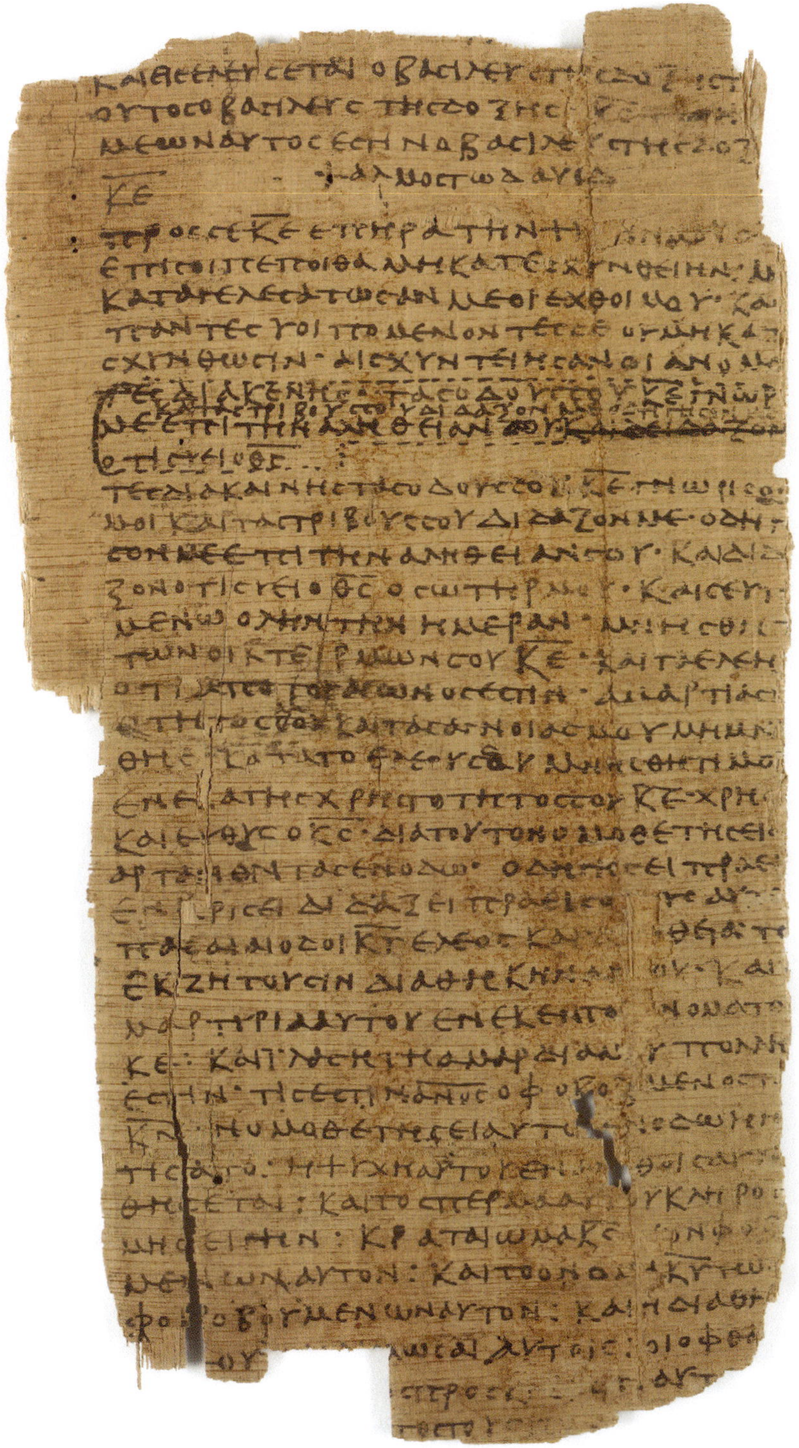

On the back of this page there is a noticeable scribal error. The scribe accidentally skipped a line while transcribing and attempted to squeeze the extra line in-between. He did not like the end result so he drew a box around the whole area and started again.

Verso (or back) side of the same leaf containing the beginning of Psalm 25.

Complutensian Polyglot Bible

BIB.001428, printed book, 1514, 1515, 1517

Initiated and financed by Cardinal Francisco Jiménez de Cisneros (1436–1517), the Complutensian Polyglot Bible became the first printed polyglot of the entire Bible. This edition presented text in Hebrew, Aramaic, Greek, and Latin in six volumes. The Old Testament (vols. 1–4) has text in Hebrew, Latin, and Greek, plus an interlinear Latin translation in parallel columns. At the bottom of each page of the Torah is Targum Onkelos, the standard Aramaic translation of the Torah. The New Testament (vol. 5) has the Greek text in a column on the left side of the page and the Latin text in a column on the right side. Volume 6 contains the appendix.

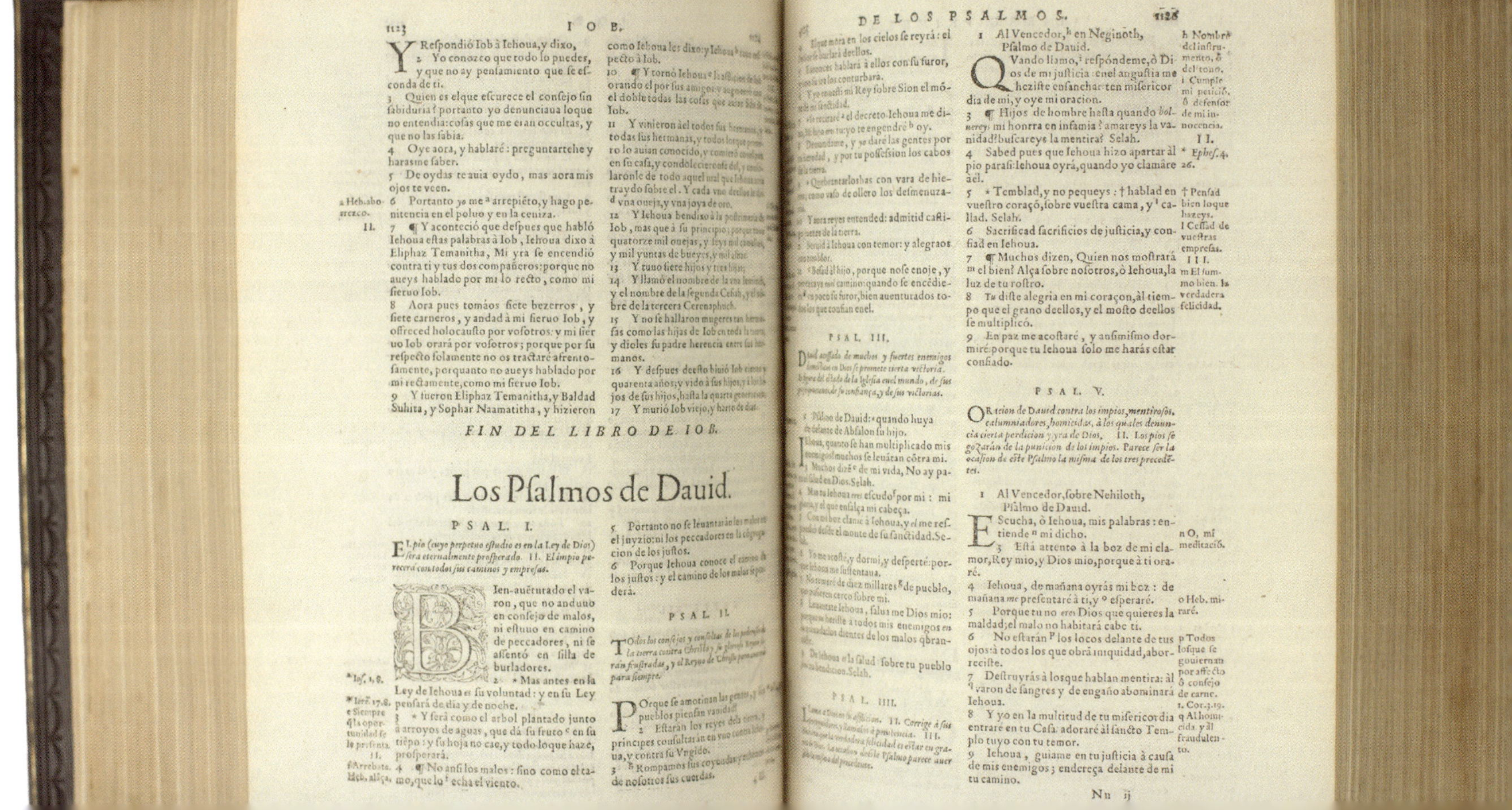

Facing page: The title page for the third volume of the Old Testament, announcing the first publication of the Greek and Hebrew texts paralleled with a Latin translation.

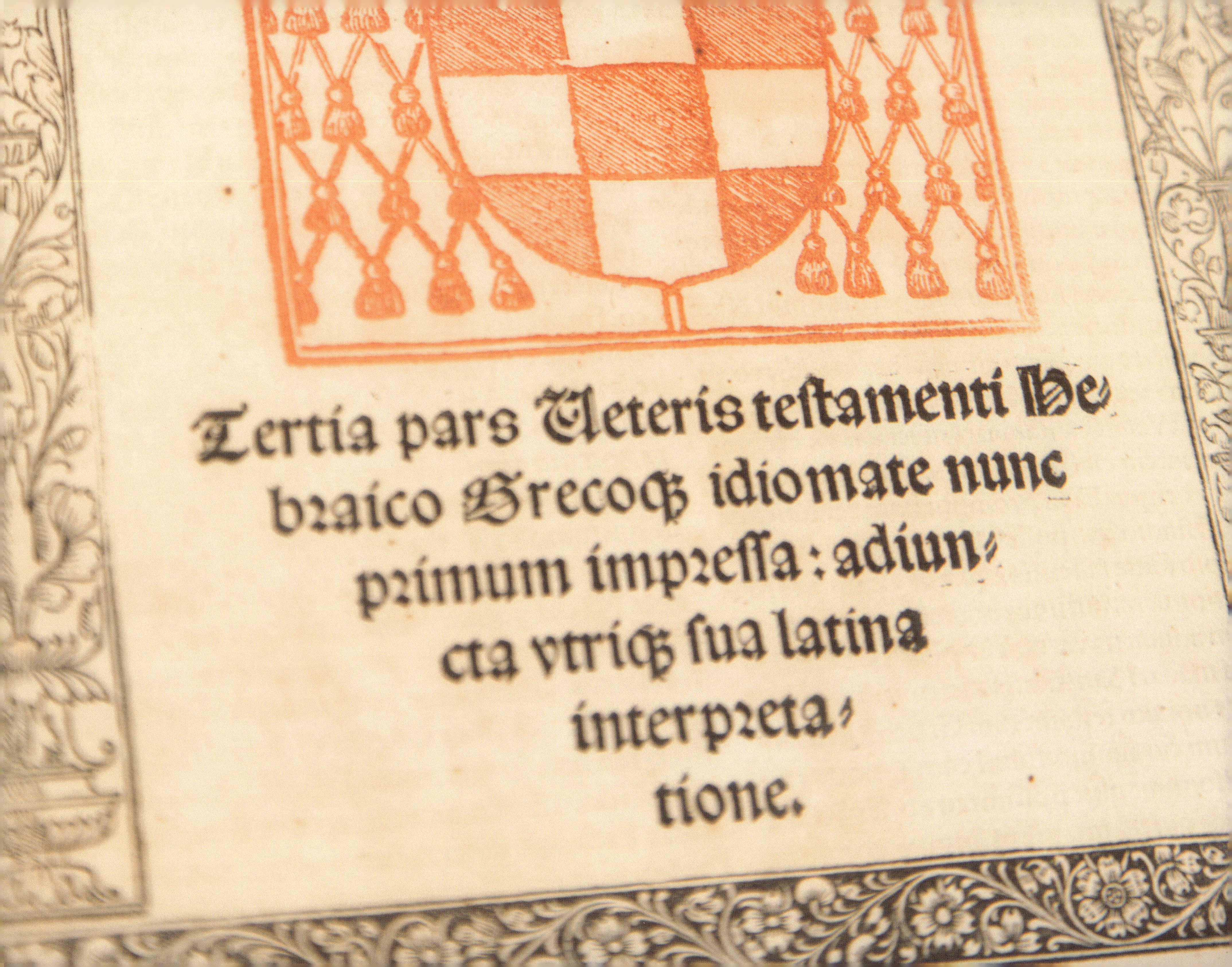
Tertia pars Ueteris testamenti He-
braico Grecoq; idiomate nunc
primum impressa: adiun-
cta vtriq; sua latina
interpreta-
tione.

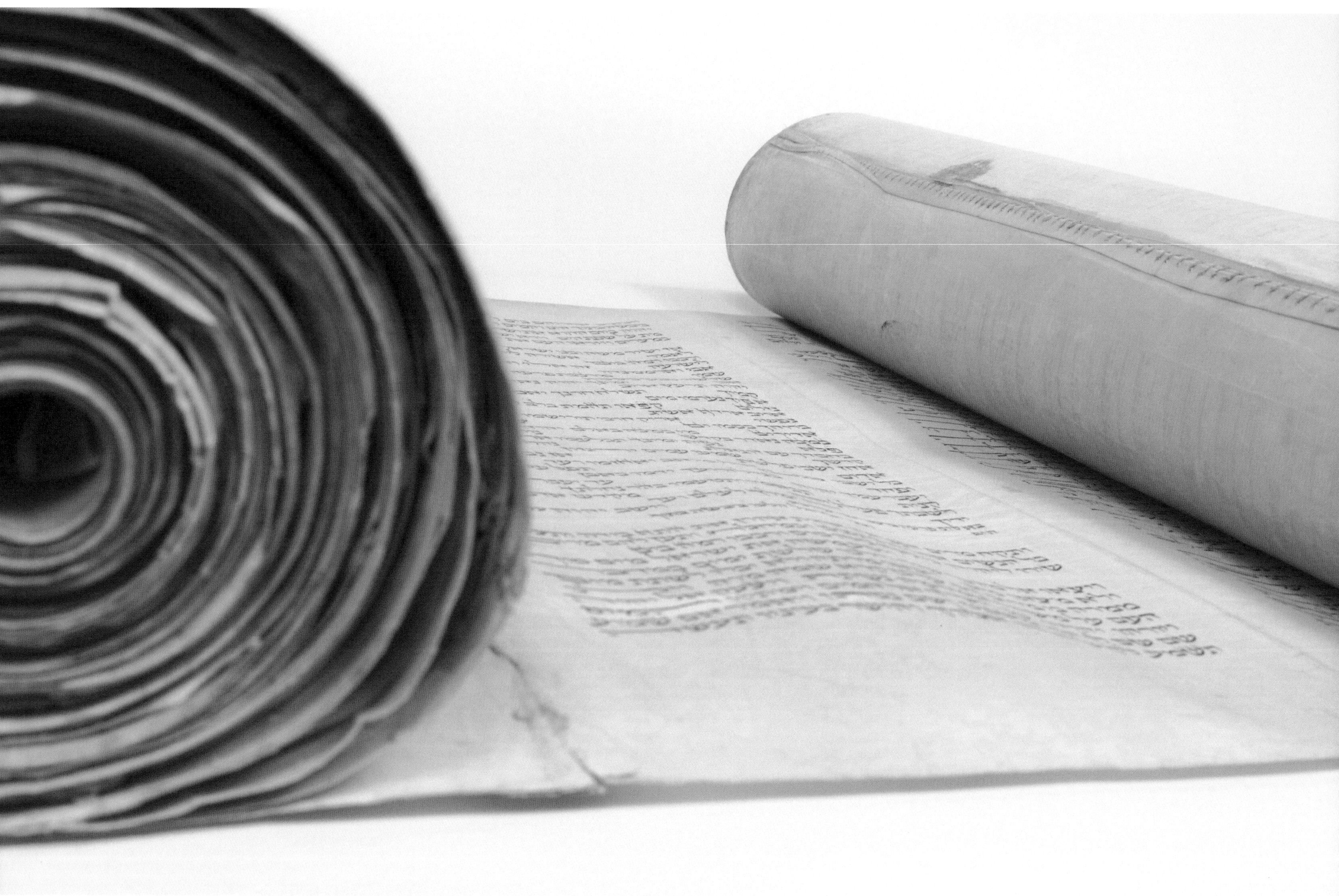

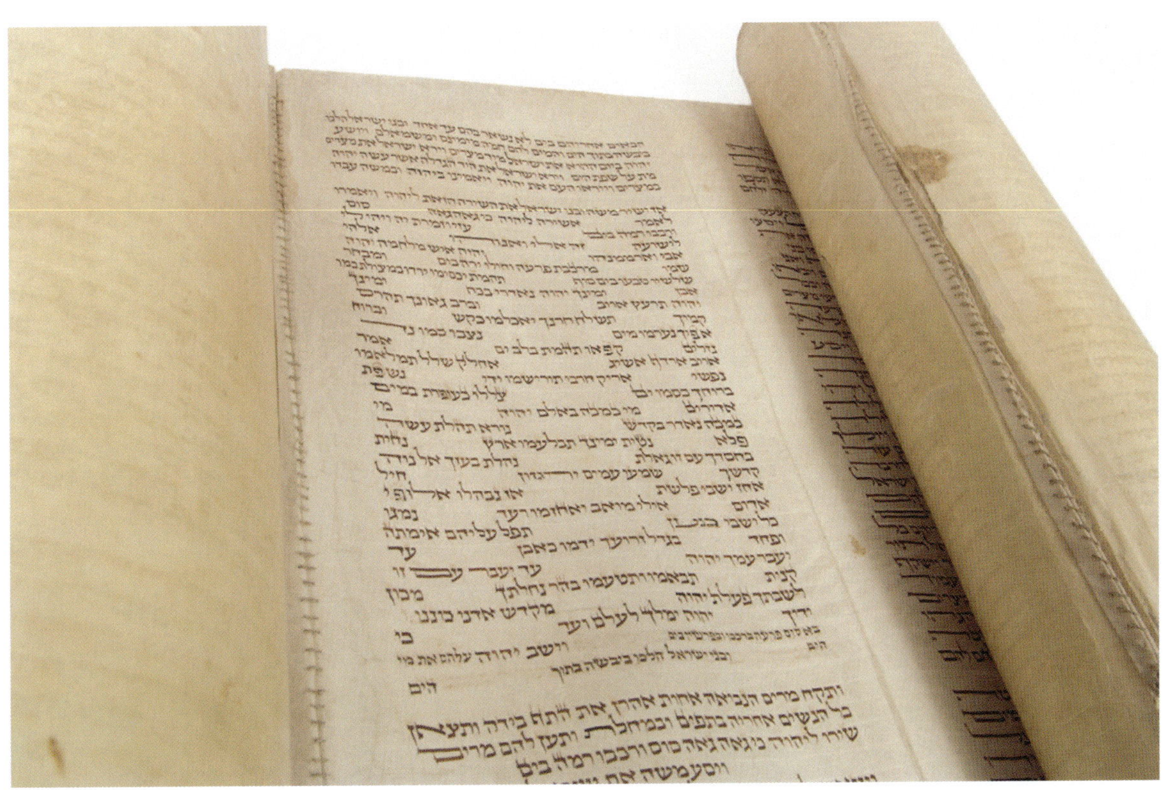

Facing page and left: Detail image of The Song of the Sea found in Exodus 15:1-18.

Medieval Ashkenazic Torah Scroll

SCR.004820, parchment scroll, ca. 1250

This beautiful scroll is one of the oldest, most complete Torah scrolls from the Ashkenazi Jewish tradition of central Europe. Its early medieval Ashkenazi origin is visible both in the ancient sewing technique used to attach the parchments and in its writing style. During later periods, portions of the script and layout were edited to adhere more closely to the teachings of Maimonides. These revisions are particularly noticeable in the Song of the Sea (Exodus 15:1–18), though fortunately the original layout is still discernible.

in to alle folkes. biginnynge at ierlm/
& ȝe ben witnesses of þese þinges: &
I schal sende þe bihest of my fadir
in to ȝou/ but sitte ȝe in þe citee: til
þat ȝe be cloþed wiþ vertu fro an
hiȝ/ & he led hem forþ in to bethanye
& wiþ his hondes weren lift up:
he blessed hem/ & it was don þe whi
le he blessed hem: he departed fro hem
& was born in to heuene/ & þei wir
schipiden & wenten aȝen in to ierlm
wiþ greet ioie. & weren euer more
in þe temple/ heriynge & blessinge god

Here endiþ luykis gospel: & here
bigynneþ þe prolog on ioon//

Ioon euangelist þat is þe gospeler:
is oon of þe disciples of þe lord/ &
god chees þis ioon a virgyn: whom
god clepid fro weddinges/ whan he
wolde be weddid/ & double witnessi
nge of virginyte is ȝouun to þis ioo
in þe gospel: in þis þat he is seid
loued of god. bifor oþer disciples/
& god þat hanginge in þe crosse: bi
took his moder in kepinge to þis
ioon: þat a virgyn schulde kepe a
virgyn/ þis ioon in þe gospel bigi
nneþ alone þe werke of vncorrup
tible word: & witnessiþ þat þe word
þe sone of god is maad man/ & þat
þe liȝte was not taken of derknes
ses/ & he schewiþ þe firste miracle:
whiche þe lord dide in weddinges
to schewe þat where þe lord is pr
eyd to feste: þe wyn of weddinges
owiþ to faile/ þat whanne elde þin
ges ben chaunged: alle newe þinges
þat ben ordeined of crist apere/ ioon
wroot þis gospel in asye. aftir þat
he hadde write þe apocalipsis in þe
ile of pathmos/ neþeles he wroot
þe gospel aftir alle þe gospeleres/
þat is: þre oþer gospeleres hadden wri
ten bifor þis ioon/ þat also an uncor
ruptible ende schulde be ȝoldun bi
a virgyn in þe apocalipsis to him: to
whom an uncorruptible biginnynge
is ȝouun in genesis in þe biginnynge
of holy scripture/ for crist seiþ in a
pocalipsis: I am þe biginnynge & ende
& þis ioon is he þat knew. þat þe day
of his departinge þat is deþ was
comun/ & he clepid to gidere his disci
ples in effesie: & schewid crist bi ma
ny preuynges of miracles/ & ȝede doun
in to þe doluyd place of his biriynge/
& whanne he hadde maad preier: he was
put to his fadris. þat is was deed
& leued/ & was so miche straunge fro
wiþ out part of sorowe of deþ: hou
miche he is founden alien fro cor
rupcioun of fleische // Here endiþ
þe prologe on ioon: & here bigynneþ
þe gospel of ioon/ c[apitulu]m primum //

In þe biginnynge was
þe word. & þe word was
at god: & god was þe
word/ þis was in þe biginnynge
at god/ alle þinges weren maad
bi him: & wiþ outen him was ma

ad no þinge/ þat þinge þat was
in him: was lyf/ & þe lyf was
þe liȝte of men/ & þe liȝte schineþ
in derknesses: & derknesses compre
hendiden not it/ a man was sent
fro god: to whom þe name was
ioon/ þis man cam in to witnessin
ge: þat he schulde bere witnessinge
of þe liȝte: þat alle men schulde
bileue bi him/ he was not þe liȝt:
but þat he schuld bere witnessinge of
þe liȝte/ þere was a verri liȝt: whi
che liȝtneþ iche man þat comeþ in
to þis world/ he was in þe world
& þe world was maad bi him: & þe
world knew him not/ he cam in to his
owne þinges: & hise resceiued him not/
but hou many euer resceiued him:
he ȝaf to hem power to be maad
þe sones of god/ to hem þat bileueden
to his name/ þe whiche not of blo
des. neþer of þe wille of fleische neþer
of þe wille of man: but ben born of
god/ & þe word was maad man: &
dwelled amonge us/ & we han seyn
þe glorie of him: as þe glorie of þe con
bigetun sone of þe fadir/ ful of gra
ce & of treuþe // Ioon beriþ witnes
singe of him: & crieþ & seiþ/ þis is
whom I seid/ he þat schal come af
tir me: is maad bifor me/ for he was
to fore me/ & of þe plente of him we
alle han takun: & grace for grace/ for
þe lawe was ȝouun bi moises: but gra
ce & treuþe is maad bi ihu crist/ no
man sai euer god: no but þe con
bigetun sone. þat is in þe bosu
of þe fadir: he haþ teld out/ And
þis is þe witnessinge of ioon. whan
iewes senten fro ierlm prestes &
dekenes to him: þat þei schulde
axe him/ who art þou/ he knowleched
& denied not/ & he knowleched for
I am not crist/ & þei axiden him/ what
þan: art þou elie?/ & he seid I am
not/ art þou a prophet: & he answe
red/ nay/ þerfor þei seiden to him/ who
art þou: þat we ȝiue an answere
to þes þat han sente us/ what
seist þou of þi self/ he seid/ I am
a vois of a crier in desert: dresse
ȝe þe weie of þe lord/ as ysaie þe
prophet seid/ & þei þat weren sent:
weren of þe farisees/ & þei axiden
him & seiden to him/ what þan baptisis
þou: if þou art not crist neþer elie
neþer a prophete/ ioon answered to hem
& seid/ I baptise in watir but in þe
middel of ȝou haþ oon stonde co
þat ȝe knowen not/ he it is þa
schal come aftir me þat was
maad bifor me/ of whom I am n
worþi to louse þe þwong of hi
scho/ þese þinges weren don in bet
hanye biȝonde iordan: where ioon
baptisinge/ anoþer dai ioon sa
ihu comminge to him: & he seid/ lo
lombe of god: lo he þat doiþ a
þe synnes of þe world/ þis is h
I seid of. After me is comen a

Wycliffite New Testament

MS.000875, parchment codex, ca. 1400–1450

IN THE 1380S, a circle of scholars associated with John Wycliffe translated the Bible from the Latin Vulgate into Middle English. This translation was more accessible to the common people than the Latin, but because its word order was influenced by the Latin, it was sometimes awkward to read. A decade later, John Purvey and others reworked the translation into a more fluent "Later Version." This beautiful early 15th-century manuscript contains the "Later Version" of the New Testament. Each section begins with a blue-and-red puzzle initial, containing elaborate patterns within the letter.

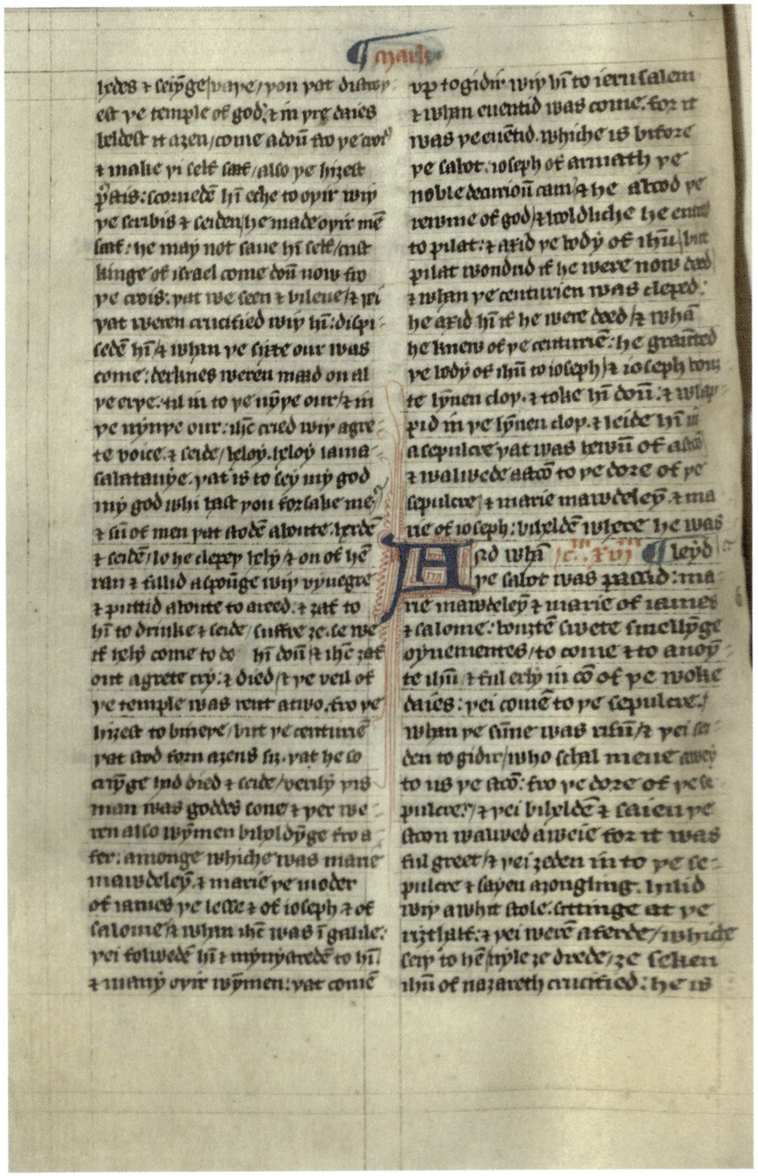

RIGHT: Detail of a decorated initial and underlined passages.

FACING PAGE: Bifolium with rubrication and scrolling ink details.

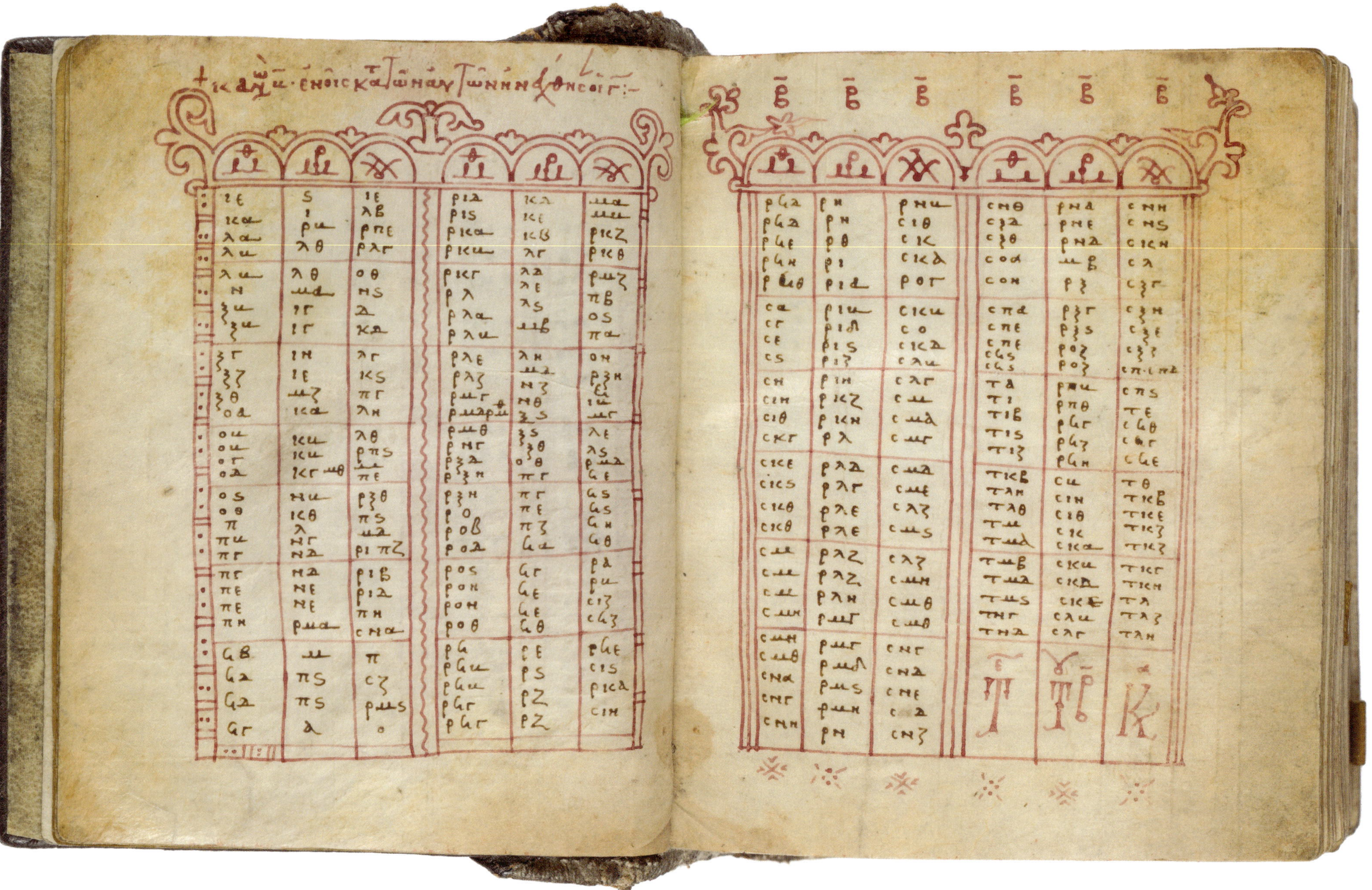

Gospel Book ("Evanis" Gospels / GA 2929)

MS.000139, parchment codex, ca. 1050–1100

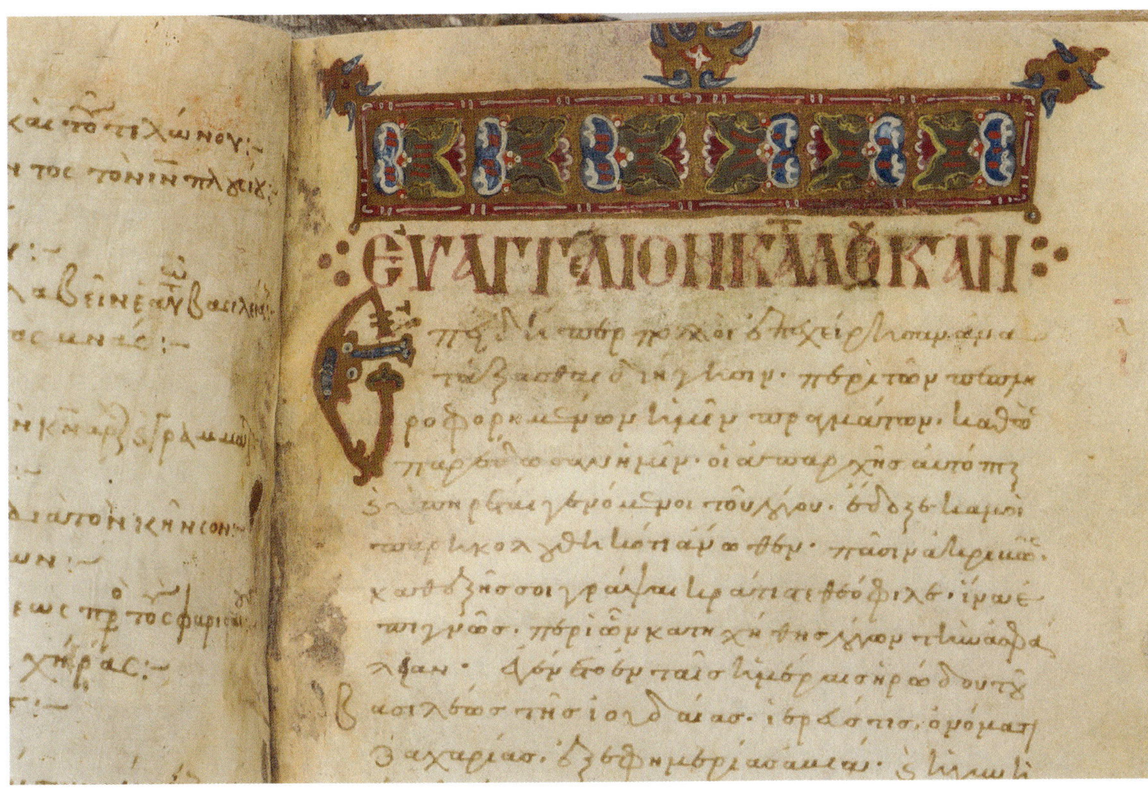

Left: Decorative header at the beginning of Luke's Gospel.

Facing page: Canon tables outlined in red ink.

This manuscript contains the four Gospels written in a small hand known to scholars as Perlschrift ("pearl script") minuscule. The scribe wrote most of the text in a light brown ink, in a single column of 22 lines. The scribe wrote the canon tables (an early concordance of parallel passages) at the beginning of the manuscript and the chapter headings (kephalaia) at the beginning of each Gospel in red ink. Section headings often appear at the top of the page in red ink, but some have been cut off when the manuscript was trimmed for rebinding at some point in the early 20th century. Miniatures of Mark and John appear at the beginning of their Gospels. The manuscript ends in the middle of John 17:22.

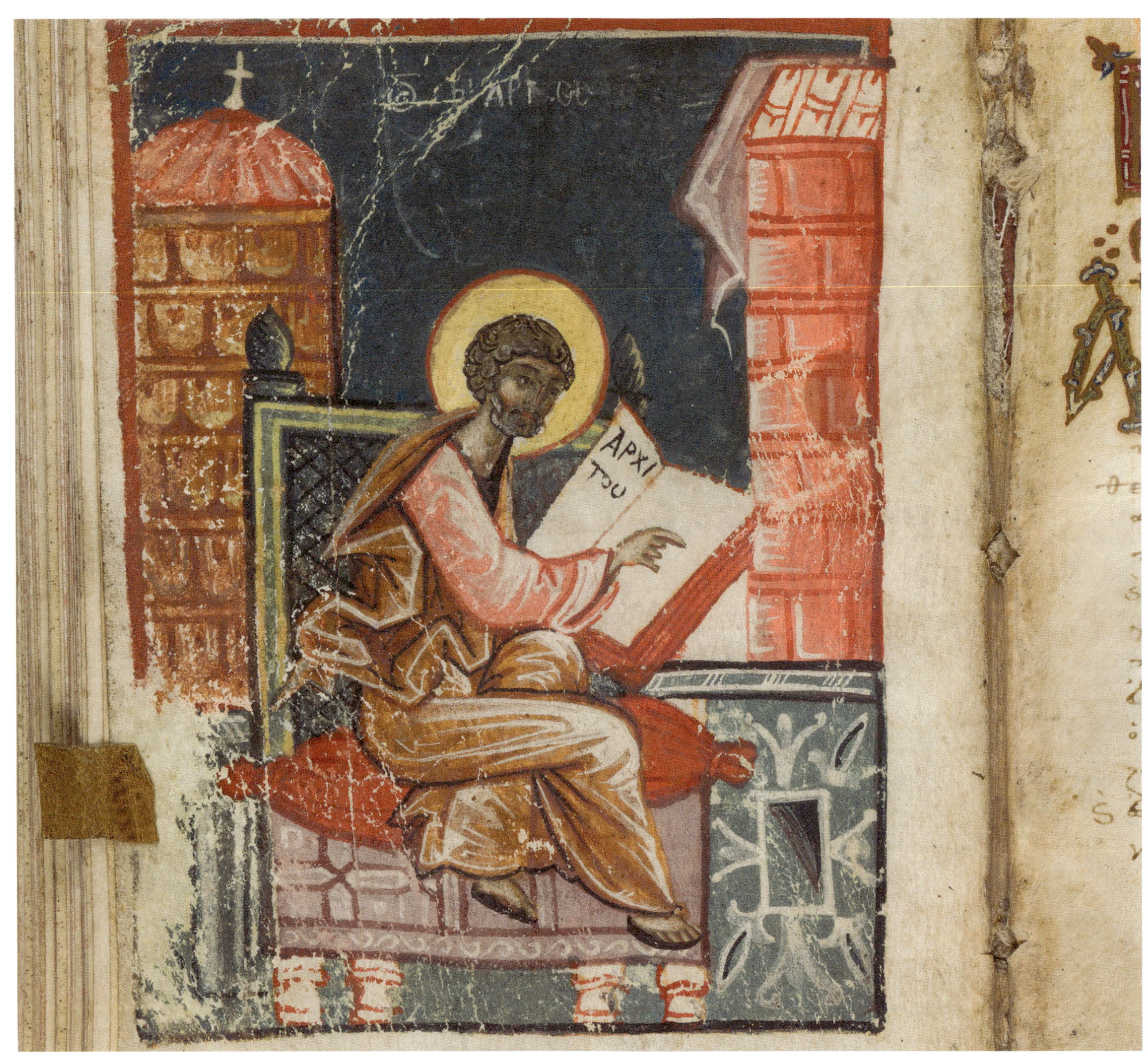

Miniature of Mark the Evangelist at the beginning of Mark's Gospel.

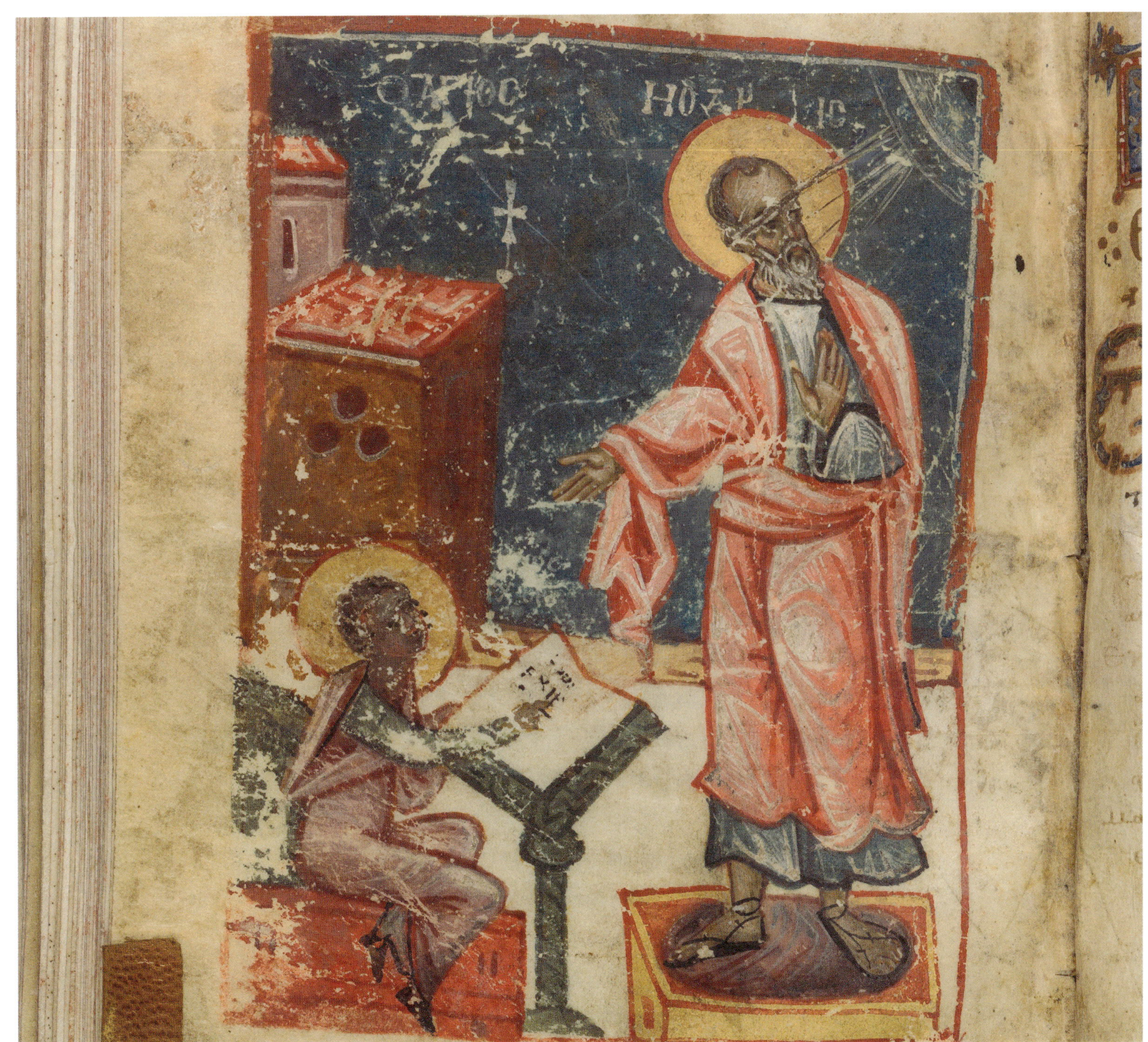

Miniature of John the Evangelist at the beginning of John's Gospel.

Novum Instrumentum Omne

BIB.000324, printed book, 1516

DESIDERIUS ERASMUS OF Rotterdam (1466–1536) was the first to prepare a complete Greek New Testament for publication. Erasmus titled this first edition Novum Instrumentum Omne. In it, he presented his own Latin translation as well as critical notes on textual variants in the Vulgate that were not supported by the Greek manuscripts he consulted. His hurried work, which was done in just ten months, resulted in hundreds of typesetting errors. After the success of the first edition, from the second edition onward, Erasmus simply called his work Novum Testamentum.

ABOVE: End of the Epistle to James, Greek and Latin in parallel columns.

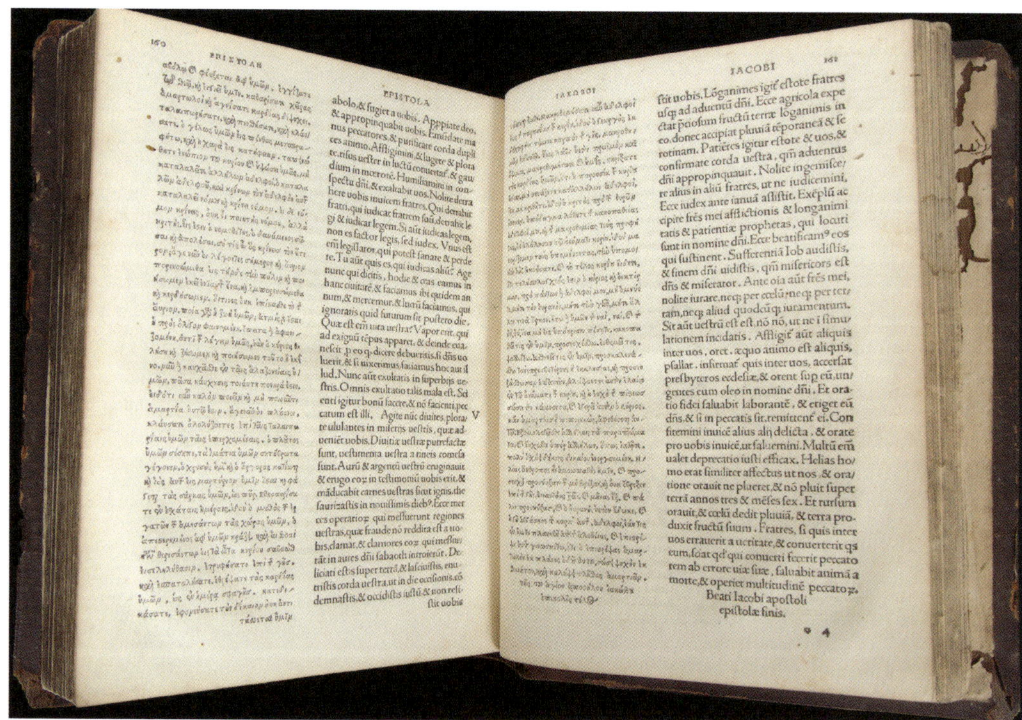

RIGHT: James 4 & 5, Greek and Latin in parallel columns.

NOVVM IN

strumentū omne, diligenter ab ERASMO ROTERODAMO recognitum & emendatum, nō solum ad græcam ueritatem, uerumetiam ad multorum utriusq; linguæ codicum, eorumq; ueterum simul & emendatorum fidem, postremo ad probatissimorum autorum citationem, emendationem & interpretationem, præcipue, Origenis, Chrysostomi, Cyrilli, Vulgarij, Hieronymi, Cypriani, Ambrosij, Hilarij, Augustini, una cū Annotationibus, quæ lectorem doceant, quid qua ratione mutatum sit.

Quisquis igitur amas ueram Theologiam, lege, cognosce, ac deinde iudica. Neq; statim offendere, si quid mutatum offenderis, sed expende, num in melius mutatum sit.

APVD INCLYTAM GERMANIAE BASILAEAM.

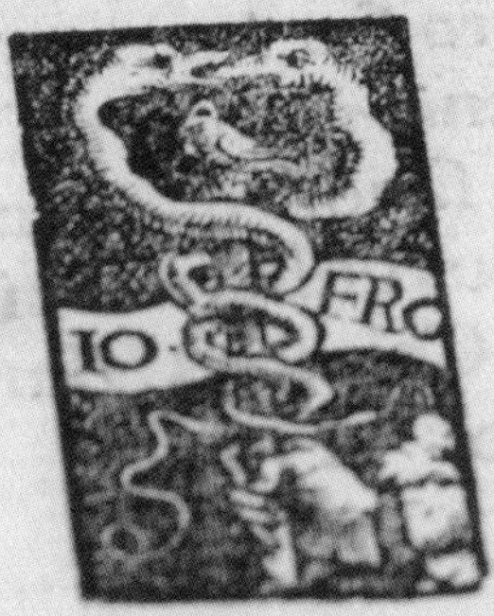

CVM PRIVILEGIO MAXIMILIANI CAESARIS AVGVSTI, NE QVIS ALIVS IN SACRA ROMANI IMPERII DITIONE, INTRA QVATVOR ANNOS EXCVDAT, AVT ALIBI EXCVSVM IMPORTET.

Indenture for "The Mayflowere"

MS.000894, parchment codex, 1610

THIS MANUSCRIPT IS an indenture, which is a legal agreement, between Peter Hills of Redriffe and his nephew, Robert Bell of Redriffe. Here, Hills sells his thirteen ships, one of which is "The *Mayflowere*" in 1610. Bell's home, Redriffe, is the same area where Christopher Jones, a known ship master and part-owner of the well-known *Mayflower*, lived. A Robert Bell also used Jones's *Mayflower* to ship French wine to England the year before the Pilgrims set sail to America on the ship. This Mayflower listed in the indenture is likely the *Mayflower* that brought the Pilgrims to New England in 1620.

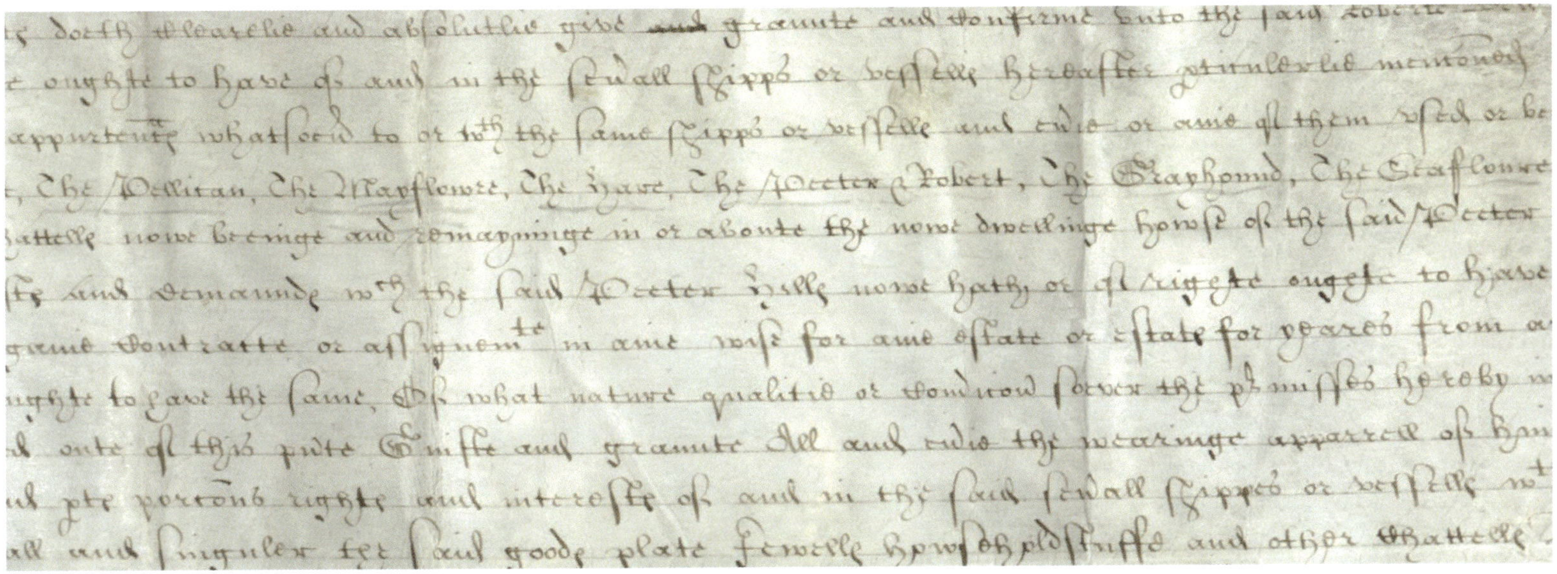

ABOVE: Detail image of "The Mayflowere," listed among twelve other ships.

FACING PAGE: Full image of the entire indenture from December 8, 1610. The *Mayflower* was a small ship used for transporting goods and possibly at one point, whaling. The last recorded entry for the *Mayflower* at the port of London is the unloading of salt in October 1621. There are no records past 1624.

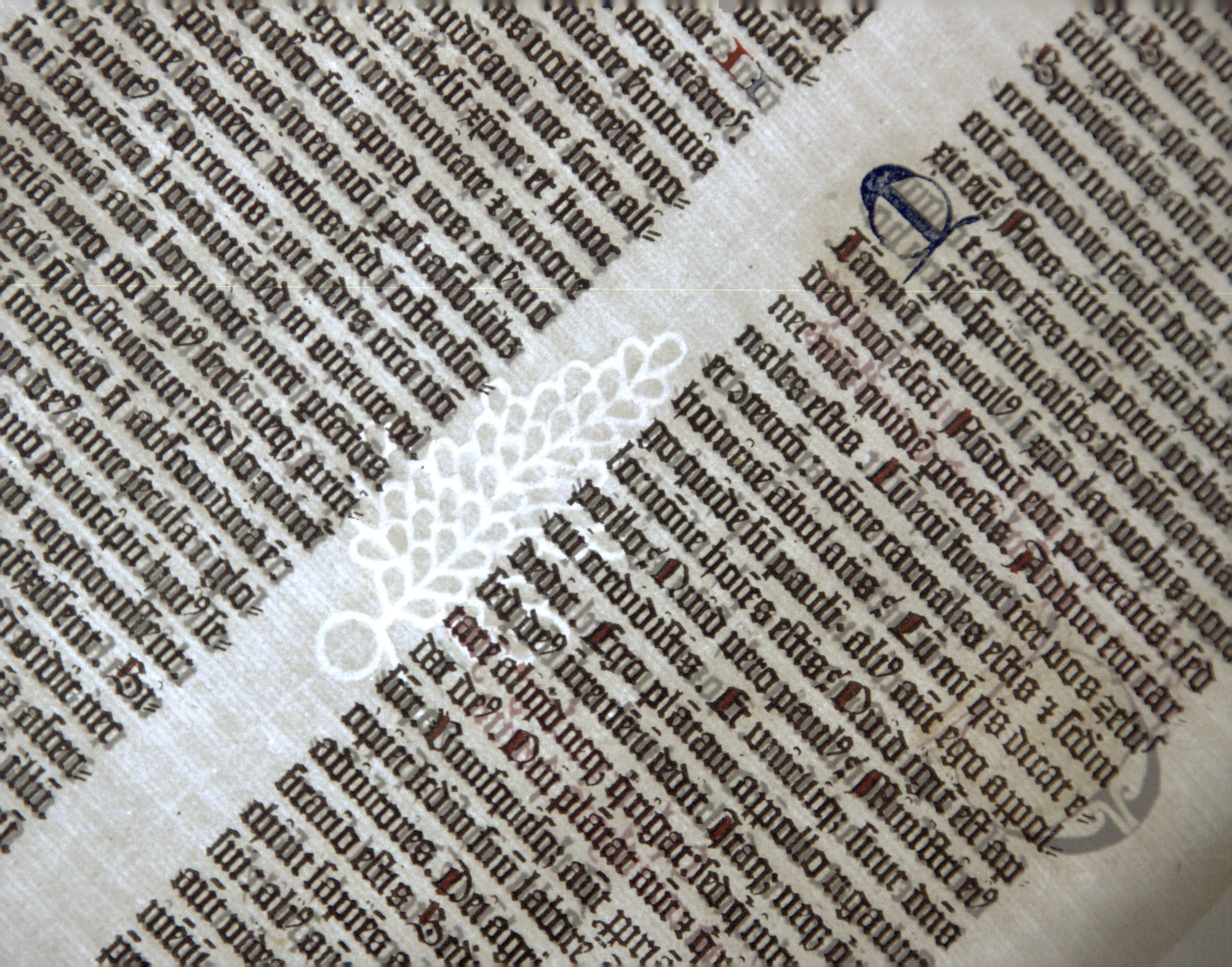

Gutenberg Fragments from the Wells Copy

INC.000142/118/117/162/162/164, dismembered printed book with hand-drawn embellishments, 1454–1455

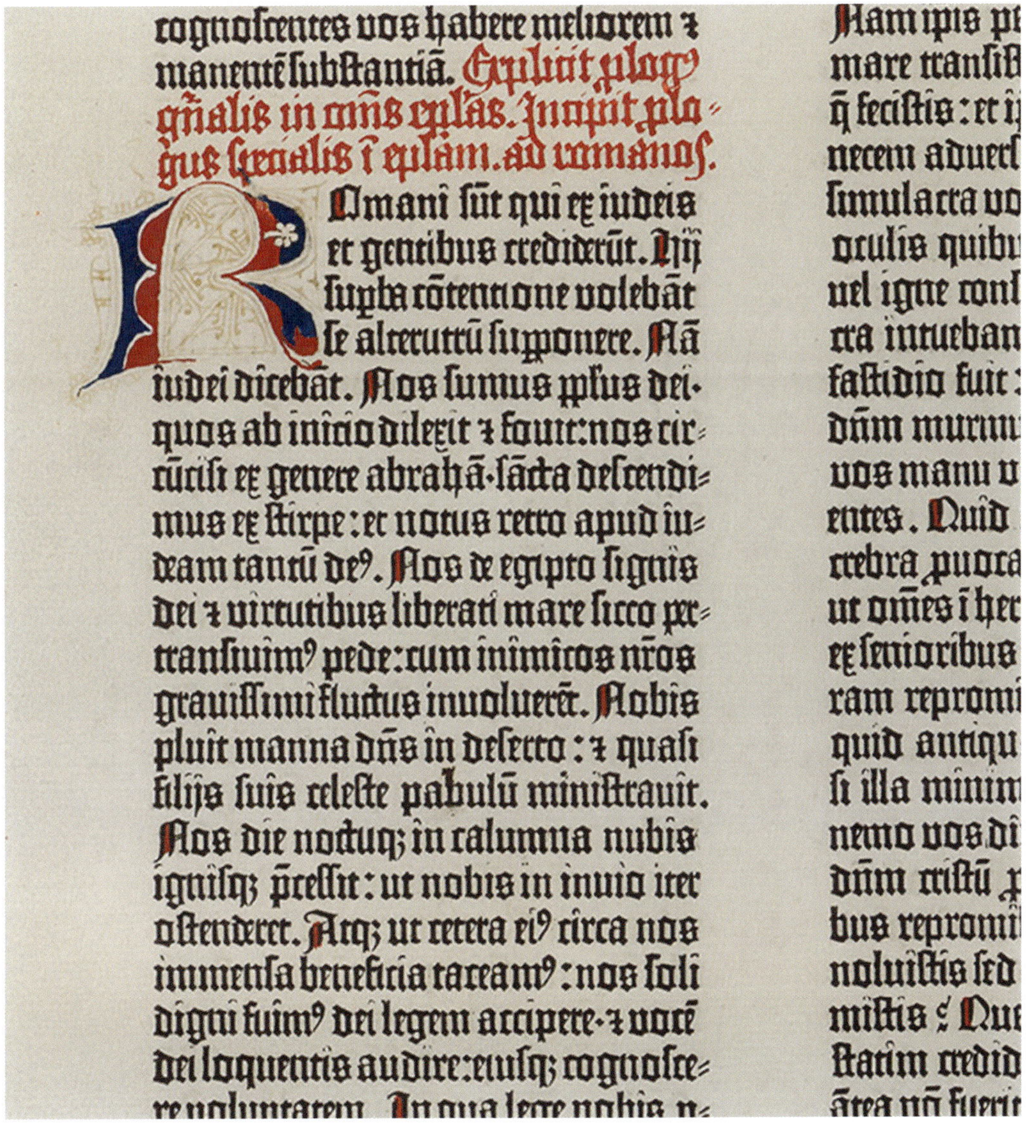

The Gutenberg Bible was the first printed edition of the Bible. The year of the first printing cannot be determined with certainty, but sometime in the middle of the 1450s, Gutenberg produced a copy of the Latin Vulgate. The Gutenberg Bible is in two columns of 42 lines and closely resembles a manuscript, using typeset that mimics period handwriting with ornamentation added by hand.

Left: Detail of a decorated initial indicating the start of a new section.

Facing page: Detail of a page from the Book of Romans highlighting an original grape cluster watermark, one of four watermarks identifying the type of paper used by Gutenberg.

A NOBLE FRAGMENT BEING A LEAF OF THE Gutenberg Bible

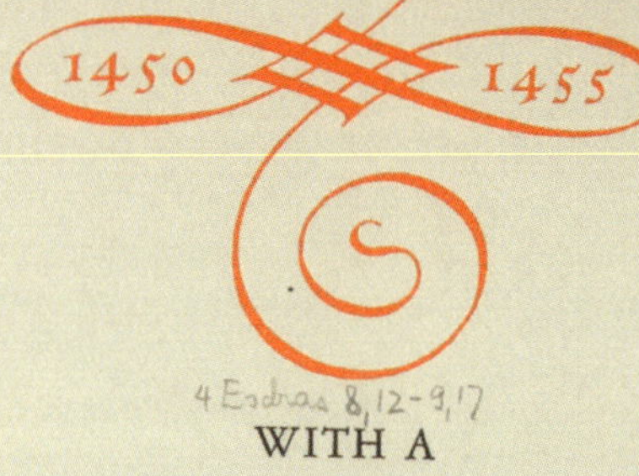

4 Esdras 8,12-9,17

WITH A

BIBLIOGRAPHICAL ESSAY BY

A. EDWARD NEWTON

NEW YORK

GABRIEL WELLS

1921

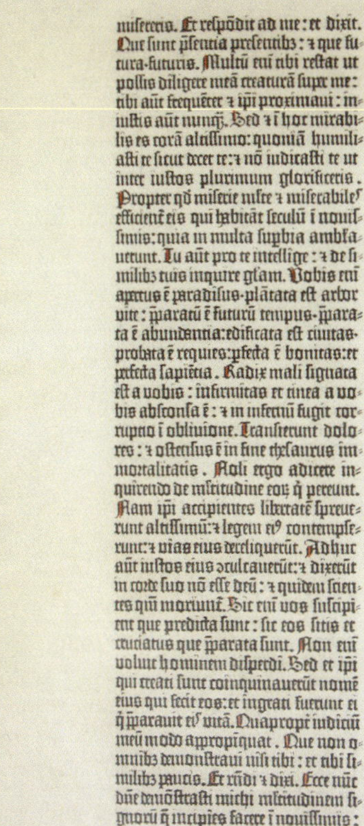

LEFT: Recto (or front) of a single page from the Wells copy of the Gutenberg Bible.

RIGHT: Verso (or back) of the same page from the Wells copy of the Gutenberg Bible.

In 1921, Gabriel Wells separated sections and pages from his incomplete copy of the Gutenberg Bible and sold them separately as "Noble Fragments," bound with an essay by Alfred Edward Newton. Many of the "Noble Fragments" in the Museum of the Bible's collection originated from this source and were once part of the same volume of Gutenberg's Bible.

The bokes of the whole Byble, how they are named in Englysh and Latyn, how longe they are wrytten in the allegacions, how many chapters euery boke hath, and in what leafe euery one begynneth.

The bokes of the first parte.

Abbreuiacion.	Boke.	Chapters.	leafe.
Gen.	Genesis, the first boke of Moses.	l.	first.
Exo.	Exodus, the seconde boke of Moses.	xl.	xxiiij.
Leui.	Leuiticus, the thirde boke of Moses.	xxvij.	xlij.
Num.	Numerus, the fourth boke of Moses.	xxxvj.	lv.
Deut.	Deuteronomion, the fifth boke of Moses.	xxxiiij.	lxxiiij.

The bokes of the seconde parte.

Abbreuiacion.	Boke.	Chapters.	leafe.
Jos.	Josue, the boke of Josua.	xxiiij.	ij.
Jud.	Judicum, the boke of the Judges.	xxj.	xiij.
Ruth.	Ruth, the boke of Ruth.	iiij.	xxiiij.
I. Reg.	Regum, the first boke of the kynges.	xxxj.	xxvj.
II. Reg.	Regum, the seconde boke of the kynges.	xxiiij.	xl.
III. Reg.	Regum, the thirde boke of the kynges.	xxij.	lij.
IIII. Reg.	Regum, the fourth boke of the kynges.	xxv.	lxvj.
I. Par.	Paralipomenon, the I. boke of the Cronicles.	xxx.	lxxix.
II. Par.	Paralipomenon, the II. boke of the Cronicles.	xxxvj.	xcj.
I. Esd.	Esdre, the first boke of Esdras.	x.	cvij.
II. Esd.	Esdre, the seconde boke of Esdras.	xiij.	cxj.
Hest.	Hester, the boke of Hester.	x.	cxvij.

The bokes of the thirde parte.

Abbreuiacion.	Boke.	Chapters.	leafe.
Job.	Job, the boke of Job.	xlij.	first.
Psal.	Psalterium, the Psalter.	cl.	xij.
Pro.	Prouerbia, the prouerbes of Salomon.	xxxj.	xxxviij.
Eccls.	Ecclesiastes, the preacher of Salomon.	xij.	xlvij.
Cant.	Cantica Canticorũ, Salomons balettes.	viij.	l.

The Prophetes.

Abbreuiacion.	Boke.	Chapters.	leafe.
Esa.	Esaias, Esay the prophet.	lxvj.	ij.
Jere.	Jeremias, Jeremy the prophet.	lij.	xxiiij.
Tren.	Treni, the lamentacions of Jeremy.	v.	xlix.
Bar.	Baruch, Baruc the prophet.	vj.	lj.
Eze.	Ezechiel, Ezechiel the prophet.	xlviij.	lv.
Dan.	Daniel, Daniel the prophet.	xij.	lxxvij.
Ose.	Oseas, Oseas the prophet.	xiiij.	lxxxiiij.
Joel.	Joel, Joel the prophet.	iij.	lxxxvij.
Amo.	Amos, Amos the prophet.	ix.	lxxxviij.
Abd.	Abdias, Abdy the prophet.	j.	xc.
Jon.	Jonas, Jonas the prophet.	iiij	xcj.
Mich.	Micheas, Micheas the prophet.	vij.	xcij.
Na.	Naum, Naum the prophet.	iij.	xciiij.
Aba.	Abacuc, Abacuc the prophet.	iij.	xcv.
Soph.	Sophonias, Sophony the prophet.	iij.	xcvj.
Agg.	Aggeus, Aggeus the prophet.	ij.	xcvij.
Zach.	Zacharias, Zachary the prophet.	xiiij.	xcvij.
Mal.	Malachias, Malachy the prophet.	iiij.	cj.

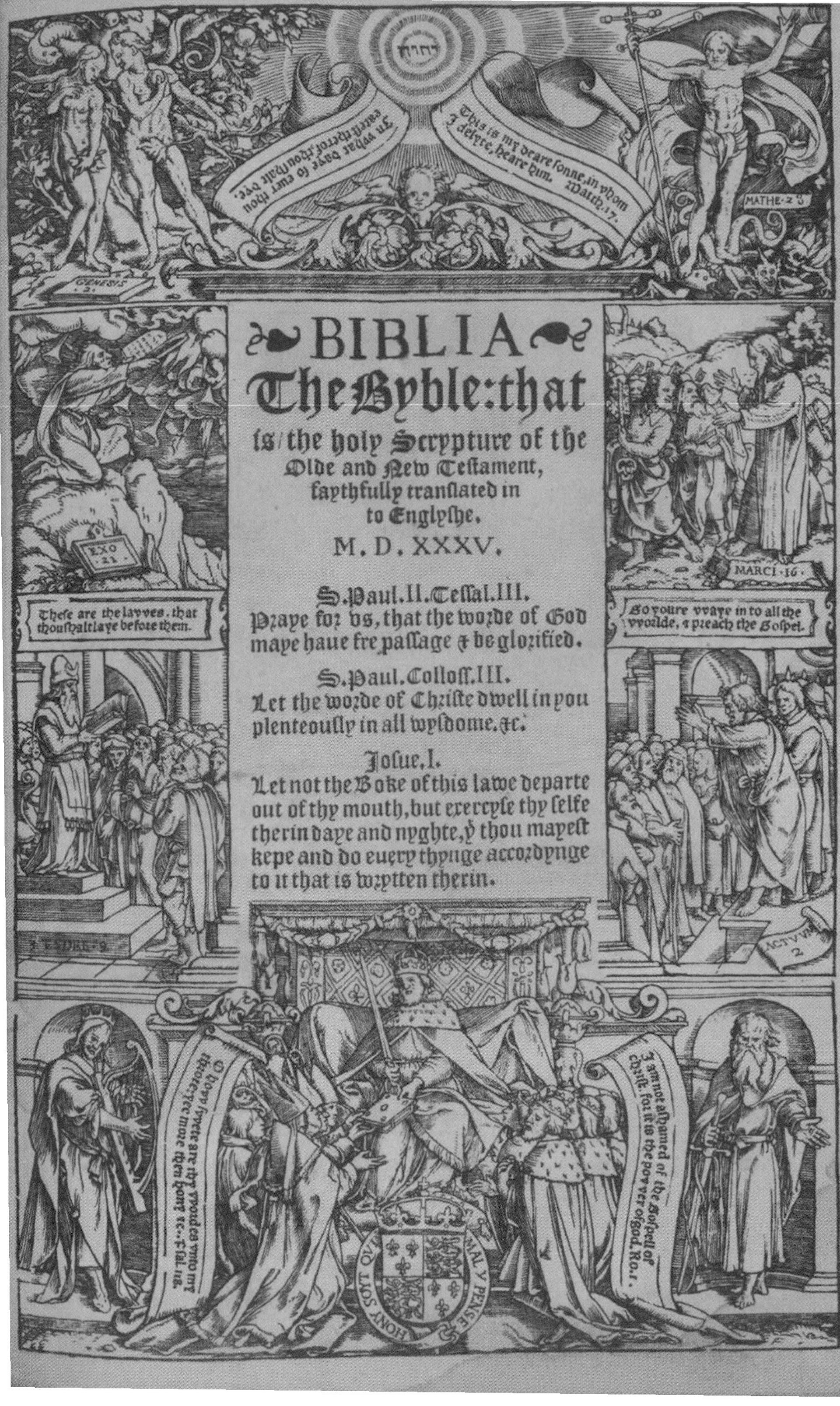

BIBLIA

The Byble: that is, the holy Scrypture of the Olde and New Testament, faythfully translated in to Englyshe.

M. D. XXXV.

S. Paul. II. Tessal. III.
Praye for vs, that the worde of God maye haue fre passage & be glorified.

S. Paul. Colloss. III.
Let the worde of Christe dwell in you plenteously in all wysdome, &c.

Josue. I.
Let not the Boke of this lawe departe out of thy mouth, but exercyse thy selfe therin daye and nyghte, that thou mayest kepe and do euery thynge accordynge to it that is wrytten therin.

The Coverdale Bible

BIB.003055, printed book, 1535

The Coverdale Bible was the first complete English translation of the Old Testament, Apocrypha, and New Testament. Miles Coverdale was an English priest and religious reformer. He published this Bible in Belgium in 1535, building, in part, upon the earlier translation work of William Tyndale. While the Coverdale Bible was not widely used, it helped pave the way for later English translations. After establishing the Church of England in 1534, King Henry VIII eventually approved the use of English Bibles in his kingdom. Coverdale would go on to supervise the publication of a new "authorized" translation in 1539. The "Great Bible," as it would become known, would draw from many sources, including Coverdale's previous work.

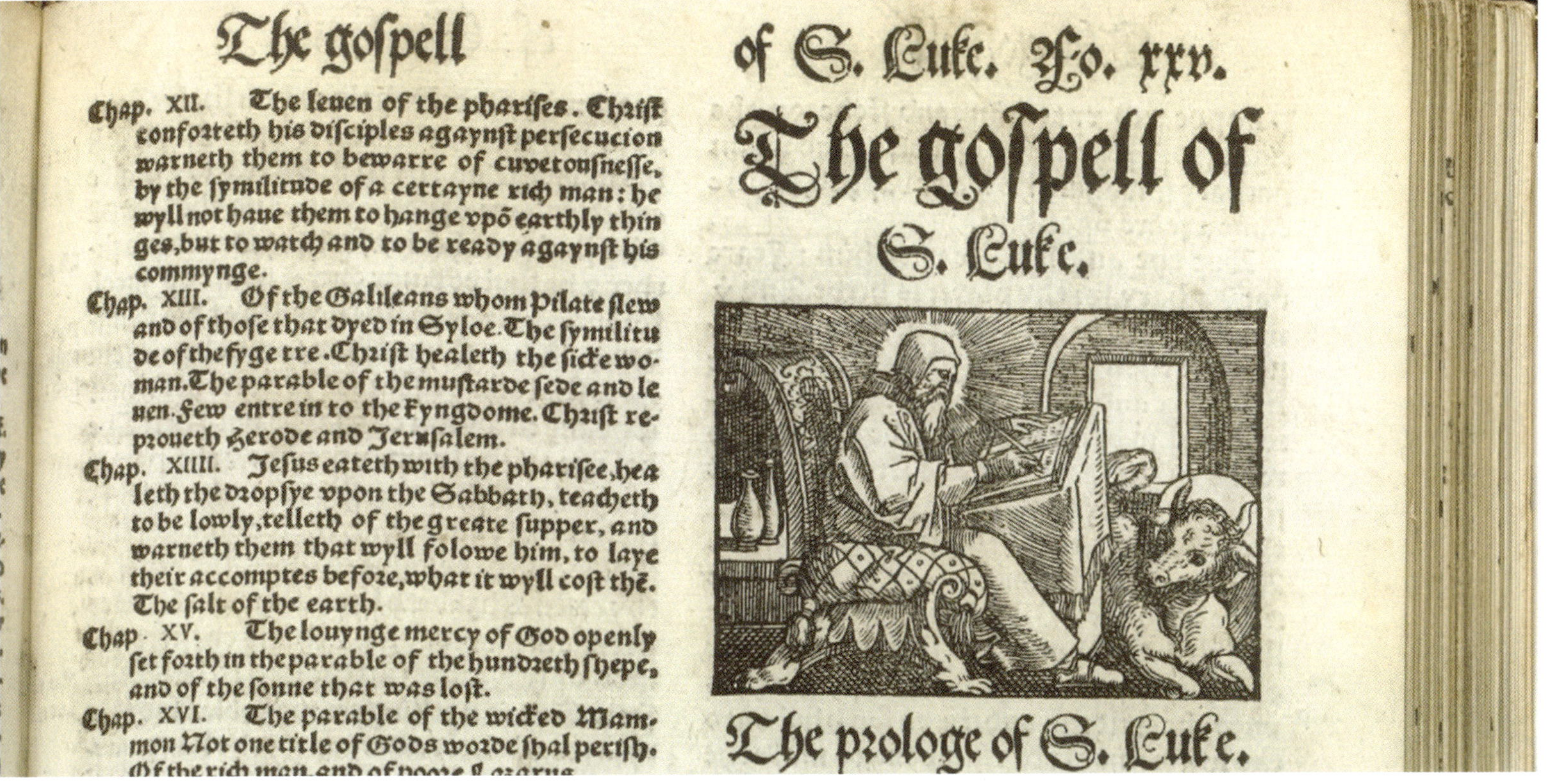

The gospell

Chap. XII. The leuen of the pharises. Christ conforteth his disciples agaynst persecucion, warneth them to bewarre of cuvetousnesse, by the symilitude of a certayne rich man: he wyll not haue them to hange vpõ earthly thinges, but to watch and to be ready agaynst his commynge.

Chap. XIII. Of the Galileans whom Pilate slew and of those that dyed in Syloe. The symilitude of the fyge tre. Christ healeth the sicke woman. The parable of the mustarde sede and leuen. Few entre in to the kyngdome. Christ reproueth Herode and Jerusalem.

Chap. XIIII. Jesus eateth with the pharisee, healeth the dropsye vpon the Sabbath, teacheth to be lowly, telleth of the greate supper, and warneth them that wyll folowe him, to laye their accomptes before, what it wyll cost thẽ. The salt of the earth.

Chap. XV. The louynge mercy of God openly set forth in the parable of the hundreth shepe, and of the sonne that was lost.

Chap. XVI. The parable of the wicked Mammon. Not one title of Gods worde shal perish.

of S. Luke. Fo. xxv.

The gospell of S. Luke.

The prologe of S. Luke.

Facing Page: Facing pages with table of contents and title page.

Left: Chapter titles (left column) and incipit (right column) of Luke's Gospel.

Paris Pocket Bible

MS.000132, parchment codex, ca. 1230–1260

THIS POCKET BIBLE is mostly complete, lacking the text of Psalms, the beginning of which was erased and the following several folios removed at some point. The small, carefully written Gothic text appears in two columns of 53–54 lines. Large blue and red initials with extensive tendrils above and below begin each book, with smaller initials alternating between blue and red at the start of each chapter. An elaborate image of acanthus leaves with an interwoven scroll lies at the bottom of the first folio's recto. On the scroll, Brother Johannes asks people to pray for him. An illuminated pointer between the columns marks the beginning of Genesis on the verso of the second folio.

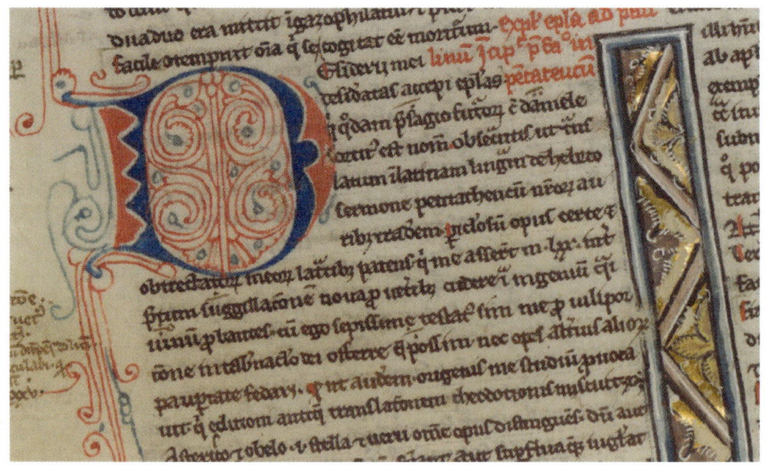

ABOVE: Detail image of a decorated initial from Genesis.

FACING PAGE: Bifolium of Genesis showing marginal notes. Pocket Bibles were used primarily by seminarians and would often contain notes from several students.

Samaritan Torah Scroll

SCR.004821, parchment codex, ca. 1160

FOR OVER 2,500 years the Samaritans, a Jewish sect that emerged in the Second Temple period, have revered the Torah. In fact, the Torah (or Pentateuch) is the only part of the Jewish scriptures that Samaritans use for worship. This scroll was likely written by the scribe Shalmah Ben Abraham around 1160 in Nablus, where many Samaritans still live. It contains Genesis 1:1–Exodus 9:35 in the Samaritan script and is one of the oldest surviving Torah scrolls from the Samaritan religious tradition.

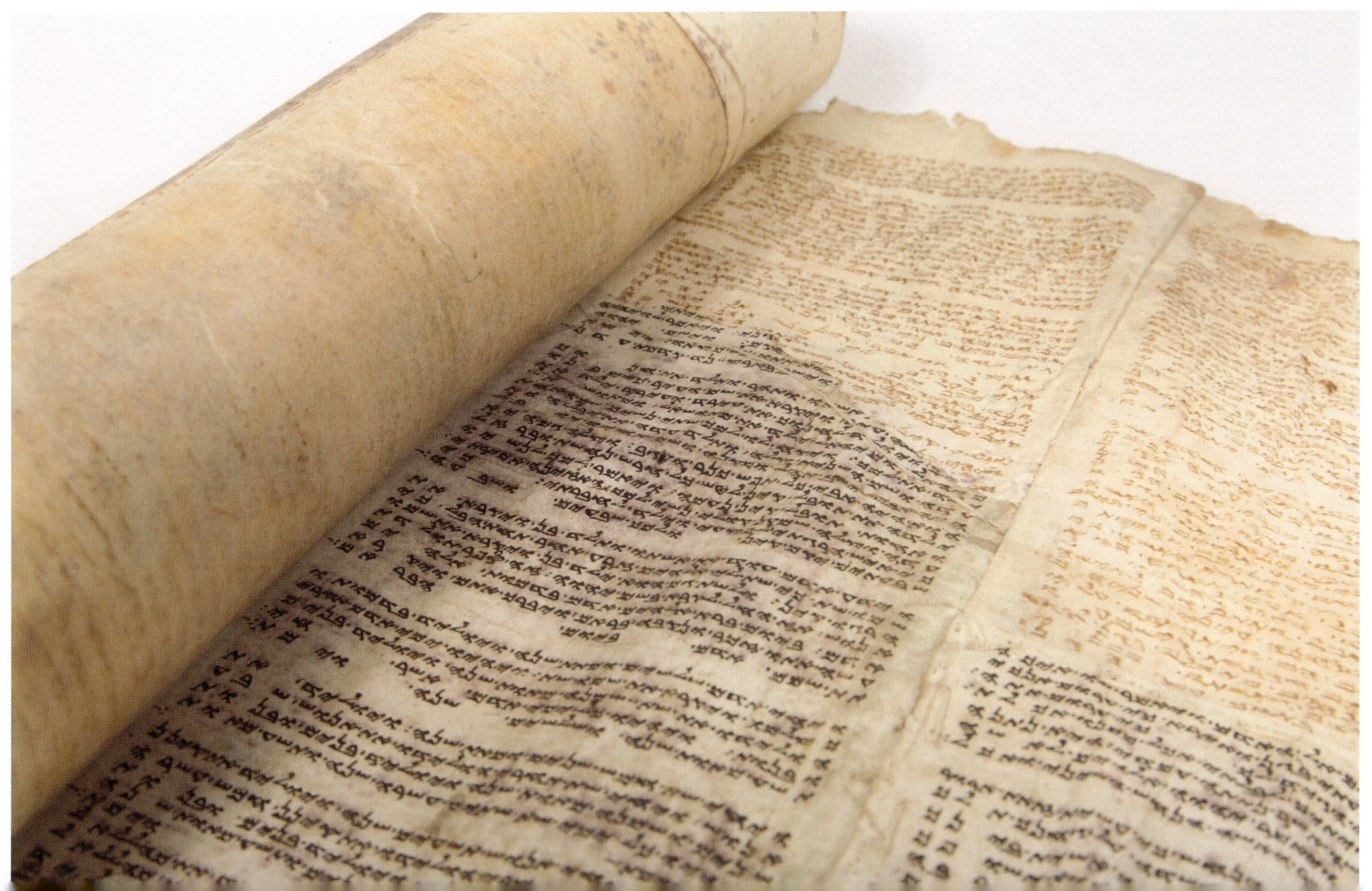

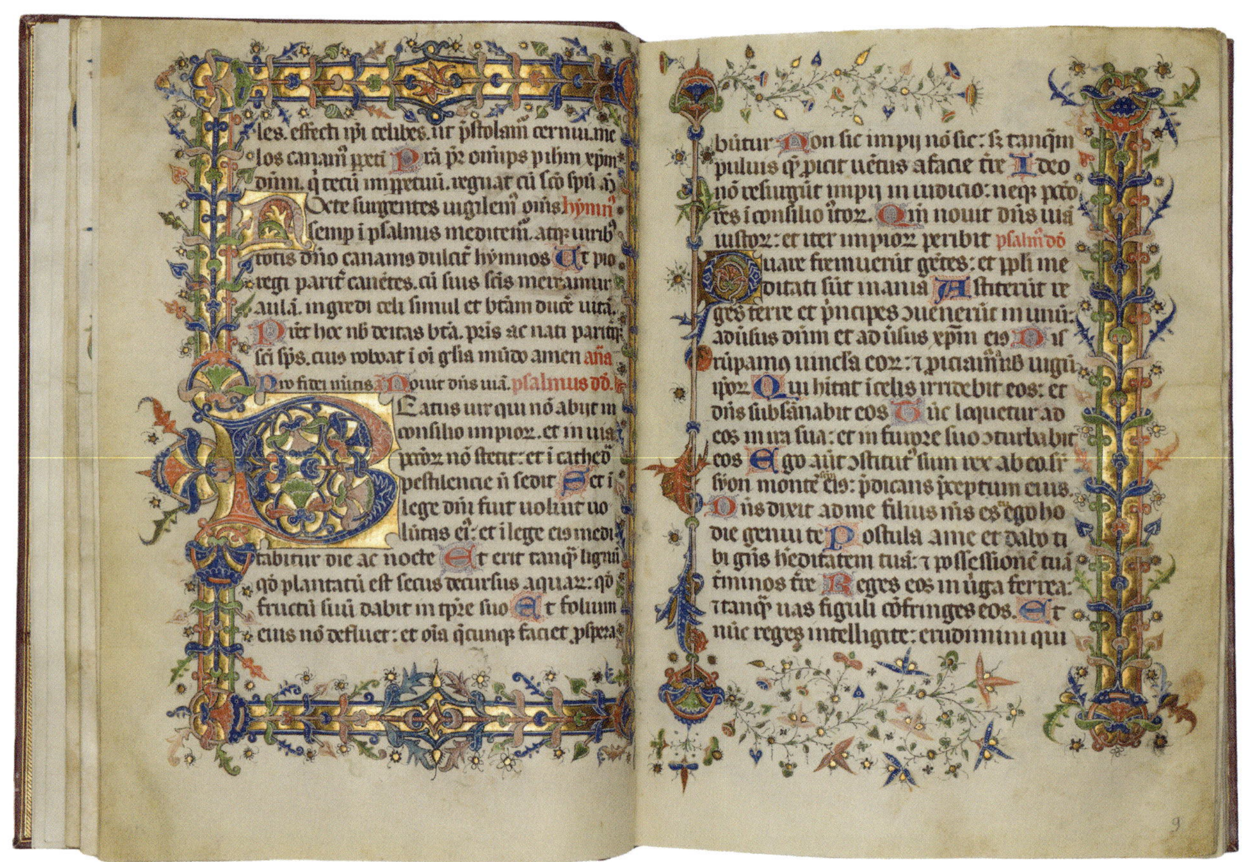

Psalterium Gallicanum Feriatum

MS.000320, parchment codex, ca. 1400–1420, with additions ca. 1440–1450

A Gallican Psalter contains the text of Jerome's second translation of the Psalms into Latin. Gregory of Tours brought this translation to Gaul (modern France), from where it takes its name. A ferial Psalter arranges the psalms in liturgical order according to the canonical hours. It also includes additional readings and chants. This gorgeous, 15th-century Psalter likely came from the region around Barcelona, although the calendar of saints' feast days also suggests an association with Santiago de Compostela. Pages bordered with a delicate floral design are interspersed with pages containing a complete border. The initials shine with gold and brilliant colors.

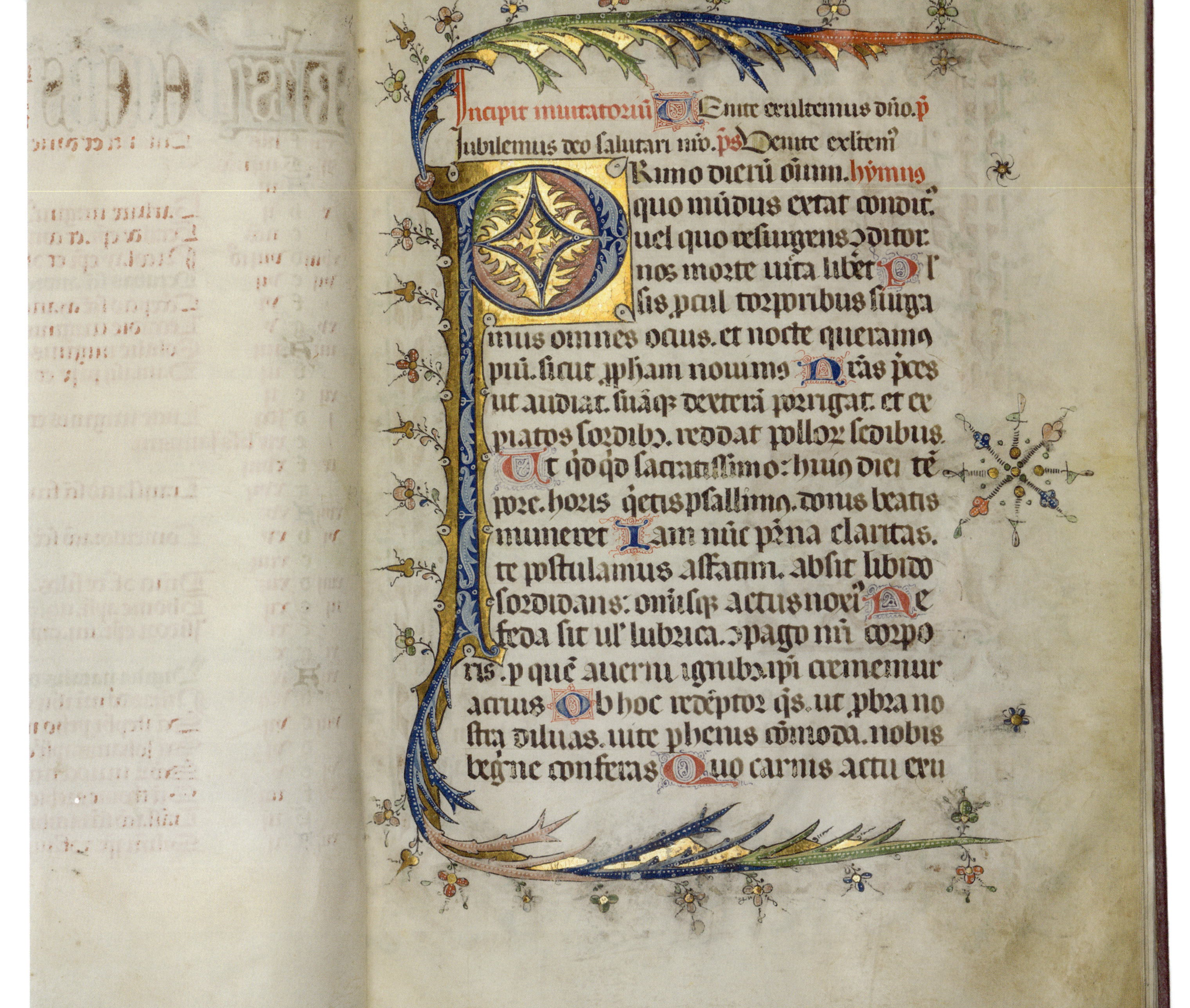
Incipit inuitatoriū Venite exultemus dño. p̄
Jubilemus deo salutari nro. ps Venite exltē
Primo dierū oīum. hymnus
quo mūdus extat condit[us]
uel quo resurgens [con]ditor
nos morte uita libet Pl
sis p[ro]cul torporibus surga
mus omnes ocius. et nocte queramus
piū. sicut p[ro]pham nouimus Nras preces
ut audiat. suāq[ue] dexterā porrigat. et ex
piatos sordibus. reddat polor sedibus.
Ut quo quo sacratissimo: huius diei tē
pore. horis quietis psallimus. donis beatis
muneret Jam nūc p̄ena claritas.
te postulamus affatim. absit libido
sordidans: omnisq[ue] actus noxius Ne
feda sit ul' lubrica. compago nri corpo
ris. p quē auerni ignibus ipsi crememur
actus Ob hoc redēptor q̄s. ut probra no
stra diluas. uite perhennis cōmoda. nobis
begnīe conferas Quo carnis actu exu

SOME PROMINENT GUESTS
FROM THE FIRST FIVE YEARS

Alan Hotchkiss Sen. Tom Cotton Miss Alabama USA (Katelyn Vinson) Miss South Carolina USA (Meera Bhonsle)
World Evangelical Alliance Secretary General, Bishop Thomas Schirrmacher David Barton Former Vice President Mike Pence
Miss North Carolina USA (Morgan Romano) Kelly Wright Fmr. Israeli Ambassador Ron Dermer Jo Anne Lyon
Dallas Jenkins Miss Louisiana USA (KT Scannell) Denzel Washington Major General (ret.) Bob Dees Os Guinness
Fmr. Sec. of Education, Betsy DeVos Mario Paredes Lt. Governor of Nebraska, Mike Foley Paula White
Bill High Michael W. Smith David Platt Harold Brinkley H.E. Daniel Mulhall, Ambassador of Ireland
His Excellency Mr. Varuzhan Nersesyan, Ambassador of the Republic of Armenia Mark Markiewicz Gil Ilutowich Congressman Jodey Arrington Shirley Hoogstra
Ann Voskamp
Sen. Mitt Romney Paul Tripp John Maxwell Jeff Brown Dan and Rhonda Cathy
Rabbi Jonathan Sacks
Tony Dungy Mark DeMoss Michael Chavis Pastor Cash Luna Philip Yancey Jack Suwinski
President Giammattei of Guatemala Congressional Wives Club Fmr. Governor Bob McDonnell Andrea Bocelli
Skip Heitzig Senator James Lankford His All-Holiness Ecumenical Patriarch Bartholomew I of Constantinople
His Excellency Keith Azzopardi, ambassador of Malta to the United States of America Congressman Matt Rosendale
His Excellency Ambassador Murat Mercan of Turkey Congressman Greg Steube
Bobby Magallanes Ambassador to Ethiopia Jay Hein Dennis Prager Ilan Goldberg
Brigadier General Tony Tata (former acting Under Sec of Defense-Founder Boundary Channel Partners) Rick Warren
Chaplain to the Queen of England
Nick Hall Matt and Laurie Crouch
Congresswoman Jackie Walorski
Alveda King Sebastian Gorka Jim Hanon
Mike Pompeo Mike Gonzales World Evangelical Alliance Secretary General, Bishop Dr Thomas Schirrmacher
Mark Burnett His Excellency President Akufo-Addo of Ghana Devin Stewart
Young Hoon Li Dansby Swanson Mark Taylor Congresswoman Yvette Heller
Judge Jeanine Piro Brad Benbow Jeremy Camp Lord Reading Roma Downey
Neal Cruz BeBe Winans Kirk Cameron
His Excellency Ambassador Alexandra Papadopoulos of Greece Lee Strobel CeCe Winans Ambassador to Malta
Tim Keller Yerry De los Santos Selah Dylan Thomas Lecrae Tom Newman
Larry Ross Governor Mike Parson Shane and Shane Mayor David Holt Ben and Candy Carson
Bob Fopma Jonathan Roumie Jim Daly John Rich Walter Kim Ben Crane
Matt Maher Rabbi Ari Lamm Phil Cooke Shannon Bream Governor Israel Ganz Jonas Beiler
Natalie Grant Congressman Kevin McCarthy Al and Lisa Robertson Don Kelly Keith and Kristyn Getty
Kay Arthur Tyler Beede Peter McGowan His Excellency Ambassador Marios Lysiotis of Cyprus
Heather Headley Chris Hodges His Excellency Ambassador Marios Lysiotis of Cyprus Stan Jantz
Jack Hibbs Congressman Blaine Luetkemeyer Governor Glen Youngkin Albert Pujols
His Excellency Ambassador Arthur Sinodinos of Australia Congressman Alex Mooney Camden Duzenack
For King & Country Michael Cromartie Jose Quintana Congressman Blaine Luetker (Auntie) Anne Beiler
Bill Reeves His Eminence Metropolitan Emmanuel Bishop Kenneth and Togetta Ulmer Scott Ligertwood
Chase De Jong Tarik Brock Adelle Banks Charles and Florence Buregeya Mugisha of Rwanda
Fmr. Congressman Randy Forbes Steve Cichek Michael Gerson Mariska Hargitay Maestro Alvise Caselatti
Mayor Muriel Bowser Byron Williamson
Scott Pruitt (Former Administrator of the Environmental Protection Agency) Scott Mathews Gov. Rick Perry Jordan Peterson David and Helen Smallbone
Willie and Korie Robertson Fmr. Ambassador & Senator Dan Coats Ranjy Thomas
Max Lucado Demi Tebow (Miss Universe) Congressman Dan Crenshaw General John E. Hyten, Vice Chairman of the Joint Chiefs of Staff His Excellency Mr. Varuzhan Nersesyan, Ambassador of the Republic of Armenia to the United States

Christopher Miller (Former Acting Sec. of Defense) Congressman Tim and Mrs. Nan Murphy San Francisco Giants Congressman Greg Stube
Her Excellency Ambassador Lilit Makunts of Armenia Fmr. Gov. Mike Huckabee Bobby Gruenewald
Bob Hoskins John Kilcullen H.E. Daniel Mulhall, Ambassador of Ireland Shirley Caesar David Jeremiah
John Jenkins, Sr. Tim Goeglein Ken Carpenter Lawrence Schiffman Billy Kim Roland Warren
His Eminence Metropolitan Emmanuel His Eminence Archbishop Elpidophoros (Lambriniadis) of America Wintley Phipps
Tim Dalrymple Naomi Schaefer Riley Menachem Wecker Peter Williams Vashti McKenzie Congresswoman Norma Torres
His All-Holiness Ecumenical Patriarch Bartholomew I of Constantinople Matt and Lauren Chandler Max McClean
Scott & Pamela Pyle Joe Mantiply Ann Graham Lotz Jack Graham Ken Hamm Atlanta Braves
Jon Erwin General Keith Kellogg (former National Security Advisor to the Vice President of the US and Director of the Defense Intelligence Agency) Peacock Cooper Arizona Diamondbacks John Piper
Johnnie Moore Congressman Jim Ryan His Excellency Ambassador Alexandra Papadopoulos of Greece
His Excellency Ambassador Arthur Sinodinos of Australia Congressman Byron Donalds
Tony Perkins Her Excellency Ambassador Lilit Makunts of Armenia Caleb Kelly Newt and Callista Gingrich
David Moberg Tony Evans Sam Sorbo Joe Knopp Congressman Matt Rosendale Dimas Salaberrios
Sealy Yates Austin Riley David Barrett Aaron Baddeley Erica Campbell Dennis Haysbert Ben Utecht Glenn Beck
Colorado Rockies Todd Ream Sammy Rodriguez
Matt Lucas Russel Moore Brian Musso Stephen Curtis Chapman
David Hamilton Josh Norman For King and Country Cast members from "The Chosen"
T. D. Jakes Mac Pier Coach Joe Gibbs A. R. Bernard Matt Maher Ambassador Danny Danon (formerly Israel's Ambassador to the UN)
John Perkins Joshua Kelley Jim Klock Chris Tomlin Jack Brewer
Jon Ponder Congressman Brian Babi Tim Kennedy Kevin Sorbo Robbie Ray Frmr. Senator Sam Brownback
Ruth Graham Nancy Lieberman Hillsong John Stonestreet Kevin Seitzer Dale Bronner
Tim Wong Senator Tim Scott Matthew West Hope Darst Curtis Loftin Loren Cunningham
Chad Robichaux Pavin Smith Sandi Patty Danny Gokey Tim Tebow Jamaal Bernard Pat Robertson
Fmr. Gov. Rick Perry Alister McGrath Norman Mintle Dylan Lee Mark Hummel Vishal Mangalwadi
Lieutenant General Michael Flynn (24th US National Security Advisor Josh Walsh Priscilla Shirer Eduardo Verastegui Eric and Lara Trump Father Paul (Chapel Royal)
Herschel Walker JD Greear Ambassador to Jordan Armstrong Williams Andy Stanley P. Eric Turner
Makoto Fujimura Israeli Ambassador Gilad Erdan Former Ambassador Craig Stapleton Congressman Arrington
Kenneth Ulmer Governor of Oklahoma Kevin Stitt Congressman Barry Moore Sammy Rodriguez
Congressman Burgess Owens Congressman Alex Mooney U.S. Chaplain Barry Black
Bob Smietana Congressman Jason Smith James E. Ward Casey Crawford Tom Holladay Fred Smith
Marty Goetz Melancon Cameron Ross Seaton David Horsager Franklin Graham Anthony Evans
Phil Vischer Pastor Joseph Prince Michael Moffitt Andrew Wommack Satish Kumar
Jacqueline Del Rosario Claude Alexander Al Mohler Eric Metaxas Amy Hollingsworth
His Excellency Ambassador Murat Mercan of Turkey Stanley Rosenberg Christopher de Hamel
Tony Lowden Emily and Daniel Master Cherie Harder Congressman Jake and Mrs. Susan LaTurner

***This is only a representative list of our special visitors. Hundreds of important scholars and authors could have been added. The same with clergy, artists, musicians, politicians, entrepreneurs, influencers, and the lists of donors displayed on the museum's walls.**

Museum of the Bible is a global, innovative, educational institution whose purpose is to invite all people to engage with the transformative power of the Bible.